/353.031P934>C1/

THE PRESIDENCY IN TRANSITION

PROCEEDINGS SERIES:

THE PRESIDENCY IN TRANSITION

JAMES P. PFIFFNER AND R. GORDON HOXIE
WITH
PERI E. ARNOLD, RALPH C. BLEDSOE,
CHRIS J. BRANTLEY, PHILIP W. BUCHEN,
WILLIAM F. BURNS, FRANK C. CARLUCCI,
DUNCAN L. CLARKE, KENNETH M. DUBERSTEIN,
WILLIAM T. GOLDEN, C. BOYDEN GRAY,
THOMAS C. GRISCOM, MICHAEL GROSSMAN,
BEN W. HEINEMAN, JR., STEPHEN HESS,
DAVID C. KOZAK, MARTHA JOYNT KUMAR,
EDWIN MEESE III, ROBERT E. MERRIAM,
RONALD C. MOE, WALTER F. MONDALE,
MARIE D. NATOLI, ALANA NORTHROP,
BRADLEY H. PATTERSON, JR., COLIN L. POWELL,
BERT A. ROCKMAN, RICHARD ROSE,
DONALD H. RUMSFELD, RAYMOND J. SAULNIER,
KATHY B. SMITH, PERRY M. SMITH,
WILLIAM C. SPRAGENS, KENNETH W. THOMPSON,
SHIRLEY ANNE WARSHAW, CHARLES Z. WICK,
EDWARD N. WRIGHT, MARGARET JANE WYSZOMIRSKI,
CHARLES H. ZWICKER

Foreword by GERALD R. FORD

Theodore Lownik Library
Illinois Benedictine College
Lisle, Illinois 60532

Sponsored by:
CENTER FOR THE STUDY OF THE PRESIDENCY
Proceedings: Volume VI, Number 1, 1989

353.031
P934
v. 6

Copyright © 1989
Center for the Study of the Presidency
208 East 75th Street
New York, NY 10021
Library of Congress Card Catalog Number 88-072368
ISBN 0-938204-00-9   Hard Cover
        0-938204-01-7   Soft Cover

"Energy in the executive is a leading character in the definition of good government. It is essential to the protection of the community against foreign attacks: It is not less essential to the steady administration of the laws. . . . The ingredients, which constitute energy in the executive, are first unity, secondly duration, thirdly an adequate provision for its support, fourthly competent powers."

ALEXANDER HAMILTON
The Federalist, #70, March 15, 1788

IN MEMORIAM

ROBERT E. MERRIAM, October 2, 1918–August 25, 1988. He fought the good fight for good government at both the local and national levels, in peace and in war. He served the Nation and the Presidency with great distinction.

Table of Contents

Preface

Eight years ago, as the transition from the Carter to the Reagan administration approached, the Center for the Study of the Presidency published its seminal volume, *Organizing and Staffing the Presidency*. It attracted both the outgoing and incoming administrations and caused Pulitzer Prize winner James Reston to devote one of his inimitable *New York Times* essays to it. He found it "summarizes all the advice from the past, and explains how to handle everything but human nature."

Now eight years later in the Center's newest volume, *The Presidency in Transition*, advice is even offered on human nature. The 40 contributors include members of every administration from Eisenhower through Reagan. One of those who offered especially cogent advice on human nature was Robert E. Merriam, who had served on President Eisenhower's staff. In January 1961, as a part of the first organized transition to a new administration, Merriam had been invited by President Eisenhower to write a little manual for future Presidential aides. Point # one in his 29 points: "Be humble." Bob died last week (August 25, 1988). A long-time member of this Center, he had volunteered his creative energies to the Center's National Advisory Council and its Fund for the Future. This volume is appropriately dedicated to Robert E. Merriam, who had served several presidencies with great distinction and had recently been named by President Reagan as Vice Chairman of the 1990 Eisenhower Bicentennial. Bob Merriam always stood for good government.

Credit for this volume rests primarily with Professor James P. Pfiffner, the principal editor, and a distinguished scholar on the Presidency and transitions. He and I are especially grateful to President Ford for his comprehensive Foreword. From his own long illustrious public career from the vantage point of the Congress as well as that of the White House, President Ford recognizes the meaning of the first words of the Constitution: "We the People of the United States, in order to form a more perfect Union." Now, for 200 years the American people have had this challenge. A part of it is in the selection of their representatives in the Congress and the two representatives of all the people, the President and the Vice President. Whoever they choose, in turn, have a mandate to help "form a more perfect Union." The Congress and the President can only accomplish this and other constitutional goals by working together. As my friend Senator Nancy Landon Kassebaum recently expressed it, "The unavoidable fact of our public life is that the President and the Congress are tied together like two men in a three leg race, if one balks, the other trips; they can argue endlessly about how to reach the final line, but ultimately they must go together or not at all."

And that brings us back to this business of human nature that James Reston talked about and that this volume talks about. Perhaps President Ford's Chief of Staff, Donald Rumsfeld, expressed it best when he wrote: "Don't speak ill of your predecessors (or successors) — you did not walk in their shoes."

Even our greatest statesmen have on occasion had difficulty achieving understanding. Such was the case of Hamilton and Jefferson. When they were both serving in Washington's Cabinet in 1792, Hamilton confided to a friend that he viewed Jefferson "as a man of sublimated and paradoxical imagination — chereshing notions incompatible with regular and firm government." Still eight years later Hamilton put the national interest above party and threw his support to Jefferson. Long after Hamilton's death Jefferson ruefully recalled that when they had served together, they had been "like two cocks in a pit."

Appointments to the Cabinet are most important for any president. The Hamilton-Jefferson experience should be an abject lesson for all future presidents. This had led to Hamilton's masterful essay on interdepartmental relations. Discord between department heads, he warned, "must necessarily tend to occasion more or less distracted councils, to foster factions in the community, and particularly to weaken the government." Washington tried in vain to pour "balsam . . . into all the wounds," finally regretfully accepting Jefferson's resignation as Secretary of State. Reflecting on this experience, Washington wrote, "I shall not, whilst I have the honor to Administer the government, bring a man into any office, of consequence, knowingly whose political tenets are adverse to the measures which the *general* government are pursuing; for this, in my opinion, would be a sort of political Suicide; that it wd. embarrass its movements is most certain."

In the concluding essay in this volume, former Vice President Walter Mondale advises the next President "your most important decisions are made before you take office in the selection of your Cabinet and key personnel and especially your White House staff." George Reedy, Jr., in this Center's First Leadership Conference in April 1970 warned that President Nixon's staff would one day "envelop him." They did.

One of the clear messages from this volume is the need not only for a good people but also sound administration. Hamilton expressed it in 1788 and Ben Heineman, Jr. in 1988: Said the former, "a government ill-executed, whatever it may be in theory, must be in practice a bad government." Said the latter, "Appropriate structures and processes are not glamorous. They are simply essential." What comes through in this volume and in other studies on transition is not only "hitting the ground running," but also a need to consider *both* continuity and change from one administration to another. There is then need for an "institutional memory." Hence, I am heartened that President Ford and other contributors to this volume have underscored what this Center has long advocated, a permanent secretariat contributing continuity from one administration to another. That is why I especially applaud Professor Pfiffner in building this volume on lessons learned *and* lessons shared.

And so we come to another election and to another transition, to another testing of what Hamilton perceived 200 years ago: ". . . it seems to have been reserved to the people of this country by their conduct and example, to decide the important question, whether societies of men are really capable or not, of establishing good government from reflection and choice. . . ."

R. GORDON HOXIE
President
Center for the Study of the Presidency

August 29, 1988

About the Authors

PERI E. ARNOLD is Professor of Government at the University of Notre Dame. He is author of *Making the Managerial Presidency: Comprehensive Reorganization Planning, 1905–1980*, and a number of articles on administration and the presidency. He is co-editor and founder of the *Journal of Policy History*.

RALPH C. BLEDSOE is a Special Assistant to the President, and Executive Secretary of the Domestic Policy Council. He has served on the White House staff since March 1981. Earlier in his career he was the first Director of the University of Southern California School of Public Administration Sacramento Program.

CHRIS J. BRANTLEY, M.A., J.D., is executive assistant to the Director of the American Association of Engineering Societies. His areas of professional interest include Congress and United States foreign policy.

PHILIP W. BUCHEN began his career in the practice of law in 1941–42 with his friend Gerald R. Ford in the firm of Ford & Buchen. He continued the private practice of law in Grand Rapids, Michigan until 1974 when he was named Counsel to President Ford. In the critical weeks preceding his appointment, he had made ready the transition from Vice President Ford succeeding President Nixon. He served as Counsel until the completion of the Ford presidency in 1977. He has since practiced law in Washington, D.C. as a member of the firm of Dewey, Ballantine, Bushby, Palmer & Wood.

WILLIAM F. BURNS is the Director, United States Arms Control and Disarmament Agency. He is a retired U.S. Army Major General. From the inception of the talks in 1981 until November, 1986 he represented the Joint Chiefs of Staff on the U.S. Delegation to the Intermediate-Range Nuclear Forces Negotiations in Geneva, Switzerland. Most recently he was Principal Deputy Assistant Secretary of State in the Bureau of Politico-Military Affairs, U.S. Department of State.

FRANK C. CARLUCCI, III is the Secretary of Defense. Immediately prior to his appointment he served as the Assistant to the President for National Security Affairs. During the past 32 years he has served with distinction in many government posts beginning in 1956 as a foreign service officer. His other positions have included Ambassador to Portugal and Deputy Director of the Central Intelligence Agency.

DUNCAN L. CLARKE is Professor of International Relations and coordinator of the U.S. foreign policy field, The American University. He was Professor of Foreign Affairs at the National Defense University, 1971–1981. His first book, *Arms Control*, won the Choice Award for Outstanding Academic Book in 1981. He has contributed to *Presidential Studies Quarterly*.

KENNETH M. DUBERSTEIN is Chief of Staff to the President of the United States. Earlier he had served in the Reagan Administration as Assistant to the President for Legislative Affairs. In the Ford Administration he had served as Deputy Under Secretary of Labor. Prior to entering government service he was Administrative Assistant to the President of Franklin and Marshall College. His private sector service also included Vice President, Timmons and Company.

GERALD R. FORD, JR. served as President of the United States, 1974–77, and as Vice President of the United States, 1973–74; he was a member of the 81st-93rd Congresses (1949–1973) and had served from 1965–1973 as the minority leader. He is the co-author of *Portrait of the Assassin* (1965). He has participated in programs of the Center for the Study of the Presidency and has contributed to *Presidential Studies Quarterly*. He is the recipient of the Center's Distinguished Public Service Medal.

WILLIAM T. GOLDEN designed the Presidential Science Advisory apparatus for President Truman in 1950. It was not, however, fully adopted until 1957 in the second Eisenhower Administration. Golden is President of the New York Academy of Sciences. He is the editor of two major volumes on science and the presidency. In 1982 he received the Distinguished Public Service Award of the National Science Foundation.

C. BOYDEN GRAY is Counsellor to the Vice President of the United States, having served with Vice President Bush since 1981. From 1969–1981 he had been a partner in the Wilmer, Cutler & Pickering law firm. Prior to that he had been law clerk to Chief Justice Earl Warren. Mr. Gray is a member of the National Advisory Council of the Center for the Study of the Presidency and like his late father, Gordon Gray, has been a participant in the Center's programs.

THOMAS C. GRISCOM is George West Professor of Communications/Public Affairs at the University of Tennessee at Chattanooga. While in college he had served as a sports reporter for the *Chattanooga Times*. After graduation he served for 7 years as a political reporter for the *Chattanooga News-Free Press*; thereafter he served for six years as Administrative Assistant and Press Secretary to Senator Howard Baker. Thereafter he served as Executive Director of the National Republican Senatorial Committee and President, Ogilvy and Mather Public Relations before being named Assistant to the President for Communications and Planning at the White House.

MICHAEL GROSSMAN is Professor of Political Science at Towson State University. He is co-author of *Portraying the President: The White House and the News Media* and of the forthcoming *The Pessimist and the Persuader: Carter, Reagan, and the Media*. He is past president of the National Capitol Area Political Science Association.

BEN W. HEINEMAN, JR. is Senior Vice President and General Counsel, the General Electric Company. In the Carter Administration he was Assistant Secretary for Planning and Evaluation of the Department of Health, Education, and Welfare. He is the co-author *Memorandum to the President* and is a member of the Board of Trustees, Center for the Study of the Presidency.

STEPHEN HESS has served as Senior Fellow, The Brookings Institution since 1972. Earlier he served as a staff assistant to President Eisenhower; as assistant to the minority whip, United States Senate; and as deputy assistant to President Nixon for Urban Affairs and National Chairman of the White House Conference on Children and Youth. He is the author or co-author of numerous books on American politics including *Organizing the Presidency*. He is a member of the Editorial Board, *Presidential Studies Quarterly*.

R. GORDON HOXIE is President, Center for the Study of the Presidency and Editor, *Presidential Studies Quarterly*. The former President of C.W. Post College and Chancellor, Long Island University, he is a Brigadier General USAF (Ret.). Dr. Hoxie is the author, editor, or contributor to more than a dozen volumes on the American Presidency. He has been a consultant to both the Department of State and the Department of Defense.

DAVID C. KOZAK is Professor of Political Science at Gannon University. Earlier he served as Professor of Public Policy at The National War College. He is the author or editor of a number of volumes on the Congress and the Presidency including *The American Presidency: A Policy Perspective from Readings and Documents; Sourcebook on Congress, Contexts of Congressional Decision Behavior* and *Bureaucratic Politics and National Security.* He is a member of the National Advisory Council of the Center for the Study of the Presidency and is a Consultant to the Chautauqua Institution on national public affairs.

MARTHA JOYNT KUMAR is Professor of Political Science at Towson State University. She is co-author of *The White House and the News Media* and the forthcoming *The Pessimist and the Persuader: Carter, Reagan, and the Media.* She is Associate Editor of *Presidential Studies Quarterly* and a member of the Editorial Board.

EDWIN MEESE III directed President-elect Reagan's transition in 1980–81. He served as Counsel to the President, 1981–85, and Attorney General of the United States, 1985–88.

ROBERT E. MERRIAM served as Deputy Director of the Bureau of the Budget in the Eisenhower Administration; also as Deputy Assistant to the President; he served as Senior Partner, Alexander Proudfoot Company (1977–87) and was Chairman, Merriam/Zuba, Ltd. until his death August 25, 1988. By appointment of Presidents Nixon, Ford, and Carter he served as Chairman, U.S. Advisory Commission on Intergovernmental Relations. He was the author of books on American government and politics and of a best seller on the Battle of the Bulge. He was a member of the National Advisory Council of the Center for the Study of the Presidency.

RONALD C. MOE is Specialist in American Government at the Congressional Research Service, Library of Congress. He is the author of *The Hoover Commissions Revisited* and a number of other books and articles on American National Government.

WALTER F. MONDALE is engaged in the private practice of law

in Minneapolis and Washington, D.C. He served as a member of the United States Senate, 1964–77, and as Vice President of the United States 1977–81. He is the author of *The Accountability of Power: Toward a Responsible Presidency* (1976). In 1984 he was the Democratic candidate for President of the United States.

MARIE D. NATOLI is Professor of Political Science at Emmanuel College. She is the author of *American Prince, American Pauper: The Contempory Vice Presidency in Perspective* and a number of articles on the presidency and vice presidency. She is a member of the Editorial Board of *Presidential Studies Quarterly* and sits on the Academic Advisory Committee of the John F. Kennedy Library.

ALANA NORTHROP is Professor of Political Science at California State University, Fullerton. She is the co-author of *The Management of Information Systems*, and she has contributed a number of articles in professional journals and chapters in books.

BRADLEY H. PATTERSON, JR. is Executive Director, The Eisenhower Bicentennial and a Senior Fellow (ret.), The Brookings Institution. For 14 years he served in the White House, most notably in the Eisenhower and Ford Administrations. He is past president of the American Society of Public Administration and is the author of *Ring of Power: The White House Staff and Its Role in American Government*.

JAMES P. PFIFFNER is Professor of Government and Politics, George Mason University. He is the author of *The Strategic Presidency: Hitting the Ground Running*, and is the author or editor of other books on the presidency. He was a staff member of the Volcker Commission on the Public Service and the Presidential Appointees Project of the National Academy of Public Administration. He is a member of the Editorial Board of *Presidential Studies Quarterly*.

COLIN L. POWELL is the Assistant to the President for National Security Affairs. A Lt. General in the United States Army, he has held many senior command and staff positions. Earlier he served as a White House Fellow.

BERT A. ROCKMAN is Professor of Political Science, University of Pittsburgh. He is the author of *The Leadership Question* and co-author of *Bureaucrats and Politicians in Western Democracies*. He is also a contributor to many scholarly journals and is on the Editorial Boards of the *American Political Science Review, Policy Studies Journal,* and *Presidential Studies Quarterly*.

RICHARD ROSE is Director of the Centre for the Study of Public Policy at the University of Strathclyde, Scotland. He is an internationally recognized expert on the politics and public policy of advanced industrial nations. He is the author of many books on the presidency and comparative public policy, the latest of which is *The Post Modern Presidency: The World Closes in on the White House*.

DONALD H. RUMSFELD served as White House Chief of Staff and then as Secretary of Defense during the Ford Administration. Earlier he served in the 88th-91st Congresses and as U.S. Ambassador and Permanent Representative to the North Atlantic Treaty Organization. From 1977–1985 he was President and CEO of G.D. Searle & Co. He is Chairman, Eisenhower Exchange Fellowships.

RAYMOND J. SAULNIER is Professor Emeritus of Economics at Barnard College, Columbia University. From 1956 to 1961 he was Chairman of President Eisenhower's Council of Economic Advisers. His many volumes include *Strategy of Economic Policy*. He is a member of the Editorial Board of and has been a frequent contributor to *Presidential Studies Quarterly*.

KATHY B. SMITH is Associate Professor of Political Science, Wake Forest University. She is the author of many articles in professional journals, including *Presidential Studies Quarterly*. She is co-editor of *The President and the Public*.

PERRY M. SMITH is the former commandant, The National War College. Presently he serves as a consultant to the W.K. Kellogg Foundation. A retired United States Air Force Major General, he has written extensively on leadership and long range planning.

WILLIAM C. SPRAGENS is Professor Emeritus of Political Science at Bowling Green State University. He is the author of *The Presidency and the Mass Media in the Age of Television* and of several other books on the Presidency and American Politics. He was also a working reporter for several newspapers. He is the political science book review editor for *Presidential Studies Quarterly*.

KENNETH W. THOMPSON is the Director of the Miller Center for Public Affairs and Wilson Newman Professor of Government and Foreign Affairs at the University of Virginia. Earlier he had served as Vice President, The Rockefeller Foundation. He has written extensively on ethics, foreign policy, and the presidency. His numerous volumes include *The President and Public Philosophy*.

SHIRLEY ANNE WARSHAW is Assistant Professor of Political Science at Gettysburg College. She is the author of several articles on the presidency and cabinet government.

CHARLES Z. WICK is the Director, United States Information Agency, a position which he has held since 1981. Under his leadership the USIA has greatly expanded its scope and services. USIA had the central U.S. responsibility in planning such major international events as the annual seven-nation Economic Summits and the four Reagan-Gorbachev Summits between 1985 and 1988. Moreover Director Wick transformed television into one of the primary tools of public diplomacy through WORLDNET broadcasts via Satellite. As a result President Reagan has been able to address foreign audiences directly.

EDWARD N. WRIGHT is Associate Professor of Political Science at the United States Air Force Academy and served as Special Assistant to the Attorney General for National Security Affairs, 1987–1988.

MARGARET JANE WYSZOMIRSKI is a Guest Scholar at the Brookings Institution. She formerly was the Director of the Public Policy Program at Georgetown University. She is the author of the forthcoming *Staffing the Presidency: Roosevelt to Reagan* and of a number of articles and book chapters on the presidency.

CHARLES H. ZWICKER is Professor Emeritus in Accounting at Long Island University. He founded the accounting programs on the University's C.W. Post Campus. He is a member of the National Advisory Council of the Center for the Study of the Presidency. He has contributed extensively to professional journals, including *Presidential Studies Quarterly*.

Foreword

PRESIDENT GERALD R. FORD

Now for two decades the studies of the Center for the Study of the Presidency have been most helpful for Presidents and more importantly, for the Nation. In 1974 I put it succinctly: "We need educators like this Center's...to promote the quality of our national life — and the quality of our politicians." In 1977 I had the pleasure to write the Foreword for Gordon Hoxie's volume, *Command Decision and the Presidency*. Seven years later the Center produced what I called, "the worthy sequel to that volume," with *The Presidency and National Security Policy*. Brent Scowcroft, who had been my Assistant for National Security Affairs, wrote the Foreword for that volume which I recommended "for all Americans concerned for our Nation's security."

The Center has also been appropriately concerned with the transition from one administration to another and how the lessons learned and the legacy of events in one administration may be transmitted to another. Unlike most of the other western democracies, like Canada, France, Great Britain, and West Germany, we do not have a permanent secretariat which continues from one administration to the next to offer the new president or prime minister advice on continuing issues. Here in the United States each new administration believes it has a mandate for change. Now it is altogether healthy for each new administration to create its own new agenda, programs and priorities and its own organization for decision making and implementing policies. Indeed, as we approach the quadrennial event of the selection of the next President, both candidates would be well-advised to have policy advisers already at work formulating recommendation on both domestic and foreign policy issues. But changes should not be made just for the sake of change. There is much to be said for the values of accumulated experience.

A president is about to leave office and a new president is about to be chosen as his successor. The departing administration will be the first full two term presidency since Dwight Eisenhower departed the Presidential office in January 1961. What should be the recommendations from one administration to another and how should they be transmitted? Without a permanent secretariat we have depended upon a transition team from one administration to another to provide continuity. At best, new administrations, particularly when they involve changes of political party, are not prone to accept recommendations from their predecessors.

It is interesting to review what President Eisenhower, who had great popular support throughout his two terms, recommended to his successor and how his recommendations were accepted. In age, he and his successor, John F. Kennedy, were like father and son. In particular Eisenhower and his security assistant, Gordon Gray, sought to transmit their sense of the vital importance of the National Security Council to President-elect Kennedy and his security assistant designate, McGeorge Bundy. In detail they sought to convey their recommendations regarding both the National Security Council policy recommending apparatus, the Planning Board (PB) and the policy implementing body, the Operations Coordinating Board (OCB). However, the new administration immediately proceeded to dismantle both bodies. As Professor Phillip G. Henderson concluded in his study on this issue, "By destroying the Planning Board and the OCB . . . Kennedy, in effect, destroyed the backbone of the NSC." Instead he relied on informal ad hoc advisers. In the case of the Bay of Pigs debacle, even the Joint Chiefs of Staff were by-passed. Had there been a small permanent secretariat which could have recalled the basic importance of the PB and the OCB, their dismantling and the disaster which followed at the Bay of Pigs probably would not have occurred. But who was there to offer an institutional memory to advise the new president? In like fashion President Johnson relied on his "Tuesday lunches" rather than the NSC in devising the strategy of the ill-fated Vietnam War.

Similarly in the area of diplomacy there is little or no institutional memory from one administration to another. My mind's eye goes back to the Vladivostock Accords which General Secretary Brezhnev and I had entered upon in November 1974. In the next two years, with the help of my Secretary of State, Henry Kissinger, and my security assistant, Brent Scowcroft, and other advisers, I had virtually completed what could have been a successful Strategic Arms Limitation Treaty (SALT) II. Indeed, on my last day in office, in a public statement General Secretary Brezhnev emphasized, "Of particular importance were the accords we achieved at Vladivostock." Instead of consum-

mating this effort, the new Carter Administration started afresh
its own SALT II designs. Recently high ranking members of the
Carter Administration, including two of the ablest, Stuart Eizenstat and Jack Watson, Jr., have acknowledged that had they in
1977–78 completed the Ford Administration treaty arrangement
rather than submit their own new treaty, which was rejected in
the Senate in 1979–80, a mutually agreeable nuclear arms reduction could have been accomplished with the Soviets. Because of
that delay, events caught up with the treaty, notably the Afghanistan invasion. The treaty which might well have been ratified
in 1977–78, could not in 1979–80. But again who was there to
provide institutional memory to so counsel?

As I noted above, in other leading democratic countries, the
administration has the benefit of a small number of permanent
under-secretaries. In the case of the U.S. Department of State,
we have something like this concept through the Foreign Service. The third ranking officer in the Department (after the politically appointed Secretary and Deputy Secretary) is a career
officer, the Under Secretary for Political Affairs. But we have
no high ranking career persons to advise the President and the
President's Chief of Staff.

In brief, I am suggesting a small permanent secretariat could
provide a valuable counsellor memory for future Presidents. This
I give as an example of the kinds of considerations that I wish
could be given regarding the future Presidency. As we approach
the bicentennial in 1989 of the first presidential administration,
we are also nearing the transition to a new administration. That
is why I deem so especially timely this new Center volume, *The
Presidency in Transition.*

Clearly I recall an important little volume, *Organizing and Staffing
the Presidency,* which the Center for the Study of the Presidency
published eight years ago as the Nation in 1980 approached the
transition from the Carter to the Reagan administration. In it
the late Milton Eisenhower pointed out the essential administrative challenge that had faced his brother as President and each
of his successors, including myself: "how to create a more responsive bureaucracy and how to relate more effectively Cabinet and
staff." After reading the manuscript for that volume, I wrote
Gordon Hoxie and told him that it "provides valuable proposals
for much needed help for the Presidential office." And I told him,
"At a time when so much is demanded and expected of the Presi-

dent concerned Americans should study this work." James Reston also read an early copy and devoted one of his columns to it. The late William J. Casey, who served as Chairman of the transition for President-elect Reagan read it and underscored the words from my commentary, "The lessons of the past decade point to the need for revitalizing the Cabinet and delegating authority." Clearly President Reagan did both, and members of the Reagan administration continue to cite that volume.

One of my own most respected mentors as I was growing up in Grand Rapids, Michigan was a newspaper publisher there, Arthur H. Vandenberg, who was to become one of the Nation's most constructive leaders in the immediate post-World War II period as Chairman of the Senate Foreign Relations Committee. Many years before Arthur Vandenberg had written a book which he called, *The Greatest American*. It was about Alexander Hamilton, and his remarkable contributions to the Nation. One of these was Hamilton's series of essays written in 1787–88 on the proposed American presidency. This included one of my own favorite quotations: "Energy in the executive is a leading character in the definition of good government." Hamilton also told us "that the true test of a good government is its aptitude and tendency to produce good administration." Hamilton emphasized that the President must have "Ist. a due dependence on the people, secondly a responsibility." And I can attest that every President must have a clear recognition both of "responsibility" and that humbling acknowledgement of a "due dependence on the people." Every new President might well read Vandenberg's volume on Hamilton and Hamilton's essays. Eisenhower did the latter.

And now I would propose that every new President-elect take time to read the remarkable essays in this volume, *The Presidency in Transition*. Gordon Hoxie advises me that principal credit for editing the volume should go to a splendid scholar who is a member of the Center's Editorial Board, Professor James P. Pfiffner, who has written the introductory chapter.

It would be presumptuous of me to try the reader's patience by commenting on each of 40 outstanding contributions to this volume. Forgive my reference to a few with whom I have pleasant personal recollection. First, there is the remarkable essay by one of my oldest friends, Philip W. Buchen, who points out, "In the last fifteen Presidential transitions, the entire number in this century, one out of every two has been unscheduled." This again points up the need for contingency planning. In this instance, a small permanent White House secretariat could again be helpful. My own transition to the Presidency was, of course, the only one entirely without precedent since it was occasioned by the first President to resign from office. Phil here records for the first time his initiative in the transition planning. He confides, "The idea for this project, with whatever guilt attaches was mine. I acted out of . . . concern that the Vice President and his staff lacked opportunity to prepare for his almost certain succession to the Presidency." Phil performed a meritorious service, and I am glad Gordon Hoxie persuaded him to here record it for publication. Only Phil, as always is too generous regarding my own contributions.

Second, I would like to record my appreciation for Donald Rumsfeld's contribution to the volume. Don was my White House Chief of Staff, succeeded by Dick Cheney when Don became Secretary of Defense. Don has set down common sense rules of conduct which every incoming White House staff member, and indeed, every incoming President, might well read and contemplate. Especially I like: "Don't speak ill of your predecessors (or successors) - you did not walk in their shoes."

Third and finally from the papers by former members of my own administration, I would like to comment on Bradley Patterson's paper. Brad recalls my role in creating the *White House Ethics Manual*, to establish standards from one administration to another not just of standards of conduct but also counselling against appearances which may be construed as inappropriate. Further, in his listing of the President's office and staff support, I am glad he includes, "His First Special Counsellor: The First Lady." Betty was and is mine! Finally, Brad recalls how after my defeat in the 1976 election, the next day we set in place in the Presidential Personnel Office a system to help relocate staff members who with the incoming administration would be out of a job. Too generously he credits this to a president who "never failed to show his appreciation to the staff members who served him." All presidents feel that way, but we hope we set an example by our conscious effort to help relocate departing staff.

Ben Heineman, Jr. carries forward a splendid family tradition with his paper on White House organization. His father back in the Johnson presidency had headed an important study on White House organization, and the 1980 *Memorandum to the*

President, which Ben, Jr. co-authored, is worth re-reading today. Heineman, now Senior Vice President and General Counsel of the General Electric Company and a member of the Center's Board, concludes, "With the wrong people, even the right rules of the game won't work. But the right people, with no rules or the wrong rules, can fail just as well. Appropriate structures and processes are not glamorous. They are simply essential."

Professor Peri Arnold further reinforces the view historians and political scientists are now coming to: the outstanding qualities of Eisenhower presidential leadership. Dr. Arnold gives Eisenhower high marks for the success of the organization studies conducted during his presidency and their effective implementation.

Professor Bert Rockman gives us a splendid paper on "The President and Permanent Government." He is, however, perhaps too generous towards me when he suggests that I am the only recent president who did not speak illy of the senior bureaucracy. His conclusion is I believe, correct when he asserts that the career service personnel's "expertise and experience can prove invaluable" and that "they can help assure that we also stay out of trouble. That seems to be part of any definition of good politics."

From the vantage point of the University of Strathclyde, Scotland, Professor Richard Rose presents some sage advise on economic planning: "Hitting the ground running is a difficult challenge for any new President, and it is doubly difficult when the President is an absolute beginner, as is the case in dealing with the politics of the economy." A much too neglected area, science advice for the President is included in the volume with two significant essays. William T. Golden had originally proposed the position of science adviser in 1950, but it was not until the Eisenhower administration that a science and technology adviser reporting directly to the President was named. Further, Eisenhower had his own Science Advisory Committee. But it was downhill all the way after that, with the science adviser finally being banished from the Executive Office of the President during my predecessor's tenure. With appreciation I here record Gordon Hoxie's account: "Realizing the mistake that had been made, Gerald Ford only five days after he became President, instituted measures to restore a science advising system in the Executive Office of the President. . . . In accordance with the President's desires, the Chief of Staff, Richard B. Cheney, gave . . . [the science adviser] access to the President." But Golden and Hoxie point out that in subsequent presidencies that access has not been fully enjoyed. They point up the relationship of science advice to national prosperity *and* security and make a good case for strengthening the science advisory role in future administrations.

National security brings me to my final observations regarding this important volume. The Constitutional Framers concerned for the security of the Nation created the office of Commander in Chief to be held by the President himself. Recent history has seen the Congress, especially since the passage of the War Powers Resolution in 1973, increasingly seeking to quarterback the commander in chief role. This led me in my final State of the Union address to declare on January 12, 1977, "There can be only one Commander in Chief."

Certainly one of the most important appointments a president makes is his Assistant to the President for National Security Affairs. In my own administration I was most fortunate in appointing Lt. General Brent Scowcroft to that position. Brent, to my mind, is something of a role model in that position, as was Gordon Gray with Eisenhower. Colin Powell, the present Assistant to the President for National Security Affairs has made a most valuable contribution to this volume by his essay. Clearly as General Powell points out, "the NSC system is indispensable for orderly policy making, and the NSC staff is indispensable for orderly working of the NSC system." Whether we like it or not every President since 1939 has had to devote the majority of his time to foreign policy and national security affairs.

The new President in January 1989 will have a demanding schedule related to national security policy. This will include the continuing challenge of Soviet military power, sabotage, terrorism, and other aspects of unconventional warfare. It will include weapons system, North-South and East-West relationships. These are all matters at the heart of peace and security. Nor can we ignore the area of public diplomacy. That is why I am glad that Charles Wick, Director, United States Information Agency, has contributed a thoughtful chapter. He wisely observes, "Public diplomacy programs can be even more effective if international public opinion is considered *before* policy options are chosen."

It was the late James C. Hagerty who first brought the Center for the Study of the Presidency to my attention while I was serving in the Congress and then as Vice President of the United States.

It has been a relationship I have enjoyed, and I commend the Center for this significant volume which will be helpful not only in the transition to the new administration but in the challenging years ahead.

GERALD R. FORD
Avon, Colorado
July 27, 1988

Introduction:
The Presidency in Transition

JAMES P. PFIFFNER
PROFESSOR OF PUBLIC AFFAIRS
GEORGE MASON UNIVERSITY

The United States is in a transition to the post-Reagan presidency; this chapter will examine how presidential transitions have developed over the past three decades and will suggest some changes in the institutionalized presidency that may be appropriate. By 1981 the transition between presidents had been institutionalized to a high degree, and the size of the transition apparatus may have reached a point of diminishing returns.

The first section of this chapter examines the growth of "presidential common law" that has led to the relatively elaborate transitions of the 1970s and 80s. The second section will lay out some of the components of an effective transition between presidents. The third section will analyze developments in the institutional presidency over the past several decades that may be ready for moderation: the centralization of policy making in the White House to the detriment of the cabinet, White House control of all political appointments, the centralization of the national security policy process, and political attitudes toward the career services.

I. The Transition Between Presidents

While the recent transitions of the presidency have been relatively elaborate, it has not always been thus. It is only in recent years that presidents and presidents-elect have cooperated very much during inter-party transitions. And it has been only since 1976 that candidates have prepared in any significant ways for the transition to the presidency.

The traditional approach to transitions was "presidential common law, confirmed by custom."[1] In 1944 Franklin Roosevelt briefed his opponent on foreign policy and national security matters, and presidents have been doing it ever since. When

Dwight Eisenhower met personally with president-elect Kennedy in 1960 he broke new ground in transition preparation. The 1960 transition contrasted sharply with the animosity of the 1952 transition between Truman and Eisenhower. In 1960 Eisenhower and Kennedy also established new precedent by designating General Wilton B. Persons and Clark Clifford as liaison between the incoming and outgoing administrations.

In 1960 Kennedy spent $300,000 provided by the Democratic National committee and his own funds. This prompted him to support the passage of a law providing funds for transitions. The Congress accepted the argument that it was in the national interest to have an orderly transition of government, and passed the Presidential Transition Act of 1963.[2] The act provided $900,000 for "the orderly transfer of a President and the inauguration of a new President." It also provided that the Administrator of General Services would provide office space wherever the president-elect wanted and staff, travel, communication, and printing services. In 1976 the funds available were increased to $2 million for the incoming administration and $1 million for the outgoing administration.

But even more important to the institutionalization of transitions has been the development of personal preparation of presidents elect for their transitions into office. In August of 1960 John Kennedy called Clark Clifford to his home and said "If I am elected, I do not want to wake up on the morning of November 9 and have to ask myself, 'What in the World do I do now?'"[3] So he asked Clifford to write him a memo on what his first steps should be in the event that he were elected. He gave Richard Neustadt the same charge, but stipulated that the two should not talk with each other about their work. Kennedy also set up a number of task forces in the summer of 1960 to report on different policy areas to help in the transition.

Richard Nixon, like Kennedy, did not undertake any elaborate transition planning; he spent most of his energies on the campaign. He did, however, designate Franklin Lincoln to be his representative for transition with the Johnson administration. Lincoln performed liaison duties and wrote a memo to the candidate, and later president-elect, about process and personnel issues during the transition. Nixon also appointed a number of task forces before and after the election to give him policy advice and to test out potential candidates for political appointments.

Jimmy Carter was the first presidential candidate to undertake systematically serious preparation for a possible transition
of the presidency. In the summer of 1976 he set aside $150,000
to establish the "Carter-Mondale Policy Planning Group." The
project would be under the direction of Jack Watson who set
up budget and policy issue groups and a personnel operation
called the "Talent Inventory Program." The TIP was intended
to set up an outreach program to locate the best and brightest
prospects for appointments in a future Carter administration.

The Watson efforts produced some good analysis and some
good candidates for political appointments, but there was also
a lot of wheel spinning. But the main problem was the perception by the campaign staff, headed by Hamilton Jordan, that
there was a group of planners "sitting in a back room somewhere
dividing up the spoils of the expected victory."[4] The planning
effort had been intentionally isolated from the campaign staff
so that fighting campaign fires would not drive out long range
planning about how to structure the new administration. But
the unfortunate effect was to create suspicion on the part of the
campaign staff that the transition group was planning to deprive
them of control of a new Carter administration. Lessons were
learned, but at the expense of valuable time lost after the election when the Jordan forces established their supremacy.

Jimmy Carter's unprecedented transition planning efforts were
modest compared to the elaborate bureaucracy created by Ronald
Reagan for his transition into office. In April of 1980 he asked
Richard Allen to begin to plan for the beginning of a new administration in the foreign and national security policy areas.
Allen organized 132 people into 25 working groups. On the
domestic side Martin Anderson organized 329 people into 23
groups to propose a policy agenda. No central planning office
was set up before the election, but all pre-election efforts were
overseen by Edwin Meese, who was also in charge of the campaign. These efforts included a personnel planning operation
headed by Pendleton James, a professional executive recruiter
who had worked in the Nixon and Ford administrations.

After the election the transition operation occupied a large,
government office building several blocks from the White House.
In an attempt to be inclusive, the transition organization was
headed by an elaborate superstructure of Reagan supporters that
oversaw operations, and 100 transition teams who fanned

throughout the government the day after the election. The listings
in the transition telephone directory numbered 588, though the
total number involved may have been twice that number.[5] This
large size led to the problem of control and communication. It
was often unclear who was speaking authoritatively for the
president-elect.

The Reagan transition bureaucracy of 1980 was the largest
in U.S. history and was presumably based on the premise that
it takes a bureaucracy to take over a bureaucracy. In 1961 Clark
Clifford thought that transitions should be more institutionalized, but in 1983 he felt that they had become too elaborate.[6]

II. Transition: What is Essential

In order for a new president to take office and get effective control of the government, several components of an effective transition must be carefully planned: personnel recruitment, congressional liaison, and transition teams in the executive branch.
If the president-elect is to be ready, planning must begin before
the election.

Personnel Planning

In order for any new president to get his policy preferences in
place and implemented, there must be people to do it. That is,
political appointments must be made. Each new administration
has three thousand appointments that it can make, but of these
about four hundred at the highest levels in the executive branch
are key to presidential success. While the career bureaucracy will
competently carry on the routines of established programs, the
new president's priorities can only be implemented through effective leadership by those appointed to policy making positions
by the president (though these people may come from inside or
outside the government).

Waiting until after the election to begin to think about this
will unnecessarily delay the new president's agenda. One of the
priorities of a presidential candidate should be to establish a personnel operation so that immediately after the election there is
a process in place ready to do the recruiting of candidates for
presidential appointments. But doing this is a delicate task. If
the names of those being considered for positions leak out, the
media will have a field day, attention will be drawn away from

the campaign, and those who are not on the lists will be alienated. There is also the considerable risk of seeming to be overconfident by taking the steps of the victor before the victory. As President Kennedy once remarked, "the last president to designate his cabinet before the election was President Dewey."

While it is useful to have data on prospective candidates for positions in file boxes or computers, what is most essential is to have a *process* ready to go immediately after the hoped for electoral victory. There must be a system set up to respond to the flood of requests and recommendations for appointments that will inevitably come from Congress shortly after the election. These requests must be handled carefully and expeditiously. A system for active outreach and recruitment must be ready to go. It cannot be assumed that the best and the brightest will be throwing themselves at the new administration. The very best will have to be sought out and actively recruited.

While it may seem presumptuous and premature to begin personnel operations before the election, it is necessary if the new administration is to hit the ground running and not flounder around after the election. Hopefully, pre-election personnel planning will become an accepted practice for prudent presidential candidates. Public funds for this function would be a good investment of the public's money.

Budget Planning

A new president taking office will be faced with a budget prepared by his predecessor, known as the "lame duck" budget. The Office of Management and Budget will have been negotiating with departments and agencies for the previous year to arrive at the budget numbers that Congress will consider in the spring and modify for the fiscal year that will begin the next October. 1. So a new president must move quickly if the new administration is to have an impact on the budget. If the lame duck budget is not affected by the incoming administration, it will be midway through the term before the new president's budget priorities will be put in place.

The first key to affecting the budget is knowing what you want to do. The campaign will presumably provide policy directions for the new administration. But it will help to have some budget experts working on how campaign promises will affect the budget and what changes in the budget are necessary to accomplish the

The second key to affecting the budget is access to the
he Office of Management and Budget. These people have
pertise to be able to translate budget priorities into specific
islative proposals and the language that is necessary to implement budgets. After all, they are the ones who have put together the lame duck budget and know most about how it can
be changed to reflect the priorities of a new administration. In
addition, the staffers at OMB, which is in the Executive Office
of the President, consider themselves to be the President's people
and are anxious to be responsive to their new chief.

But they are in an awkward position, for they work for the
incumbent president until January 20 and are at his disposal.
While this can cause problems, recent presidents have been sensitive to the needs of the incoming administration and have given
them access to OMB staffers before the inauguration. Both the
incoming Carter and Reagan administrations had some access
to OMB staffers within a month or so after the election.[7]

It will also help a new administration to have realistic expectations about what can be accomplished through the budget.
Programmatic changes are usually possible, though those programs that involve "uncontrollables" or entitlements must be approached by changes in the law or eligibility requirements rather
than through direct budget cuts. Reductions in the overall deficit
is a long term project; the deficit is not amenable to short term
fixes.

One reform that does make sense is for lame duck presidents
to submit only a "current services" budget to Congress in January
when a new president is to take office. There are all sorts of tricks
that can be attempted in the outgoing budget. Proposed expenditures can be set artificially high, raising expectations of recipient groups that must be rejected by a new president. Or proposed expenditures can be artificially low, creating expectations
for a lower deficit with little pain, leaving the new president in
the position of having to impose deeper cuts or accept a higher
deficit than was proposed by the outgoing president. A current
services budget would minimize these potential manipulations.

Congressional Liaison

It is inevitable and predictable that each new President will be
faced with a flood of immediate requests, or at least communications, from Congress, and they will not wait for the inaugura-

tion. A candidate should have made sufficient preparations so that immediately after the election there will be in place the capacity to deal with congressional correspondence. Early mistakes in this area or perceived slights can cause untold damage later in the administration, so this is not an optional activity.

In addition to the correspondence capacity, a new president needs to lay the groundwork for pursuing his agenda, and whatever his agenda is, Congress will have an impact on it. The congressional liaison people will have to go to work on making the necessary linkages with Congress and laying the groundwork for future action. Experienced people who know the Congress must be recruited, organized, and set to work on the administration's strategy. Even though immediately after the election it may be early to begin to work on specific legislative proposals, the most important work of the president's legislative liaison team is not pushing specific pieces of legislation or making deals, but rather creating an atmosphere of trust and cooperation, so that when help is needed, members of Congress will be open to requests from the administration.[8]

Transition Teams

One of the useful innovations, though one of mixed utility, in presidential transitions of recent years is the designation of transition teams from the new administration to provide liaison between the incoming and outgoing administrations. For decades presidents-elect have been designating personal representatives to act as liaison with the outgoing president; it is only for the past several administrations that transition organizations have set up teams of people to act as liaison for each major executive branch department and agency.

These transition teams serve several useful functions. One function is to gather information for the new administration. For this purpose team members are given office space in federal agencies and access to budget and programmatic data, though no access to personnel files or classified data. Another function of transition teams is to act as an occupying army and to symbolically show the flag so that the permanent government is put on notice that a new administration is about to take the reins of government, though experienced career executives are well aware of the changes that come with a presidential transition. The tone of this "occupation" can make a huge difference in how the career services react to the new administration. A third function of transition teams is to act as testing grounds, so that prospective political appointees can be seen in action before a decision is made whether to offer them a position in the new administration. If they do not perform well, it is easier to let them go than it is to fire them after they have been appointed to a position by the president.

But these transition teams are a mixed blessing, for they are hard to control. Transition is always a chaotic time, and reining in hard charging people with their own conceptions of the mandate of the president-elect or with agendas of their own, is difficult. These potential members of the new administration have opportunities to affect policy or foreclose options before the new president takes office. Thus careful control mechanisms must be established.

While it can be very useful for a new cabinet secretary to have prepared sets of briefing papers by a transition team that may add a dimension that is not covered in the briefings prepared by the career executives of the department, the newly designated chief may or may not want to keep the people on the transition team. There were several instances in the Reagan administration in which the newly designated secretary came in and said in effect: "Thanks for all of your work. Now go away, and I will run the department." These situations have the potential for hurt feelings and resentment from those whose expectations have been raised by their appointment to transition teams.

The Systemic Problem

Perhaps the most daunting problems facing a president-elect is a systemic one: everything must be done at once. In the euphoria of an election victory it is difficult to concentrate on the more mundane administrative details that are necessary to set up an administration that will be ready to govern the nation in eleven short weeks. As Benjamin W. Heineman, Jr. points out, "Appropriate structures and processes are not glamorous. They are simply essential."[9]

In that short period of time the new president must: designate and organize the core of his White House staff, designate and set ground rules for how his cabinet will relate to the White House, set up a personnel recruitment system to begin filling more than 3,000 positions, establish a legislative liaison operation, begin to put the new administration's stamp on the budget, and begin to provide leadership for the career services who will be the implementors of the new administration's agenda. The real problem facing the president-elect is that all of this must be done *all at once.*

Some scholars and participants in the presidency have proposed shortening the transition period which lasts about eleven weeks.[10] They reason that the transition period is one of ambiguity and thus danger. It would be much better, they argue, to put the lame duck administration out of its misery quickly and get on with the governing of the nation under the new president. Arthur Schlesinger argues that in 1980 and 1981 "Transition teams barged around Washington, promoting themselves for jobs, sideswiping rivals, paying off old scores, making self-serving leaks to the press and turning out reports that few people ever had time to read."[11] Stephen Hess argues that only 100 appointees are crucial to a new administration, and others cannot be nominated until these 100 are on board, and that these 100 people can be designated within several weeks.

The other side of the argument is that there are so many things that must be done and that require the attention of the president-elect that they can barely be accomplished in the ten or eleven weeks available. To presidential nominees the first priority must be to win the election. The candidate cannot take precious time off to help plan the transition, or he risks not being able to use the effort. Yet the president-elect must actively participate in the key decisions that must be made during the transition period when much of the groundwork for the administration is laid.

III. The Transition to the Presidency of the 1990s

The transition from one president to another presents a number of difficult organizational issues that must be addressed anew by each incumbent of the office. These issues have been shaped by the development of the presidency as an institution over the past several decades. The groundwork for the institutional presidency was laid by the Brownlow Committee in 1936 and the implementation of some of their recommendations by President Roosevelt in 1939. But the contemporary outlines of the institution have been influenced by major trends shaping the office since 1960. The primary trend since 1960 has been one of centralization of control of the executive branch in the Executive Office of the President and more particularly in the White House Office. While some argue that the organization of the presidency depends entirely on the personality of the incumbent, there are deep structural pressures to which each president, regardless of personality or style, must respond.[12]

White House Organization

When the responsibilities of the federal government were more limited, and when the White House staff was smaller, presidents could choose to manage the White House personally. Franklin Roosevelt acted as the chief of his own small staff. President Eisenhower chose to use a more structured approach to White House staff support, and designated Sherman Adams to be his chief of staff. At that time having a chief of staff was optional, and when President Kennedy came to office he chose to return to the Roosevelt model and be his own chief of staff.

Kennedy also chose to rely heavily on his White House staff and temporary task forces for policy development and to depend less on the permanent bureaucracies of the government. This began a secular trend of centralization of policy development and control in the White House that, with a few dips and bumps, continued for the next several decades. President Nixon greatly expanded the centralization of control in the White House, He did this in foreign affairs because he wanted to be his own Secretary of State. Though he began his presidency intending to delegate domestic policy making to his cabinet secretaries, he ended up centralizing power because he concluded that he could not trust his own political appointees with his priorities, much less the bureaucrats. The institutional mechanisms that he used were the Domestic Council and the Bureau of the Budget reorganized for more control as the Office of Management and Budget. H. R. Haldeman was Nixon's chief of staff who controlled the White House with an iron hand and who protected the president's time.

After Watergate, Presidents Ford and Carter both tried to return to a less centralized presidency and intended to be their own chiefs of staff. Each had to admit defeat after short periods of experimentation with the "spokes-of-the-wheel" approach to White House organization.

The Reagan administration began with a White House organization dominated by three people who had regular and direct access to the President, but James Baker with the office and functions of chief of staff dominated policy making in a low key and politically astute style. In Reagan's second term Michael Deaver and Edwin Meese left the White House, and James Baker was replaced as chief of staff by Donald Regan. Regan quickly moved to take tight control over all aspects of the White House at the same time that other strong members of the president's entourage left.

Regan's control extended to virtually everything the president did. His purview extended to include foreign policy and national security matters until the Iran/Contra scandal broke, at which time he quickly dissociated himself from international matters and argued that he had no idea what was going on with the National Security Council staff. Regan asked rhetorically "Does the bank president know when the teller is fiddling with the books?"

The modern presidency has experienced a range of approaches to organization, from the small and informal approach of Franklin Roosevelt to the hierarchical structure of the Nixon presidency, to the tightly controlled chief of staff system of Donald Regan under President Reagan. The presidents of the 1990s will have to choose the type of person and the type of organization they want to run the White House. There is a broad range of precedent to choose from, but some form of chief of staff will likely be as essential to the presidency in the 1990s as it was in the 1970s and 80s.

Cabinet Consultation

When presidential candidates have promised "cabinet government" they have meant to dissociate themselves from the "imperial presidency" and to promise a more collegial presidency. This includes regular consultation with cabinet members and the delegation of some aspects of policy development to cabinet departments. This approach to the executive branch is most closely exemplified by President Eisenhower.

But the presidencies since Eisenhower's have been marked by the loss of access and influence of members of the president's cabinet. Since 1960 the White House staff has come to dominate the president's time and attention and to control the policy making process. President Johnson felt he could not trust his cabinet not to leak sensitive information to the press. President

Nixon came to distrust many of his appointees with his agenda and began to replace some of them with more trusted White House aides in his second term. President Carter began his term with declarations about "cabinet government" but felt compelled to replace five cabinet secretaries in July of 1979.

The Reagan administration also began with pronouncements about "cabinet government," but ran one of the most White House centered administrations in history. Budget priorities were tightly controlled and orchestrated by David Stockman and other "keepers of the central agenda" early in the administration. Political appointments at all levels were more tightly controlled by the White House than by any other administration. The agenda of the new administration was dominated by economic priorities which were centrally orchestrated through the Legislative Strategy Group in the White House which coordinated relations with Congress. The administration began with a non-aggrandizing national security advisor, but by 1986 Admiral John Poindexter deliberately misled the Secretary of State about U.S. relations with Iran and kept important information from the Secretaries of State and Defense concerning U.S. aid to the Contras in Nicaragua. He even declared that he kept crucial information from the president, "On this whole issue, you know, the buck stops here with me."[13]

Despite this centralization of control in the White House, the Reagan administration did make a major contribution to cabinet consultation with the creation of the cabinet council system. The seven council system of the first term proved too unwieldy, but the three council system of the second term (domestic, economic, and national security councils) proved workable. The system provided forums in which cabinet secretaries could work with colleagues with overlapping responsibilities along with White House staff members working on the same policies. While some like Alexander Haig, felt that the system allowed White House staff domination, it was a system that directly involved cabinet secretaries in the policy development process. The fact that not *all* major policies were developed through the council system (e.g. the legislative agenda in 1981 or tax reform in 1985) does not diminish the value of the system for cabinet consultation.

Political Appointments

One of the most important tasks that every new administration

faces is the recruitment of political appointees to run the departments and agencies for the president. Political appointees are
representatives of the president and are responsible for providing
leadership of the executive branch and for the carrying out of
administration policies. With respect to political personnel, the
presidency is at a point of transition because the centralization
of personnel control in the White House has reached an historical high point.

The number of political appointees available for presidents
has grown significantly over the years. In the 1930s there were
about 70 high level positions.[14] In 1985 there were 527 presidential appointments in the executive branch that required Senate
confirmation.[15] Schedule C positions were created early in the
Eisenhower administration so that the Republicans could coun-
teract what they perceived to be a Democratic bias in the
bureaucracy that had been led by Democrats for the past two
decades. Schedule C positions are at the levels of GS 15 and below
and include policy determining responsibilities or confidential
relationships with political officials. They grew from several hundred in the 1950s to 900 in 1976 to 1665 in 1986. In 1986 there
were more Schedule C appointments at the GS 13–15 levels (946)
than there were total Schedule C positions in 1976.[16] In addition
to PAS positions and Schedule C positions, new administrations
can appoint non-career members of the Senior Executive Service, ten percent of the SES, about 700 of 7,000 total SES positions. In addition presidents can make a number of PA appointments, without the consent of the Senate.

Thus the president now has about 3,000 political appointments
that can be used to control the executive branch. As the number
of political appointments has grown, so has the level of White
House control and involvement. Technically, non-career SES and
Schedule C appointments are agency head appointments, rather
then presidential. In the past they were also agency appointments
in fact because the White House personnel office took little direct interest in appointing these positions, leaving them to the
discretion of departmental secretaries and agency heads. But this
changed when the Reagan administration decided that the White
House personnel office would clear, if not choose, every non-career
appointee in the executive branch.[17]

In the 1950s and 1960s assistant secretary positions, even
though they were technically presidential appointments, were

largely determined by cabinet secretaries. This happened largely for two reasons. The White House personnel operation did not have the capacity to recruit all of the assistant secretaries. But also presidents took the position that, in managerial terms, secretaries ought to have the discretion to choose their own management teams. In the 1970s the White House began to make assistant secretary choices; in the 1980s White House control extended to all levels, including non-career SES and Schedule C appointments.

In addition to the increasing numbers of political appointees and increasing White House control of political appointments, the numbers and levels of positions that were filled by political appointment rather than by career executives increased and reached deeper into the bureaucracy than before, In the 1950s and 1960s the position of deputy assistant secretary was generally a career position, that is, filled by a career civil servant with an intimate understanding of the agency and its history. By the 1980s most deputy assistant secretary positions were filled by political appointees with an average turnover of less than two years.

Thus in the 1980s there were more political appointees than ever before, they penetrated deeper into the bureaucracy than ever before, and selection was more tightly controlled by the White House personnel office than ever before. Future administrations will have to face the questions of the White House capacity to handle all appointments as well as the managerial issue of whether management teams should be put together in agencies or the White House.

National Security Policy Making

National security and foreign policy making over the past several decades has followed the same trajectory as has domestic policy making, that is, it has been increasingly centralized in the White House. When the National Security Council was created in 1947 its purpose was: "to advise the President with respect to the integration of domestic, foreign, and military policies relating to the national security so as to enable the military services and the other departments and agencies of the Government to cooperate more effectively in matters involving the national security." During the Truman and Eisenhower presidencies the NSC was used to coordinate national security policy, though the Secretary of State played the lead role, short of the president.

John Kennedy and Lyndon Johnson began to give more weight to their national security advisors, but the national security advisor really came to dominate the foreign policy making process under President Nixon when Henry Kissinger conducted foreign policy making from the White House in the president's name and overshadowed the Secretary of State. Nixon did this because he distrusted the State Department bureaucracy, but also because he wanted to be his own Secretary of State. Under Kissinger the NSC staff built up an impressive analytical capacity.

The national security advisor and his immediate staff have a number of advantages in advising the president. They are immediately responsive to the president who is their only client. There are no conflicting obligations to Congress or interest groups, and there is not the bureaucratic inertia of a large organization. They can operate without the cumbersome interagency task forces, bureaucratic consultation, and red tape associated with the State or Defense Departments.

While the national security advisor is not weighted with the bureaucratic freight that cabinet secretaries are, he is also less sensitive to the institutional apparatus necessary to implement decisions. Presidential advice that ignores the State or Defense Departments also suffers from not having access to the institutional memory and expertise that are the hallmark of these agencies. The initial purpose of the National Security Council was to coordinate policy making through departments and agencies, not replace them entirely.

Ronald Reagan as candidate had criticized his predecessors for centering policy making in their national security advisors to the detriment of their Secretaries of State. He began his administration with self effacing national security advisor who did not attempt to dominate the process. But with the perception in the White House that Alexander Haig was too aggrandizing, national security policy making began to be centered in the White House again.

The irony is that an administration that began with the intention of a department centered foreign policy, came to the point in the Iran/Contra affair that the national security advisor was misleading the Secretaries of State and Defense and that operational missions were being conducted by the NSC staff rather than by the professionals in the CIA, State or Defense departments.

The Bureaucracy

While most presidents since Truman have come to office with some degree of suspicion about the career bureaucracies they are inheriting to carry out their mandates, this natural skepticism has increased in recent years to outright distrust and hostility. President Eisenhower had some doubts about the career services that had grown under twenty years of Democratic presidents. Schedule C positions were created to give the Republicans a better hold on the bureaucracy. President Kennedy was not sure that naturally conservative bureaucracies would be able to generate the creative ideas that he wanted to fuel his New Frontier.

Richard Nixon had a legendary distrust of the bureaucracies of the federal government. He felt they were "dug-in establishmentarians fighting for the status quo."[18] He devised a number of ways to try to overcome what he was convinced was resistance to his policies, if not outright sabotage. Jimmy Carter ran for office as an outsider, campaigning against the "horrible bureaucratic mess in Washington." But the Reagan administration probably extended hostility to the permanent government to its greatest depth, arguing that government is not the solution to the problems of U.S. society but part of the problem.

Thus political appointees of the Reagan administration entered office with a great amount of suspicion toward government employees, which was, of course, mirrored back toward them. Administration backers in the Heritage Foundation tried to inoculate political appointees from the viruses carried by the career services by coaching them on "jigsaw puzzle management" that would keep career executives form glimpsing anything but small pieces of the policy puzzle until it all fell together, and by then it would be too late for careerists to sabotage it.[19]

For most political appointees in all administrations there is a "cycle of accommodation" in which political appointees gradually realize that they cannot run the government without career executives, and that they can generally expect support from them. They also have had a chance to promote those career executives most sympathetic to their policies. In the Reagan administration this cycle took longer to run its course than in other administrations.[20]

The problem with the usual approach of suspicion is that the longer it takes for political appointees and career executives to get working together as a team, the longer it will be before the president's agenda will be effectively carried out. Steps should be taken to shorten the cycle whenever possible.

One effective way to shorten the cycle would be for presidential candidates to forswear "bureaucrat bashing," that is, blaming the problems of U.S. society and disagreements with present governmental policy on those who are legally charged with implementing those policies. If political appointees take office with the expectation that career executives are there to help them run the government, they will be able to implement the president's priorities much more quickly than if they take office expecting sabotage.

Conclusion

The institutional trends discussed above have reached points where future presidents are going to have to make conscious decisions. Most of the trends involve the centralization of power and policy control in the White House, and a moderation of these trends might be beneficial to the presidency. That is, the pendulum can move slightly in the other direction to the benefit of the presidency and the country. On the other hand, most of these trends have deep, structural causes and cannot be reversed easily. We cannot turn back the clock to an era of smaller government.

The White House staff is much larger than it was in the 1960s, having reached a peak during the Nixon administration. But with increasing expectations of what the president is responsible for, the White House staff cannot be cut back too deeply. What can be done is to make sure that that staff is best organized to present issues to the president that are well staffed out and ripe for presidential decision. Experience over the past several decades has shown that a chief of staff is essential to the contemporary presidency, but not the type of chief that controls too tightly everything in the White House. Several senior aides must have direct and regular access to the president. The model for a chief of staff should be closer to James Baker of President Reagan's first term than to Donald Regan of the second term.

Several presidents since Eisenhower have tried to emulate his approach to the cabinet, but none have been fully successful at it. But that does not mean that there has to be internecine war between the White House staff and cabinet secretaries that characterized some parts of the Nixon and Carter administrations. A strong White House staff to coordinate and mediate the many departments and agencies is essential to the presidency, but staffers must have appropriate respect for the legal and political positions of members of the cabinet. Some form of cabinet council system may be the best way to achieve a balance between the cabinet and White House in policy development.

Presidents rightly feel that they have a right to loyalty from their political appointees, but attempting to run political recruitment and screening entirely out of the White House puts a strain on resources and frustrates cabinet members who want to put together their own management teams. A modus operandi can be worked out that gives the White House personnel office the presumption in all presidential appointments with the consultation of the appointee's superior in the departments and agencies. Agency head appointments can be delegated to agency heads with the understanding that they must be sensitive to White House political needs. National security advice will continue to be centered in the White House, but the style of the national security advisor can be of lower visibility and can give appropriate deference to the Secretaries of State and Defense, a style exemplified by Gordon Gray, Brent Scowcroft, Frank Carlucci, and Colin Powell.

While in many ways each president has placed his own personal stamp on the office, all presidents must respond to similar institutional pressure. A new president will be able to make his own mark on the office most effectively and avoid the pitfalls of his predecessors if he learns from the experiences of recent presidents and selects his own priorities carefully.

PART ONE
The White House

"We Welcome your Problems with Enthusiasm:" The White House Staff and the Presidential Transition

BRADLEY H. PATTERSON, JR.
EXECUTIVE DIRECTOR
EISENHOWER BICENTENNIAL

It was the late afternoon of Thursday, January 19, 1961; the scene was one of the staff offices in the Eisenhower White House. Moved by that special mixture of humor and resentfulness best understood by presidential "out-goers" on at least five January 19ths since 1953, a middle-level Eisenhower departee thought once more about the incoming opponents who would freshly appear in those very offices the following noon. He yanked open the middle drawer of his desk and taped prominently in it a copy of the well-known cartoon which portrays the bristling face of a gorilla — the brute aggressively gnashing his teeth, underneath being the caption: "We welcome your problems with enthusiasm."

Even after thirty-six years of increasingly sophisticated transition arrangements, and in spite of the oft-repeated presidential pledges of "full cooperation" with their successors, the sentiments of that snowy afternoon (and of this cartoon) still lie in the innards of every departing White House staffer when contemplating the arrival of incoming replacements from the opposite Party. If Mr. Dukakis is elected in November, those sentiments will be there again in the feelings of the Reagan crew, barely under the surface. Let no would-be reformers of the presidency pretend otherwise.

Within the White House, what measures can be taken, in such transition periods, to ameliorate the impact of these sentiments, while acknowledging their reality? Much has been written about the orientation and briefing programs which have been designed for new non-career appointees in the various departments and

agencies of the executive branch; it is assumed that such programs will be offered again in 1989 as they were in the Ford and
Reagan administrations. But this article focuses on the White
House itself. What happens there? There are three categories
of preparations: people, papers and problems.

People

Not realized by most outsiders, first of all, is the size of the White
House group which remains on duty regardless of the Party in
power. There are a whole range of support offices in the White
House the incumbents of which—while of course having no
"tenure" in the White House (nobody does)—proudly serve from
presidency to presidency. The Executive Clerk and his group
(there have been only seven Executive Clerks since 1911), the Chief
Usher and his staff in the Residence (there have been only five
Chief Ushers since 1891), the telephone operators, the men and
women of the police, the secret service details, the eight hundred White House Communications Agency technicians and the
five hundred additional military support specialists—perhaps
2,500 of the some 3,366 in the total immediate White House
staff community—will greet the new President on the afternoon
of next January 20 and will continue their skilled and professional work for him as they did for his predecessor. Some of them
will outlast him, as they outlasted Presidents before him. If, for
instance, the two distinguished women in the Appointments and
Scheduling Office—Mary Rawlins and Helen Donaldson—
continue their White House labors next January 21, Mr. Bush
or Mr. Dukakis will be the ninth President whom they will have
served.

While a tradition of continuity characterizes the White House
support staffs, in the policy offices the current practice is moving
in the opposite direction. White House secretaries used to serve
across administrations; the secretarial assistant for John Steelman
in the '50's, for instance, became the principal secretary in the
Eisenhower Cabinet Secretariat and stayed on to work for Arthur Schlesinger under Kennedy. Under President Carter, however, the secretaries in the Domestic Affairs Office were discharged
at the outset; that group in turn was ousted when Reagan entered the White House.

Recommendations have now been made (by Stuart Eizenstat,

President Carter's former Domestic Affairs Assistant, and more recently by the Center for the Study of the Presidency and the National Academy of Public Administration) that a cadre of senior officers be specifically designated to remain at the White House from presidency to presidency, even through a change of Party in the Oval Office. Such officers would have access to the papers of the previous Presidents and, as Eizenstat proposes, would be expected to point out to a new Chief Executive who wants to change a policy, the reasons why the previous President(s) instituted the policy in the first place.

Eizenstat's and the Center's and the Academy's recommendations need to be given serious attention, but from fourteen years' experience on the staff, it is the author's belief that such proposals are more visionary than practical *unless* the President himself sees it in his own interest to insist on such an experiment. The tumultous initial days of a presidency of the opposite Party, the new crew anxious to project the image of wiping the slate clean from the "errors of the past", are not conducive to welcoming the advice or even the presence of the policy officers from the White House staff of the "discredited" predecessor. Even in the National Security Council staff — perhaps especially there — insofar as new policies are initiated, new faces may have to be shown to dramatize the thoroughness of the changeover.

In a White House where policy officers and their secretaries face forced departure, a special service is sometimes made available to them by the Presidential Personnel Office: helping them find new jobs in the private sector. In 1976, when the Ford staff, the day after election, found itself facing wholesale change, Director Douglas Bennett and his colleagues in the Presidential Personnel Office turned their attention from recruiting in to placement out. Bennett assembled several executive search experts from the business world and held one or more seminars at the White House where they gave advice to fellow staffers who were seeking new employment. Resumes were collected and put into the hands of the outside "headhunters" so that individual interviews could be set up. These arrangements reflected not only the cooperativeness of Bennett and his group, but the thoughtfulness of Gerald Ford himself who throughout his presidency never failed to show his appreciation to the staff members who served him.

Papers

If the policy desks at the White House are empty on January 20, however, some of the file-cabinets (or computer disks) are not completely cleaned out before a new President arrives. The Executive Clerk's bookcase, for instance, will still bulge with the nineteen volumes of up-to-date statutory citations which authorize every one of the 2,464 Presidential appointments (including 1,565 on part-time boards and commissions). The Clerk's card-file with the precise dates of nomination, confirmation and swearing-in of each of them in the years past will still be there — dating back to 1911. His computer will nag the new President and the staff about each of the 700 reports due annually to the Congress. The Presidential Personnel Office is planning to leave behind a computer tape digest of the job descriptions of the 873 full-time executive branch positions which require Senate confirmation. The incoming Counsel at the White House will have not only a fairly new law library to use, but on his or her desk will be at least two notebooks of first-rank importance which will have been left there by those who have gone before.

The first is the White House Ethics Manual, started by President Ford. Its central precept: that for presidential staffers the *appearance* of impropriety is itself the impropriety, has been (a) unchanged throughout the years and (b) just as steadily violated by unwarned or insensitive aides. But the Manual will be there, in the Council's office, ready to be re-issued on behalf of the new President.

The second compilation is the emergency presidential illness handbook, assembled by Reagan's Counsel, Fred Fielding. From a wisdom tooth anesthesia to an assassination attempt, the Chief Executive's potential illnesses range up to and across the line which signifies a Presidential disability—and which calls for the invocation of the 25th Amendment and the temporary devolution of presidential powers onto the Vice President's shoulders. In a true emergency there would be no time to research all the legislative history and the records of past practice. Thanks to the Reagan Counsel's office (which lived through such an emergency in March of 1981) the Counsel of the future will have the needed information under tabs in the notebook—a duplicate of which will be carried on every presidential trip.

Even the papers which are removed from the White House

by the outgoing President are not beyond the reach of the new Chief Executive. In the first place almost all of the National Security Council documents since 1947 (including the briefing memoranda for the President) have been retained in an NSC depository not far from the White House; they are on call to each President in turn. Second, for even those national security affairs papers which, not having gone through the formal Council machinery, are privileged to the originating President, there has been a tradition of comity in access; the incumbent National Security Affairs Assistant can ask for and be shown them on a case by case basis. In third place, a 1978 statute (PL 95–591) is now taking effect which contains the following provision (44 USC 2205) with respect to all presidential papers:

". . . Presidential records shall be made available –" [(A) to courts through judicial process] (B) "to an incumbent President if such records contain information that is needed for the conduct of current business of his office and that is not otherwise available;" and [(C) to either House or any subcommittee of Congress if "needed for the conduct of its business . . ."]

(The affected former President can contest the granting of any such request through a lawsuit in federal court.)

Thus are changing, in some cases incrementally and in some ways dramatically, the older rules under which outgoing Presidents carted away their papers and hung onto them as private property. The White House file-cabinets are not as "empty" as they used to be.

Problems

What issues will a new President have to deal with and how should he go about organizing to tackle them?

Here the President-elect is likely to get both too much and too little advice. From the most single-minded interest group to the most distinguished "think-tank", proposals and recommendations will inundate his headquarters. Ad hoc coalitions of citizens will produce reports; transition teams will prowl through the departments. The President-elect will meet in person with the outgoing President in the Oval Office; "Transition Liaison Officers" will be designated by each of them. The departing Cabinet members will prepare briefing books for their successors; the Office

of Management and Budget professionals will have fiscal options
at the ready.

Amid this flood of exchanges, however, there is likely to be
too little advice either sought or offered about the one institution which is of greatest initial importance to the new President:
the White House itself. His Transition Liaison Officer will receive a set of the floor-plans so that allocations can be made in
the West and East Wings and in the Executive Office Building.
The citizens groups and the think-tanks, however, will, typically,
tell him that his staff should be "small"— good-sounding advice
which may in fact be wrong.

In addition to the security, military and support units mentioned at the beginning of this article, the modern White House
has twenty principal offices, each representing a core function
which has become indispensable in the contemporary presidency.
They are:

  The Assistant for National Security Affairs
  The Assistant for Domestic Affairs
  The Counsel
  The Office of Legislative Affairs
  The Press Office
  The Communications Office
  The Speechwriting and Research Office
  The Office of Public Liaison
  The Office of Appointments and Scheduling
  The Office of Intergovernmental Relations
  The Political Affairs Office
  The Presidential Personnel Office
  The Advance Office
  Czars and *ad hoc* Special Assistants (Drugs, AIDS, whatever are
    special Presidential priorities)
  His First Special Counsellor: The First Lady
  His Second Special Counsellor: The Vice President
  The Staff Secretary
  The Office of Cabinet Affairs
  The President's personal office
  The Chief of Staff

It is most unlikely that any of the analyses or recommendations of either his outside or inside advisers will deal in detail
with all of these twenty functions which the modern President

will need to include—and select early heads for—in his White House staff family.

When these officers (including the Chiefs of Staff for the First Lady and the Vice President) are picked, during the tumultuous weeks between November's first Tuesday and January 20, the men and women announced as the new principal Assistants will be preoccupied with organizing and managing the transition sub-planning which they will supervise, and with recruiting the subordinates who will be on their future staffs. If a Party change has taken place, the new senior White House designees will look at the sitting (and outgoing) presidential assistants with a certain superciliousness: "We licked your guy; we're not going to do things your way any more; this will be a reformed White House—a fresh start."

For their part, as the opening paragraphs of this article reveal, the soon-to-depart White House aides, while willing to be asked for advice, are, like the cartoon figure, not-so-inwardly tinged with resentment. Little wonder that in those especially important post-election weeks, there has long been a barrier of distance and coolness between the two groups. Carter's principal assistant, Hamilton Jordan, it is said, waved off the offer of advice about White House operations and management from his Ford predecessor—and four years later was more rueful when he, in turn, was told by the Reagan incomers: "Yeah, we'll have lunch sometime."

There have been some exceptions; incoming and outgoing White House officers have on occasion met and talked about the issues involved in operating a modern White House. But *ad hoc* arrangements are no longer enough. It is time, the author submits, to arrange a system so the new White House Assistants, and their new problems, are welcomed not just with "enthusiasm"—but with the same professional sense of commitment to good government which underlies the much more formal preparations which have long been available within the departments and agencies themselves. There should, therefore, be designated what might be called "White House Transition Conversations."

The label "conversations" is intentional; formal briefings would be out of place—at least at this tentative and experimental stage. Some non-partisan intermediary (e.g. the National Academy of Public Administration) is needed, to issue the invitations, perhaps host a series of quiet luncheons. For illustration: as soon as a new Director of the Presidential Personnel Office is announced by the President-Elect, an informal lunch or dinner should be arranged by the non-partisan moderator among the outgoing and incoming Directors, with perhaps one or two of the Directors in past White Houses also invited. The discussion would be about the issues and principles important to learn concerning the Presidential Personnel Office — and White House — organization, structure and procedures; it would not be appropriate to rake over policy issues. Books or articles about the White House patronage function, for instance the National Academy's "Occasional Paper Number Four" (the transcript of a 1984 discussion among six former White House Personnel Directors) might be provided.

Such "Transition Conversations" should be repeated twenty times — a luncheon or dinner sponsored for each of the principal staff offices just listed. If deemed permissible by the participants, notes might be made of those "Conversations"; a twenty-fold collection, published much later, would constitute an historic document about the American presidency.

There is precedent for such sharing of experience — from an office which, like the White House staff, is very much political and has to organize itself with precisely the same ten-and-one-half-week lead-time: the Inaugural Committee and Inaugural Headquarters. For many years, upon its termination in February, each subsection of each Inaugural Committee (the offices for the Parade, the Souvenirs, the Gala, the Ball, etc.) deposits in carfully preserved files the "lessons it has learned" from the frenzied weeks when it was in operation. This regardless of Party. As its first move, as soon as it is designated post-election, each new Committee opens up the manuals and scrapbooks and races into its short-deadline task having surveyed the experiences of all the Inaugurals in the recent past — both Democrat and Republican.

Over thirty-six years, the bipartisan commitment to orderly transition from one administration to another has grown stronger and the transition arrangements themselves have become more and more thorough, particularly in the Executive Office and within the individual departments. All this has happened without an iota of change in the constitutional principle that the presidential authority itself switches only at the Inaugural noon. It is now time to extend this bipartisan commitment to White House staffs themselves. Such White House to White House "Transition Conversations" would be a precedent-making step in helping to make the American presidency the effective office the voters expect.

"We welcome your problems with enthusiasm" sneers the intimidating gent in the famous cartoon. For a White House staff team contemplating its own demise, "enthusiasm" is too much to expect, but conversations are called for — even through clenched teeth — and certainly in the interest of good public administration at the apex of government.

CHAPTER TWO

Manual for Presidential Aides

ROBERT E. MERRIAM
SPECIAL ASSISTANT TO PRESIDENT EISENHOWER

Prelude to Merriam's Manual

In the summer of 1960 President Eisenhower determined that for the first time in our history he would provide his successor, whether Nixon or Kennedy, with as much information as possible about the workings of the government and the issues of the moment. To that end, every Department and Agency was required to prepare briefing papers to be handed to the next administration. These papers were reviewed by the Bureau of the Budget (now OMB) for consistency, etc. (These briefing papers are now in my papers at the University of Chicago, and I assume at the Eisenhower Library as well.)

When Senator Kennedy was elected, the President went further in offering transition help. First, he invited the President-elect to the White House (in late November as I recall) for a private meeting. He asked six or seven of us to stand by during that meeting, and when it was over he invited us into the Oval Office, and introduced us to the President-elect one by one, explaining briefly the role we played on his staff. My recollection is that the group included General Persons, Chief of Staff; General Goodpaster, Staff Secretary; Jim Hagerty, Press Officer; Tom Stephens, Appointments Secretary; Gerald Morgan, Bryce Harlow, and myself, dealing largely with domestic affairs; David Kendall, Counsel to the President; and Bob Gray, Cabinet Secretary. (The President previously had introduced Senator Kennedy to Gordon Gray, who was his National Security Advisor, and Cabinet members.)

Under General Persons, Gerald Morgan, Bryce Harlow and I were the principal persons dealing with on-going programs and issues, in Harlow's case with the Congress, and in my case with the Cabinet officers and with state and local officials. Because I had been Deputy Director of the Budget, I was also involved in most budgetary questions.

The President also asked each of us to identify the Kennedy

staffer most nearly matching our responsibilities (as nearly as we could determine), and meet with them. The Kennedy transition leaders suggested Fred Dutton in my case. I called him and invited him to my office in the West Wing above the President's office), and we met sometime in early January 1961. During that meeting I gave my memo to Dutton.

Two footnotes to this process: (1) During the Dutton meeting, the President (Eisenhower) came into my office for one last look around, and I introduced him to Dutton who, needless to say, was somewhat startled by this turn of events; (2) the meeting between Eisenhower and Kennedy took place when the vote count in Illinois was still being contested, and claims of vote fraud were in the air. Senator Kennedy knew that I had run for Mayor of Chicago against Daley, and when I was introduced to him in the Oval Office that day, he leaned over to me in the best political stance and whispered "How are things going in Chicago"?

Manual for Presidential Aides

1. Be humble.
2. Make sure the President hears both sides at the same time.
3. Be sensitive to his special needs.
4. Be aware of the complexities of issues confronting him.
5. Remember that the government has survived for a long time without you, and will survive after you have gone (get away from it all from time to time).
6. Be prepared for the lonesomeness of it.
7. Hear your critics regularly.
8. Have regular meetings with the department people with whom you relate.
9. Don't knock Cabinet meetings. They are an important forum to remind everyone that there are other parts of the government that also need guidance and advice to operate.
10. Always ask yourself, "Is this something the President really needs to involve himself in?"
11. Consciously think how you can help good decisions be made.
12. Don't be in awe of the President — talk back to him — few others will.
13. Inject some humor into the discussion.
14. Don't abuse the "This is the White House calling" gambit.
15. Assume that a call by you to an agency (however innocent)

to inquire about a friend's problem is likely to be miscon-strued and, hence, harmful to your friend.

16. When with the President, call a spade a spade - that's what you're there for - correct the facts when they're distorted even if by a Cabinet officer.

17. As you leap from mountain top to mountain top (or more properly, from crisis to crisis) try to pause now and then and think in perspective of the "big picture".

18. Remember that your role is to help the man, not second-guess him (he got the votes, not you).

19. Try to understand the role of the civil service (sometimes it is difficult, but the vast bulk of them want only to do good).

20. Remember that state and local officials are human beings; that Presidents, even Congressmen, Senators, Cabinet officers, and lesser humans, once may have been state/local officials.

21. Never forget that the Press (a) assign their best people (maybe) to cover the White House; (b) they are humans, whatever their questions; (c) under normal circumstances, i.e., not being regularly lied to, want to be friendly.

22. Assume that the Bureau of the Budget (and other executive branch offices) want to help you — trust them (until they double cross you) and use them.

23. Keep the paperwork flow to a minimum.

24. Encourage the President to have a close-in personal friend, don't try to shut him off from the outside.

25. Encourage the President to have "window out" mechanisms, whether they be stag parties or what have you.

26. Have as many generalists as you can on your staff.

27. Try to understand the political nuances of what you are doing.

28. Schedule a regular period every week when Cabinet officers may visit the President without prior appointment, perhaps do the same for Congressmen.

29. Go up to the Capitol regularly and subject yourself to their troubles. Remember that even the President is entitled to certain privacy, whether it be of his telephone calls or of who is able to visit with him.

CHAPTER THREE

Rumsfeld's Rules

DONALD H. RUMSFELD
CHIEF OF STAFF TO PRESIDENT FORD

"Rumsfeld's Rules" *have been accumulated over a period of twenty years. They are the result of experiences and observations as a Naval Aviator, Congressional Assistant, Member of Congress, Director of the Office of Economic Opportunity, Director of the Cost of Living Council, U.S. Ambassador to the North Atlantic Treaty Organization (NATO), Secretary of Defense, but, particularly, as Chairman of the transition team for President Ford and as Chief of Staff of the White House. Most are the result of trial and error, mine or others.' Others, as indicated, are recollections from readings or conversations. The attributions are best recollections and, thus, probably only reasonably accurate.*

Serving the President:
(for "the Assistant to the President"— and others)

Don't play President — you're not. The Constitution provides for only one President. Don't forget it, and don't be seen by others as not understanding that fact.

Don't take the job, or stay in it, unless you have an understanding with the President that you are free to tell him what you think, on any subject, "with the bark off"— and the freedom in practice to do it.

Learn quickly how to say, "I don't know." If used when appropriate, it will be often.

If you foul up, tell the President and others fast, and correct it.

In the execution of Presidential decisions, strive to be true to the President's views, in fact and tone. Work to handle your responsibilities as you believe he would were he in your position. It requires judgment and effort.

The White House staff and others in the Administration are likely to assume that your manner, tone, and tempo represent and express the President's wishes — conduct yourself accordingly.

Visit around the Administration. It is necessary to leadership. And, if you are not visible, the "mystique" of the White House may lead to the initiation and perpetuation of inaccuracies about you and the White House — to the detriment of the President and your ability to do your job.

Visit with White House "Assistants" from previous Administrations. They can point out some of the potholes in the road ahead — and there are many. You will benefit from their counsel.

Consider keeping your relationship with the President professional — it will probably be better for the President and for you.

Of special value to his leadership are the President's words and time — they should be expended with the utmost care.

In our free society, leadership is by consent, not command. To lead, a President must, by word and deed, persuade. Personal contact and experience are necessary ingredients in the decision-making process, if he is to be successful in persuasion and, therefore, leadership.

Be precise — a lack of precision is a good way to fall into one of the many potholes in the road. Presidential direction and the necessary accountability require precision in assignments.

Where possible, preserve the President's options — he will very likely need them.

Know that it is easier to get into something than it is to get out of it.

Know when you have a bias, pro or con, on people or issues, and make the President aware of it, so that he can take it into account.

Don't become, or let the President or White House personnel become, obsessed or paranoid about the Press, the Congress, the other Party, opponents, or leaks. Understand and accept the inevitable and inexorable interaction among our institutions. Put your head down, do your job as best you can, and let the "picking" (and there will be some) roll off.

Don't speak ill of another member of the Administration. In discussions with the President, scrupulously strive to give fair and balanced assessments.

Never say "the White House wants"— buildings don't "want."

Don't slip into trying to "run" the First Family. You will have plenty to do without trying to do that. It's the President's family—not yours. And, they'll likely do just fine without your help, anyway.

Be willing to take some of the decisions concerning the President's personal security upon yourself—from the President. He can overrule you if he wishes, but try to avoid putting him in the position of having to be the one to counsel caution.

A Vice President has a very difficult set of relationships. Do your darnedest to make things work well for him. It will take everything you have, and you still may fail.

You may never meet a person who is perfect—who is able and wise enough to advise a President—given the critical responsibilities of the President of the United States in our dangerous and untidy world. Work like the dickens to help him.

Don't blindly obey directions from the President with which you disagree, or even when you agree, when you feel he hasn't weighed all sides. If you don't tell him when you disagree, the danger is no one else will.

One price of proximity to the President is the duty to bring bad news. You fail him, and yourself, if you are unwilling to do so.

You and the White House Staff must be, and be seen as being, above suspicion. The best approach—and none is ironclad where human beings are involved—is example, vigilance, and, when problems occur, prompt action. Manage by example.

Don't speak ill of your predecessors (or successors)—you did not walk in their shoes.

Be mindful, always, of the public trust. Strive to preserve and enhance the integrity of the Office of the Presidency. Pledge to leave it stronger than when you came.

Keeping Your Bearings in the White House

Keep your sense of humor about your position. Remember the observation (attributed to General Joe Stillwell) that "the higher a monkey climbs, the more you see of his behind"—you will find it has a touch of truth.

Enjoy your period of public service — it should be a most interesting and challenging period of your life.

Don't begin to believe you are indispensable or infallible, and don't let the President, or others, think you are — you're not. It's that simple.

Help your family, staff, and friends to understand that you are still the same person, despite the publicity, and that the notoriety, good or bad, goes with the job — and don't forget it yourself.

Have a deputy and use him. Don't be consumed by the job or you will lose your balance. Maintain and tend your mooring lines to the world outside the White House — family, friends, neighbors, people out of government, people who may not agree with you. Balance is critically important to your performance.

When asked your view, by the press or others, know that what is really being sought is not your view, but rather the President's views, or, more precisely, what the Administration is likely to do next.

Don't forget that the fifty or so invitations you receive a week are sent not because those people are just dying to see you, but because of the position you hold. If you don't believe me, ask one of your predecessors how fast they stop.

Remember, you are not all that important — your responsibilities are.

Be yourself. Following your instincts should not necessarily be avoided. Success in an effort may depend, at least in part, on the ability to "carry it off." If your instincts are negative, you may well not be able to "carry off" even a relatively good decision.

Know that the amount of criticism you receive — and you will receive plenty — may bear some relationship to the amount of publicity you receive.

If you are not criticized, it could be because you are not doing much that is productive. However, the fact that you are being criticized does not necessarily mean that you are being productive.

From the inside, the White House more than occasionally looks as untidy as the inside of a stomach. Don't let the perspective you have, which is unique, or the buffeting you receive panic you. It probably looks better and is likely going smoother than it may seem from where you sit.

Accumulate and periodically review your own rules for handling the job — it can be useful. And, show them to those you work with so that they have a sense of how you are managing.

Don't stay on the job too long. Change is healthy for everyone. Identify and develop possible successors.

Be able to resign. It will improve your value to the President and do wonders for your performance.

If you are lost —"climb, conserve, and confess." (From the Navy SNJ Flight Manual.)

Doing the Job in the White House

Performance depends on people. Appoint the best, train them, tend them, support them. As errors occur, provide better policy guidance. If errors persist or if "the fit" is imperfect, be willing to help them move on — the country can afford nothing less. It cannot be "Amateur Hour" in the White House.

You must find time to help start many things, but there will be very few you will need to or be able to finish. The task is to think, plan, develop, get authorized, initiate, find good people to be responsible, give them the authority, and hold them accountable. If you try to do everything yourself, very little will be done well.

Think ahead. Day-to-day operations tend to drive out planning — don't let it happen. Plan backwards (set objectives and trace back to see how to achieve them, even though you may discover there is no way to get there and you will have to adjust the objectives). Plan forwards (to see where your steps will take you. It is seldom clear and is certainly not always intuitive).

Don't "over control" like a novice pilot. Stay loose enough from the flow that you can observe it, modify, and improve it.

A President needs multiple sources of information — work to assure adequate access. Avoid overly restricting the flow of paper, people, or ideas to the President, even as you strive to avoid wasting his time. If you over-control, it will be your "regulator" that controls, not his. Only by taking the chance that some of his time may be spent on the less important, can his "regulator" become sufficiently sensitive to the demands on him to take over.

When in doubt, you have no choice but to move decisions up to the President.

When you raise an issue with the President, try to come away with that issue decided, and more. Pose it in a way that you get from him that decision, but also the broader policy guidance necessary to answer, for you and the staff, a range of similar issues, thereby saving everyone's time.

Scrupulously serve the President, the Cabinet, and the Staff by seeing that they are informed — they must be to do their jobs competently and persuasively. If they are out of the flow of information, or feel that they are, decisions will either be poorly made, not made, or not confidently and persusively carried out. Each is damaging.

Don't allow people to be cut out of a meeting or an opportunity to communicate because their views may differ from the President's views, the views of the person setting up the meeting, or your views. Include them. The staff system must have discipline to serve the President well.

The staffing system on Presidential decisions must have integrity, and be known to have integrity. When the President is making a decision, either be sure he has the recommendations of the appropriate people, or conversely, that he knows he does not have their views and is willing to accept the disadvantages that will inevitably result, such as key people being out of phase, unhappy, or less effective as a result of being seen as having been "cut out."

Don't be a bottleneck in the flow of paper or decisions. If it is not a Presidential decision, and you are not sufficiently informed to decide it in a reasonable time, delegate the decision unambiguously, to someone who is informed. Mistakes will be made, but you will sink the President if the decision-making process clogs up. Force responsibility down and out. Find problem areas, arrange them, assign them, and delegate unambiguously. The pressure is on the reverse direction. Resist it.

Be sure the staff is given guidance — policy — against which to make decisions. Otherwise, decisions tend to be random, which ill serves the President and the American people.

One of the tasks is to separate the personal from the substance. They can easily get tangled up in policy recommendations for the President — to the detriment of the decisions. Presidents, as all of us, can make a poor decision because it is presented by one who rubs him wrong or vice versa. Work to avoid such instances.

Be willing to test ideas in the marketplace — the odds are you will learn something of value. Discussion helps assure that a final decision will benefit from a sufficiently representative range of perspectives and will merit and, therefore, have the broad support it will probably need for successful implementation.

If a prospective Presidential approach cannot be explained so that it can be understood, it is probably because it has not been fully thought out. If it cannot be explained to the American people, whose support it will require, it probably won't "sail" anyway. Send it back for further work.

Don't let the pressures of the moment deter you from weighing the longer-range implications of what is being said or done.

The people elect a President to make major choices. Staff should work to help identify the choices and see that he is aware of the real differences at the heart of the issues he must address. Staff will not necessarily do this automatically.

Most people with whom the President will be dealing will have, possibly with some cause, reasonably sizable egos before they come to government. Their experiences after they arrive, and the press notices, will probably have done little to deflate them. This includes you.

Resist the "we" (the White House) — "they" (everyone else) syndrome.

Work to strengthen the Cabinet and statutory agencies — defend them, help to move responsibility, authority, and accountability to them.

Control your own time — don't let it be done for you. If you are working off the in-box that is fed to you, you are probably working on the priorities of others — not yours. See that the staff is working off what you move to them from your out-box — or the President will be reacting, not leading.

Read and listen for what is missing. Many advisors — in and out of government — are quite capable of telling the President how to improve what has been proposed, or what's gone wrong. Few seem capable of sensing what isn't there.

Congressional relations are best handled on the "revolving door" principle. Policy decisions will require the support of each Member of the House and Senate, on some issue, at some time, regardless of philosophy or Party. Don't allow the links to any Member to be cut because he may disagree on some, or even many, issues.

Work continuously to reduce the number of people who have White House phones, White House stationery, White House Mess privileges, and the like. Only those who see the President frequently, say three or four times a week, should be in a position to represent themselves as being "White House Staff."

Work to reduce the size of the White House staff and the Executive Office of the President — from your first day to your last. All the pressures are in the contrary direction. Fight them, and the President and the country will be best served.

Assume that most everything you say or do will be on the front page of *The Washington Post* the next morning. It may well be. For many reasons, including that, conduct yourself accordingly.

Government, and therefore, government employees — that's you — are there to serve the American people.

Serving the Government

It is not easy to spend "federal (the taxpayers') dollars" so that the intended result is, in fact, achieved. This should be reread periodically — it seems to be among the least understood facts of government.

The issue, in the Congress, the press, and the bureaucracy, too often, is whether the level of effort (expenditure) is enough — instead of whether the expenditure is actually achieving the desired result for the American people.

When an idea is being pushed because it is "exciting," "new," or "innovative"— beware. An exciting, new, innovative idea can also be foolish.

Ask first: Is this a federal responsibility, or can it best be handled in the private sector, with voluntary organizations, local governments, or state governments? The Federal Government should be the last resort — not the first.

"Public money drives out private money." (Former Congressman Tom Curtis said something like this many years ago.)

Work to see that proposed solutions are as self-executing as possible. As the degree of discretion increases, so too do delay and expense.

Presidential (Governmental) leadership need not necessarily cost money. Look for — and encourage others to keep looking for — low-cost and no-cost options. They are often surprisingly effective.

"Stubborn opposition to good proposals often has no other basis than the complaining question, 'Why wasn't I consulted?'" (Senator Pat Moynihan, as I recall.)

On consultation: No one likes something unless he is "in on it" at the takeoff.

Be alert for the "not invented here" syndrome.

"The atmosphere in which social legislation is considered is no friend of truth." (Senator Pat Moynihan, as I recall.)

If in doubt, don't.

If in doubt, do what is right.

Your best questions is often "Why?"

Exercise the same care with each federal dollar as you would were it your own. This assumes, of course, that you are frugal.

Agreement can always be reached by increasing the generality of the conclusion; when this is done, the form is generally preserved, but only the illusion of policy is created. (Unknown)

"The Government are extremely fond of amassing (sic) great quantities of statistics. These are raised the Nth degree, the cube roots are extracted, and the results are arranged into elaborate and impressive displays. What must be kept ever in mind, however, is that in every case, the figures are first put down by a village watchman, and he puts down anything he damn well pleases." (Attributed to Sir Josiah Stamp, 1880–1941, H. M. Collector of Inland Revenue.)

"The objective of dedicated employees should be to analyze situations intelligently, anticipate problems prior to their occurrence, have answers to those problems and move swiftly to solve them. However, when you're up to your ears in alligators, it is difficult to remember that the reason you're there is to drain the swamp." (Unknown — possibly by preference.)

"Our troops advanced today without losing a foot of ground." (Attributed to Spanish Civil War communiqué.)

Politics, the Congress, and the Press

First Rule of Politics: You can't win unless you are on the ballot.

Politics is human beings.

Politics is addition, not subtraction.

Volunteers — like the ripples when a pebble hits the pond.

You can't lose unless you're running. Or, conversely, if you're running, you may lose.

If you tie, you do not win.

The winner is not always the swiftest nor the surest, nor the smartest. It's the one who is willing to get up at 5 a.m. and go to the plant gate to meet the workers. (Unknown)

You can't cut a swath through the hen house without ruffling some feathers. (Unknown)

Politics: Every day is filled with numerous opportunities for serious, if not fatal, error — enjoy it.

One of the often overlooked dangers for a politician is overexposure.

When someone with a rural accent says, "I don't know anything about politics," zip up your pockets.

If you try to please everybody, somebody is not going to like it.

Don't necessarily always avoid sharp edges — occasionally they may be necessary to leadership.

"The oil can is mightier than the sword." (Attributed to the late Senator Everett Dirksen, Illinois.)

Arguments of convenience lack integrity and inevitably will trip you up later.

Know where you came from.

Know that Members of the House and the Senate are not there by accident. Each managed to get there, and there is a reason — discover it, and you will have learned something important about our country and its people.

With the press, it is best to assume that there is no "off the record."

In dealing with the press, do yourself a favor. Stick with one of three responses: (a) I know, and I can tell you; (b) I know, and I can't tell you; or (c) I don't know. (The Rather Rule, Dan Rather of CBS, years ago.)

Life (and other things)

"You can't pray a lie." (From *Huckleberry Finn* by Mark Twain.)

"It takes everyone to make a happy day." (Marcy Kay Rumsfeld, age 7.)

"Persuasion is a two-edged sword — reason and emotion — plunge it deep." (Attributed to Professor Lewis Sarett, Sr.)

"The art of listening is indispensable for the right use of mind. It is also the most gracious, the most open, and the most generous of human habits." (Attributed to Robert Bart, St. John's College, Annapolis, Maryland.)

"In writing (a column) if it takes over 30 minutes to write the first two paragraphs, select another subject." (Attributed to Raymond Aron.)

In unanimity there may well be either cowardice or uncritical thinking. (Unknown)

"If you're coasting, you're going downhill." (L. W. Pierson)

"Man and the turtle are alike — they only make progress when the neck is out." (Howard Cohen, as I recall.)

The harder I work, the luckier I am. (Unknown)

"If it doesn't go easy, force it." (George D. Rumsfeld's assessment of his son's basic operating principle at age 10.)

"But I am me." (Nick Rumsfeld, age 9.)

Perspective: Maurice Chevalier's reported response when asked how it felt to reach 80 — "Pretty good, considering the alternative."

For every human problem there is a solution that is simple, neat, and wrong. (H. L. Mencken)

Simply because a problem is shown to exist, it does not necessarily follow that there is a solution.

If you develop rules, never have more than ten.

CHAPTER FOUR

Some Rules of the Game: Prescription for Organizing the Domestic Presidency

BEN W. HEINEMAN, JR.
SENIOR VICE PRESIDENT–GENERAL COUNSEL
GENERAL ELECTRIC COMPANY

The Supreme Court has well-established, clearly articulated procedures for conducting its business. So does the Congress, and its Committees and Subcommittees.

But a new Presidency starts with a clean slate and without any well accepted guide on how to structure and operate its key internal processes. A new administration often assumes that it must alter the way its predecessor organized the Executive Office of the President (EOP), and the relations between the EOP and the Cabinet Departments.

Indeed, a number of scholars and former officials believe that the structures and processes of a presidency should be largely, if not wholly, dependent on the personal style of the incumbent.[1] I disagree.

This essay argues that any Chief Executive in the late Twentieth Century should follow certain principles in structuring and organizing his domestic presidency. These prescriptions arise both from the experience of modern Presidents and from the social, economic and political environment in which future Presidents must operate. These organizing principles were set forth in detail in 1980 in a book Curt Hessler and I wrote after refracting the domestic failures of the Carter Administration through the lens of central writings on the post-New Deal Presidency,[2] and seemed valid in 1984 when I reflected on the first Reagan term.[3] Although necessarily general, I think these essential rules of the domestic presidential game will have a practical, beneficial effect if followed by the man who succeeds Ronald Reagan — regardless of his party or his personal style.

Like many others, of course, I believe that the key determinants of a successful presidency will be the President's personality and his substantive vision of how the federal government can influence the trajectory of national life. Strong presidential leadership will also turn on other key factors which can be identified but not prescribed, such as the chemistry between key appointees, the tides of history and simple good luck. Thus, I would only claim that the prescriptions which follow are necessary not sufficient conditions of an effective presidency.

*   *   *

1. *The Need for a Strategic Presidency.* The paramount task of the modern domestic presidency is to develop, and consistently test against a changing reality, a sophisticated strategy of governing that systematically incorporates and vigorously integrates in a realistic time frame the four fundamental dimensions of executive government: substantive policy (where to go); practical politics (how to get there); administrative structures (how power is distributed within the executive branch); and action-forcing processes (how to run executive government to get things done). Indeed, the nature and degree of presidential power in this era turns on the ability of the Chief Executive to forge and execute such a strategy.

A strategic approach is necessary to understand and then resolve the painful dilemmas within and between these four dimensions of the domestic presidency: for example, between the expectation that the President can effect sweeping change and the reality of multiple constraints on presidential action; between economic and social policy; between domestic policy and defense policy; between the politics of governing, renomination and the next general election; between high risk-high reward initiatives and lower risk efforts; between centralization and delegation. Most importantly, the strategy must reconcile the often contradictory demands of policy and politics—must find that marriage between them which is the acme of presidential leadership.

If properly articulated, the presidential strategy has the paradoxical effect of increasing the President's reach (by making clear to his Administration and the rest of the political world what he wants), while conserving his time (if he has made big decisions many smaller ones should follow without his intense involvement). Surely the truth of this paradox is illustrated by contrasting Carter's term with Reagan's first four years.

2. *Making the Strategy Clear From the Start.* Obviously, the first year of an Administration is crucial: Carter never recovered from 1977, while Reagan rode the successes of 1981 for a long time. For maximum effect, the strategy of governing must be developed immediately after the election and then communicated forcefully in the months after the inauguration. Thus, although this rarely happens, key personnel decisions must be made in November if at all possible, leaving two full months for strategic thinking with the new, senior members of the incoming administration. Perhaps the greatest power of the presidency—the ability to set the national agenda—is never so potent as after the initial election to office, yet that power must be wielded at a time when the new president, especially one without Washington experience, is ill-prepared for the task.

Setting the strategic course early not only influences the outside political world, but it is crucial for running an effective administration immediately. Substantively, it communicates what is the "presidential interest," and thus reduces (though it could hardly eliminate) the inevitable intra-administration disputes about what the President wants. Procedurally, establishing the rules of the game at the outset should also avoid the often debilitating, intra-administration warfare about how decisions get made.

3. *Priority-Setting to Demarcate Presidential From Sub-Presidential Decision-Making.* A key element of the strategy of governing is the division of domestic issues into first, second and third order initiatives. If the Reagan Presidency has shown anything, it has demonstrated the importance of having the President focus on a few key issues.

- On first order issues, which should be limited to five or so in domestic affairs, the President should be deeply involved and make all significant decisions. His performance, and success, on this small percentage of issues will have a disproportionate impact on how he is perceived in Washington and in the nation.
- On second order issues, which should number about 25, the President should make the basic decisions on the shape of the policy and the strategic directions. But subsequent decisions about details and implementation should be made at the sub-presidential level, with further presidential involvement limited to large problems which may arise or to select political maneuvers.
- On third order issues, the President should indicate that he regards

the issue as important to the record of the administration, and may
approve a general policy direction but he should leave virtually all
decision-making to the sub-presidential system. These third order
issues might number 100 or so, and would be specially tracked in
the EOP because of their potential importance to the administration's record.

Given his foreign affairs responsibilities, his general political obligations, the time he will spend managing crises and his duties
as head of state, it is not realistic to expect any greater involvement of the President in domestic affairs. Unless we are at one
of those rare moments like the mid-30s or the mid-60s, when
a President must race to keep up with historic change, I believe
the imperative of a slimmed down agenda applies whether a President is a high-energy person like Carter, or a low-energy person
like Reagan. There is, of course, nothing magic in the 5–25–100
numbers for first, second and third order issues, but it would
be surprising to me if the variance from those guidelines would
be great. Time — both the demands of the daily schedule and
the difficulty in changing deeply rooted historical patterns and
practices — has the President in its vise.

4. *The Need for a Strong Chief of Staff.* Given the need for a system
of sub-presidential decision-making to make executive government work, there must be a person who can, in fact, oversee this
system. This person should be the chief of staff, who is the President's most important appointment. The chief of staff must have
an aptitude for both policy and politics. He or she must be able
to develop the strategy of governing, ensure that policy is consistent with that strategy and mediate disputes that arise within
the EOP or between the EOP and the Departments on second
and third order issues. The chief of staff must also make the strategic and organizational connections between domestic and foreign policy (which are beyond the scope of this essay).

Mediation is desirable because the senior members of the EOP
and the Cabinet will be reluctant to accept a decision-maker short
of the President. Nonetheless, to make a system of delegation
and sub-presidential decision-making work, the chief of staff must
be able to resolve intractable conflicts when mediation fails on
these second and third order issues. The President will need to
make clear to his administration — first in words and then in
practice — that, once he has set policy on second order issues or
announced a general direction on third order issues, he expects

the chief of staff to compose subsequent differences within the administration.

5. *The Need for Three Substantive Policy Channels.* The first, second and third order issues should be coordinated in one of three policy channels. First, economic affairs should be coordinated by the Treasury Secretary, as chair of an EOP economic policy group comprised of relevant department heads and the heads of relevant EOP units. Second, the OMB Director will, of course, direct budget and program coordination. Third, a top presidential aide should coordinate activities within a "domestic affairs" channel. Issues in the domestic affairs channel should be limited (10–20 first and second order issues) to avoid creating inevitable conflict between the OMB and domestic affairs staffs on virtually every issue. They should be the major domestic affairs issues — such as social policy or legal or environmental matters — which are important but which cannot be given appropriate, high level attention in the economic and budget channels.

The significance of the channels is that the lead person — the Treasury Secretary, the OMB Director, the head of domestic affairs — has the responsibility for *coordinating* the *process* of policy development or implementation. Given the overlapping responsibilities of various EOP offices and cabinet departments, *advice* on those issues will come from a variety of sources which must be represented fairly by the office with the process responsibility. Although it sounds small and bureaucratic, anyone who has been in the belly of the executive branch beast knows the central importance of clarity on the simple question of who is coordinating development of an issue.

The chief of staff should decide what issue belongs to which channel (and who should be part of the intra-EOP, inter-agency process), if it is not clear.

6. *The Need for a Political Director.* A senior presidential assistant for political affairs should oversee relations with Congress, state and local governments, the interest groups, party officials and the media (although there will be separate EOP officials with specific responsibility for each set of relationships). The complexity of the political world faced by the President requires a senior aide with an overview of all the key political relationships who can creatively see how to create coalitions and political energy for innovative policy.

This person must participate extensively in the work carried on in the three substantive channels. Policy development—and policy implementation of controversial decisions—should be a continual dialogue between those with substantive and those with political responsibilities. Once again, it will be the special responsibility of the chief of staff to ensure that the political and policy officials are working closely together.

7. *The Cabinet: The Need for Access on Presidential Decisions.* Mercifully, the cry for "cabinet" government has abated since the Carter years. Proper use of cabinet officers does not lend itself to easy generalizations. The "don'ts"—don't try to use the cabinet as a whole very much, don't pretend that the cabinet is free of important issues to operate in isolation from the EOP—are easier to state than the "do's."

Simply put, the cabinet officer's role should vary depending on whether the issue is of first, second or third order importance to the President. On first and second order issues, when the President will be making the key decisions himself, the fundamental role of the cabinet officer will be to give analysis and advice. His will be an important voice, but not the only voice. Most presidential issues will implicate other cabinet departments and various EOP units. All need to be heard before the President decides, although a President is obviously going to give deference (but not automatic acquiescence) to his Defense Secretary on defense matters, on his Attorney General on legal matters.

A more complicated question is whether the EOP or the cabinet officer manages the process of policy development on these presidential issues. As noted above, all presidential issues should be *coordinated* through one of the three policy channels. Under this general principle, there are two broad alternatives. The EOP office can have the lead in the process, and direct how all other interested executive branch officials feed into that process. Or, if a presidential issue is largely the province of a particular department, the cabinet officer for that department can lead the process, but the relevant head of the EOP policy channel can provide a *process check* by ensuring that other views are fairly represented in any decision papers or presentation going to the President.

8. *The EOP and the Cabinet: The Need for a (Relatively) Clear System of Sub-Presidential Decision-Making.* An even more difficult issue than who manages the process of issue development or presidential-order questions is how the system of sub-presidential decision-making on second and third order issues operates. I be-

lieve this one of the hidden areas of the presidency which could benefit from increased historical and scholarly inquiry. The focus on the President himself obscures the vast web of sub-presidential decision-making which drives so much of the work of the Executive Branch — or causes the gears of government to lock.

Because of the potential for debilitating conflict, defining some system of sub-presidential decision-making on second and third order issues that is understood by the EOP and the cabinet officers is probably more important than any particular system. In defining roles, any system must distinguish between process management, advice-giving and decision-making. The following is one possibility.

- *Process management.* Depending on whether the issue is heavily inter-departmental in character or largely confined to a single department, the process can be managed by the head of the EOP policy channel (*e.g.*, OMB Director or head of the Troika) or by the cabinet officer with an EOP process check.
- *Advice-Giving.* EOP units and cabinet departments implicated by the issue should have the fair opportunity to provide analysis and advice.
- *Decision-Making.* Given the importance of the second and third order issues to the record of the presidency, and given the inevitability that no issue is wholly the interest of a single department, the heads of the EOP policy channels should have decision-making authority on these issues, short of the chief of staff (and the President). Obviously, however, when an issue is predominately located in a single department, a substantial degree of deference should be given to the cabinet officer's views. This proposition has greater applicability to third order issues than the roughly 25 second order domestic issues.

Given the ineluctable tension between the Cabinet and the EOP and within the EOP itself, the chief of staff, under clear direction from the President, must make this system of sub-presidential decision-making work with techniques which range from "schmoozing" to arbitrating, as indicated above. There will be lots of play in the joints, and exceptions to every rule (as the President discovers that not all his appointees are of sterling quality). But a general approach to the difficult question of sub-presidential decision-making is essential if an Administration is not to tear itself apart.

9. *Delegation to the Departments: Cabinet Level Issues.* Beyond the

first, second and third order issues which constitute the essential strategic thrust of the presidency, there are, of course, a host of other issues which often are confined to a single department. Often these involve implementation of policy, as opposed to policy development. On these, a Cabinet Secretary should not be too closely monitored by the EOP. He or she should be judged by results — but not nitpicked to death by EOP review processes. As has been noted on many occasions, executive government is simply too vast to be run out of the White House or the EOP.

If the EOP can effectively coordinate the 125–150 first, second and third order issues, it will be doing wondrous well. Recognizing the need to give discretion to the Cabinet officers on many others (when they are not very heavily inter-agency in character) is a bedrock principle of EOP wisdom. The President should insist on this — and make sure that junior members of the EOP are not mucking about in these cabinet level issues. On these, departmental performance, not polite involvement in inter-administration process, is key to the decision about whether a cabinet officer should be commended — or fired.

10. *The Vice President: Senior Advisor Without Portfolio.* The innovation of the Carter years — followed generally by President Reagan and Vice President Bush — should be continued. The Vice President should have access to all the President's memoranda, briefings, decision meetings — and to the President himself. He should ask questions, use his political antennae, and give the President his best judgment on important issues based on the work flowing from others to the President. In so using the Vice President, the President is not only getting something very important — the seasoned, inside view of a senior person who has no bureaucratic ax to grind — but he is giving the Vice President the best possible training in the event that he must assume the highest office after presidential death or disability. One of the many problems with giving the Vice President major, substantive responsibilities beyond the "senior advisor" role recommended here is that it necessarily implies an expanded, separate vice presidential staff. The last thing that the invariably overblown EOP needs is yet another large staff.

*   *   *

Some might argue that these prescriptions are too broad. I would hope, instead, that they are powerful and interrelated organizing ideas, which reflect the complexity of executive government and which have significant practical implications. Recognizing that presidential "strategy" involves linking policy, politics, structure and process in a realistic time frame implicitly asks a set of interrelated questions which must be answered. Recognizing that the strategy must be set out early underscores the critical nature of the transition — and the importance of sophisticated and substantive transition planning before the election. Recognizing that priority setting has enormous implications for executive branch processes, and for the respective roles of the President, chief of staff, EOP and cabinet officers, can shape the whole internal governance of the Executive Branch.

Some might argue that these prescriptions are too narrow and will promote legalistic disputes, rather than dampen conflict, within the Executive Branch. In my view, it is naive to think that an institution as complex as the Executive Branch can function without a shared understanding of some broad organizing ideas. The potential for acrimonious disputes — all in the name of "the presidential interest," of course — is simply too great. If all issues are treated in an ad hoc fashion, then the wheel has to be reinvented on a daily basis. Better, I believe, to have an approach which applies generally, but which is flexible enough to allow for special situations. If the President indicates early and clearly the rules of the game in his Administration, including the chief of staff's role in administering those rules, then conflict will be minimized to the extent possible in executive government, a vast, sprawling and unwieldy institution which has conflict embedded in its very structure and which operates in a fish bowl under enormous pressures.

With the wrong people, even the right rules of the game won't work. But, the right people, with no rules or the wrong rules, can fail just as well. Appropriate structures and processes are not glamorous. They are simply essential.

CHAPTER FIVE

Policy Management in the Reagan Administration

RALPH C. BLEDSOE
EXECUTIVE SECRETARY
PRESIDENT'S DOMESTIC POLICY COUNCIL

A President and a White House, like other chief executives and their front offices, generate two "products" of importance: leadership and policy. In preparing Ronald Reagan for his presidency, his staff took great pains to craft the processes by which he could readily utilize his strengths to produce these vital products. The initial triumvirate that headed Reagan's staff—Counsellor Edwin Meese, Chief of Staff James Baker, and Deputy Chief of Staff Michael Deaver—divided responsibility for these tasks. Baker and Deaver assumed responsibility for the President's "production of leadership," including identifying the force fields and the communications channels with which the President would have to contend, and ensuring that the demands for leadership made by the key individuals and organizations in the force fields were dealt with. Meese, who designed the system for "production of policy," with the aid of Caspar Weinberger, was initially responsible for coordinating both national security and domestic policy-making. In 1982, William Clark joined the White House staff as Assistant to the President for National Security Affairs, and assumed a greater share of the responsibility for national security policy-making.

Before addressing policy making in the Reagan Administration, some observations about presidential leadership are appropriate. In reality these two cannot be separated, but to more fully understand the dynamics of White House staff behavior some distinctions must be made between the two processes.

Leadership

A White House staff, if it is to effectively serve a President, must always keep in mind that leadership is demanded of a President by players in many very strong force fields. A President cannot turn leadership on and off as he pleases. The demands do not stop. Nor are they evenly scheduled to coincide with the President's mood, his workload, or his social calendar. They are constant, and there is always a lengthy queue of demands for both leadership and policy. The best a White House staff can do is sense where the strongest ones are coming from, and ensure that the staff mechanisms capably respond within a reasonable window of time. An early or late response can often lead to additional problems.

Balancing Proactive and Reactive Leadership

Rather than simply react to external demands for leadership, (and there are plenty of these to capture and envelope a President), a President is often better served when he preempts demands and presents his own vision of the direction in which he believes the country should move. However, the best a President can hope to achieve, or at least that which Americans seem to appreciate and respect most, is striking a balance between proactive leadership, i.e. proposing new national initiatives or directions, and reactive leadership, reacting in a timely manner to specific demands. Too much of either will not satisfy a large percentage of the electorate for very long. A totally proactive President who spends too much time proposing new programs and attempting to consistently surprise, or keep others in his force fields off balance, will be seen as out of touch with political realities, and will be constantly defending new proposals at the expense of maintaining existing programs. On the other hand, a totally reactive President will be viewed as captive to the agendas of others. Events that become all-consuming of a President, such as those dictated by another country, or a situation in another region of the world, can result in an image of weakness in the eyes of his constituents as well as in world opinion. Presidents will be criticized for forgetting what they came to Washington to achieve, or worse, having reneged on their promises to the American people.

The Importance of Communication

Presidential leadership, like leadership in other organizational settings, is built on a two-way communications system between the President and those in his force fields, i.e. those demanding

leadership. The staff responsibility in this process is to advise
and assist the President on how to keep the communications
channels open, despite significant differences, high-intensity
levels, and even animosity or ill-will in the demands that are expressed in the information, messages and signals that flow over
the channels. The channels to as many elements in these force
fields as possible must be kept open, because if any of them dry
up or communication is cut-off, it is likely to be the President
who suffers the greater consequences. If the President is ever completely, or even partially shut off from receiving badly needed
information about the views or moods of important parts of his
force fields, or if his vision and leadership messages are not getting to an important segment of those demanding leadership,
his influence is greatly weakened. This often extends to entities
that some may consider the least important elements in one of
the President's force fields. A complicating factor for White House
staff members is the rapidly changing and differentiated makeup
of these force fields. They influence many different issues that
the staff must deal with on behalf of the President.

The Reagan Force Fields

In the Reagan White House, the critical elements in his force
fields have pretty much paralleled recent Administrations. They
include Congress; public interest groups (religious, ethnic, voluntary, commercial, labor, management, social, and other organized entities); intergovernmental leaders such as governors,
mayors, local and state legislators; political party leaders; the press;
foreign nations and leaders; appointed members of his Administration; Federal employee groups and, by no means least, private citizens who make individual demands on the President for
leadership. Staff members are responsible for ensuring that the
channels with all these groups and individuals are kept open.
And an attempt has been made to maintain a balance between
being responsive to these key individuals and groups, and ensuring that they are aware of the President's vision and agenda,
even when there may be differences in these views. Various means
are used to keep the President informed of the demands made
by these individuals and groups, just as means have been developed for informing them of the President's initiatives and actions. Some White House staff members perform these jobs better
than others, and some have found more efficient ways of keeping

the information channels open in both directions. Of course, with a professional communicator as the leader, the task has been somewhat easier.

Staff Conflict

In the White House, understanding the linkage between leadership and policy making is important because the staff people supporting the President's production of leadership have to use a very different set of skills and talents than those who assist the President in producing policy. In support of Presidential leadership, White House staff members must react quickly to the demands and uncertainties that characterize the information and communication channels linking the entities in the President's force fields. Staff members must sense the strength of each demand for leadership, correlate it with the President's previous and current statements, policies, and thinking, and engage in a relevant dialogue that ensures the channel remains open. Staff members assisting in the production of leadership must constantly move at a fast pace, and react to a wide range of demands, often with little time to plan or consider all of the strategic implications.

Conversely, staff members who support the President's production of policy are called upon to employ skills and techniques more associated with scoping out a policy issue, using analytic approaches that produce a range of policy options for the President, and following a deliberation process that most efficiently obtains a policy decision from the President. These processes usually involve longer lead times and proceed at a different pace than the production of leadership. And, more often than not, it is the different pace at which these two functions are performed that are the real causes of conflicts between White House staff members. Staff members supporting the production of leadership usually demand faster responses from those engaged in policy production. Staff members involved in policy production usually demand more caution and want to take a cut at one more analysis, or perform one more validating step, or incorporate one more relevant background factor, or run one more check. The interagency structure and relative slowness of the policy process can be quite frustrating to those used to the helter-skelter reactive pace of ensuring that a congressman's constituents inquiry or complaint is expeditiously handled.

While there are structural and behavioral similarities in both

production processes, there are enough differences to create
conflicts that are highly visible to White House observers. And,
if a President is to be effectively served by his staff, these conflicts
must be managed, as much because of the strong dependencies
that exist as because of the image concerns.

Policy

Presidential leadership depends on effective policies, and sound
policies must accurately reflect the leadership demands made
on a President. The production of policy by a President and a
White House staff includes 1) mechanisms for producing national
security and foreign policy, and 2) mechanisms for producing
domestic policy.

National Security and Foreign Policy

The structure for national security and foreign policy production is partially dictated by a statute, the National Security Act
of 1947, and subsequent amendments. This Act established the
National Security Council (NSC), chaired by the President, and
consisting of the Vice President, and the Secretaries of State and
Defense. Additional Cabinet members may be added at the
pleasure of the President. The Chairman of the Joint Chiefs of
Staff, the Director of Central Intelligence and others serve as
ex officio advisers. Substructures are usually established under
the NSC, including interagency groups and various other committees established to suit an Administration's special purposes.

The process for producing a national security or foreign policy
begins with a tasking of one or more groups or committees. This
may be done through a National Security Study Directive
(NSSD), or by some other means. At a later stage following discussions by an interagency group, a National Security Decision
Directive (NSDD) is often prepared. NSDDs, which may address broad global issues or highly specific topics, are used to
promulgate Presidential decisions, policies, and national objectives. They are usually discussed first at a planning meeting by
selected members of the NSC and the NSC staff. When the planning group feels the issue is ready for consideration by the President, the NSDD is sent to the President and a full NSC meeting
is held to discuss the issues described in the NSDD. At this
meeting the President will hear arguments by the proponents

of various options. Following the meeting, the President may sign the NSDD, thus making it Administration policy. The contents of a signed NSDD are communicated by the Assistant to the President for National Security Affairs to appropriate organizations for implementation and/or policy guidance.

Domestic Policy

The domestic policy process designed for the first Reagan term was characterized by Cabinet Councils. Five were announced in February 1981. These included Cabinet Councils on Economic Affairs; Commerce and Trade; Human Resources; Natural Resources and Environment; and Food and Agriculture. A sixth, the Cabinet Council on Legal Policy was added in January 1982, and a seventh, the Cabinet Council on Management and Administration, was added in September 1982. All Cabinet Councils were chaired by the President, and each had as Chairman Pro Tempore a cabinet member with primary interest or involvement in the specific policy area covered by the council. Membership was overlapping, with cabinet members serving on several Cabinet Councils. In addition, each Cabinet Council was supported by an Executive Secretary who was a White House staff member in the Office of Policy Development, managed by the Assistant to the President for Policy Development. As the senior domestic policy advisor to the President, the Assistant to the President for Policy Development was to have equivalency with the Assistant to the President for National Security Affairs. Each council was supported by one or more interagency working groups, comprised of agency representatives at the deputy secretary, assistant secretary or deputy assistant secretary levels. Each working group would prepare issues and options papers that served as the basis for council discussion of an issue. During the first four and a half years these councils collectively held close to 500 meetings on well over 700 different policy issues.

As mentioned, early in the first term, the Counsellor to the President coordinated both the national security/foreign policy process, and the domestic policy process. The Assistant to the President for National Security Affairs and the Assistant to the President for Policy Development reported to the Counsellor. This was to ensure that the President would receive similar policy "products," and to enhance coordination between staff members in developing policies that had both national security and domestic implications. This also ensured that the policy production mechanisms was coordinated at a high staff level, just below the President.

Early in the second Reagan term, all four senior White House staff leaders departed, and Donald Regan became Chief of Staff. The White House staff structure changed from an arrangement in which staff members reported through one of "four stovepipes," to what could be termed a strong-chief-of-staff pyramidal model, under the Chief of Staff. National security and foreign policy management and policy making remained relatively stable except for a slightly modified structure in which the Assistant to the President for National Security Affairs reported through, rather than to, the chief of staff. Major changes were made in the management of domestic policy, however. The seven cabinet councils were merged into two policy councils—the Domestic Policy Council and the Economic Policy Council. As before, the President remained as chairman, and two chairman pro tempore were appointed. Edwin Meese, the Attorney General, became chairman pro tem of the Domestic Policy Council, and James Baker, Secretary of the Treasury, became chairman pro tem of the Economic Policy Council. Cabinet members were assigned to one of the two councils, although the general practice was to encourage all cabinet members to participate in both councils. The executive secretaries and staff members supporting both councils were to report to the Chief of Staff through the Cabinet Secretary, instead of through the Assistant to the President for Policy Development.

In the second term, the two Councils have met about 275 times, addressing an additional 150 different policy issues. As is evident and expected, many more issues were handled in the first term when the Administration was making its major moves to turn the country in a new direction. In the second term there has been more concentration on fewer issues, using the experiences gained in the first term.

The operating processes used by the two policy councils have not changed a great deal. Interagency working groups are still the primary means by which policy issues are identified and scoped. Working groups and task forces are responsible for preparation of the issues and options papers to be discussed by the councils. As with the cabinet councils, issues are usually discussed in one or more council meetings without the President in attendance. When an issue is ready to be forwarded to the President for discussion and/or a decision, the council directs that a paper be prepared reflecting the council's views. If the President is being asked for a policy decision, the paper is in decision memorandum format, usually including a statement of the issue, background information, a discussion of decision options with advantages and disadvantages of each, and a recommendation, if appropriate. Following a meeting with the President, at which council members present their advice and views, the President will usually make a decision that is then communicated to the appropriate departments and agencies for implementation.

It should be noted that the imposition of structure on the policy making process, such as that described above, is very important in the management of a White House. If such a structure is lacking, White House staff members will tend to create different paths and processes for nearly every issue or type of issue, thus significantly increasing their individual power over the policy process, as well as the specific policy issues. This relegates Cabinet government to staff control instead of Presidential control.

President Reagan has been better served by the structures like those described above, since he firmly believes in control through Cabinet government. He is a leader who prefers expressions of opinions by a wider range of staff and line advisors about the policy choices he may be considering. While the formal nature of the system frustrates some White House staff members, especially those who prefer small "rump groups" as a means for controlling the processes, and more significantly, the outcomes and decisions, the policy making councils have performed very steadily throughout the full Reagan Administration. Though many policy issues are still handled by a less structured (or a differently structured) process, and while some of these have been major policy decisions, e.g. tax reform, they have been far fewer in number than they would have been under a less structured policy management process. And perhaps of greatest importance, although similar systems have been used by previous Presidents, this process seems to fit the "style" of policy and decision making that worked best for Ronald Reagan when he was Governor of California, and it has worked throughout the nearly two full terms he has served as President of the United States.

PART TWO

Presidential Transitions

CHAPTER SIX

The Making of an Unscheduled Presidential Transition

PHILIP W. BUCHEN
FORMER COUNSEL TO PRESIDENT FORD

Gerald R. Ford came to be President of the United States as the result of an extraordinary sequence of events, each one an historic first:

- Adoption in 1967 of the Twenty-fifth Amendment to the Constitution, which in Section 2 provides the first and only method of filling a vacancy in the office of the Vice President without waiting for the next-scheduled quadrennial election.[1]
- The first resignation from office by a Vice President because of charges against him of criminal misconduct, this on October 10, 1973 when Spiro Agnew resigned as a condition to having his prison sentence suspended.[2]
- Implementation for the first time of the Twenty-fifth Amendment when President Nixon on October 13, 1973 nominated Congressman Gerald Ford to be Vice President and both Houses of Congress, after extensive hearings, voted by December 6, 1973 to confirm his nomination.[3]
- The first resignation from office by a President, this on August 9, 1974 when Richard Nixon resigned to avoid impeachment proceedings by the Congress.[4]

Despite the novelty of the circumstances that gave President Nixon the opportunity to send to the Congress his nomination of a Vice President, his selection, although not inevitable, was hardly surprising. In August of 1968, Richard Nixon, then Republican nominee for President, had once before asked Ford if he would join the ticket.[4] Five years later, after the Presidency had become mired in the Watergate affair and a suspicious Congress was threatening impeachment, Nixon needed for his Vice President a person who would be well received by the Congress. No Republican could have filled that need better than Ford. Also, the confirmation proceedings produced no surprises, except possibly for the unprecedented thoroughness of the investigation into Ford's background and qualifications.[6]

What gave these initial proceedings under the Twenty-fifth Amendment added significance was their connection to an imminent change in the Presidency. The feeling was abroad that President Nixon could not long survive the exposures then coming out of various Watergate investigations. Among those who knew the feeling well was the Speaker of the House of Representatives, Carl Albert. During the 58 days from October 10 to December 6, 1973, when this country had no Vice President, he was next-in-line to become President.[7] He took seriously his potential responsibilities, as he should have, and quietly prepared himself for a transition to the Presidency.[8]

Members of the Senate and House Committees who conducted the hearings on Ford's nomination talked as if they were actually selecting the next President of the United States. An example comes in testimony before the Senate Committee on Rules and Administration, early in the confirmation hearings, from Senator Birch Bayh, who had been a leader in passage of the Twenty-fifth Amendment, and in a remark from Chairman Cannon:

> *Senator Bayh* . . . "[A]s we were debating the 25th amendment, I think we anticipated a great many eventualities. . . We could have imagined the possibility of a Vice Presidential resignation, but who could have imagined that at the same time the future of the Presidency itself was being questioned by a number of people and a number of news sources throughout the country? However, in my judgment these unexpected factors only serve to dramatically increase the importance of our responsibilities to see that the 25th amendment is functioning properly during the initial implementation. . . Can the nominee serve our country as President? In my judgment, that is the fundamental question that all of us are faced with today". . . *The Chairman.* "I pointed out in my opening statement before we heard Mr. Ford that we could well be selecting the next President of the United States". . .[9]

However alluring such sentiments might have been for anyone else in Ford's position, they seemed to have no effect on the Congressman from Michigan. After his swearing-in as Vice President, he remarked to his Congressional and television audience: "I am a Ford, not a Lincoln."[10]

Problems of Being Vice President During President Nixon's Final Days

As matters turned out, Ford's tenure as Vice President lasted little more than eight months, from early December to early August. For all that time until word came to him of Nixon's pending resignation, he remained disinterested, it seemed, in his prospects of becoming President. He spoke out as if he expected and wanted Nixon to stay in office until the end of his term.[11] His support and defense of the President troubled his friends, especially after transcribed recordings of Oval Office conversations about Watergate increasingly implicated the President in wrong doing. Growing numbers of Americans feared the harm being done to the country from having a distracted and weakened President, incapable of effective governing, remain in office. On the other hand, a large band of Nixon loyalists remained convinced of their President's right to stay in office and critical of the mischief being done to unseat him.

A Vice President is supposed, of course, never to give an impression of seeking the Presidency so long as the incumbent is alive and breathing.[12] The next-in-line is expected at all times to act unassuming. It is only if and when death strikes down the incumbent President, that a Vice President can with propriety act differently. Then without any preparation he must make an impromptu transition to the highest office in the land.

In keeping with that tradition, Vice President Ford eschewed even the semblance of preparations by his staff for his imminent succession to the Presidency.[13] Moreover, Ford had not been brought into the President's confidence to share his information on public issues of the day and learn of the decisions he was making or contemplating. The tradition of nothing-much-to-do Vice Presidents, largely isolated from the President, was not broken until President Ford did so on gaining Nelson Rockefeller as his Vice President.[14]

In the last fifteen Presidential transitions, the entire number in this century, one out of every two has been unscheduled.[15] Each of the others has followed an election when the winning candidate has had time from early in November until inauguration date, now the following January 20th, to prepare for his entry into the Presidency. It is this more frequent kind of a transition that receives attention.[16] Such is not the case in respect to the unscheduled transition and its problems, even though a Vice President, who may have to step into the Presidency with virtually no time for preparation could well use some advance help and forward planning.

The succession to a President in Nixon's situation, whenever he did resign or became impeached, was sure to pose problems more difficult than in the case of a vacancy caused by death. If a President dies from illness or assassination, particularly one who has not lost public favor, Americans will regard the event as a national tragedy, will not feel the need for a confidence-restoring transition, and will ordinarily expect continuity, at least for a time, of policy and personnel. In the circumstances of President Nixon's resignation, Ford was faced with having to undo the effects of an administration that had broken the public trust and had brought on widespread distress over lack of integrity in high places. At his swearing-in to be President, Ford responded to the plight of the country by assuring Americans: "Our long national nightmare is over."[17] So in taking over the Presidency when he did, Ford took on a responsibility unique to his transition into that office.

Planning in Secret for a Change of Presidents

On August 26, 1974, a couple of weeks after President Ford had taken office, *The New York Times* carried on its front page an account of plans made for a Ford Presidency starting months beforehand. The idea for this project, with whatever guilt attaches, was mine. I acted out of friendship and admiration for Gerald Ford, as well as concern that the Vice President and his staff lacked opportunity to prepare for his almost certain succession to the Presidency. Helpful collaborators in this surreptitious undertaking were Clay T. Whitehead, who had worked on the prior Presidential transition from President Johnson to Nixon and who had served on the latter's White House staff, along with Brian P. Lamb, Laurence E. Lynn, Jr., and Jonathan Moore. All were knowledgeable about the workings of the White House, and none was likely to attract notice from the press of his movements in and out of meeting places.

A series of meetings of this group involved comprehensive discussions and presentation of papers on a range of topics. They

covered the mechanics of getting a new President in place, organization of the White House staff, dealings with press and public,
getting control of the government machinery, and introduction
of fresh policies. Although this effort was only preliminary, it
permitted Whitehead to have ready a complete agenda, with
recommendations on points to be decided early, for use at the
next stage of planning when advisers of the Vice President's selection took over.

As matters turned out, the next stage of planning did not start
until Wednesday evening, August 7, 1974, scarcely 40 hours before Ford was to become President. Not until the evening of August 6th had Ford become sure enough of a Nixon resignation
to share his information with me. At the same time he decided
on the team of advisers he wanted to tackle the task of changing
Presidents in quick and orderly fashion and authorized me to
bring them together. The persons he chose, whom I called later
that night for a meeting the next evening, were Robert Griffin,
Rogers Morton, John Byrnes, and William Whyte, former colleagues of Ford's in the House, along with William Scranton who
had been Governor of Pennsylvania and Bryce Harlow who had
earlier served on President Nixon's and on President Eisenhower's
staffs.

Even at that time, Ford wanted us to keep the transition
gathering out of sight, because the President was having second
thoughts over his initial decision to leave office. No matter that
a Vice President knows it is in the public interest for him to be
well prepared to assume the Presidency, he still feels inhibited
from having any forward planning take place. This feeling in
Ford's case comes through in his telling of the occasion when
he first learned, during his talk with me on August 6th, about
the transition effort I had instigated:

"Phil hit me with a real surprise. The resignation, he said, had seemed
likely to him for the past several months. He'd been so concerned
about it, so mindful of all the things that would have to be done,
that early in May he had formed a sub rosa 'transition team' . . .
And secrecy, Phil went on, had been a vital consideration. They
realized that had I known of their activities, I would have demanded
that they stop. If Nixon or any one of his supporters found out,
it would have been construed as an act of disloyalty on my part,
and the results could have been disastrous."[18]

Making the Change of Presidents

The uncertainty of when a change of Presidents would occur did not end until late on Thursday morning, August 8, when President Nixon first told the Vice President of his decision to resign, effective at noon the next day.[19] By that time the group that had met the night before had ready for the President-to-be an option paper and recommendations. The topics covered were the swearing-in (where, when, and before whom?), the new President's initial remarks, relations at the outset with the former President and his staff, the appointment of a formal transition organization, and early meetings with the Congressional leadership, the Cabinet, and other official groups. The first action came with the Vice President's call to Chief Justice Warren Burger, then attending a conference in the Netherlands, to seek his return by Air Force plane in time to administer the oath to the 38th President of the United States. The second urgent step was a call to Jerald TerHorst of the *Detroit News* asking him to accept and start filling that very day the position of Press Secretary. This appointment was crucial because of the overwhelming press and public interest in this historic making of an instant President.

Robert T. Hartmann, Chief of Staff for the Vice President, had already prepared a draft of suggested remarks for the new President to make as soon as he took office. The draftsman experienced at once the work hazards that beset every Presidential speech writer, as his draft underwent the critical scrutiny, not only of the man who was to utilize the work, but also of everyone in the transition group, each with his own preferences for what should be said. In Hartmann's vivid account of that busy day before the change of Presidents, he summarizes the happenings:

"There were so many urgent things to be done; somehow we did most of them. The Vice President himself was calm and decisive, the coolest head in the crowd."[20]

To provide the new President with further advice after his inauguration, August 9th, for completing the operational transition from the Nixon to the Ford Presidency, he called upon Donald H. Rumsfeld, then temporarily back from the NATO headquarters in Belgium where he served as this country's ambassador, Rogers Morton who was Secretary of the Interior, Governor Scranton from the earlier transition group, and John O. Marsh,

Jr. from the Vice Presidential staff who soon became Counsellor to the President. L. William Seidman, also from the Vice Presidential staff who soon became Assistant to the President for Economic Affairs, worked in a staff capacity with this latest transition team, as did Whitehead and I.

This last of the three successive transition teams finished its report and presented it to the President on August 20th.[21] After that the team disbanded, lest it start to become directly involved in operational matters, which was not its purpose. Problems with which the report dealt thoughtfully were: overlap and competition between the Office of Management and Budget (OMB) and the Domestic Council; the need to resolve the confusion of roles among economic policy advisers and spokespersons; the need for restaffing and elevating the President's organization for legal affairs in the aftermath of Watergate and the damage it had done to the Presidency; and the need to raise the stature and competence of the White House personnel operation. Specific ideas proposed in the report were to reduce the White House staff in size, including the number of military officers assigned to the staff; to reduce the trappings of the Presidency; to hold visits with top career Civil Servants; to use "straight talk" with the American people on key problems of the nation; and to take policy initiatives in respect to national parks and historic preservation, pension reform, and automobile safety.

Evaluation of the Ford Transition to the Presidency

The final transition team had cautioned in its report that its efforts did not complete the transition to a Ford Presidency. The rest was up to the President and to the people he decided upon to fill the key staff positions in his White House. The report had presented no recommendations as to persons who should be appointed to serve in particular positions or as to which, if any, incumbents from the Nixon administration should be kept on. Nevertheless, everyone with whom I worked during the whole transition took it for granted that with the exception of Henry Kissinger, the new President would keep few, if any, holdovers from before August 9th.

Contrary to this assumption, the President was reluctant to seek resignations from incumbents who had taken no part in the misdeeds that had brought down the Nixon administration, and he was slow to transform the staff and the Cabinet into ones of his own making. Hartmann had been particularly critical of this result after the transition team disbanded:

> "I sometimes wonder what might have happened if President Ford had rejected his transition advisers' desire to fade quickly into the background and instead installed most of them immediately as the nucleus of his new Administration, along with dedicated veterans of the Vice Presidential staff. . . The Nixon-to-Ford transition was superbly planned. It was not a failure. It just never happened."[22]

I am inclined instead to put part of the blame on the way the transition was planned, largely because the Vice President and his staff dared not become involved early enough. It would have made a substantial difference if in advance of changing Presidents, Ford had decided, with the help of trusted advisers, whom he would want to hold each of the key positions on his White House staff and in his Cabinet and what his first policy moves would be. The same work that takes place on the part of a President-elect between his election and his inauguration should have occurred, in a low-key and confidential manner, during the Ford Vice Presidency.

In its report on August 20th, the transition team made a point that the President should *plan backwards:*

> "Plan backwards from where you want to be next February, after the State of the Union, Economic, and Budget messages, to identify an orderly sequence of events between now and then."

Such "backward planning" would affect when and how the President made his major policy decisions and how promptly he made appointments for filling positions necessary to meet the goals he set for the next February.

Nothing like such strategic planning occurred after that, so far as I could tell, and it is unlikely that it could have. Once the President had taken office, the rush of day-to-day events and demands caught up with him, just as it did for his few new appointees to the White House staff. That kind of extended thinking never comes easily in the White House. A better place and time for it is the Vice President's office before he is impelled to make a sudden transition into the Presidency.

Even though President Ford delayed putting his stamp on the

administration he had inherited, whenever he did bring in a person of his own choice, he appointed someone of exceptional competence and high integrity. Particularly noteworthy were his selections of Nelson Rockefeller to be Vice President, Alan Greenspan to head the Council of Economic Advisers, Edward H. Levi as Attorney General, Donald H. Rumsfeld as Secretary of Defense, John T. Dunlop as Secretary of Labor, William T. Coleman, Jr. as Secretary of Transportation, Carla A. Hills as Secretary of Housing and Urban Development, George Bush as Director of the Central Intelligence Agency, and David Mathews as Secretary of Health, Education, and Welfare.[23]

No matter what weaknesses Ford's transition to the Presidency may have had, and no matter what caused them, he brought to that office unusual strength and qualities of his own, much-needed at the time. They were not the product of any transition team's efforts; nor could they have been, however much time and care had gone into the preparation. In that respect, the preparation was all Ford's, extending over a quarter-century of his dedicated service in Congress and during years before then of inspired character building. As James Reston wrote soon after Ford came into the Presidency:

"Within the first days of his unexpected — and probably unwanted — Presidency, Gerald Ford has demonstrated the force of principles of open discussion and moral example. His approach is different. His language is different, the voice is strong, the eyes straight and steady, his religious faith proclaimed openly to an unbelieving generation."[24]

CHAPTER SEVEN

The Transition from President Nixon to President Ford*

KATHY B. SMITH
ASSOCIATE PROFESSOR OF POLITICS
WAKE FOREST UNIVERSITY

The study of presidential transitions is the study of communication in a particular environment. This paper will examine the peculiar environment of the Nixon-Ford presidential transitions and the efforts that were made to transfer presidential power with the least disruption of governmental operations.

The paper will be organized around the following research questions: 1) What are the elements involved in a presidential transition? 2) In what ways was Gerald Ford's transition similar or dissimilar to other transitions? 3) What process was used to implement the Nixon-Ford transition? 4) What major problems were encountered and how were these problems addressed? 5) How successful was the Nixon-Ford transition and what lessons can be gleaned from this episode?

The method of investigation included an examination of public evaluations of the Ford transition as discussed in *The New York Times* and *The Washington Post* for the six months following Ford's assumption of office. A study of the theoretical articles dealing with the nature, significance and historic use of transitions was conducted. Finally, papers from the staff members of the Ford Administration were used to study the mechanizations of the transfer of power. This normative process will hopefully permit the advancement of findings not only about the specific Nixon-Ford transition but of subsequent presidential transitions as well.

Transition Period

The presidential transition period can be defined by length of time or by functional assumption of tasks. A difficulty with focusing upon transitions is this amorphous nature of its definition. While some writers use the phrase transition to cover the period from election night to inauguration day, others discuss transitions as the first few (usually three) months of the new administration. This "100 day" approach is still shorter than the period from inauguration to 6 months later used by official sources or the first two years discussed by Neustadt.[1] However, a transition is not simply a calendar described period, but instead encompasses the ability to handle inheritance problems, present a new agenda, and place a personal stamp on the presidency. This personal stamp involves both structural and symbolic changes in the operation of the White House. Laurin Henry argues that while presidential responsibilities may be transferred with the oath of office, the presidency must be recreated by each president.[2]

The tasks of the transition period are both varied and essential. People must be hired and fired. The organizational structure of the White House needs to be fitted to the personal decision making style of the new president. A policy agenda must be compiled and campaigned for within the limitations of task commitments. Inherited foreign and domestic policy directions must be maintained or smoothly altered without evoking international alarm. New roles and expectations need be established for smooth governmental operations. Personal influence must be nurtured and expanded through personal presidential contacts, public addresses and close attention to image portrayal. These are some of the tasks confronting a new president in his first weeks under the spotlight of national media attention.

Although definitions of transition may vary, there is little disagreement that transitions are very significant for a new president. In discussing the transition from President Ford to President Carter, Donald Haider concludes with the following line, "If the 1976-77 transition suggests anything, it is that transitions may be critical to the fate of the administration."[3] Walker and Reopel agree based on their work on the Reagan transition, that Reagan's "carefully planned and effective transition was a crucial precursor for Reagan's legislative and budget successes during the presidential honeymoon."[4] Why would this be the case? Many reasons are advanced, but central to this answer is a perception of control and direction rendered by the Washington media and president watchers on and off Capitol Hill. The tone or style of the new presidency is set during this early period, and its hard to alter if the portrayal is not flattering.

Internationally, our nation is at a vulnerable point as the retiring president, although still in constitutional control of the executive branch, loses personal momentum and desire to commit his successors to major policy directions. While the president elect has no authority to address national issues, and as a newly inaugurated president may be unfamiliar with the foreign policy mechanisms. Our foreign neighbors ask for continuity and maintenance of relations at a time of domestic political turmoil.

Transitions, therefore, are important to a new president, to our foreign neighbors and to the American people. How can we judge the success of this vital transition period? Perhaps following the focus of the Presidential Transition Act of 1963 a concern for being orderly and insuring continuity of governmental operations is a good beginning. But from a democratic perspective, a successful transition should also be responsive to the American people, sensitive to the ethical demands of the situation and conscious of the importance of a positive symbolic image for the American presidency. Thus, successful transitions, include both smooth government operations and a democratically consistent persona.

Ford Situation: Both Common and Unique

The transition from Richard Nixon to Gerald Ford illustrates both the common elements in transitions and the unique nature of this particular event. Turning first to the elements shared by all presidents when they assume the presidency, we encounter both positive and negative features. The American tradition of election and transferring power is marked by a concern for giving the new person a "fair" chance to succeed, even if the elected official was not a personal favorite. This honeymoon perspective demands that the sharp claws of criticism be kept sheathed for the early days of the new presidency. Some mistakes are forgiven as examples of the problems of being new to the job.[5] But there are still withdrawals from what Neustadt terms the bank account theory of power. But after the initial, often awkward, experiences are accomplished by the new president, the expectation is that a learning experience has occurred and next time will be better handled. Whether it's a matter of protocol, such as omitting an invitation to a White House dinner or an awkwardly timed legislative initiative, multiple errors spell trouble for the image of a competent new administration.

Just as a honeymoon is common to presidential transitions, so are the problems of satisfactorily fulfilling role expectations and handling the changeover of personnel. How things have been done in the past can become the expected behavior for the future. For example, cabinets, lacking a constitutional base, have been included in every president's organization and wearing blue jeans in White House photographs was criticized during the Carter administration as inappropriate attire. Many expectations and routines are widely known by the president and his advisors, but the sheer number of constituencies and diversity of functions of the White House mean that many role expectations are discovered only when they are violated.[6] The routing of correspondence from one office to another is often charged with undertones of relative power position in the White House, and a new crew may violate and, therefore, offend the existing office staff.[7] Successfully meeting the initial role expectations is time consuming but very important for establishing an image of competency in the Washington community. President Ford was confronted with the time commitments of meeting Congressmen's expectations when he was informed by his staff that he must personally sign a portrait of Gerald Ford and have it hand delivered to each Congressman "as soon as possible." This broke down to 25 signatures per day for three weeks[8] — quite the pleasant program.

The matter of dealing with executive personnel has two facets. The staff of the old administration must be skillfully managed while recruiting and correctly placing the best possible new team. Since the old staff has the experience and intimate knowledge of government operations, the cooperation with the new team is vital. Although important, it is not automatically forthcoming in cases of transitions from radically different presidents or even from one party control to the other party.[9] Ideally, however, the old staff can be used for their expertise and removed before incessant problems ferment. President Johnson would probably have benefitted from a more timely changeover from the old loyal Kennedy team to the establishment of his own personal team. But the nature of the times (a martyred president) can dictate a path that may not have initially been desired.

The building of a new administration requires the recruitment of the best personnel in a rapid fashion. Public employment with its fish bowl existence and relatively low compensation, compared to the private sector does not assure an acceptance of a presidential offer to join the administration. So often the task was one of locating the individual that fits the list of requirements (ranging from party and ideology to gender and home region) and persuading that individual to become part of the new government. An administration will be fairly judged by the caliber of the individuals recruited to the available posts, so the early choices help form lasting impressions of that administration. Additionally, there are political costs in making widespread changes in the initial team. These actions can be seen as indications of a lack of good judgment in the early hiring process. Worse is the case where recruits dishonor the president or produce feuds within the executive office. Thus, personnel decisions are both difficult and central for a successful administration.

To summarize, the features held in common by any presidential transition, including the Nixon-Ford transition, include the condition of being new to the post, the honeymoon period, assuming role expectations and dealing with personnel questions.

The Nixon-Ford transition, however is also noted for its unique nature in the history of the American presidency. Issues of legitimacy, shortness of time, and an aroused public mood towards the national government, set the stage for Ford's presidency. The United States prides itself on the orderly manner of transferring power and the attendant legitimacy granted to each succeeding president. This legitimacy is grounded in the precedent of having been duly elected by the electoral college. President Ford, however, assumed office under a far different situation. Other Vice Presidents have assumed the presidency, but no one previously had become president without the benefit of a national election. Following Section 2 of the Twenty-fifth Amendment to the Constitution, the resignation of Vice President Spiro Agnew led to the appointment by President Nixon of Gerald R. Ford for the vacant vice presidency. The Watergate episode led to the ultimate resignation of President Nixon and the transfer of power (under Section 1 of the Twenty-fifth Amendment) to Vice President Gerald Ford. Thus, Gerald Ford rose to the presidency without ever being elected by a national constituency. The legitimacy of this transfer of power rested on the proper use of the Twenty-fifth Amendment, but not on the stronger democratic base of a electoral success. Louis Koenig describes this sequence of events as "abhorrent to democratic standards."[10] This historic chain of events led scholars and President Ford, himself, to challenge the wisdom of retaining the Twenty-fifth Amendment.[11]

Besides the cloud left by the legitimacy question, Ford entered the presidency with a very brief period for preparation. Granted his preparation time was longer than President Johnson's unanticipated assumption following Kennedy's death, but it was very short by historic standards. In contrast, President Reagan began plans for entering the White House during his presidential campaign, including the preparation of dossiers on perspective candidates for office. The Transition Act of 1963 provides for government funds to be spent for office space, staff, and other expenses incurred in planning the new administration from the November 4 election onward until six months after inauguration. While President Ford saw the Watergate scandal unfold he was not in a position to publicly work on his own assumption of power, without appearing disloyal to President Nixon and overly ambitious.[12] He cannot be criticized for either of these charges since he maintained a distance from transitions plans until the time immediately before his inauguration. Thus, Ford was left with the rare problem of no time for active transition efforts prior to his assumption of office.

Finally, President Ford also entered the presidency when public opinion was generally disenchanted with the actions emanating from the presidency. As a position of great importance in the socialization of America, Nixon's fall from the high pedestal of the presidency was a hard one, attendant with many aftershocks. A wariness toward government honesty and a particular distrust for the presidency aggravated Ford's transition problems.

President Ford was forced to deal with the problems of legitimacy, lack of preparation, and public disenchantment as he began his presidency. The approach he took in dealing with these problems determined the success of his transition period.

Transition Process

President Ford's transition preparations began in secret in May, 1974, not on August 7, 1974, the day before President Nixon's resignation, as earlier reported in the press.[13] The planning was started by a past law partner of Ford's from Grand Rapids, Michigan, Philip Buchen.[14] Mr. Buchen was working on a study of The Rights of Citizens to Privacy under a committee chaired by Mr. Ford. He was not part of the Vice President's staff, but his concern focused on the possible plight of his friend, Gerald Ford. In May, Buchen approached Tom Whitehead, whom he knew well, a Nixon staff official working in the office of Telecommunication Policy. Buchen knew that Whitehead had been a part of the team for the Johnson-Nixon transition and discussed Ford's need for contingency planning. Whitehead reluctantly agreed to help, but both men agreed that the planning would be kept secret. Secrecy was dictated since Nixon was still contending he would not resign and Ford said he would not show a lack of confidence in President Nixon. Buchen, Whitehead and three individual participants (unidentified to the press) met four times in the summer at Whitehead's house. Their discussions ranged widely, but Whitehead summarized the discussion into a nine point list he called the "Index."

On Tuesday, August 6, a day after Nixon disclosed the tapes showing his participation in the cover-up, Ford was informed that "within 72 hours he could be president." Buchen immediately contacted Whitehead, who honed the Index down to the points on the "transition team" and "first week." Ford was now told by Buchen of the earlier transition efforts and volunteered five names of people he wanted working on the transition. These individuals were Mr. William G. Whyte, U.S. Steel; former Governor William Scranton, of Pennsylvania; Senator Robert Griffin of Michigan, the Senate Republican Whip; former Representative John Byrnes of Wisconsin; and, Bryce Harlow of Procter & Gamble and a former aide to both Presidents Eisenhower and Nixon.

Wednesday, August 7, this newly formed group of Ford friends met at Mr. Whyte's home from 5:00 p.m. until midnight working from the Whitehead Index. They still had no indication of how imminent the turnover might be, but they knew time was short. From this meeting came many decisions that set the base of a successful transition. These decisions included a discussion of the role of the Chief Justice. It was decided that the Chief Justice of the United States, Warren E. Burger, must return from his trip to the Netherlands to officiate at the inauguration. The consensus of the group was that President Nixon should not be present at Ford's swearing-in ceremony. It was recommended that Ford would quickly need a brief speech to the American people and a new press secretary to replace discredited Ronald L. Ziegler. Furthermore, an ongoing team would be needed to assist Ford in the continuing problems with transition.

Thursday, August 8, Nixon informed Ford that he would announce his resignation in a televised message that evening. Following the speech Nixon would leave for California for the last time as President of the United States since the formal letter of resignation would not yet have been delivered to the Secretary of State. The group of five met in Whitehead's office from the afternoon hours until 3:00 a.m. Friday, with only two brief breaks. During this time the decision memorandums were drawn for Ford's actions and notices were drawn to be sent to every federal department and agency informing them of the change of power.

Friday, August 9, Byrnes and Buchen went to Mr. Ford's house to discuss the transition plans. The three men discussed these plans while being driven into the city of Washington where that day Mr. Ford would become the thirty-eighth President of the United States.

President Ford followed the recommendations of his friends closely in the following days. The new transition team consisting of John Marsh, Rogers Martin, Donald Rumsfeld and William Scranton was an illustrious group with considerable prior governmental experience. This group began meeting with President Ford regularly, beginning with his inauguration day. The change of press secretaries also happened quickly as ter Horst replaced Ziegler within one hour of Ford's inaugural address.[15] As suggested by the transition group, former President Nixon was not present at the swearing-in ceremony of Gerald Ford.

The constitutional presidential transfer of power occurred with very little time for advance planning. How successful was this process? *The Washington Post* described the event as "an orderly thing, this passing of power."[16] On August 10, *The Washington Post* editorialized the "transfer of power proceeded with dignity, as everyone assumed it would, and concluded on a strongly reassuring note."[17] According to *The New York Times*, "in his first hour in the presidency he seemed to be saying and doing everything right."[18] The reason for this success will be the subject to which we turn next.

After Inauguration

President Ford began his presidency with the advantage of having good advisers provide politically feasible advice which he could expediently put into action. His reliance on the informal transition team report, close attention to personnel problems, continuing efforts to establish his legitimacy, and influence the public mood helped account for his successful transition.

The group of five working on the transition produced a report entitled "Memorandum for the Vice President" on August 8, 1974.[19] This memo is interesting both for its brevity, a mere three and a half pages, and its attempt at facilitating two-way communication between the writers and Vice President Ford. Four areas are addressed and under each heading a direct recommendation for action is presented, a brief rationale for this decision is presented, options are presented, and space provided for "Your Choice: ." The first section "Transitional Organization" called for a temporary operational group interposed between the new and the old White House staff.[20] Following was a list of functional positions to fill with recommended names only one of which had a star beside the entry. These starred recommendations became a part of the new Ford Administration.

The second section on "the business of government" argued that "you should have a series of meetings the first few days to assert your personal direction and control of the executive branch of the government."[21] An order of proposed meetings was then given and, again, followed by Ford, along with the suggested meetings with "a number of key American and foreign individuals." A summary of presidential activities for Ford's first two weeks indicate a total of 120 presidential events during that period.[22] The business of government was discussed as establishing personal contact and direction over a wide range of constituencies. *The New York Times* described these meetings as "steps to show he was in control of government."[23] And he was credited with obtaining this initial control.

The third section "Old White House Staff" deals with inheritance problems. Ford is advised to "walk a delicate line between compassion and consideration for the former president's staff and the rapid assertion of your personal control over the executive branch."[24] The staff should be asked to initially stay on, but given the understanding that they may soon be expected to leave. Al Haig was singled out for separate attention and described as having "done Yeoman's service for his country." However, "he should not be expected, asked, or be given, the option to become your *Chief of Staff.*"[25] The staff was reassured and Al Haig continued doing his job during the transition period, but he did not become the Chief of Staff.[26] Ford's situation of having no prior time to recruit new personnel made him more dependent than usual on the good will and cooperation of the old staff.

The final section, "Vice Presidential Search Process" does not address the question of whom to consider, but instead deals with the question on how and when. Specifically, the recommendation was to follow the procedures used by Mr. Nixon in eliciting suggestions from a number of sources, and having this correspondence by a date "a week or so hence." The concern was that "this cannot deter you and your transition team from the business of government."[27] The vice presidential selection must be done quickly but not at the expense of attending to the business of government. Ford's response was to give himself 10 days to come up with a vice presidential nomination.[28]

President Ford began office with the assistance of politically astute advisors who winnowed down an immense task into four main areas. The task of transition was made to appear manageable and orderly as long as, among other things, careful attention was given to skillfully dealing with the old and new personnel. The major considerations for any new president is the use of old personnel and the hiring of a new team, but for Ford, the recruitment process had to occur after inauguration. The immediate need was to get Nixon's staff to cooperate in insuring the smooth continuation of government services. To this end, "Memorandum for the White House Staff" was sent out on August 9 by the Vice President prior to his swearing in. After acknowledging their joint feelings of sorrow and encouraging them to be "proud of the president you served and of your efforts for him and the country," Ford asked each of them "to stay long enough to assure a steady and uniform transition of the presidency." One rationale given to stay on the job is summed up in the following line: "You can still serve him (Nixon) and the nation by helping me to carry on the essential function of the presidency."[29] Acknowledging their shared feelings and using their continuing loyalty to Nixon, helped President Ford bridge the gap from the Nixon to Ford Presidency.

On August 10, the day after inauguration, Ford held his first meeting with the cabinet. The main purpose of the meeting was to: "1) reassure the cabinet of your respect for their abilities, your need for their help, and the importance of an orderly continuation of the work of government. 2) Inform the cabinet of the transition staff arrangements and how they should interact with the transition staff and you."[30] Ford asked for written reports from each cabinet member conveying the department's activities and problems which would go directly to the president.

The advice was given to establish the authority of the transition group as a presidential representative and change the old pattern of working through the Domestic Council and Al Haig.[31] New routing of information, new contacts but existing personnel were identified as problem areas to be addressed. William Timmons complained that the President and other new staff officials had made contact with Congress without clearing his office. Additionally, duplication of effort occurred with two different offices, sending colored photos of President Ford out to Congressmen.[32] Problems still occurred in the duplication of efforts, and in the stepping of personal turf, but widespread lack of cooperation did not occur. Ford's transition efforts seem to follow the words of Thomas Jefferson, which Ford evoked in remarks to the executive employees on August 13: "That government is strongest, he said, of which everyman feels himself a part."[33]

The other side of the personnel question also received attention in the Ford Transition Team Report. The report on personnel begins with the admonition "nothing you can plan and organize will be more important to the success of the Ford Administration than your selection of personnel."[34] After the perfunctory praise for the old staff, some forthright appraisals of the Nixon staff are discussed, including the fact that "they're exhausted," "some may have vulnerabilities from the past two years," and "some have difficult relationships with the rest of the government." So the report continues "the time to recruit is now." The good feeling existing immediately after the inauguration may not last and the best people must be tapped immediately. Sixteen suggestions are made, but the list is headed by a suggestion that is both important and heeded by President Ford: "The most important thing you can do with respect to personnel is for you to resolve to spend a significant portion of your personal time on the subject of personnel. The better job that is done, the less time you will have to spend during the remainder of your Presidency on problems."[35] Many changes are suggested dealing with recruiting pools, hiring provisions and staff reductions but an interesting suggestion dealt with the issue of handling those individuals leaving office. The report called for,

> careful, humane, decent treatment of those individuals who will be leaving. It is not complicated, but it takes a little time and has to be organized. . . It is critical to recruiting that those who are thinking about coming into the administration, see clearly that the people who are there and have been there, were well treated. Further, it is the right thing to do.[36]

The advice is sound and the Administration followed this process with quiet consideration for the old staff. James Reston writing in an article entitled "Ford's Noble Beginning" said "Gerald Ford has demonstrated the force of those principles of open discussion and moral example."[37] The new Administration's attitude towards personnel seems to justify Reston's description.

Besides from following the transition group's suggestions and tending to the pressing personnel problems. Ford also dealt with the question of legitimacy and the tarnished public image of the presidency. Constitutionally, the legitimacy of his authority came from his confirmation by Congress as Vice President. But as *The Washington Post* editorial stated, "in the larger sense, legitimacy lies in his acceptance by the people of this country, and that overwhelming and warm acceptance cannot be doubted."[38] Although not doubted, it also may not have been maintained without careful attention. President Ford's remarks on taking the oath of office were part of the process of establishing his legitimacy and putting the American people squarely behind his new presidency.

President Ford's inaugural address began with a reference to the oath he was taking being the same as the one taken by George Washington, but the circumstances being different. Thus, in the introduction he both establishes the continuity of our government and acknowledges the uniqueness of his personal situation. He responds to questions of his lack of election with the request that "you confirm me as your president with your prayers."[39] A request which is easy to grant and impossible to measure the levels of non-compliance. Ford calls for unity and pledges "an uninterrupted and sincere search for peace." The quotable line "my fellow Americans our long national nightmare is over,"[40] tries to provide closure to the Watergate episode and prepare for a new beginning. The new Administrative style of "openness and candor with full confidence that honesty is always the best policy in the end" was a welcome change and a signpost for the future. Finally, this address is a successful one because it portrays the human side of Gerald Ford to a public eager to learn more about their new chief executive. His request for prayers for Richard Nixon and for Nixon's family was a compassionate request that blended well with his humble yet confident concluding line, "God, helping me, I will not let you down."[41] The address confronted the problems of legitimacy, the Watergate legacy, the need for a new style of White House operations and revealed the humanity of the speaker.

During his first days in the White House, President Ford met personally with a host of groups putting the stamp of his presence on the new Administration. Just as the portraits of Nixon were quickly exchanged for those of President Ford, the face and style of the new President was imprinted on both domestic and foreign audiences. The call for a more open Administration was given reality through the operations of the Press Secretary's office. Press Secretary J. F. ter Horst wrote in a "Memorandum to the White House Staff" that "the President supports and encourages increased accessibility to the media, balanced, of course, with the need to ensure proper and timely flow of information to the public."[42] After explaining the five types of attribution ter Horst "strongly recommends that White House officials speak on the record. It is by far the safest route." The memo concludes with the encouragement "to speak to reporters openly and fully about matters within your area of responsibility and personal knowledge," "but to use caution when speaking outside your expertise."

The Press Office also helped build support for the Administration by apologizing to the press corps when their daily briefings were delayed. This is not a major action, but one that was notable in contrast to the lack of such actions by the preceding Press Secretary, Ron Ziegler.[43]

The speech following the oath of office, numerous personal contacts, and the operations of the press office helped promote legitimacy and national support, as did the change in style of the Ford Presidency. President Ford moved to decentralize the decision-making process and return more policy initiatives to the departments.[44] Transition team recommendations called for a substantial reduction in size of the White House Staff and the Office of Management and Budget. These measures were implemented with close initial contact between the President and the individual cabinet members. During the first two weeks Ford met with individual members of the cabinet 23 times. The image of the distant, majestic Nixon presidency and the desire to change the tone of the Ford Presidency produced a series of constructive suggestions. These included cutting the trappings of the presidency by reducing the use of limousines and reducing the number of military men assigned to the White House. Additionally, it was recommended that the military people in the White House dress in civilian dress for all but formal occasions.

Measures suggested to humanize the President including giving "a series of small informal dinners with national leaders and top officials of your Administration;" "having a few dinners with your children and *their* friends"; "taking occasional walks in various D.C. neighborhoods (not just inner city problem areas) to meet your new neighbors;" "returning to Grand Rapids, possibly on Veterans Day or Thanksgiving. Richard Nixon did not have a hometown." And "play golf occasionally on the South Lawn, for relaxation or while talking business."[45] Some of these were followed by President Ford, but they all highlight the importance given to changing the image of the presidency. Journalists wrote after the first week of transition of "the relative ease of changing the presidential atmosphere after the poisoned days of Watergate."[46] The achievement of an improved atmosphere emanating from the White House is less a testimony to ease than it is a triumph of planning and skillful execution.

Conclusion

This paper focused upon the Nixon-Ford transition as an example of both the common features, and the unique nature of each presidential transfer of authority. The problems inherent in being new to office, having little preparation time, dealing with both old and new personnel, establishing Administrative legitimacy, and moving national opinion in a supportive direction were discussed during the Nixon-Ford transition period. Other important problems dealing with policy positions, developing new routines, organizing a personal-decision making structure and dealing with the many problematic "Nixon questions" await later exploration. But this discussion does lead to the advancement of the following conclusions. The Nixon-Ford transition can be viewed as a success based on the earlier established criteria of being orderly and keeping the machinery of government moving. Additionally, this transition meets the more stringent requirement of following high moral and ethical standards of behavior and attempting to respond to public needs.

From a practical perspective, the transition indicates the importance of having a transition coordinated by a few, able individuals close to the president with no direct, personal career stake in the advice being offered. Ford's transition team was close enough to the President to be listened to and to speak to the President in his own language, based on common experiences as elected officials and associates. The transition was implemented quickly but actions had to be taken rapidly to insure the clean break with the past and in anticipation of future events. Although 61 hours is not a long time, much was accomplished through the use of prioritizing and delegating of tasks to trusted advisers. The advisers laid the groundwork for a successful transition but one other crucial factor was required — a president who was willing to learn from his advisers, teach his new and old colleagues and lead the American people in a new direction. A successful transition does not a successful presidency make, but a successful presidency is not possible without a well-planned and executed transition process.

CHAPTER EIGHT

Presidential Transition: Guidelines for a New Administration

EDWIN MEESE III*
CHIEF OF STAFF, 1980–81 TRANSITION

EDWARD N. WRIGHT*
ASSOCIATE PROFESSOR OF POLITICAL SCIENCE
UNITED STATES AIR FORCE ACADEMY

The period between the presidential election and inauguration is a time of great vulnerability and fundamental importance in the orderly process of leadership succession. During this time the president-elect must prepare to assume the powers and authority of the presidency while the outgoing president must continue to exercise that authority up to the moment the president-elect takes his constitutional oath of office.

Many challenges exist for both the outgoing and incoming presidents in a personal sense, and for their administrations in the larger view of the presidency as an institution. As was witnessed in the transition from President Truman to Eisenhower, these transitions have the potential for conflict and bitterness. This is especially true when hard-fought campaigns produce a new occupant of the White House from the opposite political party to that of the incumbent. Fortunately, since 1960 successive presidential transitions have increasingly developed a more cooperative environment which best serves the national interest by an orderly transfer of governmental power from one political leader, and party, to the next. This article is based primarily upon the experiences of and lessons learned from the Presidential Transition of 1980–81, which extended further this norm of increased

* Edwin Meese III directed President-elect Reagan's transition in 1980–81. He served as Counsellor to the President, 1981–1985, and Attorney General of the United States, 1985–1988. Edward N. Wright is an Associate Professor of Political Science at the United States Air Force Academy and served as Special Assistant to the Attorney General for National Security Affairs, 1987–1988.

cooperation. Both President Carter and President-elect Reagan were committed to a cordial and constructive relationship between their respective staffs throughout the transition period.

In assessing presidential transitions and thinking about how to organize and plan the enormous and challenging task of such an enterprise, the available literature is somewhat sparse. There are, however, some excellent sources of information which should be noted. The work of the Center for the Study of the Presidency—its journal and other publications—is particularly helpful.[1] While a limited number of studies of various transitions over the past three decades have been written, the 1980–81 transition served to inspire several articles and publications on this subject.[2] An important source for any student of presidential transitions is the report of the 1980–81 effort, *Transition of the President and President-Elect*, which resulted from the agreement between the transition directors for Presidents Carter and Reagan.[3] The purpose of this article is not to review that report, but to reflect on the 1980–81 transition and to draw from that experience an overview and certain practical lessons which should be considered in the approach to future transitions.

The Transition

President Eisenhower observed that there is really no transition of the presidency, as an institution, rather there is a transfer of presidential authority from one president to the next while the institution remains intact. The degree to which the new president is prepared to take control of the machinery of governing— political leadership of the bureaucracy, policy initiative within the executive branch and with the Congress, mastery of the budgetary process, and communication with the public—will determine his ability to control the governmental agenda and to achieve the objectives he articulated in the electoral campaign. Ideally, the work undertaken in the transition continues the development of themes and policy positions set forth during the campaign which are expanded into plans for the first year of the administration.

The transition, which represents roughly 70 days of preparation, is not only a time of preparation for the president to assume the office but a time in which he must assemble the team to support him in the White House and throughout the executive branch. The most pressing need is to identify personnel to fill cabinet and subcabinet positions, as well as the White House staff, but attention to non-career appointments at the program level of the governmental structure is also critical to the successful management of the bureaucracy. The first 180 days of the administration are crucial to the ability of the administration's success in achieving its goals. The extent to which this period will be productive depends to a great extent on the planning and preparation that takes place during the 2½ months of the transition.

A Precautionary Note

A note of caution is perhaps appropriate in anticipation of the hectic and heady days which follow an election. The transition, when viewed from the perspective of the newly-elected president and his team, is often filled with the exhilaration of victory and a sense of righteousness, as well as an eagerness "to get to work" on the problems of government. The transition also requires a shift in the approach of the newly elected president and his team from the campaign mode, driven by a frantic schedule and the need to react to the latest political crisis, to an analytical and deliberate focus on policy objectives and program initiatives, organization, and personnel.

By the time the transition begins, the federal bureaucracy has already begun to shift gears to mesh with the new administration by such steps as delaying actions that are opposed, developing issue papers for future appointees, and institutionalizing positions to be protected. Similarly, many decisions will be delayed until the incoming administration arrives — either through bureaucratic inertia or by intentional decision of the outgoing administration. The transition team must identify these and other pressing, current issues so that the incoming administration will be prepared to deal with them. Special targets of scrutiny should be personnel and budgetary decisions made during the last weeks of the outgoing administration.

Looking at the transition from the perspective of the outgoing administration other considerations prevail. While the incumbent president and his officials must govern effectively until the

Inaugural on January 20, the temptation of other matters will intrude on their attention, including future plans, post-election introspection, and the desire to institutionalize projects and policies that they fear may be lost in the next administration. The incumbents have governed for the past four, or eight, years and feel a sense of accomplishment which they will readily defend. There is the potential for understandable resentment at having to turn the leadership of government over to "inexperienced, unseasoned newcomers." The outgoing president must see that such distractions are resisted if he is to govern effectively throughout the remainder of his term and respond appropriately to the challenges that will continue until Inauguration Day.

The newly-elected president and his staff must be careful not to interfere with the outgoing administration's continued operation of the government. Likewise they should cultivate the goodwill of the incumbent officials to develop a constructive relationship with the White House staff and with the personnel of each executive department and agency.

Going outside the executive branch, there is also anticipation on the part of Congress, which will watch closely for indications of how the new administration will work with the legislative branch. Therefore good Congressional liaison is important from the first days of the transition throughout the president's term.

A final matter to be anticipated by the transition is the desire of the press to gain as much insight as possible into the structure and operation of the new administration prior to its assuming office. Responding to the news media will require great tact, since many personnel decisions will take considerable time before they are ready to be announced and the president will want to avoid premature statements of policy.

Essential Tasks to be Addressed

The 1980–81 transition sought to accomplish five objectives: (1) provide a period of adjustment following the campaign during which President Reagan would be provided with the knowledge and resources he would need when he assumed office, (2) wind up the campaign apparatus, (3) select personnel to fill the key positions in the new administration, (4) plan for the first 100 days of the Administration so that we could implement the President Reagan's policies and programs as quickly as possible, and (5) establish working relationships with groups outside the Administration that would be critical to its success. In pursuing these five objectives a number of functions were identified as essential to the success of the transition and in turn the successes enjoyed by President Reagan in his first several years in office.

Transition Staff and Organization. Only limited transition planning should be initiated before the election actually occurs. Decisions about the transition should be limited to those which must be activated immediately following the election — identify who will direct the transition, structure the policy and issue development organization and develop a plan for the use of campaign supporters for easy expansion into the transition effort (for example, to man the Departmental Transition Teams and overall policy development staffs).

White House Staff. First and foremost, the transition must identify how the president can best operate in the White House and to establish early who the leaders of that effort will be. The White House organization must reflect the personal style of the president — how he makes decisions, who he wants to rely on for information, and how he wants options raised to him for decision. Advisory systems, and accompanying staff structure, must reflect and serve his decision-making style.

Policy Development. The transition must address a process for developing policy — for planning during the transition and subsequently for implementation from the White House itself. Domestic, economic and national security policy issues must be identified and administration approaches and initiatives developed. Especially important here are issues which will offer early opportunities for or require early action. In addition, a more expansive list of specific actions the president may want to take in the early days of the administration must be developed to enable him to put his stamp on the government.

Executive Branch Liaison. Transition teams, organized around leaders with substantive knowledge of the various executive branch departments and agencies, must move quickly to assess issues, budgetary concerns, and personnel needs in their areas of responsibility so as to be useful in the development of a coordinated strategy by the president-elect and principal transition leaders.

The Budget. Although a policy document, the budget deserves and requires separate attention because the new administration must react almost immediately to the outgoing president's budget and bring to bear its own set of priorities in its budget submission to Congress. Access to budgetary data is often difficult for the transition team because the Office of Management and Budget must complete the outgoing president's budget before it can turn to consideration of the plans and needs of the incoming administration.

Personnel. Personnel functions must be divided into two separate operations: selection and preparation. The selection process is one of the most important opportunities the president has to accomplish his objectives, to change the direction of government policies, and to pursue his own agenda. Who the president chooses to head cabinet departments and federal agencies has an enormous impact on their activities throughout the term. Appointees must be selected for the levels below department and agency heads who are responsive to the president's priorities. If this is done, the appointive leadership will form an effective chain-of-command that can give direction to the program-level supervisors and ultimately the entire work force.

A separate personnel function is to prepare newly selected administration officials to assume office. Security clearances are essential and must be expedited. A program of briefings on how to approach their new positions and work with federal personnel is essential. Intensive courses on the Congress and its operations, information on the department or agency to which they have been nominated, and instruction on dealing with Congress and the press must be provided.

Strategic Planning. It is essential that strategic plans be developed, which coordinate all the various elements of the new administration's policies and objectives as well as the overall concept of activity for the first year. White House organization and Cabinet staffing must be incorporated into the planning effort as well as decisions on the budgetary issues confronted by the new administration.

Congressional Relations. The transition must address the need for effective liaison with Congress, particularly how to work with the leadership of both Houses and the members of the president's party. An essential element of good relations is the selection of a team knowledgeable about how Congress operates and how to work harmoniously with the legislative branch in developing policy initiatives that carry forward the president's agenda. Initial impressions are important and a spirit of cooperation and communication will set the course of this critical relationship throughout the president's tenure.

Public Affairs. There must be a central point of contact for the news media in the transition and for managing the public pronouncements of the incoming administration. Any public statements by incoming officials or transition team members must be cleared through this organization. Only selected individuals, such as the assigned public information officers and the transition director, should be designated as official spokesmen for the new administration.

Administration and Finance. To support the transition effort, consideration must be given to internal administrative and fiscal arrangements. Current laws relating to the transition will require careful accounting of all expenditures from governmental appropriations. In addition, there must be careful recording of all funds used in the transition from sources other than the Federal Government. An early responsibility is the establishment of liaison with the General Services Administration which provides the logistical support to the transition team. Personnel management services for both paid workers and volunteers must also be provided.

Lessons Learned

Based on the experience of previous transitions, certain approaches are suggested to provide for a harmonious and productive joint effort.

The new Administration should arrange, if possible, with outgoing officials to defer appointments and changes in status (i.e., from "non-career" to "career" status) and to postpone all policy, program, and regulatory decisions that are not urgently required during the last 2½ months of the President's term.

Newly selected officials should avoid making statements or answering news media questions about the policies of the new administration. Information to the press should be limited to biographical information about the individual concerned. This will avoid premature or conflicting accounts of the plans of the incoming administration and will provide maximum flexibility for the new president in formulating and communicating his program.

Special attention must be given to assisting the new officials after they have been selected. A central point of contact, which maintains a telephone "hotline," should be established to provide assistance and advice on the many questions that arise as to the status of appointees, processing of clearances, briefing plans, etc. A significant component of this assistance is the provision of experienced congressional liaison advisers to prepare nominees for legislative courtesy calls and hearings, as well as to accompany them on all Capitol Hill contacts.

Finally, the new team preparing to manage the Executive Branch should avoid comments on the incumbent administration or any other actions that might hinder a harmonious relationship between outgoing and incoming officials. It is particularly important for the "administration-in-waiting" to refrain from any statement or activity which might interfere with the effective management of the government by those still in office or cause confusion in the minds of the public as to "who is in charge" in Washington.

Conclusion

The presidential transition provides a great opportunity for two groups of national leaders and their appointees, perhaps from different political parties, to work together in the national interest and to effect a smooth transfer of authority from a serving president to the new chief executive whom the people have elected. Conversely, this situation also holds the potential for disputes and antagonisms that could not only disrupt an orderly transition but cause great damage to the country if the national leadership is impaired or confused during any sort of domestic or international crisis that might occur.

The 1980–81 transition provided a model of cooperation and constructive joint activity, despite the great political differences between the presidents involved. This spirit of accommodation and accord can be achieved through careful planning, good communication and the clear designation of responsibility by the transition teams of both administrations. If handled properly, the transfer of presidential authority can reflect well on the officials involved and contribute greatly to national unity. If this effort is successful, Inauguration Day will see the dignified departure of one leader and the optimistic assumption of office by the other.

CHAPTER NINE

Proposal: A New Presidential Selection Timetable

STEPHEN HESS
SENIOR FELLOW, THE BROOKINGS INSTITUTION

The presidential transition that takes place between election day and inauguration day is much too long. I believe this for the "standard" reasons — it creates an unnecessary period of danger abroad and drift at home — but also because I believe these 10 weeks may actually increase the difficulty of forming a new administration.

The most basic work of this period is the choosing of less than 100 executives for the agencies and White House, a task that can only be accomplished by the President-elect, assisted by a small group of intimate advisers. The rest of the administration should not take shape until these 100 appointees have been selected and can take part in choosing their subordinates. Most of the other activities amount to "make work," tasks created to keep people busy while the inner circle goes about its business. Some of these duties are marginally useful, but others can and do cause problems for the president-elect.

My major recommendation is a constitutional amendment to change the inauguration date. This was done once before, in 1933, and so it is hardly a pie-in-the-sky notion.

A transition, by definition, is a transitory state, a passing from one stage to another. Altering the transition, then, is likely to affect what comes before and what comes after. Examining transitions presents the opportunity and the obligation to look at the whole process. A very good social scientist, who became a U.S. Senator, often noted that in urban policy everything is interconnected, everything relates to everything else. It is in the spirit of Daniel P. Moynihan's injunction that this proposal for a new presidential selection to timetable is offered.

Copyright (©) 1988 by The Brookings Institution. This is an original essay prepared expressly for this volume.

The plan calls for elections of the president, vice president, U.S. Senators, and Members of the U.S. House of Representatives on the last Monday in May (Memorial Day), the swearing-in of the new Congress on June 29th, and the inauguration of the president and vice president on July 4th (Independence Day). Other changes in the timetable of presidential selection are suggested.

Election Day (last Monday in May)

Objective: to encourage greater voting participation by holding elections in better weather and on a nonwork day.

According to the computations of Walter Dean Burnham, the high point in voting for President came in 1860 when the turnout rate was 81.8 percent; 40 years later in 1900 the voter turnout had dropped to 73.7; 40 years later in 1940 the voter turnout had dropped to 62.5; and 40 years later in 1980 the voter turnout was 54.3.[1]

Most experts no longer believe that the country's pathetic record of voting participation is caused by structural roadblocks that have been placed in the path of potential voters who otherwise would get to the polls. Yet there are still some impediments that deserve attention.[2] Americans living across the nation's northern tier must contend with weather that is predictably unpleasant on the first Tuesday after the first Monday in November. For example, on election day, 1984, some low temperature readings

TABLE 1: ELECTION DAY WEATHER[3]

Present (Nov.) (high/low average in degrees)	City	Proposed (May) (high/low average in degrees)
28	Anchorage	49
49	Albuquerque	68
54	Atlanta	69
46	Cleveland	61
46	Detroit	61
65	Jacksonville	77
57	Little Rock	77
55	Memphis	73
55	Norfolk	74
45	Pittsburgh	62
41	Portland, Me.	58

were 19 in Fargo, 29 in Billings, 23 in Chicago, and 22 in Minneapolis-St. Paul. But in almost all parts of the country, the weather is nicer in late May than in early November, as table 1 illustrates. There is no reason to turn the act of voting into an unpleasant chore by picking a date for elections that might discourage some citizens, especially the elderly and those in poor health.

That people are more likely to vote if the weather is good than if it is bad is an assumption: We cannot conduct a controlled experiment in which the same election with the same electorate is held once in rain and once in sunshine. But we are not a nation of masochists and we have the right to want to conduct democracy's work in good weather.

Holding elections on Memorial Day will be an unattractive notion to some. The idea behind the proposal, of course, is that using a day on which most people do not have to go to work could increase voter turnout. There are other ways to accomplish the same goal, however, such as weekend voting or adding another national holiday.[4]

An act of Congress will be needed to change the election day for federal offices. It is assumed that states will choose to conform with the federal schedule. This is desirable, but not necessary.

Congressional Transition (Election Day to June 29)

Objective: to discourage lame-duck congressional sessions by cutting in half the time between election day and the swearing-in of the new Congress, from roughly two months to one month, or more precisely from 62/57 days to 34/29 days.

The 2nd section of the 20th Amendment would be changed to read: "The Congress shall assemble at least once every year, and such meeting shall begin at noon on the *29th day of June* [presently the 3rd day of January], unless they shall by law appoint a different day."

Since the ratification of the 20th Amendment in 1933, Congress has held 10 post-election sessions. At the last lame-duck session in 1982, 19 percent of the House of Representatives were lame-ducks (i.e., had not sought reelection or had been defeated) and there were 5 lame-duck senators. "Lame-duck sessions," in the opinion of Senator Claiborne Pell, a veteran of four lame-duck sessions, "are nearly always unproductive, sharply criticized by public and the news media, and may result in actions unrepresentative of the will of the people."[5]

Inauguration Day (July 4)

Objective: to insure that the President will be inaugurated in better weather and to enhance the significance of this act.

Section 1 of the 20th Amendment would be revised to read: "The terms of the President and Vice-President shall end at noon on the *4th day of July* [presently the 20th day of January], and the terms of Senators and Representatives at noon on the *29th day of June* [presently 3d day of January . . ."

The revised inauguration date will shorten the term of some future (unknown) President, but there is precedent for this in the cases of George Washington and Franklin Roosevelt.[6]

Having five days between the beginning of the congressional term and the inauguration of the President comes from a proposal (S.J. Res. 71) introduced by Senators Pell and Charles Mathias in 1984.

Some of us still shudder when recalling the paralyzing snowstorm that struck the capital on the night before John F. Kennedy was to be inaugurated in 1961. Those whose memories do not go back that far need only reread two headlines from the front page of *The New York Times*, January 21, 1985: Reagan Sworn For 2d Term; Inaugural Parade Dropped As Bitter Cold Hits Capital and Shivering Visitors in Washington Mostly Relieved on Cancellation. The following table reviews what the weather was and what it might have been over the past five inauguration days.

TABLE 2: INAUGURATION DAY WEATHER[7]
(Washington, D.C.)

Present (Jan. 20) (high/low average in degrees)	Date	Proposed (July 4) (high/low average in degrees)
36	1968/69	74
42	1972/73	75
27	1976/77	75
47	1980/81	82
9	1984/85	81
32	average	77

Laurin L. Henry writes of the "rituals of democracy, affirming the public faith that this electoral process, despite its imperfections, offers significant choices that lead to the designation of a leader, legitimate and politically responsible enough to merit the allegiance of the entire nation. On inauguration day, personal and partisan differences are temporarily submerged; all unite in saluting the new President."[8]

What would be more appropriate than to use every fourth Independence Day to celebrate this "ritual of democracy"?

Presidential Transition (Election Day to July 4)

Objective: to shorten the period of drift and possible danger between the election and swearing-in of a president. Also to strengthen the political parties and to facilitate the relocation of personnel entering or leaving Washington when administrations change.

There is some discussion in political science circles of presidential transitions as "potentially periods of grave danger . . . open invitations to unfriendly or hostile actions by other nations."[9] More often, transitions are simply looked upon as periods of drift, a time when the U.S. government treads water despite the public concerns that require high-level attention. This is especially true when the outgoing president is of one party and the incoming president is of the other, which since 1952 has happened with some frequency (1960, 1968, 1976, 1980).[10]

Table 3, using the last five elections (1968–84), shows how this proposal would have reduced the number of days between the election and the inauguration on average from 76.2 to 36.2.

My observations from various vantage points during the last four transitions lead me to believe that the value of the work performed is greatly exaggerated.[11] In the 1980 transition, by far the largest and most elaborate in history, Carl M. Brauer rightly notes, "What residents and observers of Washington often saw was the blizzard of task forces, committees, and teams that [Edwin] Meese devised in part to reward, flatter, and occupy the conservative faithful." Transition organizations are ad hoc arrangements by definition. Yet as the apparatus becomes larger and larger, there are some who see this as an end in itself rather than as a means to establishing a more useful presidential administration. There is an analogue to this in the temporary arrangements of campaign organizations out of which many of the

TABLE 3: DATES OF ELECTION DAY AND INAUGURATION DAY

Year	Election Day	Present System Inauguration	# Transition Days
1984	Nov. 6	Jan. 20 ('85)	75
1980	Nov. 4	Jan. 20 ('81)	77
1976	Nov. 2	Jan. 20 ('77)	79
1972	Nov. 7	Jan. 20 ('73)	74
1968	Nov. 5	Jan. 20 ('69)	76
		Average # days	76.2
		Proposed System	
1984	May 28	July 4	37
1980	May 26	July 4	39
1976	May 31	July 4	34
1972	May 29	July 4	36
1968	May 30	July 4	35
		Average # days	36.2

transitioners have come. Within the transition organizations there are now conflicts between "the politicians" and "the experts," those who are there because they helped the candidate get elected and those who are there because of special knowledge of how government works. The transition organization is under added stress because many of its workers are also hoping to find jobs in the new administration. Much time is spent bickering and gossiping. Indeed the production of misinformation is so substantial as to eat into the energy of the small circle of those who really are advising the president-elect. As Ed Meese, the transition chief in 1980, was fond of saying, "Those who know aren't talking and those who are talking don't know."[12]

No new administration "hits the ground running."[13] To get some quantifiable notion of how much is actually accomplished during a transition, at least in terms of personnel selection, I added up the nominations that Presidents Nixon, Carter, and Reagan submitted to the Senate during their first month in office (1969, 1977, 1981). There are about 500 jobs in the cabinet and subcabinet that rank in the executive schedule levels I-III. Nixon sent 85 names to the Senate; Carter and Reagan 40 each. In rough terms, then, the election-to-inauguration period probably only produced between 8 and 17 percent of these key jobs. Since very few of these names were surprises — persons who had not been friends of the candidate, campaign workers, contributors, or previous government officials — there is no reason why they could not have been produced by a shorter and leaner transition.

A shorter and leaner transition would mean more reliance on holdovers and members of the permanent government. Exiting officials are usually anxious to impart the nitty-gritty and the pitfalls of their jobs to their successors, even if they are of an alien party. The successors are usually uninterested in learning from others' experiences. (Eventually they too become exiting officials and feel otherwise.) At any rate, a shorter transition might alter this relationship; it would not make it worse. The relationship between incoming personnel and the civil service depends, in part, on the degree to which the president-elect had campaigned as an outsider, running "against" Washington as did Carter in 1976 and Reagan in 1980. But, as Lincoln P. Bloomfield writes, "The outsider's glib assumption that career civil servants will be disloyal to a new administration is an unwarranted calumny based on ignorance."[14]

A presidential transition, of course, is more than a 10-week-period between the election and the swearing-in. Generally some transition work (though not much) is done before the election, while most of the really hard labor comes after the inauguration. A sensible transition plan, in addition to decreasing the election/inauguration period, should aim to increase pre-election planning, if possible. The problem obviously is that the candidates and their inner circles must dedicate themselves to the job at hand, getting elected. Transition planning is low priority and even may be counter-productive if it causes squabbling among the staff. The Meese operation in 1980 produced the best record to date, partly because of Meese's closeness to the candidate. Similar offices in the future should be folded into the parties' national committees and paid for with federal funds. (Funding might be in the range of $1-million for each party.) The inducement of public money (which would be audited and could not be used for other purposes) gives new responsibilities to the national parties. The separation between the candidates and their parties has been of growing concern to political scientists of late. Perhaps transition planning can be used as one bridge to narrow the gap.

Starting presidential and congressional terms at the beginning of summer has another benefit that will be appreciated by new legislators, their staffs, and those who will be coming to

Washington to work in the new administration. The federal government will be in phase with other major employers who have figured out that this is the best time of year to transfer workers to new locations. It is the least disruptive of families. There will be fewer forced separations. Children can settle into new homes during the summer and enter new school with their new friends in the fall.

Presidential Selection Timetable

Considerable criticism has been leveled at presidential selection for being too long. No other nation devotes two years to choosing a chief executive. Advances in communications technology allow us to speed up the process, it is said. The extended campaign bores the electorate, it is said. A shorter campaign would be a cheaper campaign and we now spend too much money, it is said. I am not among the critics, feeling that there is a better chance of the least political voters learning what they need to know about the candidates under the present system. But I also recognize that I am in the minority.

It may be that we would prefer to hold the national nominating conventions in April preceded by the state primaries and caucuses in January, February, and March. If so, the period from the Iowa caucuses and the New Hampshire primary to the inauguration would be compressed to less than six months. It now takes nearly a year.

At any rate, changing election day to late May automatically forces us to rethink the rest of the presidential selection schedule.[15]

Taking the Reins of Organization: Reorganization Planning in Presidential Transitions

PERI E. ARNOLD

PROFESSOR AND CHAIR, POLITICAL SCIENCE
UNIVERSITY OF NOTRE DAME

"Better decision-making involves drawing on history to frame sharper questions. . . ."[1]

This essay will examine executive reorganization planning as a tool within presidential transitions. Executive reorganization is central to the presidential role within the bureaucratic state. From the first decade of this century, presidents have used ad hoc groups of experts to plan for reform of administrative organization.[2] As well, reorganization planning has appeared in several modern transitions, adopted as a means for preparing a new administration to govern. Analyzing these several cases, 1952–53, 1968–69, and 1976–77, we shall inquire about the lessons they hold for a president-elect organizing his transition to power. But, before broaching these cases, we have a preliminary concern. What is it that executive reorganization planning might contribute to the process of presidential transitions?

Transitions and Bureaucratic Government

A president-elect has two and a half months to move from the role of campaigner to the head of a government.[3] In that brief period, a president-elect will create a White House and Executive Office staff, decide how to treat the departing president's budget, and identify the issues to be given priority now that the campaign is past. But, the task facing the president-elect that is most fundamental, and upon which much else rests is this one: how will these successful partisans govern the administrative state? This question is most acute when the president-elect represents a change in party control of the White House. Then,

this question hangs the ability of a new adminis-
national problems and direct the development
cy.

ition is more than the period from the election to
Ja   )th, inauguration day. It is the time necessary for a
preside   to establish his administration. Pfiffner observes that
"the effective period of transition actually extends well into the
new president's first year in office."[4] The success of transitions
lies in the efficacy and speed with which a new president is capable
of establishing an approach to governance. More than anything
else, the time it takes to grasp the reins of government's organizations will determine the length of a new president's transition
into office. Two related problems must in turn be solved to fully
accomplish the goal of taking direction of the bureaucratic state.

The first problem in attempting direction of the bureaucracy
is its sheer scale. It is a mass of agencies and a myriad of organizational forms.[5] While the overwhelming proportion of the
personnel of the system is permanent, the president is responsible for almost four thousand appointments. These appointments
are crucial because success of the agencies of government will
depend on the ability of the new people to take over and give
direction to organizations and their programs. They are crucial
also because through them the president is speaking to the universe of actors who observe, and are affected by, the federal agencies. Each presidential appointment will seem an omen to legislators, the interest groups, journalists, and not least, the permanent
civil servants.[6]

A second problem that must be addressed by a president-elect
acting to fill the roles of federal organization is that of making
choices about individuals, and the organizations they will direct, with an eye to his own personal style, needs, expectations,
and limitations. Each president-elect brings political and policy
goals, styles of work, and background experiences which will shape
their needs and expectations regarding the federal agencies. First,
and even more pressingly, those personal aspects — character —
will determine how a president-elect will organize and staff the
apparatus most immediate to him, the White House Office and
the elements of the Executive Office of the President. As Colin
Campbell observes: "no president . . . can be fully understood
without thoroughly linking character and performance to the
task of governance."[7] As a corollary of Campbell's thought, no

president will fully succeed without understanding the way his own character affects his approach to governance.

Executive Reorganization and the Tasks of Transition

In staffing the organizations of government, the president-elect must also ask what he can expect from organizations and how he wants to direct key agencies. It is in this reflexive element of the transition experience — the fitting of agencies to the new administration and *vice-versa* — that reorganization planning might appear attractive for presidential transitions.

Indeed administrations-to-be need guidance about what organizational choices will most enhance the new president's capacity to govern. Reorganization planning's attractions lay in its promise to aid the new president in taking over direction of the government. The president-elect can design reorganization planning to address his particular needs. In turn, the chance that an instance of reorganization planning will substantially aid a new president depends on his ability to understand his needs and designate uses of reorganization planning consistent with them.

In its most familiar and grand forms, such as the Brownlow Committee, the two Hoover Commissions, and LBJ's Heineman Task Force, reorganization planning constitutes a long term effort within an administration to reform the executive branch. This type of reorganization planning can be thought of as operating within the time frame of a whole presidential administration. But transition-oriented reorganization is a very different use of reorganization planning and necessarily works within the briefer time frame of the transition itself. Grand, multi-year, reorganization planning efforts characteristically seek broad improvement in government's organization, addressing generic problems across the departments of government. In contrast, transition-oriented reorganization planning aims for the immediate adaptation of organization to a new administration. Thus the use of reorganization planning within transitions ought to be considered as distinct from grand reorganization planning. While the latter has come under criticism from expert observers in recent years for failing to produce sought after results, transition-era reorganization planning has received no such attention.[8]

Once a president-elect has chosen to pursue reorganization

planning within the transition, several decisions follow. It is in making these choices that he must consult the consequences for governance of his personal style, needs, and values. He must also ask, what will be the mandate or goals of this group? Can reorganization planning achieve those goals? Who will be chosen to gather information and recommend reforms of the federal agencies? When will the reports of this group be most useful to the new administration? What form should their recommendations take, and to whom should they go? Every reorganization planning effort entails these choices, whether it be launched during a transition or not. However these choices are most critical in transition period reorganization planning because the operative time frame is short and the possibility of benefits for a new administration depend heavily upon a president-elect's ability to ascertain his needs and preferences.

Reorganization planning has appeared three times in modern transitions, in the preparations for the Eisenhower, Nixon, and Carter administrations. The next section will present these cases through brief sketches. Besides relating the course of reorganization planning in each case, these sketches will highlight how a new president's approach shaped choices about reorganization planning. In a final section we shall ask about the lessons that might be drawn from these instances of transition period reorganization planning.

Three Cases of Transition Period Reorganization Planning

1.   Eisenhower and the Advisory Committee on Government Organization

Dwight Eisenhower's preparations for entering the presidency were the most ambitious up to that time. To effect his transition, the president-elect created a staff organization with five main elements.[9] Joseph Dodge oversaw the transition in budgeting. Senator Henry Cabot Lodge headed a group dealing with foreign affairs. Sherman Adams, who had directed the campaign, was charged with building a White House staff. Herbert Brownell and General Lucius Clay led a personnel search for cabinet and sub-cabinet appointments. Finally, a committee was created to examine the federal agencies with an eye towards proposing desirable changes as well as for the purpose of preparing the new people for their duties. This committee was titled the Special Advisory Committee on Government Organization, and Nelson Rockefeller, Arthur Flemming, and Milton Eisenhower were its members. While reorganization planning groups such as this had become fairly routine in the modern presidency, never before had a reorganization planning group been created by a president-elect.

Eisenhower gave to the advisory committee wide ranging responsibilities. The committee was to attempt to improve presidential administrative authority, streamline departmental organization, and recommend the elimination of unnecessary activities. It would also brief administration appointees on the organizational issues they would confront in their assignments.[10]

As with all three of the cases to be examined below, the 1952–53 transition entailed a change in the partisan control of the White House. The Republicans were returning to the presidency for the first time since Hoover left in March 1933. Twenty years of Democratic control of the White House made the president-elect sensitive to the fact that he and his partisans were entering unknown territory. The executive branch over which Dwight Eisenhower would preside had been shaped by Franklin Roosevelt. Seen in this light, President-elect Eisenhower's elaborate transition organization becomes understandable, as does his creation of a committee to investigate and think critically about executive branch organization. But, the committee's role was not to duplicate the first Hoover Commission which had recently finished issuing its recommendations for reorganization, many of which had not been implemented.[11] The committee's role, rather, was to think about organization in light of the particular needs of the president-elect.

In a sense Dwight Eisenhower was coming to the presidency as an outsider. In important ways no one was more experienced, more the "insider," than he. He had worked closely with the preceding two presidents. He had been involved in high diplomacy, and he had just returned from command of NATO. But with the exception of a brief period on General George C. Marshall's staff before World War II, Eisenhower had not worked in Washington since the 1920's when he had been an aide to General Douglas MacArthur. One of President-elect Eisenhower's most pressing needs was to find a way to orient himself to that new Washington. More than anything else, it was to fill these needs that Eisenhower created the Special Committee on Government Organization.

Eisenhower's lack of touch with the post-New Deal state was symbolic of the situation of his whole party. The Republicans who had been in Washington after 1933 had been outsiders, and many had become increasingly embittered. Who of them could serve the president-elect and his administration by helping them prepare for governing the state from which they had been alienated?

For the committee's members Eisenhower turned to three Republicans who had recently been on the inside of executive government. As important, these were people who Eisenhower trusted. Nelson Rockefeller had served in the Department of State during the war. Arthur Flemming had been a Civil Service commissioner, responsible for defense mobilization in the Truman administration, and was also a member of the Hoover Commission. Milton Eisenhower, the president-elect's brother, was president of Penn State University. He had begun his career working in the Department of Agriculture and had consulted on farm policy with every administration since Coolidge's.

Eisenhower needed his reorganization consultants to have extensive knowledge of the executive branch agencies, and he also needed them to have good judgment. He composed the committee with people he trusted, and he expected to be able to use it often and informally. A key part of the committee's basic mission was to be on-call. Arthur Flemming said of their relationship to Eisenhower: "If Ike had an idea or problem he would bring it to the committee. If the committee had an idea or saw a problem, it would bring it to Ike."[12]

The Special Committee's assignment was to serve Eisenhower. Every prior reorganization planning vehicle had a facade of expert neutrality and the duty of preparing recommendations that would have wide distribution. This committee had only Eisenhower as its client. It had no public mission, only the duty to strengthen the president-elect's preparation to create an administration and govern effectively.

Between its creation in November 1952 and April 1953, the Special Committee prepared twenty memoranda for Eisenhower. Each dealt with a single agency or organizational issue, and each contained recommendations for reform.[13] Because the committee was highly confidential and trusted by the president-elect, he could consult it on matters that could be politically sensitive. For example, the issue of domestic Communists in government employment was potentially troublesome. Senator Joseph McCarthy had savaged the Truman administration on this issue, and now Eisenhower had to walk the tightrope of satisfying the Senator from Wisconsin while also acting responsibly in the conduct of government. The committee was asked to consider means for addressing the domestic security issue.[14]

The recommendations of the advisory committee gave Eisenhower the impressive advantage of being able to enter the presidency with a clear agenda of organizational initiatives. In his first year in office, President Eisenhower presented ten reorganization plans to Congress. Six of these came within three months of the inauguration. Among these was the creation of the Department of Health, Education, and Welfare as well as important changes in Agriculture, Justice, and Defense. Considering Eisenhower's problem of creating and guiding the first Republican administration in two decades, these immediate organizational changes were significant. They signalled that the administration had found its way and had established a sense of purpose. It is of particular interest that in transforming the Federal Security Administration to a cabinet-level department, H.E.W., this Republican president succeeded where President Truman had failed. What his advisory committee helped President Eisenhower do was orient himself to ongoing issues of governance in a context of policy and organization. In succeeding to establish a welfare policy department where a Democrat could not, Eisenhower was signalling that he could work within the context of the contemporary domestic government and, perhaps, improve it.

In addition to its recommendations for specific organizational changes, the committee advised the president-elect on a general approach to organizational concerns. It proposed to Eisenhower that improving administration was "a perpetual, day-after-day job."[15] It argued that there ought to be constant monitoring of the administrative operations of government's agencies. But, in addition to watchfulness, the committee cautioned: "A Government must be able to think as well as act."[16]

President Eisenhower was so convinced of the utility of his experiment with transition period reorganization planning that he transformed his advisory committee into a permanent part of his administration. Choosing to make it the instrument for fulfilling its own injunction "to think as well as act," President Eisenhower gave the committee official status and renamed it the President's Advisory Committee on Government Organization (PACGO). [17]

Eisenhower's use of reorganization planning in a presidential transition was innovative for two reasons. It was the first use of reorganization planning in a transition. But, it was also a highly innovative use of reorganization planning in that Eisenhower made a tool for personal advising out of what had until then been wrapped in symbols of a neutral, expert, management science. That Eisenhower gave the committee permanent status in his administration was the final demonstration of the committee's remarkable success in pleasing its client.

PACGO's members remained within Eisenhower's inner circle of advisers. The committee continued to focus upon formulation and advising rather than research, and its staff never grew larger than three or four. For informational needs it developed a close relationship with the Bureau of the Budget. The committee, augmented by the director of the budget, would annually propose to President Eisenhower an agenda of organizational changes. It would steadily monitor and discuss organizational aspects of the administration's policy concerns, and it continued to serve Eisenhower as a forum that could prudently handle politically sensitive matters. For example, between 1954 and 1956 the committee served as an intermediary between President Eisenhower and the very touchy second Hoover Commission. [18]

2.   Reorganization Planning in Nixon's Transition

After the 1968 election Richard Nixon faced problems that were like those confronting Dwight Eisenhower in 1952. Like Eisenhower's, Nixon's victory heralded a Republican return to the White House. Also like Eisenhower, Nixon entered the presidency after a period of Democratic sponsored expansion of public policy. In the 1968 campaign, Nixon had decried Lyndon Johnson's War on Poverty. Looking back upon the campaign, Nixon wrote: ". . . America in the 1960's had undergone a misguided crash program aimed at using the power of the . . . federal government to right past wrongs. . . . The problems were real . . . , but the method was foredoomed . . . its costs had become prohibitively high in terms of the way it had undermined our federal system."[19]

Richard Nixon's transition to the presidency was shaped ⹁, his view that the expansion of federal social programs in the 1960's had been a failed project. Also, the transition was colored by the president-elect's predisposition towards managerial order. Nixon sought policy solutions to what he saw as the undesirable consequences of the War on Poverty, and he wanted to build a clear and orderly managerial system for his White House and the executive branch. In other words, Nixon's strategy to overcoming what he viewed as bad domestic policy contained two prongs. He would seek different substantive policy—a legislative path, and he would make government work better—a managerial path.

From the beginning, President-elect Nixon sought a transition image that conveyed competency and a rational ability to make government work. John Osborne described Nixon as thinking: "Disciplined order and precision within his immediate establishment . . . [were] prerequisite to the promise and appearance of orderly administration that he succeeded from the start in conveying to the country."[20]

President-elect Nixon planned for his transition through ten task forces. Composed largely of businessmen, each task force was assigned to a policy or organizational problem. Among them was a task force focusing on the organization of the Executive Office, chaired by Frank Lindsay of the ITEK Corporation.[21] The Lindsay task force recommended improvements in the White House-Executive Office system as a key to overall improvement of the management of the executive branch.[22] In this the task force reinforced the president-elect's tendencies towards a highly structured organizational system in domestic affairs.[23]

Nixon moved on the Lindsay task force's advice by appointing Roy Ash, president of Litton Industries, as a transition period consultant on matters of organization and management.[24] Rather quickly, Ash echoed to the president-elect the advice he had gotten from the Lindsay task force, and urged that Nixon pursue reorganization of the Bureau of the Budget and create cabinet-level councils as arena for policy consideration.[25]

When Dwight Eisenhower had sought transition advisers on government organization he turned to three trusted individuals with extensive government experience. Conventionally, presidents who have gone outside government for advice on government organization have shown preference for public administration experts. But Richard Nixon turned to successful private sector managers for help on making government's organization work better.

As a candidate, Richard Nixon had attacked government's policies and operations that were the work of Democratic administrations. Presidential transitions that are also transitions of partisan control face the challenge of having to transform heated partisan rhetoric into reasonable approaches towards ongoing governmental activities that were the subject of that rhetoric. Presidential transitions from Democratic to Republican control entail the most strain because it has been the Democratic agenda to expand social policies while the Republicans have attacked that expansion. When returned to power, Republicans are prone to look with suspicion at public policies created by Democrats but also to consider suspect the bureaucrats administering those policies.[26]

From Nixon's critical perspective, experts on government organization and policies are likely to be intellectual captives of the assumptions that Republicans had attacked during the campaign. However, private sector managers might be different. Nixon's assistant for personnel matters, Frederick Malek, exemplifies this view. Government decisions ought to be like those in the private sector, he thought. The question is "one of how best to allocate . . . resources; . . ." But in fact government's decisions are ". . . predicated on politics."[27] Richard Nixon sought guidance in disciplining government to the standards of the private sector by turning to accomplished private sector managers. Lindsay and Ash were among the country's most successful conglomerate managers. They were successful at running organizations that were concerned with the best way to allocate resources, and they were untainted by Washington. These were exactly the qualities sought by President-elect Nixon as the intellectual basis for his approach to management.

Management considerations were central to Richard Nixon's approach to governance in the domestic arena. Through the first two years of the administration his approach was to develop improved policies *and* to improve the management of government. But, after 1970 he sought to change government through managerial control directly. In describing this change, Richard Nathan observes: ". . . in many areas of domestic affairs, *operations is policy.* Much of the day-to-day management of domestic programs — regulation writing, grant approval, and budget apportionment —

actually involves policymaking."[28] In the administration's first phase, management was an important side issue for President Nixon. But in the second phase it became a prime concern. Through both stages, reorganization planning specified the instruments upon which the president would rely in his conduct of domestic governance.

The medium for reorganization planning in the Nixon administration was the President's Advisory Council on Executive Organization, which he announced on April 5, 1969.[29] It was a natural outgrowth of the advising system on management that Nixon had created after the election, and its initial mandate was to strengthen presidential management. Roy Ash was named the council's chairman and four additional members were appointed, George Baker, dean of the Harvard Business School, John Connolly, former governor of Texas and ex-Secretary of the Navy, Frederick R. Kappel, chairman of the executive committee of A.T. & T., and Richard M. Paget, partner in the management consulting firm of Cresap, McCormick, and Paget. In June a sixth member was added, Walter Thayer, president of Whitney Communications. Thayer's specific assignment was to organize the council and get it operating. Roy Ash's business obligations had, in fact, kept him from the task, and President Nixon was pressing the council for guidance. Thayer hired the council's staff, and belatedly, the Ash council turned to its work.

In creating the Ash council within his third month in the presidency, Richard Nixon apparently sought guidance for improving management in the early stage of his administration. It is in this sense that the council should be seen as an outgrowth of transition advising on management. It is also an outgrowth of transition advising in a second sense. The council's membership underlines and punctuates President Nixon's strong preference for private sector managerial approaches. Its members were business managers. Roy Ash's own views of the council's role were in perfect tune with the president's, and he assumed that the lessons of good business management could be transferred to government.[30]

In his first message to Congress, President Nixon requested a renewal of the presidential reorganization authority that had lapsed on December 31, 1968.[31] On March 27th Nixon signed into law an act of Congress extending the authority for two years. The renewal of reorganization authority was a prerequisite for creating the Ash council. Without that authority the president would lack the most efficient means for effecting the council's recommendations. But, creating the council prior to the renewal of reorganization authority might invite Congress to impose further limitations upon its use. Within days after approving the renewal of reorganization authority, President Nixon announced the council. The resources supplied for the council's work were stunning when compared to PACGO in the Eisenhower administration. Its FY 1970 appropriation was a million dollars, and by the end of 1969 its staff numbered twenty-five people.[32]

The Ash Council's first recommendations to President Nixon concerned the organization of the Executive Office of the President. Meeting with the president on August 20, 1969, the council described some general approaches to reform, and Nixon approved them. In the following October the council presented detailed plans for a reorganization of the Bureau of the Budget and the creation of a new Executive Office agency for policy development, the Domestic Council. These proposals were sent to Congress on March 12, 1970 as Reorganization Plan no. 2 of 1970.

The proposed reorganization of the Bureau of the Budget aimed to strengthen the agency's responsibilities for management and policy coordination. The chiefs of the operating divisions of the bureau were made subject to presidential appointment, reversing the practice of career people serving in high positions of the agency and increasing the agency's responsiveness to the incumbent's interests. To signal its broadened responsibilities the bureau's name would become the Office of Management and Budget.[33] Reorganization Plan no. 2's other major component was the Domestic Council. Based on the example of the National Security Council, it was meant to bring together the views of cabinet heads of the domestic departments. The council would have an executive director who was a presidential assistant and a staff to aid in the development of policy proposals.

In a message accompanying Reorganization Plan no. 2, President Nixon described the proposed reorganizations as providing the means for improved presidential governance. He explained that these reorganizations would allow him to govern through management rather than by attempting direct control of government. He said:

A President whose programs are carefully coordinated, whose information system keeps him adequately informed, and whose organizational assignments are plainly set out, can delegate authority with security and confidence. A President whose office is deficient in these respects will be inclined, instead, to retain close control of operating responsibilities which he cannot and should not handle.[34]

The reforms of the Executive Office were accepted by Congress, albeit with some controversy. Yet the reforms did not appear to satisfy the president's expectations of them. A year later he presented sweeping recommendations for changes in the cabinet-level departments in what seemed to be an admission that he needed means of direct control over government. In his 1971 State of the Union address, President Nixon called for reform of the "framework of government itself . . . to make it again fully responsive. . . ."[35]

In March of 1971 the president sent to Congress bills containing Ash Council recommendations for creating four functionally organized super departments that would swallow most of the traditional domestic departments. Here were the changes in government's framework that had been promised in the State of the Union address. New departments of natural resources, economic affairs, human resources, and community development were aimed at destabilizing traditional bureaucratic ties to political interests. The president and his reformers hoped that newly centralized and integrated departments would give the president substantial leverage in departmental priority setting.

In his first months as president, Richard Nixon had sought managerial means for allowing the president to govern over a system of dispersed authority. But just a year after he introduced reorganizations meant to achieve that end, he sought departmental reorganizations that aimed at increasing the president's direct control over the departments. As might be expected, a Democratic Congress rejected these sweeping changes in governmental organization.

The 1971 departmental reorganization proposals ought to be seen as the midway point in President Nixon's movement toward what Richard Nathan called his "administrative presidency" strategy. At the beginning of his second term, Nixon adopted practices that would strengthen his hand over government changes that necessitated congressional approval. Through increased and changed staff responsibilities, impoundments, and relatively small scale reorganizations, the president attempted to achieve direct controls over the departments without recourse to legislation.[36]

Richard Nixon's transition period use of reorganization planning failed to fulfill his own apparent expectations for it. Through Frank Lindsay and Roy Ash, and then through the Ash Council, Nixon called upon private sector managerial advice to strengthen the president as a manager. President-elect Nixon's hopes rested upon frail assumptions about the promise of private sector managerial systems. His own experience was wholly in the public sector, and his assumptions about private sector management were founded in his own values rather than in any experience with managing organizations.

The president had hoped that private sector managers would have a key to solving government's bureaucratic problems. If people like Ash and Kappel could make effective organizations out of giants such as Litton Industries or American Telephone and Telegraph, was it not likely that they could see a solution to the problems of government's giant organizations? Despite the president's hopes, the evidence suggests that rather than calling upon their own experiences with corporate organization, these members of the Ash Council chose recommendations that evoked the classic public administration reform tradition of expanded presidential organization and centralized bureaucracy. As Richard Nixon's eventual turn to an "administrative presidency" strategy indicates, reorganization planning in itself had not fulfilled his initial hopes for it.

3. Jimmy Carter's Uses of Reorganization

In 1976 Jimmy Carter promised that if elected he would transform government, simplifying it, making it more understandable, and more accessible to the people. Carter's strategy in his run for the presidency was a pure form of an outsider's appeal.[37] He offered his lack of Washington experience or national service as his advantage, his guarantee of purity. In effect, he presented his inexperience as a privileged vantage point which allowed him special insight into government's failings.

From the beginning of his presidential campaign, Jimmy Carter offered executive reorganization as the tool he would use to make government right. Never before had reorganization figured so prominently in presidential electoral politics. During the campaign Jimmy Carter spoke of his intended reorganization as one that would comprehensively remake government. He rejected "incremental efforts" that would fail because narrow interest groups would mobilize against them while the general public would remain uninterested. On the other hand, he told an interviewer: "If it's clear, comprehensive and it's presented in such a way as to arouse the support of the people, then the special interests quite often back off."[38]

Why did the promise to reorganize become so central to Jimmy Carter's quest for the presidency? Several different factors explain this. First, as governor of Georgia, Jimmy Carter had conducted a major reorganization of state government. He had made reorganization his chief priority as governor and had successfully fought for reorganization authority from the state legislature. He claimed that he had reduced the number of Georgia's state agencies to 22 from 300.[39] Second, promising reform is an ideal recourse for an outsider seeking the presidency. An outsider's disability is lack of experience (and knowledge). To promise reform is to promise great change without having to be specific about government's details and policies. Third, one should not overlook the apparent degree to which Jimmy Carter took very seriously his promises to reform and reorganize.[40]

Thus Carter's promises to reorganize government constituted a fundamental claim upon his administration. He had not just used reorganization, he believed in it. Even before the November 1976 election, Carter created an Atlanta based transition planning staff. According to Jack Watson's description, it had the job of thinking about public policy and government while the campaign staff's job was to win the election.[41] The transition staff included a seven member group focusing upon executive reorganization planning headed by Harrison Wellford. The reorganization group gave its first recommendation to Jimmy Carter in September, proposing the creation of an energy department. Candidate Carter announced that the new department would be among his first initiatives as president.[42] Between the election and inauguration the reorganization planning team's most important product was a plan for reorganizing the Executive Office of the President. This proposal directly inspired President Carter's mid-1977 Executive Office reorganization.[43]

As was also the case for Richard Nixon, Jimmy Carter entered the presidency at a time when the presidential reorganization authority had lapsed without renewal by Congress.[44] If executive reorganization was going to be one of his major endeavors in the presidency, President Carter would have to seek legislation re-establishing presidential reorganization authority. Furthermore, and as a separate concern, he would have to create an organization capable of the large scale reorganization planning task that he envisioned.

Before inauguration, Carter called for congressional renewal of the reorganization authority. On February 5, 1977 he submitted to Congress a bill that would create broader authority for the president than had been granted by earlier legislation. In April Congress responded with a less generous grant of authority than had been proposed.[45]

To develop and coordinate his reorganization activities, Carter grafted an entirely new organization to the Office of Management and Budget. Titled the President's Reorganization Project, it would be headed by an executive associate director of OMB and would contain its own capacities for congressional liaison and publicity as well as a number of divisions with responsibilities for studies in various functional areas.[46] While OMB and its predecessor, the Bureau of the Budget, had long had responsibility for management improvement, presidents pursuing reorganization planning had favored ad hoc planning reorganization planning groups such as the President's Advisory Committee on Government Organization and the Ash Council. Among other motives, reorganization planning through such groups allowed the president to fit reorganization planning into his own political agenda. In contrast, President Carter's arrangement for reorganization planning implies a denial that reorganization planning has a political dimension. With the Reorganization Project in OMB, Carter signaled that he saw reorganization planning as a technical exercise that ought to be conducted at some distance from the president.[47]

Given the attention that reorganization received in Carter's campaign and transition, there are surprisingly few reorganization proposals in Carter's first year in office. True to his promise, the president proposed a Department of Energy on March 1, 1977. This fit nicely with his call for strengthened energy policy. His justification for the department was that new, effective policy would need a coherent organizational framework.[48] In short, this reorganization effort was linked to a conception of public policy development. James Schlesinger, Carter's specialist on energy policy, took the lead in espousing the new department, and he became its first secretary after Congress established it in August 1977.

On two occasions in 1977 President Carter used the renewed presidential reorganization authority. In only one of these instances is reorganization clearly linked to the preparation for governance. Through Reorganization Plan No. 1 of 1977 President Carter reorganized the Executive Office of the President. The plan's thrust was twofold. It reduced the size of the EOP's personnel by about 15 percent. It also created a consolidated administrative office in the EOP to eliminate redundant housekeeping activities among the several EOP agencies. The second use of the reorganization authority, Reorganization Plan No. 2 of 1977, effected changes in the public information activities of the Department of State. Two preexisting bureaus were joined into a new International Communications Agency.

In fact, the reorganizations conducted during 1977 are a minor sidelight to the story of the Carter administration's reorganization planning. The main story lies in the enormous effort ongoing in the President's Reorganization Project. With over 300 staff members and a supplemental appropriation of $2,172,000, the Project was deeply enmeshed in planning for very large scale reforms.[49] In the next few years the study teams within the Project would produce recommendations for expanded new departments, natural resources and trade-technology. While neither of these large scale proposals found favor in Congress, the Reorganization Project also produced a number of small scale reforms that were implemented by Reorganization Plan after 1977. Of course, the president's reorganization planners were also preparing what would become the 1979 reforms of the civil service. Whatever else its accomplishments, reorganization planning in the early Carter administration had little to do with governance.

The Utility of Transition Reorganization Planning: Lessons for Future Presidents-Elect

What guidance do these cases of transition reorganization planning offer a future president-elect? Dwight Eisenhower, Richard Nixon, and Jimmy Carter sought quite different aims in planning for executive reorganization during their transitions into the presidency. Were their goals themselves appropriate to the transition period? Was reorganization planning a reasonable instrument towards their goals?

President-elect Eisenhower's use of reorganization planning was linked to his assessment of his personal needs. He had little Washington experience and virtually no contact with the domestic side of government. Moreover, many of the Republicans he would appoint would also have limited Washington experience and need orientation to the organizations they would head. To build into the transition a way of gaining an overview of the governmental establishment might address some of these problems. In this critical matter of establishing a working overview of governmental organization, Eisenhower needed people who knew Washington and whom he trusted. His Special Advisory Committee became the instrument for meeting these goals.

Richard Nixon's transition use of reorganization planning was guided by two related aims. First, he viewed the administrative establishment with hostility, and he aimed to change it. The bureaucracy represented for him profligate social spending, ill-conceived policies, and ideologically liberal administrators. Second, Nixon's view was that government's policies are at least in part formed in implementation; to change policy one had to change bureaucracy. Consequently, he sought organizational changes that would increase his leverage over bureaucracy. Nixon's instruments for reorganization planning were logically related to his ends. He sought to break with the long-term (and liberal) habits of government's organizations. During the transition President-elect Nixon turned to distinguished corporate managers to advise him.

Jimmy Carter sought to make government better through executive reorganization. At different times during the campaign and transition Jimmy Carter attributed different benefits to executive reorganization, but they always amounted to variations on efficiency and virtue. Government should be simple and accessible he would say, and presumably a government with those qualities would also be less likely to be wasteful. Executive reorganization was less a means to other ends for Jimmy Carter than it was an end in itself. President Carter promised to reform government. By establishing a reorganization planning group even before the election, he was getting a head start on fulfilling a goal of his presidency. However, it is not apparent that reor-

ganization planning had any short term or instrumental purposes in Jimmy Carter's transition to the presidency.

Does anything about these cases suggest that reorganization
may be worth considering as a transition tool? Did reorganization planning as used in these cases enhance the early months
of the Carter, Nixon, or Eisenhower administrations?

Jimmy Carter embraced reorganization as a symbol of change,
and he created a large group in OMB for reorganization planning. He invested his political currency to achieve several large
reorganizations — the Department of Energy in 1977, the Department of Education in 1979, and the Civil Service Reform in 1979.
However, Jimmy Carter's use of reorganization does not give encouragement that reorganization planning enhances a new president's capacity to govern. Much of what the President's Reorganization Program aimed to accomplish looked far beyond the
immediate needs of a new president. Finally, few of PRP's plans
aimed at making the president more efficacious, either in the
short or the long run.

In contrast to the Carter experience, Richard Nixon's uses of
re-organization planning in his transition and early presidency
were aimed at enhancing the president's ability to achieve his
ends. For Richard Nixon reorganization was an instrument for
enhanced control over the bureaucratic apparatus of government.
Mastering the unruly bureaucracy seems like an obviously appropriate aim for a president-elect. However it is not only a goal's
appropriateness that determines its utility for a president-elect.
One must also ask if the goal is attainable through executive reorganization.

Reorganization planning *per se* did not achieve President
Nixon's goals. Bureaucratic organizations are difficult to harness,
for reasons of politics, law, organizational habits, and legislative
expectations. It is unlikely that a group of business managers
such as the Ash Council could find a formula that could make
of the president an effective (that is, controlling) manager of the
executive branch. As Richard Nathan has shown, President
Nixon turned to a more direct effort at directing the bureaucracy
after two years of experimenting with reorganization planning.[50]
Using what Nathan terms an administrative presidency approach,
he attempted to gain direct hold of key agencies through a political strategy in the selection of personnel and the guidance of

their actions. In short, reorganization failed as an instrument to forward President Nixon's goal of making the bureaucracy controllable.

For both Nixon and Carter reorganization planning's large-scale reformist purposes overshadowed possible short term, transitional goals. Neither president accurately identified immediate needs that might be fulfilled through reorganization planning. Dwight Eisenhower's use of reorganization planning presents a rather different case.

Eisenhower turned to reorganization planning as a transition tool for quite different reasons than Carter and Nixon. The ends adopted by Carter and Nixon, different as they are in other respects, are alike in their abstractness. They both hoped to transform bureaucracy in fundamental ways, and their views of government organization rested on critiques of the habits, character, and political tendencies found in them. In contrast, as he began his transition experience, Dwight Eisenhower looked at governmental organizations as problems and opportunities about which he had to gain information. He sought trusted and experienced advisers to prepare him for the organizational aspects of the presidency. In contrast to Carter's and Nixon's abstract concepts about bureaucracy, Eisenhower's perspective was informed by the insight that organizations, issues, and people must be addressed in terms of their distinct characteristics — their histories.

Eisenhower used reorganization planning in a way that mined its fullest utility for a transition. He had two aims, to change government's organizations and to prepare himself and his people to govern those organizations. The committee gathered information that would familiarize the president-elect and his appointees with government's organizations, and it was to recommend changes in those organizations. The committee operated within a context of concrete organizations and immediate problems. Its mission was not to overcome bureaucracy abstractly conceived but rather to enhance the fit between those who would govern through specific agencies and those agencies themselves. That President-elect Eisenhower's expectations about reorganization planning's utility were fulfilled is suggested by the high level of reorganization activity in his administration during its first year and by his establishment of the Special Advisory Committee as a continuing fixture of his administration. In contrast to Eisenhower's experience, Presidents Nixon and Carter established reorganization planning mechanisms that were appropriate for grand, long-term reorganization planning and tried to gain short term guidance from them.

Richard Neustadt and Ernest May have written that public agencies have histories — past events and submerged details that have shaped those organizations and conditioned their responses.[51] To govern effectively through organizations requires knowledge of their pasts. In the American regime those who govern do not "come up" through a regimented career ladder. There is no ordered way through which those elected to the presidency gain knowledge appropriate to governance. This disadvantage is even more acute for presidents-elect who are "outsiders." Whatever their backgrounds, presidents, their staffs, and their appointees must themselves act to grasp information about their organizational context that is sufficient to their needs. It was this problem that Dwight Eisenhower's use of reorganization planning addressed with evident success while the failures of the Nixon and Carter efforts rest on the degree to which they failed to take account of the realities of the organizational context of the presidency.

What lessons can be learned about reorganization planning's general utility from the Eisenhower transition? First, reorganization planning might be useful when it can be designed to address the specific experiential and informational characteristics of the incoming administration. Second, its utility might be enhanced by a tight mandate that focuses reorganization planning activity onto concrete questions about why specific agencies work as they do and how they might be improved. Third, the product of reorganization transition era reorganization planning will have the most effect if it can be used to prepare the cabinet and sub-cabinct officers who will be charged with managing the agencies under study. Finally, the Eisenhower case suggests that these possibilities for transition period use of reorganization will be most likely if those who conduct reorganization planning have political sophistication, Washington experience, and ready access to the president-elect.

Experience teaches that reorganization planning might prove attractive to a president-elect for two very different reasons. As in the Nixon and Carter cases, reorganization planning might seem like an appropriate weapon for confronting the evils we often attribute to bureaucracy. On the other hand, as in the Eisenhower case, reorganization planning might seem like an appropriate instrument for preparing an administration to work within a bureaucratic context. The Eisenhower case suggests that this purpose is to be recommended for consideration by a president-elect. The Nixon and Carter cases suggest that the transformational uses of reorganization are inappropriate for transition planning and likely to be quixotic.

PART THREE

The Presidency and the Executive Establishment

CHAPTER ELEVEN

Cabinet Government in the Modern Presidency

SHIRLEY ANNE WARSHAW
ASSISTANT PROFESSOR OF POLITICAL SCIENCE
GETTYSBURG COLLEGE

The phrase "Cabinet Government" is one which has emerged relatively recently within the context of the American political structure. Americans had consciously stayed away from using the term for fear of evoking an image of similarity between the British system of Cabinet Government and our system of separation of powers. Cabinet Government, within the British context, referred to a system of power sharing between the chief executive and the Cabinet and between the executive and legislative branches. In essence, the British have a plural executive. The American governmental structure was framed to ensure that we had a singular, not a plural executive, with all power emanating from a single chief executive. The role of the Cabinet within the American structure was advisory only.

However, in spite of this traditional aversion to power-sharing within the executive branch between the President and his Cabinet, the term "Cabinet Government" has emerged to distinguish between a President who relies on his White House staff for policy advice and one who relies on his Cabinet. A President who has a relatively small White House staff, whose primary role is policy coordination rather than policy development, is said to advocate "Cabinet Government."

The concept of Cabinet Government in the United States is one that has only been possible since the creation of the Executive Office of the President in 1939. Prior to that time, Presidents did not have the staff capabilities to question or to independently develop policy options. The President simply accepted the policy recommendations of the executive departments. The emergence of a White House staff after 1939 allowed the President the choice of accepting departmental recommendations or using his own staff to refine or develop new policy options.

Throughout the first two decades in which the Executive Office of the President existed, the advisory role of the Cabinet remained essentially unchanged. The EOP served primarily as a coordinative rather than a policy-making office. Harry Truman commented specifically that he had to delegate a substantial amount of authority to his Cabinet because "government was simply too large" to be run from the White House. Truman's Cabinet, not the White House staff, handled policy development.

His successor, Dwight Eisenhower, similarly delegated a substantial degree of policy-making authority to the Cabinet. Eisenhower relied heavily on his Cabinet and, in October 1954, created the Cabinet Secretariat within the White House to coordinate the Cabinet's preparation of policy recommendations. The Cabinet Secretariat was responsible for establishing the agenda for the Friday morning Cabinet meetings and for ensuring that each Cabinet officer who had a major issue to discuss had circulated a background paper to the President and other Cabinet officers.

Eisenhower made the fullest use of the Cabinet of any modern president. He not only sought the advice of individual Cabinet officers in policy decisions, but used the collective Cabinet as a means to bring opposing viewpoints into the open. Cabinet officers were encouraged to debate and discuss a wide range of national issues during the Cabinet meetings, a technique which Eisenhower felt ensured that he had been exposed to all sides of an issue and which enhanced the sense of teamwork among his Cabinet members. The Reagan White House took a leaf from the Eisenhower system when it molded the Cabinet Council system thirty years later. Ronald Reagan re-instituted this system of discussion-oriented Cabinet meetings which had been systematically eliminated by Presidents Kennedy, Johnson, Nixon, and Carter. Ford was an exception.

Eisenhower also created two especially significant White House staff positions, Special Assistant for National Security Affairs in 1953 and Special Assistant for Science and Technology in 1957.

However, not until the administration of John F. Kennedy did the White House staff become a sizable enough unit to question or initiate policy proposals. Presidents Roosevelt, Truman and Eisenhower had been reluctant to move policy development from the executive agencies to the White House.

John F. Kennedy, however, was concerned that the growth of the federal bureaucracy during the Eisenhower administration had stagnated policy innovation. He increased the size of the White House staff in order to circumvent the career bureaucracy, which he perceived as reluctant to develop creative solutions for social and economic problems. Kennedy became the first President to significantly alter the advisory role of the Cabinet in the years following creation of the Executive Office of the President. Kennedy enlarged his personal staff to provide limited policy and management advice and created advisory committees within the White House, and enlarged others. On the one hand he removed the Special Assistant for Science and Technology from the White House staff, placing the Office of Science and Technology in the Executive Office of the President where there was less accessibility.[1] On the other hand he brought into the White House a group of special assistants whose role was, according to Kennedy, to make certain that "important matters are brought here in a way which permits a clear decision after alternatives have been presented."[2]

The pendulum toward greater utilization of the White House staff for policy development continued during the Johnson administration. Johnson expanded the size of the White House staff and encouraged its active participation in the preparation of administration policies, working both with the departments and the Executive Office of the President (EOP) staff to that end. White House staff members emerged as major participants in both policy review and policy development. Prior to the Johnson years, the role of the White House staff had been limited to advising the President on the merits of departmental recommendations.

The trend toward a White House based policy-making system was in large part the product of the dramatic increase in federal expenditures during the 1960s and the subsequent increase in departmental responsibilities. Due to defense spending from the Vietnam War and mandates stemming from the Great Society legislation, the federal budget grew from $92 billion in 1960 to $195 billion in 1970. In contrast, the Eisenhower administration had shied away from federal expenditures for social programs during its eight years in office. The growth in the federal budget from 1947–1964 was primarily in its defense programs as a result of escalating fears of Soviet expansionism.[3] However, the trend began during the 1960s toward the expansion of government activities, particularly in the area of income maintenance.[4]

Such increased programmatic and regulatory responsibilities within the executive departments led to an increased role for the bureaucracy and special interest groups in the policy-making process.[5] Lyndon Johnson became extremely concerned that these bureaucratic and constituent pressures on the departments were detrimental to Presidential policy objectives. He considered many of his Cabinet officers "captured" by the permanent government and subsequently sought to bypass the Cabinet for major policy initiatives.[6] Johnson preferred to rely on the White House staff for policy advice and for the development of policy proposals. Joseph Califano, for example, was a key member of the White House staff who led the Department of Health, Education and Welfare in the creation of numerous social welfare programs. Without Califano's leadership, few programs would have emanated from HEW.

The Johnson era marked the emergence of the centralized policy-making system, one which challenged the traditional leadership of the Cabinet in policy development. Cabinet officers were replaced by White House staff, such as Joe Califano, as the President's prime source of advice on major policy issues.

Creation of a Centralized Policy-Making System

Lyndon Johnson's decision to establish a centralized policy-making system was implemented through the resources available within the Executive Office of the President. Johnson's decision to expand the policy-making responsibilities of his staff reflected his concern that the bureaucracy shaped departmental policy to, as Francis Rourke notes, "expand their own jurisdiction," rather than to meet presidential goals.[7] The growth of the bureaucracy as a political entity was the major, although not the sole factor which contributed to the emergence of a centralized policy-making system. Preparation of departmental policy initiatives tended to be a long, time-consuming process due to the number of people involved in the process. Each layer of staff involved in the preparation of the policy document spent time writing, reviewing, and re-writing its ideas. Before the proposal reached the President the departmental Secretary, staff members, division chiefs, bureau directors, deputy assistant secretaries and assistant secretaries had read the material and met to discuss changes. The process took weeks, generally months. It was a process that frustrated Lyndon Johnson, particularly during the first year of his administration.

Johnson also turned inward to his staff rather than to his Cabinet because he was convinced that only his staff had a clear idea of the direction that he wanted government to take. Presidents with a broad vision for government, such as Franklin Delano Roosevelt and Lyndon Johnson, relied on their immediate staff for innovative ideas in policy development. White House staffs differ from the Cabinet in that they are usually close associates "who know the President and his thinking well and have frequent access to him. They have a sense of how he views problems and which issues and factors he considers most important," as former White House staff member Roger Porter noted.[8] White House staff have been more astute at understanding the types of policies that the President wants developed than Cabinet officers.

Creation of Cabinet Government
(or a Decentralized Policy-Making System)

In spite of the advantages which Lyndon Johnson found in the centralized policy-making system, his successors found that the Johnson system had numerous disadvantages. Policy had been too closely managed from within the White House for the effective operation of government. The exclusion of Cabinet members from regular contact with the President on policy issues redirected the allegiance of many Cabinet officers from the President to their departments. Cabinet officers turned inward to their own staff and established stronger bonds with departmental staff than with the President or with White House staff.

Successive Presidents were convinced that a centralized policy-making system which alienated the Cabinet and their executive agencies was detrimental to the office of the President and to the policy goals of the President. As a result, Presidents Nixon, Ford, Carter and Reagan campaigned on a promise of a return to a Cabinet-based policy-making system such as existed prior to the Kennedy/Johnson years.

The most serious problem that the centralized policy-making system had encountered was the inability of the White House staff to build the coalitions of support necessary for their policy initiatives. Policy proposals developed in the White House could not be fine-tuned as they had when departments were the center of policy deliberations. The departments provided, as William Carey described, "the pluralistic decision structures" which allowed presidential proposals to be modified through interaction and consensus.[9] In policy initiatives which were developed through the departments prior to the centralized policy system, departmental staff, special interest groups, government agencies, and others were given the opportunity to influence the final product.[10]

Ironically, one of the major reasons that Johnson turned to his White House staff for policy development was his concern that bureaucratic and constituent pressures on departmental policymaking were resulting in policies which did not meet Presidential objectives. The result of the centralized policy-making system, however, had been to create policies for which minimal political support existed even though the policies met with Presidential approval.

In addition to the problems caused by policies developed without departmental support, a number of other major problems were identified by successive Presidents with the centralized system. First, the White House staff, most of whom were personal and political associates of the President, lacked the depth of technical expertise that was available at the departmental level. Despite the size of the White House staff and that of the larger Executive Office of the President, their expertise rarely equaled that of the departments. White House aides tended to be generalists rather than programmatic specialists and therefore had a limited expertise in any given area.

Second, policies developed by the departments frequently failed to account for the management problems in the implementation stages. Most members of the White House staff lacked departmental experience and had not assessed the administrative problems that changes or modifications in policies might cause. Policies that created administrative problems were slow to be implemented and resulted in unfavorable reactions at the local level.

Third, by relieving the Cabinet officer of responsibility for key departmental policymaking and by placing that responsibility with the White House staff, the Cabinet officer's command became impaired. In its study of presidential management of the executive branch, the National Academy of Public Administration cited the importance of agency heads being an integral part of the policy-making process. As the study said,

> Agency heads . . . must be at the center of the flow of information and advice from constituent units of their agency to the Executive Office. If any agency head is not in such a position, his authority and effectiveness will be quickly eroded and his or her ability to represent the President's program rapidly destroyed.[11]

Fifth, the expansion of the White House staff into diverse areas of policy development resulted in a system which became a mini-bureaucracy. As Jack Valenti, a senior member of the Johnson White House noted,

> Large White House staffs breed an inner bureaucracy that can get as crusted with official barnacles as a Cabinet department . . . The ideal White House operation is one with just enough bodies to do the work and with the capacity to call on the executive departments and the OMB for detailed research and information gatherings.[12]

The advantage of speed, which Johnson felt to be a major reason for implementing a centralized policy-making system, was substantially mitigated as several layers of staff within the White House became involved in policymaking. Each layer of staff in the White House prepared and reviewed the material before it reached the chief domestic policy adviser, which was substantially the same process as occurred within the executive departments. The White House domestic policy adviser was faced with reviewing numerous pieces of material, which required meetings with staff to clarify, and subsequently he himself became a bottleneck in the policy process which the President had created to speed up executive decision-making.

Sixth, the original purpose of the centralized management system was to use the White House staff for the development of major administration policies. However, many issues with which members of the White House staff became involved were minor and distracted their attention from larger issues.[13] As Rexford Tugwell and Thomas Cronin point out, large presidential staffs "create conflict, make line administration more distant, and attract more duties to the White House than can be administered effectively."[14] The bureaucratization of the White House staff led the staff to try to influence not only major departmental activities but minor ones.

In short, the effort to establish Cabinet Government during the post-Johnson years was designed to limit the authority of the White House staff over departmental policy-making. The Cabinet's advisory role had been minimized with centralized policy making. Cabinet Government was an attempt to restore the Cabinet officers to their status as "assistant presidents," as Alexander Hamilton first proposed, and to re-establish the Cabinet as the President's principal source of advice on policy issues.

Since there was ample evidence indicating that centralized policy-making staff within the White House was detrimental to Presidential policy goals, recent Presidents have endeavored to implement Cabinet Government. Without exception, each successive President since Lyndon Johnson has tried to reduce the influence of the White House staff in policy development. But only one has been moderately successful. The White House continued to be a major influence, and at times primary initiator, of administration policy. What happened?

The Nixon Experience with Cabinet Government

Richard Nixon entered the Presidency in 1969 with a commitment to reduce the size and the influence of the White House staff that had flourished during the Johnson administration. He did this for two primary reasons. First, it was a politically advantageous strategy to promise the electorate that decisions would be broad-based. The White House staff would not dominate policymaking without regard to departmental recommendations on implementation problems and legislative concerns. Second, Nixon sought to focus his attention on international issues, and leave domestic issues to the Cabinet to resolve. Cabinet Government afforded Nixon the opportunity to direct his efforts at solving a myriad of foreign affairs issues, such as containing the cold war, resolving the Vietnam War, and re-aligning U.S. interests with mainland China. In an interview with Theodore H. White during the 1968 campaign, Nixon summarized his plan to rely on the Cabinet for domestic policymaking:

> I've always thought this country could run itself domestically without a President; all you need is a competent Cabinet to run the country at home . . . the President makes foreign policy.[15]

Nixon saw relatively few problems with allowing the Cabinet the freedom to develop domestic policy proposals. Since his domestic goals were straightforward and few in number, he believed that his Cabinet could easily manage domestic affairs. Once in office, Nixon endeavored to implement Cabinet Government in domestic policy by giving his Cabinet officers control over departmental personnel and policy decisions. The role of the White House staff domestic advisors was to provide the Cabinet officers a framework for policy development based on Nixon's 1968 campaign pledges and long-range goals for the administration. Their role in actual policy development was minimal.

The system of Cabinet Government lasted less than one year before Nixon increased the policy-making role of the White House staff, in a staff system similar to that in the Johnson White House. The Cabinet lost access to Nixon, departmental personnel management, and control of major policy development by 1970.

The single most important factor which led Nixon to alter his decision structure was his concern that the Cabinet officers had been captured by their department's bureaucratic and constituent interests. Three departments in particular (Interior, HUD, and HEW) were criticized by Nixon for developing policies which were more liberal than Nixon wanted. HEW's decision to strengthen enforcement of the 1964 Civil Rights Act which governed public school desegregation was a classic example of an agency advocating a policy which Nixon considered too liberal.

Rather than seeking to resolve policy differences with his Cabinet officers, or to offer clear direction in policy, Nixon simply changed the policy development system. He absolved the Cabinet of policy-making responsibility within nine months of taking office, and transferred that authority to the White House. He did not endeavor to work within the Cabinet Government structure to resolve policy differences with his Cabinet officers.

Although Nixon was quick to blame his cabinet for the failure of Cabinet Government, his management style was a major factor in its demise. Nixon failed to help Cabinet officers gain support in Congress for many of their legislative proposals, he allowed White House staff to offer conflicting advice to Cabinet officers, and he provided poor overall direction on policy matters. He gave his Cabinet a broad mandate at the start of the administration to reduce the size of the federal bureaucracy and cut the number of federal programs, but offered little specific policy direction. When the first major conflicts began to develop in the spring and summer of 1969 between Nixon and members of the Cabinet, Nixon was in the midst of developing an international policy and was embarking on foreign tours. Not until the fall of 1969 did

he focus his attention on domestic affairs. Rather than resolve
the conflicts in policy development, Nixon changed the organizational structure and abandoned Cabinet Government.

In early 1970 Nixon created the Domestic Council within the
White House to develop the administration's domestic policy objectives and specific policy initiatives. The Domestic Council had
a staff of seventy to prepare and coordinate domestic policy, a
function which had been handled previously by the Cabinet.

The Cabinet's decreasing role in policy development was
matched by the increasing role in policy development of the Executive Office of the President (EOP) during the second year
of the administration. The number of personnel within the EOP
rose from 1,298 in 1969 to 1,768 in 1971, a fifty percent increase.
During the same period, Nixon increased the EOP budget from
$31 million to $45 million.[16] He also increased the number of
advisory committees within the White House and the size and
budgets of existing White House advisory groups. For example,
the Special Representative for Trade Negotiations on the EOP
staff went from a budget of $482,000 and a staff of twenty-eight
in 1968 to a budget of $757,000 and a staff of thirty-five in 1971.[17]
General Presidential advisory panels similarly proliferated during
this period, growing to 198 advisory groups and 1,500 lesser commissions by 1971. Thomas Cronin discussed such a bureaucratization of the White House stating that,

> Under President Nixon, in fact, there has been an almost system-
> atic bureaucratization of the Presidential Establishment, in which
> more new councils and offices have been established, more special-
> ization and division of labor and layers of staffing have been added,
> than at any time since World War II.[18]

In spite of the problems that Nixon saw with the centralized
policy-making system which Lyndon Johnson had established,
and in spite of Nixon's commitment to Cabinet Government,
the system failed in the Nixon administration. After nine months
in office Nixon was convinced that the Cabinet needed strong
leadership from the White House in policy development.

The Ford Experience with Cabinet Government

Because of the brevity of the Ford administration, it is unfair to assess whether or not Cabinet Government was successful during the two and one-half years in which Gerald Ford held office. However, it is important to note that he, as did his predecessor, entered office with a pledge to reduce the authority of the White House staff and to rely on the Cabinet for policy advice.

His first move to implement Cabinet Government was to establish a system in the White House in which each member of the senior staff had equal access to the President. Ford called the system analagous to the Knights of the Round Table. He had summarily rejected the concept of a chief of staff, in the Haldeman mold, opting for a "spokes of the wheel" approach similar to that used by John F. Kennedy. Such a system, he hoped, would keep information from being bottled up with the chief of staff and ensure that he had access to a wide range of viewpoints.

His next move to implement Cabinet Government was to choose experienced federal executives for his Cabinet, such as Elliot Richardson and William Coleman, who he believed could control the bureaucracy and deal effectively with Congress. Each member of the Cabinet was given free access to Ford, without being subjected to several layers of White House staff before receiving clearance to enter the Oval Office.

Ford viewed the Cabinet meetings as another important tool to implement Cabinet Government. They provided an opportunity for him to hear a broad spectrum of ideas on policy issues and their political implications. The Cabinet was designed to be a collegial system for policy discussion, in a manner similar to that used by President Eisenhower.

However, by the end of his brief tenure in office, Ford had increasingly turned to his White House staff for policy advice. He reverted back to the chief of staff system, increased the number of staff within the White House, reduced the frequency of Cabinet meetings, and spent less time meeting with individual members of his Cabinet. As had his predecessor, Gerald Ford concluded that the parochial interests of his Cabinet officers often took them in directions which were unacceptable to the White House and thus required closer control by the President. Ford never totally abrogated Cabinet Government, as Richard Nixon had, but he did dramatically reduce his reliance on the Cabinet during the last months of his administration. Whether or not he could have

Theodore Lownik Library
Illinois Benedictine College
Lisle, Illinois 60532

salvaged Cabinet Government during a second term remains speculation, for he never had the chance to modify Cabinet Government to a system with which he could work.

The Carter Experience with Cabinet Government

For many of the same reasons that Richard Nixon chose to implement Cabinet Government, Jimmy Carter chose to implement Cabinet Government. At the swearing-in ceremony for his Cabinet Carter firmly stated,

> I believe in Cabinet administration of government. There will never be an instance while I am President where the members of the White House staff dominate or act in a superior position to members of the Cabinet.[19]

In an interview two months later with *U.S. News & World Report* Carter reiterated his preference for a strong Cabinet and decentralized management. In that interview he said, "I would not establish a 'palace guard' in the White House with the authority to run the departments in the federal government."[20]

Carter's views on Cabinet Government were discussed in detail both with his White House staff and with the Cabinet prior to the inauguration. Jack Watson, a senior member of the White House staff, described the role of the White House staff as "supportive, not command . . . They will not be running the departments."[21] Cabinet Government also meant that the Cabinet officers were responsible for personnel selection and other management decisions at the departmental level. One Cabinet member quoted Carter as telling him, "I intend to keep my promise of Cabinet Government to the American people."[22]

Carter's primary reason for supporting Cabinet Government was political expediency. The 1976 election was the first presidential election following Richard Nixon's resignation. As a result, both Jimmy Carter and his Republican opponent, Gerald Ford, sought to establish clear differences between their governing styles and those of Richard Nixon. The fact that Nixon had resigned in disgrace, partly for the organizational mechanism he had established, was ample reason for Carter and Ford to seek organizational structures which were significantly different from the one used by Nixon during the majority of his term.

Carter pledged that Cabinet Government would facilitate his commitment to open government and the openness of the decision-making process. Cabinet Government, Carter felt, would permit "full participation by our people in their own government's processes."[23] Cabinet Government provided Carter the means for having an "open government" and allowing the public to have a greater influence in departmental policy decisions.

In addition, and perhaps equally as important to Carter, were the administrative benefits which Cabinet Government would provide. Carter's top two priorities for his administration were "achieving maximum bureaucratic efficiency and reorganizing the government."[24] Since Carter's primary concern was making administrative changes rather than policy changes, the departmental staff rather than the White House staff were the logical place to implement his plan.

Carter also had as a major goal of his administration to revise and streamline the "procedures for constantly analyzing the effectiveness of its (government's) many varied services."[25] Carter believed that the in-depth organizational procedural changes that he wanted to make in the delivery of public services were most appropriately handled at the departmental rather than the White House level. Carter was willing to delegate to the Cabinet the authority to make the changes in departmental budgeting, auditing, and management changes that would result in substantial cost savings and in improvements to service delivery. Cabinet Government was, therefore, an appropriate organizational structure to accomplish the major goals of his presidency.

However, Cabinet Government during the Carter Administration lasted barely six months, three months less than it had during the Nixon administration. In a reorganization of White House staff on July 15, 1977, policy development and departmental oversight was reassigned within the White House from the Cabinet secretariat to the White House Domestic Policy Group. Jimmy Carter gave Stuart Eizenstat, his Domestic Policy Council director, "clear responsibility for managing the way in which domestic and most economic policy issues are prepared for presidential decision."[26] *The Washington Post* noted of the staff reorganization that "Eizenstat's new domestic policy process is aimed at increasing the President's ability to oversee and control every step in framing major domestic programs."[27]

The White House Domestic Policy staff grew following the

1977 reorganization from twenty to forty-three full-time positions in order to manage not only domestic policy but also economic policy development. By the fall of 1977, Eizenstat had restructured the manner in which Cabinet officers participated in presidential policy-making. Cabinet clusters remained the primary mechanism for convening Cabinet officers on policy issues, but they were convened only at Eizenstat's request. Policy issues were discussed in clusters which the White House staff, rather than the Cabinet, developed. After meetings with the Cabinet cluster, Eizenstat's staff prepared an issue definition memorandum which outlined the questions to be answered, the agencies to be involved, the timetable to be met, and the organization that would serve as a lead agency. If approved by the President, basic research on the policy issue was handled by the lead agency under White House supervision with the White House staff synthesizing the departmental material into a Presidential Review Memorandum (PRM), a term coined by Eizenstat.

The PRM outlined the policy options for Carter, giving the pros and cons of each option. Cabinet officials had an opportunity to review the Presidential Review Memorandum, and to recommend changes, before it was sent to Carter. The final memo, however, on all policy issues went from Eizenstat to Carter, not from a Cabinet member or cabinet cluster to Carter. This was the crowning blow to Cabinet Government, for White House staff controlled the final policy product submitted to the President after the July 15, 1977 reorganization.

The Reagan Experience with Cabinet Government

Ronald Reagan followed the Nixon-Carter tradition of campaigning on the promise of Cabinet Government. He too capitalized on the political expediency of decentralizing policy-making to minimize the implementation of policies that lacked popular support. When introducing his Cabinet appointments to the nation on December 20, 1980, Reagan noted that "I am more confident than ever that Cabinet Government can and will work."[28]

Reagan promised to reduce the size and the influence of the White House staff to rely on his Cabinet officers for policy advice. His reasons for pursing Cabinet Government were three-fold. First, he sought to project a difference in governing styles between himself and the Democratic presidential candidate,

Jimmy Carter. Second, as had Carter, Reagan's primary goals for his presidency were administrative and procedural: cutting the budget, reducing the size of the federal bureaucracy, and curtailing social welfare programs as much as possible without affecting the "safety net," as he called it. The Reagan agenda was easily managed from the departments in Reagan's organizational structure.

Unlike his predecessors, Richard Nixon and Jimmy Carter, Ronald Reagan was successful at establishing a modified version of Cabinet Government. Throughout his two terms in office, Reagan sought the advice of the Cabinet in policy decisions, and reduced the role of the White House staff in policy development. The White House staff served to offer broad direction in policy objectives and to coordinate interdepartmental issues. Although the White House staff clearly played a major role in policy development, they were partners with the Cabinet officers, which could not be said of either the Nixon or Carter administrations after the first year.

Although the Reagan system of Cabinet Government was a highly modified one, one in which the White House had significant input in policy, with the possible exception of Ford's brief tenure, it remains the only successful system of Cabinet Government since Eisenhower. The most important reason that Cabinet Government failed in both the Nixon and Carter administrations was the concern by each President that their Cabinet officers were initiating policies which were inconsistent with presidential goals. There is, in fact, ample evidence to indicate that Cabinet officers did develop policies which Nixon and Carter did not support, but not because the Cabinet had become "captured." The problem was the lack of direction which both Nixon and Carter provided their Cabinet in policy matters and with the relatively weak personal relationship between Nixon and Carter and their Cabinet officers.

Reagan endeavored to remedy both of these problems. First, he chose Cabinet officers with a clear understanding of the policy direction that he sought to take. Cabinet selection was not premised on racial, religious, or gender diversity as in other administrations, but on ideological compatibility with the President. In addition, ideology was the dominant consideration when filling vacancies in sub-Cabinet policy-making positions. The White House Personnel Office, under the direction of E. Pendelton James and later John S. Herrington, controlled all departmental appointments and ensured that each appointee was in tune with the Reagan philosophy.[29] This was not the case in either the Nixon or Carter administrations, where Cabinet officers were free to choose their departmental staff.

The staffing of the Reagan presidency was notable not only for its ideological consistency but also for the depth of political expertise that it inserted in policy-level positions. Many sub-Cabinet appointments had policy-making experience on Capital Hill or other executive agencies. This was in sharp contrast to both the Nixon and Carter administrations where departmental staff frequently moved in to policy-making positions from within their departments and had minimal experience in other agencies or in Congress. The majority of sub-Cabinet appointments in both the Nixon and Carter administrations were technocrats rather than political executives.

The second means by which Reagan ensured a workable system of Cabinet Government was to constantly provide his Cabinet officers direction in policy matters. Reagan created five Cabinet councils, later expanded to seven and eventually reduced to two in the second term, which focused around broad policy areas. The White House provided small staffs for each of the councils through the Cabinet Secretariat. Cabinet councils met frequently throughout Reagan's two terms, providing a constant forum for policy options to be collectively discussed and refined. This system had two ancillary effects on the policy process. First, it instilled into each Cabinet officer a sense of teamwork in policy development. Cabinet officers believed that they personally had contributed to each of the administrations' major policy initiatives and were willing to support those initiatives within their departments, Congress, and with the public at large. This led to a sense of camaraderie and solidarity within the Cabinet.[30] Cabinet members believed they were part of a team, each contributing to the "team agenda." Second, individual Cabinet officers had little opportunity to move policy away from, as one scholar noted, the "overarching focus" of broad ideological goals when policy was subjected to collective review.[31]

The success of Cabinet Government in the Reagan administration can be attributed to a careful structuring and nurturing of the White House-Cabinet relationship. The frequent meetings of the Cabinet Councils allowed the White House staff to reinforce the policy objectives of the administration and to provide a forum for policy options to be discussed within the framework for the policy objectives outlined by the White House staff.

Cabinet Government in Perspective

The promise of Cabinet Government by Presidents Nixon, Carter and Reagan shared the common theme that each sought to structure their policy-making system very differently from that of their predecessor. In each case, political expediency was an over-riding factor in their decision to implement Cabinet Government.

However, each also believed, quite sincerely, that Cabinet Government was the most effective organizational structure for the administration. For Nixon, Cabinet Government freed his time from domestic policy issues to focus on foreign policy. Nixon, who had a fairly limited domestic agenda, was confident that his Cabinet officers could handle domestic policy with minimal direction from the White House. For Carter, who also had a limited domestic agenda, Cabinet Government provided the optimal means for implementing his goals of reorganizing government and streamlining the federal bureaucracy. These were issues, he felt, that had to be tackled by the Cabinet officers rather than White House staff. Reagan, who also had a limited domestic agenda, saw the Cabinet as the most logical structure for developing and implementing policy.

Reagan, however, was the only President of the three who used his White House staff as a mechanism to develop broad policy objectives and to ensure that the Cabinet was constantly attuned to those objectives. Reagan's style of governing cannot be ignored, either, in evaluating why Cabinet Government was more successful in his administration than in that of Nixon and Carter. Reagan chose not to become involved in the majority of policy issues, and thus was not informed of most departmental proposals. Reagan was satisfied that Cabinet officers and sub-Cabinet officers had been thoroughly screened to ensure their ideological commitment to administration goals, and that these goals were constantly reinforced through Cabinet Council meetings.

In reviewing the success of Cabinet Government in the Reagan administration, it must be noted that the White House was a major participant in policymaking. Cabinet Government in its pure sense is not a workable system. Cabinet officers need clear policy direction throughout their tenure in office from the White House, and they need a forum to coordinate interdepartmental issues, which the Cabinet Council system provides. The White House staff must play a strong role in offering policy direction to the executive agencies, in resolving inter-agency conflicts, and in offering programmatic coordination for issues that cross jurisdictional lines. However, for all of the reasons outlined earlier in this chapter on the problems with a centralized management system, the White House staff cannot become the dominant actor in the policy-making process.

The lesson learned from the Cabinet Government experience of the Nixon, Ford, Carter, and Reagan presidencies is that the White House staff must be large enough to guide the departments in their policy considerations but small enough so as not to create a counter bureaucracy. Reagan defied tradition by not selecting his Cabinet for the political strength it would add to the administration. The Cabinet was chosen primarily for its commitment to Ronald Reagan and the Reagan ideology. Neither Nixon nor Carter ever trusted their Cabinet officers. Each chose the majority of their Cabinet to diversify the political base of the administration rather than for their commitment to presidential objectives. The result was to produce a Cabinet which never had the support of the President. Again Ford was the exception.[32]

The complexity of federal policymaking leaves no doubt that the President must rely on his Cabinet for the development of policy proposals. The White House staff is simply not skilled in either the technical details or the institutional conflicts that are involved. But the Cabinet needs clear and constant direction from the White House on the short and long term policy goals of the President. Cabinet Government is a term that means policymaking will be focused in the executive agencies with broad policy direction coming from the White House. It is a public statement by the President that overall policymaking will not be focused in the White House.

CHAPTER TWELVE

The Waning Political Capital of Cabinet Appointments

MARGARET JANE WYSZOMIRSKI

GUEST SCHOLAR

BROOKINGS INSTITUTION

Cabinet appointments are publicly and politically regarded as the single most important action of a new president.[1] Cabinet appointees symbolically bridge the transition from election to administration, from the politics of campaigning to the politics of governance. Despite the actual as well as symbolic importance of cabinet recruitment, the cabinet as a political institution, exhibits little organizational coherence and only a tenous claim on presidential influence since it rests on the shifting sands of a "completely customary basis."[2]

The process of selecting presidential appointees (including cabinet members) has undergone important changes during the last half century. While cabinet recruitment has become part of a more institutionalized staffing system, it nonetheless retains strong idiosyncratic and personalistic aspects. While post-World War II presidents have developed (and increasingly relied upon) elaborate personnel recruitment and talent scouting systems to fill specialized administrative and sub-cabinet positions,[3] they continue to prefer managing the cabinet appointment processes more directly. Hence the process of cabinet-making is one of the most personal and least institutionalized aspects of presidential staffing. It is also one of the most variable since cabinet agencies vary considerably with regard to importance, whether judged in terms of size, age, complexity or programmatic responsibilities. Similarly, the members of the cabinet exhibit an array of origins, abilities, and loyalties. Furthermore, cabinet secretaries perform a variety of roles with varying degrees of proficiency and have had quite disparate relations with their respective presidents. Despite the cabinet's discontinuous and variegated character, one constant seems to prevail. A major purpose of the cabinet has been to provide presidents with political capital. Each president requires political capital if he is to fulfill his roles and responsibilities as executive, as legislator, as policy designer and advocate, and as preeminent democratic politician. Although the cabinet is surely not the sole source of a president's political capital, it is, nonetheless, an important source.[4]

In addressing its primary purpose, the cabinet (and its members) is called upon to act in the following capacities, either singly or in combination:

- political coalition representative
- political operations assistant
- departmental administrator
- expert policy adviser

The prospect for effective performance in each role can be associated with certain skills, experience, and other individual characteristics. If situational factors do not generate hindering or countervailing conditions, then cabinet appointees who possess such qualities and qualifications should be assets to the president, increasing his political capital in terms of policy expertise, administrative competence, political skills, and/or political support. Ideally, cabinet secretaries will be able to augment the president's resources on more than one of these dimensions. Certainly it is logical to assume that presidents might seek to maximize their capital accumulation by means of appointees who represent resources of more than one type.

It must be recognized that such political capital can be useful both in affirmatively advancing a president's agenda as well as in protecting his balance of resources from unnecessary depletion through error or mischance. Such "preventive assistance" would include using political skills to help keep Congressional-Executive relations cordial so as not to prejudice later prospects for positive cooperation. It would also include the use of administrative skills to conduct departments in such a way as to avoid unnecessarily taxing the president with managerial detail or with the political costs of scandals. These preventive contributions to the president's political capital are rather like tax exemptions — their impact is "measurable by contrast to what the consequences (or costs) might have been if the situation were otherwise."[5]

Using the concept of political capital to orient an examination of cabinet recruitment and circulation reveals a number of both long and short term patterns. For example, the varieties of political capital that the cabinet members can provide are not of fixed or equal portions. Rather, the relative portion of different kinds of political capital acquired through cabinet recruitment varies both with time and with specific cabinet position. Circulation patterns can also be discerned and related to such factors as the ideological distinctiveness of the president's political philosophy, the character of a president's requirement for the loyalty of his "lieutenants", the impact of other interacting political institutions, the influence of partisan differences, or the effect of circumstantial elements (such as whether it is a first or a second term for a given president, or whether it is the term of the accidental president).

A comprehensive analysis of patterns of presidential capital accumulation of all four types of capital during the last fifty years is beyond the scope of this paper, which will instead, focus on a selection of patterns pertaining to the most explicitly political types of political capital that cabinet appointees have represented.

Political Skills

One can think of such political skills — persuasion, negotiation, consensus formation, and coalition building — as possibly being directed at three types of "targets"— independent decisionmakers in other political institutions (e.g. congressmen, governors), public officials in ostensibly subordinate executive positions (e.g. bureaucratic administrators), or the public (either in general or in special interest constituencies). It seems logical that political skills are best acquired and polished through active engagement in public affairs. This may be done from authoritative bases or from informal ones. Authoritative bases may include tenure as the member of a legislature or as a political executive who has dealt with the legislature, such as a governor or a big city mayor or as the director of a federal agency who has had extensive contact with Congress. Informal experience is most likely gained through experience as a lobbyist for an interest group or as congressional liaison staff for an executive agency. In their application, political institutions other than the presidency are those most likely to be of use in governance, while those applied to ostensibly subordinate public officials are of primary concern to administrative tasks. While political skills employed with regard to the public are a necessary and valuable support to governance functions, they are, first and foremost, indispensable to success in the campaign and electoral process.

Given the necessity for collaboration between the President and Congress, skills pertaining to the legislative process are highly valuable. It seems logical to assume that those who have acquired these skills via authoritative experience are likely to have additional qualitative advantages in that they have established reputational and social networks to draw upon and which enhance their credibility with other political officials. It therefore follows that Congressmen are a most valuable source of political skills, that the utility of non-federal elected executives may be limited by their relative unfamiliarity with the specifics of the national political scene, and that informal craftsmen (such as lobbyists or experienced congressional liaison staff) may have considerable skill but comparatively little independent legitimacy for its exercise.

Thus, to maximize their investment in political skills capital, presidents would be wise to recruit Congressmen and, secondarily, Governors. Furthermore, incumbent officials are likely to carry greater cachet than former officials, with the utility of their social networks and legitimacy declining in proportion to the length of time out of office and the circumstances under which they left office. Conversely it would increase according to their institutional position and seniority (e.g., as chairman of a congressional committee or as governor of a major state).

It should also be noted that judicious recruitment of cabinet officers from the ranks of incumbent federal legislators might also indirectly facilitate positive congressional action on a president's agenda. That is, the recruitment of certain committee or subcommittee chairmen or even of congressional party leaders (including the Speaker of the House) who might be less than enthusiastic proponents of policies high on a president's agenda could have the added effect of removing strategically positioned potential legislative obstacles while simultaneously opening up those positions to more active supporters. Concurrently, such appointments often have the advantage of bringing in individuals knowledgeable both in policy and in politics. If of differing political philosophical persuasions, such officials might broaden the administration's governing coalition, whether actually or merely symbolically. Although few presidents seem to have recognized the full direct and indirect utility of such an appointment strategy, this does seem to have been part of Roosevelt's personnel recruitment calculations in 1932–33. For example, the selection of Senator Claude Swanson not only brought the Senate's naval affairs specialist in to head the Navy Department but simultaneously "made room in the Senate for Roosevelt's old friend, to whom he now looked for support, former Governor Harry E. Byrd."[6] Similarly the selection of fiscal conservatives House Speaker John Garner as Vice President and of House Appropriations Committee member Lewis Douglas as Director of the Bureau of the Budget removed two conservative-oriented leading Democratic legislators, thereby both facilitating passage of Roosevelt's more liberal economic measures and while also reassuring fiscal conservatives that their views were well represented in the president's advisory circle.

During the past fifty years, Democratic presidents have sought political skills capital with more frequency than have Republican presidents. For example, in an unlikely pair, FDR and Carter made the greatest efforts to recruit individuals with reputations and skills in congressional affairs. FDR recruited Senate committee chairmen Cordell Hull and Claude Swanson in 1933. Later he brought in Henry Stimson and Jesse Jones—two highly respected federal executives known for their abilities to work with Congress. Carter initially recruited the chairman of the House Budget Committee (Brock Adams to Transportation) and later appointed Senator Edmund Muskie as a replacement Secretary of State. Additionally, Carter appointed one incumbent Congressman (Bob Bergland—Agriculture), one Governor (Cecil Andrus of Idaho to Interior), and later two big city mayors (Moon Landrieu of New Orleans to HUD and Neil Goldschmidt of Portland to Transportation).

Although other Democratic presidents sought to recruit politically skilled individuals, they followed less prestigious patterns. Truman generally settled for former Congressmen who had gone on to federal judgeships, such as Lewis Schwellenback (Labor), Fred Vinson (Treasury), James Byrnes (State) or James McGranary (Attorney General). He supplemented these with the acquired skills of a number of experienced federal administrators. JFK mixed one relatively junior Representative (Stewart Udall—Arizona), with three governors (incumbent Abraham Ribicoff—Connecticut and former governors Luther Hodges—North Carolina and Orville Freeman—Minnesota), and a big city mayor (Anthony Celebrezze—Cleveland). While these appointees were quite successful in terms of preventive political assistance, they were less able to move Kennedy's policies through Congress to enactment—a record reflecting not only their extra-Washington experience as well as the generally conservative and uncooperative mood of Congress at that time. Surprisingly, Lyndon Johnson paid scant attention to political skills amongst his cabinet personnel, retaining only two of Kennedy's original political appointees but recruiting none himself. Perhaps, given Johnson's own considerable legislative skills, he felt little need for additional political skills among cabinet members.

In contrast, Republican presidents have made fewer and weaker efforts to use cabinet appointments to increase their political skills capital. Throughout his eight years in office, Eisenhower only had the services of an interim-appointed, former Senator (Fred Seaton at Interior) and two Governors (Christian Herter—Massachusetts and Douglas McKay—Oregon). Nixon also tended to tap governors as his initial appointees (John Volpe—Massachusetts, George Romney—Michigan, and Walter Hickel—Alaska), as well as selecting Congressman Melvin Laird. Later, Nixon brought in former Texas Governor Connally, retiring junior Senator Willian Saxbe, and incumbent Congressman Rogers Morton. Although the total number of politicians in the Nixon administration was substantial, the record of their performance was less so. Both Saxbe and Morton were brought in to attempt political damage control. Governors Romney and Hickel apparently used their political skills to work for policies not high on the president's agenda and thus came to be regarded by the President as political liabilities rather than assets. Thus, the net political advantage of these appointees was considerably less than it might appear. Finally, Presidents Ford and Reagan each recruited few legislators. Ford tapped his former House colleague Donald Rumsfeld, while Reagan recruited incumbent Senator Richard Schweiker and former Governor Richard Thornburgh.

A possible explanation for the infrequency with which Republican presidents appoint members of Congress or Governors into their cabinets lie in the relatively small recruitment pool of such individuals. For the last 50 years the Republicans have been the minority party. As such, Republican presidents have fewer elected partisans to consider for possible executive appointment. For example, in 1966 only 17 states had Republican governors and in 1981 only 21 states did. Thus when Presidents Nixon and Reagan came to office there were relatively few Republican governors to select from and even fewer who had served long enough to be available for federal office. Similarly, the Republicans have held majorities in either Houses of Congress for only eight of the past 55 years. Thus there are fewer Republican congressmen for Republican Presidents to recruit and few of those will have had the opportunity to have exercised leadership as committee chairmen. Furthermore since Republican capture of both Houses in 1952 and of the Senate in 1980 coincided with the election of new Republican Presidents, many Republican congressmen in those years were essentially unavailable for cabinet office since they were only just assuming the powers and prerogative of seniority and majority control. Paradoxically, because Republican presidents have so frequently faced Democratic controlled Congresses, their need for extra political capital of the political skills variety is likely to be more acute than that of Democratic presidents.

An alternative source of political skills has historically resided in the political parties. Indeed, party functionaries, even if they have never held elective office, are likely to be adept political operants. However, their practice in coalition-building has often been gained through activity in nomination and campaign politics rather than in governance. Virtually every president has recruited such political operants into the cabinet, with the campaign director, the party chairman, or the party campaign finance chairman being most frequently rewarded with cabinet office.

Historically, the Postmaster-generalship went to one of these party officials (e.g., James Farley-FDR, Robert Hannegan-HST, Arthur Summerfield-Eisenhower, and Lawrence O'Brien-LBJ), but with the conversion of the Post Office Department to a government corporation, this cabinet appointment is no longer available. Alternatively, modern presidents have sometimes appointed party leaders/campaign supporters to inner cabinet posts (e.g., Robert Lovett to Defense-HST, Robert Kennedy-JFK and Herbert Brownell-Eisenhower as Attorneys-General). One must, however, note that in a period of declining political parties and of increasingly individualized campaigning, the political value of political skills gained in party positions are likely to be particularly attuned to the mobilization of candidate-centered electoral coalitions and not as readily transferable to the task of assembling and maintaining governing coalitions.

Although the decrease and diminution of political skills capital in the cabinet has been erratic and subtle, the significance of this change is nonetheless apparent. A growing chorus of observers and critics have pointed to the difficulty presidents have in forming "a government"[7] or in converting their electoral coalition into a governing one.[8] While some attribute this problem to split partisan control of the institutions of Congress and of the presidency (e.g., during periods in the Truman, Eisenhower, Nixon, Ford and Reagan presidencies), it is equally true that Kennedy and Carter fared no better with solid Democratic party control of both Congress and the White House. Indeed, as the cases of Presidents Nixon and Carter demonstrate, even if politically skilled cabinet members are recruited, they may use those skills for other purposes than support of their president and his programs or else they may find themselves unconsulted and underutilized. Conversely, Presidents Truman and Eisenhower seemed to have dealt effectively with opposition controlled Congresses. Thus, awareness of a less politically efficacious presidency with regard to Congress seems to coincide with the noted decline in the political skills capital available in the cabinet. While not the sole cause of this worsening performance, changes in cabinet recruitment patterns certainly seem to be a contributory factor.

Aside from the frequency and the potency of political skills in the cabinet, anecdotal evidence indicates that the advantageous use of such resources has declined. For example, recent presidents seem highly prone to firing or losing skilled politicians-turned-cabinet-members. Conversely, one encounters frequent references to bad congressional relations as a reason for the turnover of cabinet personnel.

The development of the administrative presidency is another factor contributing to the apparent difficulties modern presidents seem to encounter in effectively capitalizing on politically skilled cabinet appointments. As postwar presidents have sought to realize bureaucratic control and assert political direction implied by the idea of an administrative presidency, they have exhibited increasing difficulty in tolerating, much less collaborating with, potent political allies within their "official family." As Colin Campbell has astutely observed, all modern presidents except Eisenhower and to some extent Ford and Truman, have regarded cabinet secretaries as "barons to be dealt with one-on-one or to be forced into passivity" rather than as allies or colleagues.[9] Thus, it would seem that in the quest for greater administrative control, presidents have diminished their ability to accumulate political capital through cabinet appointments.

The decline of political skill capital in the cabinet has, no doubt, been affected by the expansion of political advice and assistance available within the Executive Office of President (EOP). Since the establishment of a White House staff, it has been customary for presidents to move key campaign aides into staff positions. With the proliferation of agencies within the EOP as well as the growth of the White House staff, presidents have had many opportunities to retain and reward campaign assistants with staff jobs. Indeed, campaign chairmen were appointed to senior White House staff positions by Kennedy and Carter, while both Carter and Reagan appointed the national party chairman as EOP Special Trade Representative.

Within the White House staff a special office for Congressional liaison was initiated by President Eisenhower and maintained and expanded by subsequent presidents. Thus it would appear that presidential staff agencies have become a locus of political skills capital rather than the cabinet. Such presidential staff resources are not, however, completely comparable substitutes for political allies in the cabinet. First, the skills of many such campaign assistants are geared to electoral politics rather than governance. Thus, the newer breed of political operants tends to be candidate-centered and politically dependent upon a specific president rather than its appointive alternative who were more politicaly independent and party-centered. Second, the White House Congressional Liaison Office, unlike cabinet politicians, seldom adds to a president's political capital; rather they assist him in utilizing already available resources when dealing with Congress. Indeed, the existence of such an office does not guarantee that it will function successfully. For example, President Carter's congressional assistants were notorious for their ineptitude and consequently for drawing-down the president's political capital.

Political Support

It is commonly held that "the chief significance" of the cabinet is that it "offers an opportunity for consolidating political strength through a coalition of leaders whose adherence brings the strength of their political following to the administration."[10] During the last 50 years, however, there has been a decreasing tendency to recruit actual political leaders who can command either partisan or constituency support. The decrease of partisan leaders is, in part, related to the declining incidence of former elected officials with their attendant political skills. But it is also related to the increasing tendency (and indeed necessity) of presidents to seek support both beyond their own party base and among special interest groups. Hence most modern presidents have deviated from the historic norm of partisan purity when appointing their cabinet.

Perhaps the most common strategy has been to appoint representatives of "opposition" party factions that have already begun to shift their allegiance. For example, FDR's appointments of Progressive Republicans, Henry Wallace and Harold Ickes, were meant to confirm both their personal and their constituency's support during the 1932 election campaign. Likewise Roosevelt's June 1940 appointment of former Republican Secretary of State Henry Stimson and former Republican vice presidential candidate Henry Knox were designed to attract bipartisan support both for an unprecedented third electoral bid and for the anticipated war effort. Similarly Eisenhower's appointments of Oveta Culp Hobby and Robert Anderson brought nominal Texas Democrats into his administration, while seeking to consolidate the electoral support of moderate Southern Democrats who had voted for Eisenhower in 1952 and 1956. Richard Nixon sought to appeal to the very same geographic constituency with his appointment of a Democrat and former Governor of Texas John Connally.

Again, a subtle shift in the potency of such partisan representative capital must be noted. Beginning with Eisenhower, the tendency has been to seek to appoint nominal members of the opposition party, rather than leaders within the opposition. Both Hobby and Anderson were active in Democrats for Eisenhower but this represented a candidate-centered group rather than an enduring partisan realignment. While Kennedy appointed registered Republicans, such as Douglas Dillon and Robert McNamara, these gentlemen were not party leaders or spokesmen, but rather symbolic representatives of the opposition party. Johnson's appointment of Republican foundation executive, John Gardner, was of a similar cast. Ford appointed not only symbolic Democrats like William Usery and F. David Mathews, but the avowed independent, Edward Levi. Finally, Carter appointed veteran Republican administrator James Schlesinger to serve as his first Energy Secretary. Thus presidents have retained the appearance of bipartisan coalition-building through appointments but have seldom enjoyed the additional partisan support that would attend actual, as opposed to merely symbolic, coalition partners.

A related development indicative of an era of shifting partisan allegiances involves the recruitment of former members of the opposition party who have switched party identification shortly before being appointed or who do so soon after appointment. This phenomenom is especially noteworthy within Republican Administrations. For instance, Democrats-turned-Republicans include Secretaries Hobby and Anderson of the Eisenhower administration; and cabinet members Blount, Hodgson, and Connally in the Nixon administration. Of course President Reagan and his first UN Ambassador Jeanne Kirkpatrick are well-known ex-Democrats. With the exception of Progressive Republicans-turned-Democrats Wallace and Ickes of Roosevelt's presidency, none of the Republicans in Democratic administrations underwent such conversions.

Aside from partisan representatives, political support capital can also be accumulated through the appointment of interest group representatives. Indeed this would seem particularly appropriate among the nominees to head the constituency-oriented departments of Agriculture, Commerce, Labor, and Education. Indeed there is strong precedent for the recruitment of just such representatives at Agriculture and Labor, although interest group leaders can be placed in any cabinet position. Here again it would seem that presidents have had an increasing tendency to discount the potential value of such appointments by selecting symbolic representatives or special interest administrators.

The trend toward special interest administrators rather than leaders is, perhaps, most clearly seen at two of the historic clientele departments. For example, while each Secretary of Agriculture is expected to own a farm and figuratively "to have dirt under his fingernails," Henry Wallace (FDR) may have been the last actual agricultural leader to head the department. Since then, the secretaries have generally been state or national agricultural administrators (e.g. Claude Wickard-FDR, Ezra Taft Benson-

Eisenhower, Charles Brannan-Truman, and John Block-Reagan) or academic agricultural economists (e.g. Clifford Hardin-Nixon, Earl Butz-Ford). Occasionally a former congressman who had served on food or agriculture committees (e.g. Clinton Anderson-Harry S Truman, Robert Bergland-Carter) have been recruited to this post. While such appointees are usually acceptable to the farm constituency, it is clear that they function as the president's spokesman to farmers rather than as farm leader-as-member-of-the-administration. At least one recent Secretary of Agriculture was actively opposed by farmers upon his nomination (Earl Butz).

Somewhat similarly, the Secretaries of Labor display a rather paradoxical pattern, with union leaders often recruited by Republican Administrations while Democratic presidents tend toward naming labor lawyers and mediators. FDR started this line of non-labor leaders with the appointment of Frances Perkins. Truman followed with Lewis Schwellenbach, a former Senator who would stay clear of the then-current factional struggles within labor, and later Maurice Tobin, a former mayor who had good ties to labor. Kennedy first appointed labor lawyer Arthur Goldberg; then he (and later Johnson) turned to lawyer and labor negotiator Willard Wirtz. Carter tapped an academic labor economist who had served on a number of governmental advisory commissions concerning manpower issues (F. Ray Marshall). Thus, the Democrats, long identified as the party of the working man, have not appointed a single labor leader to head the Labor Department during the last fifty years.

In contrast, Republican presidents have named nearly as many union leaders as industrial management specialists to this post. For example, Eisenhower's first Labor Secretary was Martin Durkin, a Democrat and the President of the United Association of Plumbers. Similarly, Nixon recruited Peter Brennan, who was also a Democrat and the head of the Building and Construction Trade Council of Greater New York, while Ford selected International Association of Machinists activist, W. J. Usery. Since the tenure of all these recruits has been short and relatively stormy, one may question the ultimate utility of what is clearly a bold bid to attract unorthodox coalition partners. Alternatively, other Republican Labor Secretaries have been industrial relations experts and administrators, such as, James Mitchell, George Shultz, James Hodgson, Jon Dunlop, and Raymond Donovan. Thus, with the exception of gestures to demonstrate an "above politics as usual" style (as with Eisenhower's appointment of Durkin) or to woo electoral support in an upcoming election (Usery), the labor secretary has at best, been only a symbolic representative of his nominal constituency. As such, they could bring little additional political support capital to the presidents who appointed them. Conversely one might point to the succession of Labor Secretaries as evidence of the waning political clout of organized labor itself: a trend apparently reflected in the two most recent secretaries of Labor, William E. Brock, III and Anne McLaughlin, who demonstrate the tenuousness of labor's claim on a cabinet seat since neither evidenced any prior linkage to labor interests or issues.

Minority interests have also come to be represented in the contemporary cabinet, though these appointees have been scarce, tend to cluster in issue-area departments, and to occupy outer-cabinet influence status. During the past half century, nine woman have been named to the cabinet, seven of these since 1975. Four of the nine presidents since FDR have not appointed even one woman to their cabinets, while the two most recent presidents (Carter and Reagan) have each named more than one. The incidence of female cabinet members is indicative of both the persistent under-representation of women in the highest councils of government as well as recognition of their growing political significance in modern American society.

Despite their symbolic importance, none of the appointees could be considered representatives of women in any politically organized sense. Rather, they were symbolic representatives of their gender constituency. As such, they added little in actual political suport capital to the administrations for which they were recruited. Indeed, most were appointed for a complex of reasons and attributes of which their gender was a contributory, rather than a decisive, factor.

For example, FDR had wanted a woman in his cabinet in recognition of their relatively recent enfranchisement. He also needed a competent labor administrator, but did not want a union leader. In Frances Perkins, he found the combination of characteristics that he sought. From a different perspective, Oveta Culp Hobby (HEW, 1953-55) and Patricia Harris (HUD, 1977-79; HHS, 1979-81) were recruited for the political positions they represented rather than for the gender group they symbolized.

Hobby had helped bring many Texas Democrats into Eisenhower's winning electoral coalition, while Harris was a respected civil rights activist, Black Democrat. President Reagan's midterm selection of Elizabeth Dole (Transportation, 1983–86) and Margaret Heckler (HHS, 1983–86) marked an attempt to bridge the "gender gap" as well as to enhance party unity and to cushion the impact of losses at the congressional elections in 1982.[11]

Finally, it must be noted that both the utility and influence of these women were limited by factors other than the political support capital which they represented. Virtually none had experience in electoral office and hence had little opportunity to acquire proficient political skills. Only Margaret Heckler had successfully run for elective office, while Patricia Harris has gained some experience in party politics. Although Perkins, Hobby, and Dole could claim some administrative capital via prior service as appointive public administrators, none had experience with the agency they were to head. Furthermore, none of the female cabinet members could make a strong claim to substantive expertise in their areas of responsibility. Thus, these individuals possessed few administrative, expertise, or political assets that might have enhanced their utility to or influence with the president. The relatively weak political influence of women secretaries is evident in the fact that they have rarely been positioned to become part of a president's inner circle, either by personal friendship or by departmental stature. Only Frances Perkins (FDR) could be considered a presidential confidant or the head of department central to the president's early policy agenda. The others were not only relative strangers to their presidents, but were appointed to head departments that were low-to-antagonistic to the president's priorities or else were newly established and beset by the problems of bureaucratic birth. In other words, female cabinet appointees have seldom added substantially to a president's political capital and have rarely exercised significant influence within an administration.

Even fewer Blacks and only one Hispanic have been appointed to the modern cabinet. Lyndon Johnson was the first president to make such an appointment, naming Robert Weaver to head the then-new Department of Housing and Urban Development. With the exception of Nixon, subsequent presidents have each named one Black to their cabinets: William Coleman Jr. (1975–77), Patricia Harris (1977–81) and Samuel Pierce (1981–88). Each of these has been appointed to head an issue-area department responsible for programs of particular importance to minorities. Most frequently, this post has been the Housing and Urban Development Department (i.e., Weaver, Harris, and Pierce). In addition, Coleman, a respected transportation lawyer, headed the Transportation Department, while Patricia Harris served at HHS as well as at HUD. Reagan was the first President to name an Hispanic as a cabinet member when in 1988 he selected Lauro Cavazos as the Secretary of Education.

As interest group representatives, Harris and, especially, Coleman brought considerable political capital to their appointing presidents. Harris, in addition to being a symbolic representative of women, had been active in Democratic Party circles on civil rights issues. Whereas both Weaver and Harris might be considered well-educated, successful and prominent members of the Black community, neither had the constituency stature of William Coleman. Educated at Harvard Law, then a law clerk to Supreme Court Justice Felix Frankfurter, Coleman had co-authored the brief for the hallmark desegregation case of *Brown* v. *Board of Education* in 1954. In 1971, he was elected president of the NAACP Legal Defense and Education Fund. In recruiting Coleman (who was also a life-long Republican), President Ford gained considerable political support capital from an interest group that seldom identified with the modern Republican Party. Reaching out to Blacks (and women) through executive appointments was but one of the many efforts made by President Ford to help restore legitimacy and public support for the discredited government he had inherited in the wake of the Watergate scandal and President Nixon's resignation.

In contrast, the Reagan Administration gained little political capital from the appointment of Samuel Pierce in 1981. A New York labor lawyer who had served in the prior Republican administrations of Eisenhower and Nixon, Pierce was no minority leader and did little to improve relations between the Reagan presidency and Black Americans.

The Declining Political Character of Cabinet Recruitment

Despite its discontinuous character, the president's cabinet has persistently functioned as a mechanism and resource of presidential governance. Cabinet personnel have been treated herein as bearers of political capital that may add to a president's capacity to govern. Although the discussion has focused on capital of the political skills and political support variants, even this limited focus is suggestive of broad aspects of the evolution and problems of the modern presidency.

The scarcity of experienced politicians as well as of interest group leaders illustrates one way in which the quest for managerial control by the Chief Executive has hindered the presidency as a political institution. Indeed, the evidence suggests that the cabinet has atrophied as a political institution whose members are skilled political operants and/or potent political allies. Rather, the political qualities of cabinet personnel have become virtually residual: constituency representatives are merely symbolic (not actual) group leaders, while politicians who have lost or are losing their political base are more frequently recruited than those who can command independent power bases. While this tendency deprives presidents of certain political assets, it nonetheless has the virtue of producing cabinet secretaries who are likely to be dependent, and, therefore, relatively controlled, by presidents. Since this is in contrast to the historic independence of self-sufficient politicians who have served in earlier cabinets, the trend toward technocrats might be viewed as a move toward more manageable bureaucracy.

Since the 1937 Brownlow Committee's declaration of the president as the managerial head of the executive branch, presidents have sought to realize and exercise control over the so-called "fourth branch of government"—the bureaucracy. Theoretically, cabinet officers were to be a president's chief field officers in exercising this control. As administrative control became an increasingly important presidential goal, presidents have sought greater managerial resources to employ towards its achievement. Hence cabinet recruitment in the post-war period has come to emphasize the accumulation of administrative capital. Concomitantly, it has de-emphasized those political assets which might incur bargaining costs if a president were to secure political alliances with other elective, factional, or interest group leaders.

A second modern development has cast the president as the chief policy designer—a role that requires expertise in such a variety of fields that it is beyond the capacity of a single individual. In many ways, the growth of the Executive Office of the President can be explained as the cumulative effect of repeated efforts to provide presidents with the expert resources needed to function as chief policy designer. The Council of Economic Advisers, the National Security Council staff, and the Office of Science and Technology Policy are each prominent examples of new institutional assets available to presidents requiring diverse expertise capital. Similarly, the search for expertise capital has carried into cabinet recruitment as presidents have sought technocrats rather than political allies. Indeed, the search for technocrats such as labor, industrial, and agricultural economists, may have been pursued at the cost of seeking political allies, particularly with major political interest groups.

In a related development, the apparent substitution of expertise capital for political skills capital may have indirectly had an additional erosive effect on the political capabilities of an administration. Particularly during the last 20 years, policy expertise has tended to be recruited from the ranks of professional policy analysts, particularly those in think tanks and research institutions. The change from an "establishment" based set of policy experts to alternative sets of professional policy analysts has been most commented upon in the realm of foreign and national security affairs, where the shift was seen as symptomatic (if not catalytic) of the breakdown that occurred in the 1970s in the positive, bipartisan consensus of foreign policy.[12] Yet domestic issue networks have also become evident, each with its sets of competing policy professionals.

With so many intellectual and professional analysts now involved, policy making acquired something of the atmosphere and norms of academic politics. Whereas the old "establishment" prided itself on anonymity (or at least avoided notoriety), the new professionals sought public recognition and reputation. Whereas the "old" expertise had performed what it regarded as informed service in the public interest, the "new" expertise prided itself on espousing analytical, partisan and ideological distinctions to advance its own careers and causes. In other words, the prime strategy of academic politics — drawing distinctions and emphasizing differences while simultaneously intellectualizing and personalizing disagreement — was transferred into the political arena with the recruitment of professional policy experts into administrative and decisionmaking counsels. As a consequence, the norm of the new policy experts — to develop and emphasize differences — was largely incompatible with the old political skills of compromise, accommodation and consensus-building. Thus the shift in the kinds of resources recruited into the presidential cabinets would seem to be reflective not only of waning political capabilities and capacities but the more fundamental displacement of operating norms supportive of productive politics and effective governance.

In sum, these two related trends are illustrative of and contributory to one of the central paradoxes of the modern American presidency. Against enormous structural and customary impediments, presidents have enhanced their managerial control of the executive branch and with it, significant influence over the direction of public policy. This managerial gain has apparently been realized at the cost of the capability to govern effectively. As one recent commentator noted, presidents form "administrations" rather than "governments."[13] But in a political system of separate institutions sharing power, it is only "governments" that have both the capacity and legitimacy to govern.

CHAPTER THIRTEEN

The President and the Permanent Government — "Hitting the Ground Standing"

BERT A. ROCKMAN
PROFESSOR OF POLITICAL SCIENCE
UNIVERSITY OF PITTSBURGH

Presidents and the Career Executive — A Disengaged Relationship

American presidents are almost never directly engaged with their senior career officials. The relationship of presidents to the permanent government is a remote one at best. Except for an occasional ceremony, for example, civil servants do not keep company with American presidents, nor are they even greatly involved directly with their cabinet secretaries. Certainly senior civil servants are not a presence in the fashion that is the case in most European countries or Japan. From time to time, of course, exceptionally agile career officials from the foreign service or the civil service make their way into high and visibly infuential posts. Frank Carlucci, who has served in important posts across four presidential administrations — Republican and Democrat — is an example of this rare breed of highly influential and visible career official. In the American system, unlike others however, the price of engagement is usually the loss of one's civil service tenure.

To presidents, the permanent government is something that is out there. It is a distant and remote *them* — almost an alien creature. The White House tends to be suspicious of the *them* out there. Consequently, the White House usually seeks to reduce the role of senior career officials in policy making on the premise that there already is a surplus of advice and advisers. Who needs more? As I shall note a bit later, this skeptical perspective lends itself toward limiting the civil servant's role to a strictly managerial one.

Presidents also want to have as much flexibility as possible to manage programs they believe are central to their interests in ways that they also believe are compatible with their interests.[1] Presidents, however, are rarely experienced in management. They are most likely to act as chiefs, not chief executives.[2] Manipulating symbols, not managing details, is the forte of most aspirants to, and successful incumbents of, the White House. To the extent that presidents are likely to be involved in managing, it is organizing their entourage in the White House with which they will be most concerned. Any president's sense of "the government" inevitably is a constricted one. It consists largely of that small handful of people with whom the President has direct relations.

From Distance to Distaste

Despite the seeming distance of the rest of government, at some point in the 1970s bureaucratic distance somehow became equated with bureaucratic resistance. Because the Federal government grew so rapidly in terms of programs and especially expenditures from the mid 1960s to the latter part of the 1970s,[3] the federal bureaucracy became a favorite subject for abusive political rhetoric — more favored as a target by the Republican Right than the Democratic Left, to be sure, but not immunized from criticism by either wing. As a general attack on the growth and perceived intrusiveness of the Federal government, the Republican Right frequently portrayed the bureaucracy as symptomatic of a malignant growth of government that sapped initiative and productivity, eroding both the private sector and the discipline provided by markets. Bureaucracies and career bureaucrats, consequently, were viewed as either self-interested in their programs and their budgetary expansion or ideologically committed to them.[4]

At the same time, the Democratic Left increasingly grew critical of the career bureaucracy, suspecting it of being more interested in its perks than its programs and more apt to respond routinely than innovatively. From both Left and Right, then, the bureaucracy was viewed as a deadweight on change, in desperate need of being transformed. Because bureaucracies are stable elements resistant to short term change, a path of lesser resistance, that of shifting responsibility increasingly to politically appointed decision makers came to be emphasized with increasing vigor. Whether these accusations about the career bureaucracy are true is of lesser significance than the fact that the career bureaucracy had become a source of contention at a time when political positions had themselves become increasingly contentious.

In such a climate, this anti-bureaucratic sentiment has been reflected by presidents, especially the most recent presidencies of Reagan and Carter. Each demeaned the established government in rhetoric, and each made appointments of some non-career personnel who were notably antipathetic to the career bureaucracy. It was earlier, however, during the Nixon administration that resentment against the career bureaucracy became evident. This resentment stemmed from Nixon's view of the career bureaucracy as politically biased against the policies of his administration.[5]

Pluralism Among Career Executives

The career bureaucracy is not a monolith. While it is natural for career officials to be committed to the activities they are engaged in, government itself is almost never traveling along a clear trajectory. Its career officials, as a collective entity, tend to be committed to the various multiple and sometimes contradictory objectives that the government, overall, is committed to.[6] For the most part, officials in spending agencies generally prefer more to less; those at the Office of Management and Budget (OMB), on the other hand, prefer less to more.

Martin Anderson, in his memoirs of the Reagan Presidency, notes, in this regard, that the drastic budget cuts proposed early in the Reagan administration relied extensively upon a strategy of coopting OMB early into the process of budget analysis. This meant relying heavily on the career professionals at OMB. Anderson asserts that, "In effect, that first year we acted as if the OMB professionals were part of the White House staff and treated them that way."[7]

Note that bureaucrats in the spending agencies are treated rather differently. Shortly before the passage quoted above, for example, Anderson notes that in prior administrations "it did not take long . . . for the cabinet officers to be seduced by the professional bureaucrats and the natural constituencies of their departments."[8] In other words, bureaucrats' interests and the logic of their roles are frequently conflictual and competitive. The im-

plication is that a wise president will invest substantially in officials
whose roles favorably dispose them to support of presidential
goals — whatever these may be.

Interdependence Between the Chief Executive and the Federal Executive

Certainly, who sits in the oval office — what that president's priorities are and how clearly they are articulated, what his staff
and appointments are like, what his style of policy management
is, and even (perhaps most important) what his rhetoric is
about — affects the senior civil service. Although many senior civil
servants, at any point in time, are engaged in matters that are
far from the president's priorities, they are hardly immune from
either the style or goals of the political leadership.

When the style is one of command and the goals are radical
departures from the status quo, relations between senior careerists
and the presidential administration will be delicate at best, and
hostile at worst.

Equally, however, presidents are affected by the willingness
and ability of career executives to adapt to new directions, their
capability for derailing or seeing through presidential initiatives,
and their motivation (or lack thereof) for helping their appointed
superordinates and keeping them out of trouble. This is indeed
a strange relationship, if relationship is even the right word.
Though presidents and senior civil servants rarely see one another, each is dependent upon the other. Presidents are reluctant to admit that, of course, in large part because they are incapable of seeing what experienced civil servants can do *for* them
rather than *to* them.

Factors Governing the Political-Administration Nexus

Regardless of the exact nature of the relationship between any
given president and the career bureaucracy, the relationship is
governed perhaps most powerfully by broader factors. One of
these factors is the theory that legitimates the career bureaucracy.
The largely analytic distinction between administration and politics is, among the industrial democracies, most firmly planted
in the United States, whatever the actual state of affairs. This
distinction implies that senior career officials are to be public
managers, possessing limited discretion. What they decidedly
are not to be are molders of policy. In the Federal Republic of

Germany, by contrast, senior bureaucrats are not only expected to be molders of policy, they are legally required to be involved. In general, in other industrialized democracies, the politics-management distinction is less evidently in vogue as an operating theory of the political leadership.

A second factor has to do with the institutional nature of the American political system and its division of political authority. This division, operationally, means that there are multiple and sometimes conflicting authorities (and thus ambiguous directions). When there is conflict, bureaucrats will be suspect in someone's eyes because two conflicting directions cannot be simultaneously obeyed. The system of divided authority, however, also means that senior career officials in the U.S. often can have better access *outward* toward the Congress than *upward* through their departments.[9] The distance between senior career officials and department secretaries is very large; between senior career officials and the White House, it is cavernous.

A third factor has to do with rhetorical context. Big government is a negative symbol in the United States. Rhetorically, therefore, the career bureaucracy is an inviting target for ridicule or worse.

Beyond these broader factors are also ones that reflect the existing atmosphere — salary compression, limited opportunities for promotion, and losses of influence. These conditions have soured senior career officials to some degree. Many of them have been in senior positions only during a period in which the bureaucracy and bureaucrats have been subject to conditions of strong budgetary constraint, limited discretion, and low morale. Whether there is a crisis of the senior civil service or not cannot easily be answered, but is a problem that the next president will need to address if, in the longer term, the proficiency and quality of the public service are to be preserved or enhanced. The difficulty, though, is that, for reasons to be discussed below, presidents have no obvious short-term incentives to try to remedy the underlying malaise of the senior civil service.

Presidential Interests and Civil Service Interests — A Mismatch of Incentives

Presidents and senior civil servants begin their distant relationship with very different incentives. For presidents, their aim is to make change or at least to make it appear as though they are making change. Campaign slogans are filled with the language of change, particularly, but not exclusively, in the candidacies of the opposition party.

Civil servants, on the other hand, have invested in the past and have little incentive to change, which is not exactly the same thing as saying that they will not change. Naturally, then, these two distant participants in the executive branch — the President and the senior career bureaucrats — have a certain mismatch of incentives. This natural awkwardness has been fueled especially in recent years by the anti-government, anti-Washington rhetoric of the past decade and a half. Many civil servants have tended to see presidents, their White House entourages, and some of their appointments in the departments as inexperienced and unwilling to listen to advice regarding alternative pathways to their objectives. For their part, presidents believe the career bureaucracy is obdurately opposed to new directions.

Both perspectives — that of the president and that held by the career officials — have some truth attached to them. Presidents have a short time to make their mark; bureaucrats have a longer perspective. Presidents trust *their* people — those who form their entourage. To the extent, however, that career bureaucrats become identified with a given administration's policies or personalities, they will lose their ability to be viewed as effective servants of any other administration's policies. From the bureaucrat's perspective, the problem is summed up in the picturesque analogy drawn by a senior career official in the Interior Department:

> If I'm a politician and you're a bureaucrat, I'm gonna stand over there and I'm gonna wave at you and I'm gonna say, 'come on over here in the burro pen,' and I'm gonna get you as far in that burro pit as I can get you. But you better not get there. If you do, you're gonna be in trouble. . . . The more I think about that, that is a tremendous philosophical statement . . . because I know that the administration is gonna try to pull you to their way of thinking as far as they can, and the next administration when there's a turnover is gonna do it the other way. I think it's our job to keep the objective . . . without getting into the burro pit.[10]

The fundamental problem for presidential management is to find an acceptable balance between what it is that a president needs to know and what it is that he wants to do.[11] When presidents hold intense and passionate convictions, they may be less likely to tolerate "wimpish" bureaucrats who fail to share their own, or perhaps even any, convictions.[12] If leaders know what they want to do, it also may be that they think they have correspondingly less need to know about alternatives or feasibilities. As a species, politicians are inclined to do, not to doubt.

In the long run, of course, if government is to achieve intelligent direction, the prudence and conservatism of civil servants and the more radical instinct of politicians are complementary. But this desirable long term equilibrium is not likely to be seen in the short term, and it should be remembered that presidents generally have a strong short-run interest in pushing their own objectives. Equally, career executives tend to have an interest in the protection of their own projects and programs. When these are threatened, there are potential allies to be summoned. As noted already, of course, any president's policy agenda will displease some civil servants more than it will displease others. Defense department, law enforcement, and OMB bureaucrats generally have fared better during the Reagan years than have other sectors of the bureaucracy. Technical or management specialists, arguably, may be faring better than program generalists. This probably is inevitable.

The matter of mismatched incentives, however, remains as a general problem. One way of dealing with that, of course, is for a president to encourage turnover in the senior civil service by making the job less attractive — in other words, continuing present tendencies. Evidence has surfaced in Great Britain of vastly increased turnover in the civil service during the nine years of Margaret Thatcher's prime ministership.[13] Although interpreting turnover rates is more ambiguous in the United States, there is strong evidence of a transformation in the ideology of American senior career officials over the course of a decade and a half in the direction of greater receptivity to the agendas of Republican presidents.[14]

In the long run, however, the effects of accelerated turnover and diminished attractiveness of career positions are bound to be negative. A less attractive career will likely reduce the yield of highly qualified candidates, and those most likely to leave are apt to be among the most talented. That, in short, is the omnipresent danger in a strategy of devaluing the career service.

Ironically, it may be that both Mrs. Thatcher in Britain and

Mr. Reagan in America have sought not to politicize the civil service but to depoliticize it by sharpening the distinction between politics and administration. In this formulation, politicians make policy, and civil servants are supposed to manage it efficiently.[15] But, at least within the United States, less and less room is available for managerial judgment as increased control over the management of details is being centered within OMB. OMB's initiatives, however, often have been rejected by equally precise countermanding instructions from Congress. This growing tendency for micro-management has come to limit the ability of civil servants in the departments to make judgments. Hence, it also has increased the frustrations and reduced the attractiveness of the job.

Without a massive and unforeseeable institutional change in the relationship between senior career officials and presidents (resulting in more extensive career penetration of political decision-making bodies such as exists in Europe), senior career officials will be mostly out of sight and out of mind for presidents. The career service will be a distant *them*. The ability of senior career executives to have their experience felt in higher decision-making councils of government will depend upon the quality of presidential appointees in the departments and their relationships to the White House. High quality appointees can help steer the presidential agenda while mediating the perspectives of the political leadership to the civil servants and vice versa. But high quality, experienced, and judicious political executives are hard to find, sometimes difficult to appoint (because ideologues see them as 'sell-outs'), and extremely problematic to retain.

Finding Common Ground

In spite of the short term mismatch of career service incentives and presidential interest, the country needs to have the leadership that presidents can provide and the dedication and detailed knowledge that career officials can bring to government. The difficulty lies in synergizing these traits. Careerists have the knowledge to steer political leaders away from trouble if they are trusted to do so. To do that, civil servants cannot simply be managers in the most technical sense, but, instead, also must be sensitive to the politics of governing. For political leaders, however, one aspect of their leadership is generating motivation. Presidents,

of course, are more naturally attuned to motivating their political followers than the bureaucracy—and spurring one often runs
counter to stimulating the other. In this regard, if the machinery
of government is to function effectively, it is necessary for presidents to motivate career officials and to prevent a longer term
degradation of the public service. The actual operations will be
in the hands of appointed intermediaries but that, as has been
noted, requires careful selection of the appointees.

From the newly-elected president's perspective, it is important to realize that the role of the civil service and the machinery
of government (other than the arrangement of personalities on
the White House staff and in some of the cabinet departments)
is on the farthest back of all the back burners. Such issues have
no direct popular political impact. Party constituencies have an
interest largely in patronage or furthering ideological goals, and,
increasingly, the latter. Thus, of all the things a president-elect
is likely to consider during the period of transition, this is clearly
among the very least unless, of course, it is seen as intrinsically
important to the accomplishment of the presidential agenda.

There is good reason to believe that these issues were more
central to the Reagan team before entering the White House
than to just about any other presidency for several reasons. The
first is that the Reagan team wanted to disconnect sharply from
past policies in certain areas. Secondly, to do this, the Reagan
team needed to find a set of appointees who were firmly committed to this disconnection. Thirdly, the Reagan team needed
to placate, as the Carter team before it had, certain voluble party
constituencies of a highly anti-establishment bent. Appointing
individuals who represented these constituencies to positions
within the bureaucracy was perceived as a necessary and perhaps also desirable strategy. Fourth, the Reagan team, for either
budgetary or symbolic political reasons (or both), wanted to cut
the size of the administrative corps, thus, instituting fairly significant reductions-in-force (RIFs). Fifth, in areas of special interest to the politics and policies of the Reagan Presidency, it
was important to have in place senior career officials who could
accommodate well to the policy changes that a Reagan Presidency would push. Consequently, the Reagan team paid unusual
attention to the bureaucracy, although not in a form that senior
bureaucrats necessarily found desirable. By virtue of their efforts
(and undoubtedly other powerful factors in the environment),

the Reagan Administration ultimately found itself working with a senior bureaucracy less instinctively hostile to its general policy objectives than, for example, had been the situation faced by Richard Nixon by the time he turned his attention to the bureaucracy late in his administration.

How presidents ultimately connect to the permanent government depends immensely on their own personal styles, their experiences, and their agendas. A so-called *conviction* politician such as Reagan need not act as though there is a permanent government at all. Those of a more consensus-building style (or with views still in the process of formulation) may be more inclined toward making use of a broad set of advisory channels. The advice of civil servants, in this context, almost never is direct. Rather, it is funneled through departmental agents who may bring these views (though never advertised as such) to the White House.

A President Bush or Dukakis would be temperamentally very different than President Reagan and neither would be engaged in a powerful effort to disconnect from the past. A President Bush would be a President with extensive experience in working with senior career officials—foreign service operatives in his diplomatic posts in China and the U.N., and senior career officials at the C.I.A. Moreover, he also had been a member of the House of Representatives with some feel for the relationships that bureaucrats and appointees must maintain with congressional committees and subcommittees. For his part, a President Dukakis clearly exhibits some of the tendencies that civil servants have; for example, an appreciation of the fact that details make a difference.

None of this, of course, need predict anything—and it well may not. But if it does, it probably means that the style of governance brought to the White House is likely to be more compatible with the perspectives of career officials than those that most recently have been on exhibition. It is most unlikely that 'revolutions' will emanate from a Bush or Dukakis White House. That prospect offers real opportunity for either a Bush or Dukakis Administration to seek to revitalize the career service. Unlike the Reagan administration's emphasis on "hitting the ground running," a Bush or Dukakis presidency, less filled with a sense of certainty about its agenda, is more likely to "hit the ground standing." That offers an early chance for stability and competent management.

Although there is common ground to be reached between the White House and the permanent government, the issue, being one of low salience, faces two obstacles. Thus, the memo writer who handles this aspect of the presidential transition will first face the problem of getting the president-elect's attention, and secondly, convincing him that the problem of the career service should be responded to. Such a memo-writer will no doubt need a deft hand, but a rough draft of that memo might have features in common with the one below.

A Memorandum to the President-Elect

TO: The President-Elect
FROM: Transition Team on the Career Bureaucracy
RE: Relations with the Permanent Government

In the next two months you will need to address a number of issues and problems, the effective handling of which will be crucial to the success of your presidency. Most of them will seem more immediately pressing than that which is the subject of this report—how to deal with the career government. Obviously, substantive policy areas of central importance no doubt will occupy much of your time—the budget, revenue options, the trade deficit, health care financing, U.S.-Soviet relations, the Middle East, etc. Formulating policy strategies and initiatives certainly are of foremost importance. Understandably, so also are strategies needed to deal with our political constituencies, the media, and, especially, with Congress.

Beyond these, however, is an issue of considerable, if not always self-evident, importance. That is, how can we strengthen our ability to manage competently our programs and policies and avert, to the extent possible, avoidable mistakes? These issues are not front end ones. They do not appear pressing for now. But a failure to effectively engage the apparatus of government will produce problems later. It is necessary, therefore, to develop an effective management strategy.

Critical to achieving such a strategy is the organization of workable relations between our political appointees and the senior career officials. This a delicate relationship because while we need good working relationships to get things done and to avert mistakes, we also want to make sure that our appointees stay on the administration's track and avoid being merely spokespersons for the existing department view. John Ehrlichman referred to this during the Nixon administration as the problem of "marrying the natives." As we will note later, it is important to get political executives who are in tune with our goals, yet experienced in public management. No administration has been blessed in recent times with an abundance of such people. It also will be important to develop regular small group structures, such as the Reagan Cabinet Councils, so that cabinet members and their subordinates regularly work together with cross-cutting issues.

There are no simple formulas for ensuring that those to whom we delegate, in fact, work on our behalf. There have been a variety of presidential models ranging from Eisenhower's so-called board of directors style to Johnson's frenetic entrepreneurial style. All have strengths and weaknesses and, in turn, are dependent upon presidential temperament and agenda. On the whole, however, it seems less and less possible for presidents to draw everything toward themselves. If appointees are not given authority, it will be increasingly difficult to get high quality personnel. At the same time, mechanisms for coordination and integration are vitally important. These must be run from the White House but in a manner that draws in rather than removes cabinet members and their deputies from the action.

Let us return to the problem of the career service, however. We need to have their experience working for us, not against us. Clearly, we will need self-discipline which also means a larger definition of responsiveness than John Ehrlichman's postulate, "When we say 'jump,' they should ask 'how high?'"

What steps might be taken?

Boost the Profession of Government

For reasons alluded to earlier, low morale within the career executive is a growing problem. Relatively low pay, a compressed pay scale, diminished status, scapegoating (Reagan in Moscow blames oppression in the Soviet Union on *their* bureaucracy!), and loss of influence are taking their toll, and there is real worry that the future quality of the career executive will be eroded.

Unfortunately, the present budget crisis and Gramm-Rudman provide little leeway to tackle the problem of material incentives. For the foreseeable future, reducing budgetary deficits will have to take priority over spending claims, especially ones as unpopular as pay increases for bureaucrats. Only the minimum can be done here, and that no doubt means a loss of some individuals on the General Schedule (GS) salary scale. Having recently accepted salary increases for the federal judiciary and federal executives (greatest among cabinet secretaries and subcabinet appointees), Congress will be reluctant to soon approve such increases again.[16] In view of these generalized constraints, we will not be able to do much except to offer our sympathy. (Alas, we cannot do this too publicly since the public has a notable shortage of sympathy for tenured executives who may be making $65,000 or $70,000.) The true comparison, of course, is with what these individuals could be making (though without the grant of tenure) in the private market. But that comparison will not carry much weight. Although some modest experiments regarding salary incentives can be implemented, these are unlikely to affect the system as a whole.

Given that we will not be able to alleviate problems of salary in the foreseeable future, are there other means of compensation for preventing erosion of civil service quality?

Fortunately, some simple and even symbolic steps may be possible. What are these?

Beginning with Kennedy (with an exception during the brief Ford Presidency), every president has spoken ill of the government and, by implication, of those who have chosen government as a profession. Distrust of the senior executive has been especially rampant during the latter stages of the Nixon administration and the earlier stages of the Reagan administration. Carter's anti-government rhetoric was more diffuse, but certainly not flattering to the civil service.

The anti-government tone of the 1970s and early 1980s may now be spent. Some of the social and economic regulatory excesses of the 1960s and 1970s have been harnessed and, if anything, there could be some support for reestablishing modest government intervention. In any event, there seems little short-term political profit to be gained by any further bureau-bashing and a great deal of cost.

Taking the opportunity to say some good things about the dedication and competence of civil servants and foreign service officers ought to be considered on appropriate occasions. This can be taken as a signal of trust and confidence in the career service — evidence of an outlook that they count and that their work is appreciated even when it cannot be matched by financial compensation. In general, when confidence is offered by political leadership, it is likely to motivate the career officials to do a better job in furthering the goals of the administration and in protecting against political vulnerabilities.

In its earlier stages the Reagan administration adopted a command style toward the career service which, in general, paralleled the last part of the Nixon Presidency. This clearly produced resentments, sometimes produced illegal behavior, and certainly generated strong reaction from political opponents and powerful restrictions when the opponents were able to gain the upper hand. During the early Nixon administration and throughout the Carter administration, the mode of treatment was one less obsessed with control and more characterized by indifference. One engages the bureaucracy but not in constructive ways; the other largely ignores the permanent government. Is it possible that a view of government as a partnership between our ideals and goals and the experience, savvy, and expertise of civil servants might actually work best? Under the circumstances of a moderate presidency, that could be an operative formula.

Leadership Counts, So Make Good Appointments

The point of interface in the administration between career officials mostly will be at the assistant secretary or deputy assistant secretary level in the departments. This means that whoever the assistant secretaries are, especially, will be important. Care should be taken to ensure that the assistant secretaries are not only in tune with administration objectives but that they also are temperamentally inclined to work with others around them and to be accessible to careerists. Prior experience in the federal government is no guarantee as to how individuals will work out, but it is likely to incline them to some understanding of the role that civil servants have to play. It is important for individuals to have management skills and interpersonal skills in addition to the particular political or policy expertise they bring to their jobs.

As a general matter, effective department secretaries bring with them a high quality team of subcabinet appointees. And effective subcabinet appointees learn to get along with their senior career officials, or to work the system until they do get career people they feel comfortable with. The implication is that department secretaries should be politically experienced and judicious of temperament. (An example of this in the Reagan administration had been the appointment of Bill Brock to replace Ray Donovan as Secretary of Labor.) Department secretaries need to be able to provide policy leadership yet also appreciate the importance of management.

Vetting through a White House personnel office, of course, will (and should) continue to be an important function. (The Reagan White House elevated personnel vetting to a high art form.) But the Reagan White House provided very narrow criteria for vetting. One of the Reagan appointees, however, conceptualized the selection criteria properly:

> I think fundamentally we do a whole lot more to further the Reagan administration agenda by being careful than not. There certainly is a way to be responsive in terms of strategic thinking and that's the way I think we are responsive as opposed to the kind of nickel and dime stuff that [happens], and I don't think it's our obligation to hire every . . . party activist that comes down the pike just because they're party activists. [I mean] I'm glad that they got in and fought the good fight but I'm not sure that that means that they become the next assistant secretary for whatever.[17]

Increase the Responsibility of the Civil Service

Ultimately, it certainly will not hurt to consider the possibility that over time some consideration should be given to increasing the number of assistant secretary and deputy assistant secretary posts that might go to career officials (who could then be moved out of those posts but not out of the career service with changes in presidential administrations). Over the long run, this well could strengthen the capabilities of the civil service without weakening the capabilities of an administration's political leadership.

The search for politically appointed executives from the outside is never an easy one. A further balancing between "in and outer" entrants into the executive and career service personnel could reduce some of the pressures of executive search, and might well prove to be acceptable across the parties. Any reduction in executive positions upon which the Senate must pass could be seen, however, by the Congress as a potential infringement on the rights of confirmation.

The idea here might be to set up something equivalent to a

Royal Commission to syndicate across the parties, the Congress, the Executive, and outside experts on public administration the responsibility for long term planning toward the future of the senior career service. With proper care, there is no way this can be a loser. Taking the initiative in combination with other measures should be viewed by the permanent government as a confidence-building step meant to strengthen its status. If it fails, then it is not the fault of the Bush/Dukakis administration but is attributable to the inability to develop a consensus around these issues system-wide.

Consult with Congress

As part of a larger strategy, advance consultation with Congress is advisable. That will not by itself guarantee success. Much depends upon the political character of the present Congress and the extent to which your election is viewed as decisive or, alternatively, as marked with ambiguity. Attempts to dominate Congress by breaking through subgovernments and so forth through exclusively administrative means, though, are likely to prove counterproductive over the course of your administration.

One of the reasons past administrations often have been suspicious about senior civil servants is that the White House perceives the careerists to be doing an "end-run" around administrative channels to the Congress. There is no doubt that there is an active relationship between senior career program managers and congressional staffers. Constitutionally, that is inevitable because, regardless of what we might like the situation to be, Congress shares authority over the bureaucracy with the Chief Executive. Confrontation between the White House and Congress will probably promote end-running behavior when interpretations of the law conflict. In this regard, it is probably likely to prove counterproductive to change statutory intent through administrative means and to set off confrontation with Congress. As part of a general strategy with Congress, it would be wise to avoid unnecessary friction because over the long haul there is no clear evidence that the executive can dominate the Congress simply through fiat.

We should avoid placing civil servants in the exceedingly difficult position of being caught between two implacable bosses (the White House and Congress), each requiring their allegiance but not getting that fully requited. The best way we can do that

is by avoiding precipitous and unilateral action toward Congress
and by working to get acceptable changes. Obviously, an election outcome in which the members of our party think that they
might owe us something is the best situation from which to
bargain.

In any event, the simple facts are that we cannot do better
in negotiation with Congress than our political situation permits.
Enticing as it is in the short run, however, we can make matters
substantially worse by seeking (as the Nixon and Reagan administrations sometimes did) to govern exclusively through executive means.

Let us turn briefly to a few final points.

Think Through What Your Goals Imply

The clearer the signals received by career officials, the more likely
they are to be able to respond to them or at least establish a frame
of reference to deal with issues of implementation. In this respect, President Reagan's goals were remarkably transparent. He
came to public life as an advocate. His philosophy was straightforward and in its structure very basic. This compensated a lot
for his own passive management style. One did not need to ask
often where he was going. That was a known.

But Mr. Reagan is a rare specimen of the presidential species
in that regard. No matter how long a presidential candidate has
been in the public eye, his image is not likely to be as sharp or
as predictable as Mr. Reagan's has been. Neither Lyndon Johnson
nor Richard Nixon, who certainly were around a long time, were
very predictable in their policy goals. The same probably is true
for a Bush/Dukakis presidency.

It is important to think through what your goals are. Inevitably
these will go through mutation. But it is important to think about
them in an integrated way; that is, what do they imply for each
other? This provides a way to sort out priorities and clarify objectives. Others in Washington (as well as in the country) will
be dependent upon the signals you send about your priorities.
(That was a key part of Mr. Reagan's success.) The price of not
thinking in this way can be seen in the Carter Presidency. The
result was an overloaded agenda and a great deal of confusion
about what the president actually wanted. If appointees are to
help the White House, they need to know what objectives they
are to be serving. And the President needs to know what the

implications of his objectives are if the goals are to be effectively and realistically monitored. In essence, effective delegation occurs when goals are clear and priorities are well developed. Signals that are mostly ambiguous, by default, grant large amounts of uncharted discretion to the administrative agencies. That will beget an inordinate amount of inter-agency squabbling.

Coordination Must Accompany Delegation

In most respects, the White House cannot run the government directly. But mechanisms for coordination and integration are essential. At the very least, there is a need for central clearance. Working groups of administration officials need to be regularized. In general, it would not be a bad idea to bring career officials into these meetings as well. The Reagan cabinet councils seemed to operate more effectively than similar mechanisms had in the past. They provided a basis for inter-agency policy operations. For them to run smoothly, however, policy guidance from the White House is essential.

Deploy Existing Levers When Necessary

The Civil Service Reform Act of 1978 gives a presidential administration more leverage over the deployment of personnel than previously had been the case. The Reagan administration used provisions of the Senior Executive Service component of the act to good effect in advancing its goals in the departments. Among its provisions, a 10% non-career component with the Senior Executive Service and a limit of 25% non-career within any given department is permitted. The Reagan administration, naturally enough, tended to top-load departments with political appointees in those situations where they wanted to achieve a great deal of change and were skeptical that such would be carried out by the career officials.

These provisions should be used prudently but must be used from time to time. Moreover, this degree of flexibility is common in continental systems. Top civil servants in West Germany, for example, who are identified with the previous government are retired from their posts *but not from the civil service*. Nevertheless, there is no *a priori* need to shuffle people around, nor is there even an inherent need to bump up against the limits of non-career deployment, at least if over the long term we wish to leave a legacy of a strengthened, more esteemed, and excellent civil service.

In Sum

The strategy offered here for dealing with the permanent government is softball rather than hardball. Playing softball has better long range prospects than playing hardball—an analogy that should be carefully considered in this context. So instead of hitting the gound running with much frenzy, there is a need to softly hit the ground standing and to consider how to engage the resources of the career bureaucracy to further administration goals. This is especially relevant to a moderate presidency that is less dogmatically anti-government than its predecessor.

There is no doubt that hitting the ground running provides some instant gratification and certainly comports well with cynical attitudes in Washington. The expectation that the bureaucracy belongs to a presidential administration is dangerous stuff because it will allow the erosion of experience, quality, and institutionalization in our government when those traits appear to be more necessary than ever. If it is simply a case of *ours* being replaced by *theirs* when administrations change, no President will be able to have confidence in the competence of the executive branch. There is no doubt that a strategy of hitting the ground running can produce instances of stretching or even violating existing laws or, at least, of making bad judgments. The career service is there to help place bounds on that. Its expertise and experience can prove invaluable, and because senior bureaucrats are sensitive to the ways of Washington, they can help assure that we also stay out of trouble. That seems to be part of any definition of good politics.

CHAPTER FOURTEEN

The President and the Bureaucracy: Enemies, Helpmates or Noncontenders?

ALANA NORTHROP

PROFESSOR OF POLITICAL SCIENCE

CALIFORNIA STATE UNIVERSITY, FULLERTON

The bureaucracy, the vast support staff in the executive branch which runs the wheels of government, has been under attack since the founding of the United States. But the attack has recently been gaining new steam. Public opinion polls over the last quarter century have charted an increase in the public's mistrust of the bureaucracy.[1] And starting with Nixon's presidency, the White House has purposely sought to end run the bureaucracy.[2] Carter and Reagan, in turn, even campaigned for the presidency by saying the problem with government was government.

Professional students of government have also contributed to this growing critique of the bureaucracy. A common argument in any textbook that deals with the bureaucracy is that bureaucracies seek to maintain themselves and that bureaucrats independently shape public policies. Both these characteristics of bureaucracies are said to work against the public will or the will expressed through elected officials. For example, in order to maintain or enhance their agencies, bureaucrats are said to seek larger budgets irrespective of broader social needs. Moreover, they can use their expertise to make a self interested case to Congress or the White House, neither of which have the parallel level of expertise to see through the self interested presentations.

The iron triangle argument, also found in government textbooks, complements the above bureaucratic characteristic argument because it too sets the bureaucracy in opposition to the president and his political appointees. Essentially, this theory suggests that interest groups and their relevant administrative agency and congressional committee form an alliance that is so strong that the president cannot dictate or direct change. In fact, if this theory is valid, it provides a rationale for presidents or their staffs executing sweeping end runs around the bureaucracy.

In summary, we have an old but growing view of the bureaucracy as uncontrollable and in opposition to the public will. Moreover, this view is supported by a preponderance of professional scholarship on American government. No wonder a major concern of a newly elected president is how to wrest the reins of government from the bureaucracy.

While the preceding view of the bureaucracy may be overwhelmingly popular, it would be a mistake for presidents to act on its premise. A solid case can be made for the bureaucracy actually being a helpmate to the White House instead of an enemy. Moreover, most day to day operations of government do not involve disputes, discussions, or debates over what elected or appointed officials want to accomplish and what bureaucrats will let them accomplish. This chapter argues that if presidents continue to maintain negative views of the bureaucracy, the ability of presidents to direct the bureaucracy and thus to govern will decline.

The Bureaucracy as Helpmate

Let us first consider the argument that bureaucracies seek to maintain themselves. This argument makes instinctive sense. Man has a need for self preservation and security. Not only is one's job and career clearly related to these needs, but also one forms an identity with his/her organization. Thus, we would expect career civil servants to seek to maintain their programs when they were threatened. Yet, civil servants do in fact help to end their own programs and even do so willingly. Take three recent cases under the Reagan Administration.[3]

Housing Secretary Samuel Pierce decided that housing vouchers for low income housing made more sense than federally subsidized new construction. Thus, in his 1982 budget request he asked for support for housing vouchers, not new construction. Congressional approval for the voucher program took two years. During those two years career civil servants designed the voucher program. Eventually they even ran it. Moreover, given the quick turnover of political executives in HUD, the careerists had to literally pick up the ball when the changing political leadership left a managerial void.[4] Thus, here is a case in which bureaucrats not only helped kill their own program but also directed the political executives in how to do so.

An example of bureaucrats actually ending federal involvement in an area versus supplanting one program for another comes from the Department of Transportation. Under Secretary Dole's leadership the careerists worked effectively with her staff to transfer authority of National and Dulles Airports from the federal government to a regional authority.[5]

Bureaucrats also helped end the Regional Health Planning Program. The demise of this program was an early agenda item of the Reagan administration and was strongly supported by some of the career staff who were affiliated with the program.[6] A career manager was even given the sole objective of managing the elimination of the program.

Bureaucrats can, consequently, end programs. In each of the above cases, the career civil servants did not oppose change.[7] Although bureaucracies may seek to maintain themselves, the maintenance is not necessarily static. Bureaucracies can and do willing change. One conclusion is that the survival of organizations may take an evolutionary form as does that of humans.

The results of a 1982 survey of members of the Federal Executive Institute Alumni Association, who were typically senior level administrators, complement the preceding three cases. The executives ranked organizational stability, budget stability, and organizational growth at the bottom of eleven organizational goals.[8] As the authors of that study concluded, "Being able to count on certain levels of funding and/or expanding one's organization are either not highly desired or, more likely, not realistic in today's era of tight budgets and less government."[9] Thus, we have evidence that bureaucrats, both in their actions and values, do not always seek to maintain their agencies or programs.

The professional values of civil servants may help to explain the bureaucracy's "helpmate" role. James Pfiffner found that "most career executives will willingly support a new administration and not resist its legitimate policy initiatives."[10] In essence, he found that serving your boss is a professional value held by many civil servants. So when policy directives change, the career bureaucrat continues to do his or her job even though it may have a new content or direction. This aspect of administrative professionalism may help explain why bureaucrats work dedicatedly to end or alter their own agencies' programs.[11]

The changing character of career bureaucrats may also help explain their adaptability. For example, Aberbach, Rockman, and Copeland have found today's careerists and political appointees moving to the right in ideological values.[12] Hence, as the president with a new agenda reflects changes in social values, as Reagan did, so too will the personnel in the bureaucracy. These complementary shifts can therefore result in shared agendas between the administration and the career bureaucrats, not inherent conflicts in their policy positions.

Finally, it should be noted that dissemblers do choose to leave government service.[13] Thus, another explanation for the adaptability of careerists is continuing self selection to serve. Of course, this explanation can only explain the helpmate nature of the bureaucracy to a small degree, since we do not see massive retirements or self terminations with each change of administration.

The Bureaucracy as Noncontender

Not only can bureaucrats be helpmates rather than enemies, they can also be in a noncontentious relationship with the president. For example, although the federal government performs thousands of tasks and services, the president and his cabinet can only concentrate on a few policies due to time and political limitations. In addition, the more energy and political know-how one exerts on even a smaller subset of policies, the more successful a president or cabinet secretary will be. Reagan's first term legislative successes demonstrate this phenomenon, as does Elizabeth Dole's successes as Transportation Secretary.[14] However, time and strategy limitations also mean that thousands of policies are not in question. In other words, the potential for bureaucratic opposition to the directives of political appointees is not present in a vast range of policy areas.

The noncontentious nature of the bureaucracy is also due to the fact that the need for change grows out of past administrative experiences. Changes in the housing program, the transfer of National and Dulles Airports, and the ending of the regional health planning program all had roots before Reagan took office. Moreover, public policy was generally ready for change and moving in that direction before Reagan took office. "Jimmy Carter earned Arthur M. Schlesinger Jr.'s rebuke that he was the most conservative Democratic president since Grover Cleveland, because in important respects he represented that shift."[15] Thus, so-called political control of the bureaucracy evolves from the bureaucracy. A new president or cabinet secretary may "supposedly" initiate dramatic changes in policy, but many times the groundwork is already there. In fact, some scholars argue that almost all dramatic changes in policy come from policy succession rather than new ideas.[16]

The Role of the President in Successful Administration

So far we have evidence that the commonly held view of bureaucrats in opposition to the administration is supported more in theory than in practice. This being the case, it may be possible for the president to capture the bureaucracy and therefore implement his campaign promises. What type of presidency will have a greater chance of successfully holding the reins of government?

To begin, a potentially effective president must have a clear ideological mindset. This is important on two counts. First, a clear ideological mindset allows the president and his staff and perhaps even the bureaucracy to interpret his election as a mandate to accomplish policy change. Second, a clear ideological mindset allows his political appointees to think as he does or would. In essence, a president is extremely dependent on his political appointees to carry out his policy agenda and to control the bureaucracy on a daily basis. A president does not have the time to set or review all the policy agendas of the cabinet departments, nor is he interested in doing so. Thus, he must depend on his appointees.

For example, Treasury Secretary Donald Regan recalls that he never met alone nor discussed with President Reagan aspects of economic, fiscal, or monetary policy.[17] Regan, like other political appointees, had to discover on his own what the president would like to have done. The task is obviously easier as well as more likely to be accomplished if there is a clear presidential ideological framework to begin with and if the political appointee shares that perspective. For instance, the three cases earlier cited about policy change in the Reagan administration fit the Reagan framework of deregulation and transferring federal authority and were viewed as such.[18]

To be effective, a president must also take care to appoint politically experienced men and women. If the bureaucracy is amenable to changes in directives, then the keys to the bureaucracy-president linkage are the political appointees. The political appointees must be politically experienced for several reasons. First, they receive little or no training prior to starting their new duties. One day one is a congressperson, and the next day one is Director of the Office of Management and Budget. Secondly, their tenure in position is short, and so critical time is lost if they have to not only learn their new job but also about policies, bureaucracy, Congress, etc. And thirdly, external politics are as important as the internal politics for effective administration. Thus, an effective private sector manager is often ill prepared for running a government agency or department.

Finally, a president and his appointees who seek to redirect public policy need a supportive bureaucracy. As noted earlier, there is empirical evidence to suggest that active support exists.

In conclusion, a president can be an effective administrator but much depends on him. He must have a clear ideological mind set; he must pursue only a few issues; and he must carefully select compatible political appointees with political experience. Finally, presidential effectiveness also rests on the recognition of the helpmate role of the bureaucracy.

Recognizing the Real Problem with Bureaucracy: Its Critics

We have argued that career bureaucrats are helpmates of the White House due to their professionalism, their values that parallel societal value changes, and because dissemblers leave government. But we have also noted the increasing criticisms of the bureaucracy, as well as the campaign denunciations and tendencies of the White House to circumvent the bureaucracy. These negative attitudes and actions do not bode well for the helpmate role of the bureaucracy.

First, the increasing attack on the bureaucracy over the last quarter century is paralleled by the decline in working conditions and morale.[19] In fact, only one quarter of a recent sample of senior level federal administrators advise "bright, competent young people" to seek careers in federal government (only 5% recommend careers in state or local government).[20] Paralleling this, "the percentage of students interested in public service has dropped over the last 20 years from 12% to 6%."[21] Second, organizational changes instituted by recent administrations to gain more firm control over the bureaucracy actually have had the opposite effect. For instance, an argument can be made that the capacity of the bureaucracy to change direction is impaired if the bureaucracy is decapitated with each change of administration. The net effect of such organizational changes is to reduce the sheer number of career bureaucrats in critical leadership positions, leaving managerial responsibilities to new, inexperienced political appointees.[22] Third, the view of the bureaucracy as standing in the president's way has led to White House machinations resulting in scandals on the level of Watergate and Iranscam.

What these three trends suggest is a situation that threatens the effectiveness of the bureaucracy, the presidency, and therefore government. To the extent that the career civil service is populated by less skilled professionals, there may not be as many bureaucrats who want to (1) do their jobs well, (2) work *with* the political appointees, and (3) pass on the organizational and political memories and know-how necessary for implementing the president's agenda. And to the extent that energies are directed to reorganizing the bureaucracy, then energies are diverted from the real task of governing. Finally, end runs risk scandals. The net result is the president's agenda is sacrificed. Thus the real problem with bureaucracy is its critics. And if the criticisms are not countered, the chance of an effective presidency will be greatly reduced.

Conclusion

Presidents need bureaucrats. But on most day to day issues, bureaucrats are noncontenders with presidents and their political appointees. And on many other issues, bureaucrats are helpmates, not enemies standing in the president's and his appointees' ways. In fact, many policy changes and ideas come from the bureaucracy. And it is the bureaucracy's expertise, experience and professionalism that is critical to the effective administration of new as well as old policies.

Yet, what is more critical to effective administration is the president. In this chapter we have tried to dispel the myth that the bureaucracy stands in the way of a president's success. We have actually turned that myth on its head. For much depends on the president. What he represents in terms of world view, the kind of men and women he appoints to office, and how he chooses to administer (e.g., proactive versus reactive, overload versus underload) are all critical to a president's success. And how very nice for him, for *he* can control these critical ingredients to his success.

PART FOUR

The National Security and Foreign Policy Processes

CHAPTER FIFTEEN

The National Security Council: Introductory Survey

R. GORDON HOXIE
PRESIDENT
CENTER FOR THE STUDY OF THE PRESIDENCY

A. Introduction

The Presidency was created by the Constitutional Framers largely because of the critical need for an executive, for a chief diplomat and commander in chief. At the same time, advice, consent and oversight roles were given the Congress. Led by Alexander Hamilton, an early need was recognized for covert operations and for an intelligence service. Hamilton readily acknowledged the Congressional role of oversight in intelligence operations but emphasized it should be limited by reasons of security to three members from the lower house, three members from the upper house, and none other.

Today there is a vast array of Congressional committees engaged in foreign affairs and an enormous amount of the time of the Secretary of State, The Secretary of Defense, and the Director of Central Intelligence is expended in testifying before these committees. A decade ago, this editor stated, ". . . instead of fifteen different congressional committees converging on foreign affairs, perhaps there should be a composite committee which would represent congressional interests with the President in these matters."[1] A joint committee made up of the chairs of those several committees might well consider this issue of consolidation of at least some of these committees. As a first step the Senate and the House select committees on intelligence might well be combined. In our time, as in Hamilton's some members of Congress find it difficult not to speak publicly on security sensitive issues.

In the nearly two centuries of the operation of the federal government under the Constitution there has been a constant struggle between the Congress and the President over the formulation and direction of national security policy. The most notable periods of Presidential dominance have been in times of total war: Lincoln in the Civil War and Franklin Roosevelt in World War II. The period since 1973, signalized by the War Powers Resolution of that year, has been characterized by Congressional dominance. In his own final State of the Union Address, January 12, 1977, President Ford urged Congress to "reexamine its constitutional role in international affairs. . . ." He asserted, "There can be only one commander in chief," and concluded, "In these times crises cannot be managed and wars cannot be waged by committee, nor can peace by pursued solely by parliamentary debate." Subsequent Presidents have underscored these views.

B.   Origins of the National Security Council

The National Security Council had its origins in the experience of World War II. President Franklin D. Roosevelt had largely run the war through the Joint Chiefs of Staff (JCS), which was an ad hoc and de facto body, without statutory basis; personal advisors, such as James F. Byrnes and Harry Hopkins; and in association with Winston Churchill. Congress was concerned that the ad hoc advisory system of the Roosevelt era should, with President Truman, be replaced by more formal structures. Thus, for example, in 1946, the Council of Economic Advisers was created by statute.

As early as 1944, both War Department Secretary, Henry L. Stimson, and Navy Secretary, James L. Forrestal, had perceived the need for a high-level national security policy planning body which should extend beyond the armed services. Largely through Stimson's efforts that year, the State-War-Navy Coordinating Committee (SWNCC) had been formed. Stimson, who had served from 1929–1933 as President Hoover's Secretary of State, appreciated, as did few other Americans in the early 1940s, the vital relationship between diplomatic, military, and political affairs.

The war-time experience had also shown the need for unification of the armed forces. However, the Navy Department resisted Congressional, Presidential, and War Department initiatives. Forrestal, in 1945, turned to his friend, Ferdinand Eberstadt, to counter these proposals. In what came to be called "Forrestal's revenge," Eberstadt proposed the creation of the National Security Council; also a Central Intelligence Agency (CIA).

In the ensuing two years, the NSC was the least contentious portion of the proposed national security legislation. Only President Truman, who viewed with suspicion any possible limitation on Presidential prerogatives, viewed the NSC proposal with some reserve. Reluctantly, the Navy came to accept an independent Department of the Air Force, while successfully resisting the military departments giving up autonomy to a National Military Establishment (Department of Defense). In November 1946, the Republicans had gained control of the Congress. As enacted by the 80th Congress and signed into law on July 26, 1947, the National Security Act included the creation of the NSC, "to advise the President with respect to the integration of domestic, foreign, and military policies, relating to the national security. . . ." Although "domestic" policies were recognized as vital to national security, the only executive department heads designated as members were State, Defense, Army, Navy, and Air Force. The President could, however, "from time to time" name other executive department heads to sit on the NSC.

While the National Security Act did create the CIA, the Director of Central Intelligence (DCI) was not named as a statutory NSC member. The CIA, which was an outgrowth of the wartime Office of Strategic Services and the National Intelligence Authority that had succeeded it at the war's end, was to serve in an advisory capacity to the NSC.

C.   The Truman Years, 1947–1953

Since the NSC is an advisory body, its organization and use has undergone change, according to the concepts of each President. Although President Truman chaired the first session, he viewed the NSC with continuing reserve. He believed only the President made policy, and he looked at any creation of the 80th Congress with especial suspicion, as seeking to circumvent his authority. Reflecting his opinion, he named the Secretary of State to chair subsequent NSC sessions. St. Louis insurance executive, Rear Admiral Sidney W. Souers, ably served as the first Executive Secretary of the NSC, 1947–50, followed by James S. Lay, Jr., from 1950–53.

The first review of NSC operations came in January 1949 from the Hoover Commission (Commission on Organization of the Executive Branch of Government). The Commission found the NSC lacking in developing comprehensive national strategy plans. The Commission was concerned with the intense rivalries among the armed services and the lack of authority by the Secretary of Defense. It recommended dropping the Army, Navy and Air Force service secretaries from membership on the NSC. Its recommendations were reflected in the August 1949 Amendment which added the Vice President, dropped these service secretaries, making the Secretary of Defense the principal spokesman of the armed services, and recognizing the JCS as "the principal military advisors to the President." On this basis, with the advent of the Korean War, the JCS began attending NSC meetings.

Further, with the outbreak of the war, the NSC met more frequently and Truman began presiding on a regular basis. He did so in 62 of the 71 meetings between June 1950 and January 1953. Nonetheless, the NSC under Truman remained of subordinate use. The doctrine of limited war, which he espoused, was largely that of his Secretary of State, Dean Acheson. Moreover, the most important strategic planning document, NSC 68, which was produced on the eve of the Korean War, was not the work of the NSC or its Senior Staff but rather that of a joint State-Defense study group. At no time under Truman was the NSC a decisive policy instrument.

D.   The Eisenhower Era, 1953–1961

It remained for President Eisenhower to bring to fulfillment the promise of the NSC as the principal instrument in both the formulation and implementation of national security policy. He institutionalized the NSC and gave it clear lines of responsibility and authority. He created the position of Special Assistant for National Security Affairs, replacing the Executive Secretary, and he related the succeeding incumbents in that position, Robert Cutler, Dillon Anderson, and Gordon Gray, to his Staff Secretary, General Andrew Goodpaster. The Special Assistant coordinated the NSC studies and the Staff Secretary, their implementation. Moreover, he greatly expanded the staff to its largest number of permanent positions (76) in the entire history of the

NSC. Emphasizing the vital importance of the Council, he convened its sessions weekly throughout the eight years of his Presidency and, except during his illness, personally presided. On a regular basis he included in the meetings not only the statutory members plus the Secretary of the Treasury, the Chairman of the JCS, and the DCI but also many second and third level members of the executive departments. He established two major NSC adjuncts: the Planning Board and the Operations Coordinating Board. Until his last year in office the Operations Coordinating Board had been chaired by the Under Secretary (since designated as Deputy Secretary) of State. In his last year in office Eisenhower made his Special Assistant for National Security Affairs, Gordon Gray, Chairman of the OCB. "The new assignment," Eisenhower wrote Gray, "is one step which I feel should be taken toward enabling the President to look to one office for staff assistance in the whole range of national security affairs."[2] Moreover, President Eisenhower established the Board of Consultants on Foreign Intelligence Activities, later redesignated as the President's Foreign Intelligence Advisory Board (PFIAB).

Although critics of the Eisenhower NSC admit there was a high volume of work, they level charges of mediocrity, lack of innovation, and of achieving consensus at the cost of imprecision and vague generalities. Such charges have scant basis. Indeed, one of the 1960 critics, then Associate Professor Henry Kissinger, testified 20 years later as to the vigor of Eisenhower's leadership. A part of the quality of Eisenhower's leadership was that everyone, including the Secretary of State and the Special Assistant for National Security Affairs, clearly understood who was in charge.

E. The Post-Eisenhower NSC

Meeting with President-elect Kennedy, Eisenhower emphasized the especial importance of the NSC. However, the young President, presumably on the advice of Professor Richard E. Neustadt, proceeded to dismantle the NSC apparatus. As a result, there was scant long-range planning. Emphasis was on current operations and crisis management, with ad hoc groups. For example, Kennedy utilized what he termed the Executive Committee (ExCom) in the October 1962 Cuban Missile Crisis.

The Kennedy downgrading and deinstitutionalizing of the

NSC was accompanied by the politicizing of the position of the Special Assistant for National Security Affairs. It would never have occurred to Eisenhower's aides to make public pronouncements. However, beginning with McGeorge Bundy (1961–66); Walt Rostow (1966–69); and Henry Kissinger (1969–75), incumbents were increasingly public advocates of particular policies and came to dominate the Secretary of State as administration spokesmen. Rostow's title was simply Special Assistant to the President. Beginning with Kissinger, the title was elevated to Assistant to the President for National Security Affairs.

President Johnson essentially continued Kennedy's ad hoc system, but, by contrast, relied heavily on his Secretaries of State and Defense, Dean Rusk and Robert McNamara. Policy leadership was left to the State Department, and there was little or no long range planning as the Nation drifted in the quagmire of the protracted Vietnam conflict. Thus, by 1969, the NSC was practically nonexistent as a policy instrument.

President-elect Nixon and Dr. Henry Kissinger, his designated Assistant to the President for National Security Affairs, went to the dying President Eisenhower for counsel on national security organization. The result was a revitalization of the NSC, much in the Eisenhower image. This complemented Nixon's own views to transform the Kennedy-Johnson focus on current operations and crisis management to longer range planning, for which the NSC had been designed. Nixon and Kissinger, with talented aides, including Helmut Sonnenfeldt and Brent Scowcroft, developed an impressive series of national security policy studies. These included brilliant initiatives with China, in the Middle East and Eastern Europe. Inevitably Kissinger rather than Secretary of State William P. Rogers became the President's principal foreign policy adviser. However, Rogers continued to serve until September 1973. For the balance of the second Nixon Administration and the first year of the Ford Presidency Dr. Kissinger served as both Secretary of State and Assistant to the President for National Security Affairs. Kissinger's deputy at the White House since 1973, Lt. General Brent Scowcroft, succeeded in 1975 to the position of Assistant to the President for National Security Affairs. Scowcroft, like Kissinger had a scholarly background. They worked effectively together and with President Ford. President Ford reaffirmed the NSC overall control of policy as related to foreign intelligence and created the Intelligence Oversight Board with three civilians as members to review the legality and propriety of the intelligence community's operations.

President Carter avowed to restore a sense of collegiality among the executive departments and to reduce the presumed dominance of the NSC over State and Defense. He did reduce from six to two the NSC committees (Special Coordinating Committee (SCC) and Policy Review Committee (PRC), but this change was largely cosmetic. Actually, he ended up by elevating rather than downgrading the Assistant for National Security Affairs, making Dr. Zbigniew Brzezinski (1977–81) the first incumbent with Cabinet rank. Brzezinski presided in the White House Situation Room over the SCC, including the Vice President, the Chairman of the JCS, and the DCI in such sensitive areas as intelligence, arms control, and crisis management. The relationship between Brzezinski and Secretary of State Cyrus Vance became reminiscent of that between Kissinger and Rogers. In both instances, the Secretary of State eventually resigned. President Carter discontinued the President's Foreign Intelligence Advisory Board.

F. The Future

The Reagan Administration committed itself to a fundamental restructuring of the National Security Council and its staff. According to the Eisenhower concept, in which President Reagan concurs, the NSC should serve not as the decision making, but rather as the decision facilitating instrument of cabinet government. By the Eisenhower and Reagan conceptions, the NSC staff serves as the secretariat of the NSC, coordinating policy formulation among the agencies represented in the NSC and ensuring that decisions taken by the President are effectively implemented. The goal is to provide the President with the means to make the most vital decisions as related to national security, including defense programs, budget, force structures, and resource allocations, in brief, to create and implement national strategy. Further, to strengthen the institutional aspects of the NSC, Reagan restored the PFIAB.

This return to an institutional role, as compared to a policy advocacy political role is, of course, easier said than done. A necessary part of this effort has been the subordination of the position of the Assistant to the President for National Security Affairs.

Cabinet rank was eliminated. Management responsibility for the National Security Council staff was placed by President Reagan in the Counsellor to the President (with Cabinet rank). The Counsellor, Edwin Meese III, and the Assistant, Richard V. Allen, conceived of the NSC Staff much as did Gray and Goodpaster in the Eisenhower years: as a catalyst of interagency activity, initiating or accelerating interagency coordination of national security issues, but not as an independent policy agency and not as the instrument for exercising direct White House control of the interagency process.

Even with these assurances, however, in the first months of the Reagan Administration the Secretary of State, Alexander Haig, went to great lengths to assert his own dominant position, not only at State, but also in the White House Situation Room. A subsequent directive from President Reagan placed the Vice President in charge of crisis management. Perhaps a part of Secretary Haig's dilemma in these first months was his recollection of his former service with Assistant to the President Kissinger, who, from the White House vantage point, dominated the senior executive department. Haig was determined that this kind of experience would not be repeated and that he would emerge as the "vicar" of foreign policy. According to Brzezinski, "The control wielded by McGeorge Bundy, or Henry Kissinger, or myself was not due to any special personal talents, but was largely derivative of the Presidents' [Kennedy, Nixon, and Carter] involvement."[3]

The Congress has found little comfort in such a view, and in the last year of the Carter Administration, conducted hearings on the role and accountability of the Assistant for National Security Affairs. This was followed by an excessive amount of publicity on possible indiscretions of Mr. Allen as related to Japanese visitors during the first days of the Reagan Administration. Although Mr. Allen was cleared by the Attorney General of any wrong doings, lamentably his continued service had been imperiled by the politicization of the Assistant's position, begun 20 years before in the Kennedy Administration. On one occasion, when a reporter had asked whether McGeorge Bundy was getting "too powerful" and becoming too much of a policy spokesman, Kennedy, with his adroitness responded, "I shall continue to exercise some residual functions."[4]

Bundy's successors, Kissinger and Brzezinski, by their dominant roles, had contributed to the resignation of Secretaries of State (William P. Rogers and Cyrus R. Vance). The Reagan Administration quite soundly had sought to depoliticize and subordinate the position. In this instance, Allen's difficulties were exacerbated by his relationship with the Secretary of State. His resignation was accepted with regret. William P. Clark, who had served ably as Deputy Secretary of State, was named on January 4, 1982 as the Assistant to the President for National Security Affairs. In 1983 Clark accepted the appointment as Secretary of the Interior, and Robert C. MacFarlane succeeded him as Assistant to the President for National Security Affairs serving through 1985. He in turn was succeeded by Rear Admiral John M. Poindexter.

The relationship between the President's NSC assistant (NSA) and the Secretary of State continued to be troublesome until midway in the second Reagan administration with the appointment of Frank C. Carlucci as the NSA on December 2, 1986 and the appointment of Lt. General Colin L. Powell as his deputy. Carlucci brought to the position an extensive experience as a foreign service officer and ambassador, also with the Office of Management and Budget and the Central Intelligence Agency. The then Secretary of Defense Caspar W. Weinberger rightly predicted that Carlucci would "constitute the NSC staff in a way that we thought it should be. That is to say that it would be a staff to the President concerned primarily with sorting out and presenting to the President differing views and giving the President expert staff advice in these matters and working extraordinarily well with all the elements of the security community."[5]

A year later Carlucci succeeded Weinberger as Secretary of Defense and Powell was named as Assistant to the President for National Security Affairs. Powell has had broader administrative experience in security related affairs than many of his predecessors. Earlier he had served as executive assistant to the Secretary of Energy and military assistant to the Secretary of Defense. With outstanding qualities of intelligent discernment, like those of Gordon Gray three decades before, Powell has enjoyed considerable success.

CHAPTER SIXTEEN

The NSC System in the Last Two Years of the Reagan Administration

COLIN L. POWELL
ASSISTANT TO THE PRESIDENT FOR
NATIONAL SECURITY AFFAIRS*

The structure and operation of the National Security Council (NSC) and the NSC system in the last two years of the Reagan Administration reflect both continuity and change. The continuity stems from President Reagan's long-held view of the NSC's role in the formulation of national security policy. This role has been defined by the need to balance a fundamental commitment to cabinet government with the requirements of Presidential policy guidance and control.[1]

The change stems from the damage suffered by the institution in the wake of the Iran-Contra affair. The prominent NSC role in this foreign policy failure, and the ensuing public and congressional concern, argued for immediate changes in the workings of the NSC system. President Reagan fully understood this. Even before the Tower Board issued its report (see below) the President had ordered changes designed to ensure the integrity of the NSC and the NSC process. He also accepted the recommendations of the Tower Board in their entirety, and went beyond them, as he told the nation in a March 4, 1987 address, to put the NSC system in even better order. Indeed, it was with this mandate to restore the NSC to its proper role in the development of national security policy that Frank Carlucci and I were brought on board as the National Security Advisor and his Deputy in January 1987.

The NSC Process

Before discussing the changes we implemented—at the Presi-

* The author would like to express his appreciation for the assistance of Peter W. Rodman and John E. Herbst in this essay.

dent's direction — in the NSC process, it would be useful to review both the nature of the NSC system and the problems revealed during the Iran-Contra affair.

The National Security Act of 1947 established the National Security Council. By this statute, the NSC consists of the President, the Vice President, the Secretary of State and the Secretary of Defense. Its function is to "advise the President with respect to the integration of domestic, foreign, and military policies relating to the national security. . . ." But its role is strictly advisory. As Gordon Gray put it, "the National Security Council is the *President in Council*. The National Security Council does not exist apart from the President himself."[2] In our constitutional structure it could not be otherwise.

The term "NSC" is sometimes used loosely to refer to the NSC staff, or the Security Advisor and the staff. Strictly speaking, however, the NSC is the Cabinet-level body headed by the President.

Both by law and by tradition, the Council is advised by other senior officials such as the Director of Central Intelligence, the Chairman of the Joint Chiefs of Staff, the Director of the Arms Control and Disarmament Agency, and the Director of the United States Information Agency. Of course, as each President shapes the NSC to his own requirements, other senior members may be added. President Eisenhower, for instance, included the Secretary of the Treasury in his NSC because he wanted the economic dimension of national security issues factored into each decision. President Reagan has regularly invited the Attorney General, the Secretary of the Treasury, the White House Chief of Staff and other senior officials to his NSC meetings.

An important player in the NSC process is the Assistant to the President for National Security Affairs, also known informally as the National Security Advisor. This job, of course, was not established by the National Security Act of 1947 or any other statute. President Eisenhower created the post of Special Assistant to the President for National Security Affairs in the White House to monitor, on his behalf, the operation of the NSC and the various subcommittees. While the position has evolved since then, growing in power and responsibility, the Security Advisor remains in formal terms a mere member of the White House staff. He is not a statutory member of the NSC or even a "principal," except as the President may give him authority in practice.

The National Security Act of 1947 authorizes a staff to support the Council. Historically the staff has fluctuated in size in the range of 30–60 professionals. Its job, strictly speaking, has been to help ensure the smooth running of the interagency process. Since the Eisenhower Administration, the NSC staff has worked *de facto* under the supervision of the President's Assistant for National Security Affairs.

I take very seriously the traditional view of the responsibility of the Security Advisor and NSC staff, namely that our job in the first instance is to ensure the integrity and running of the interagency process. Now, the "interagency process" works in many different ways. It includes supporting subcommittees that bring the departments and agencies together at the working level; it can mean more informal ways of ensuring consultation coordination, deliberation, and advice to the President. But it means, in any event, that in an important sense a National Security Advisor and the NSC staff are accountable to *all* senior members of the National Security Council.

We must make sure that all the relevant departments and agencies play their appropriate role in policy formulation. We must make sure that all pertinent facts and viewpoints are laid before the President. We must also make sure that no Cabinet official completes an "end run" around other NSC principals in pushing a policy line on which they too have legitimate concerns. All Cabinet Secretaries are somewhat ambivalent about the interagency process. They welcome it as a restraint on others, but less so when it restrains themselves. If I make sure the interagency process works well and fairly, I sleep well at night regardless of who is mad at me, and someone usually is.

Yet the Assistant for National Security Affairs inescapably has another responsibility. He is also a personal advisor to the President on his staff (and the NSC staff is part of the Executive Office of the President). As custodian of the interagency process, the National Security Advisor makes sure the President hears everyone else's opinion; but then he also gives the President his own view. And the NSC staff supports him in this role.

Every modern President has needed a staff to support *him* in his personal duties and in the heavy burden of making the final decisions. A President's staff helps him put in perspective the different recommendations of his Cabinet officers; it helps him understand the real choices he has; its job is, in short, to give him the very special support and preparation he needs to make sound decisions and maintain his control of the process. This Presidential need for personal advisors with a White House view is as important on foreign policy issues as on domestic issues. The delicate task of the National Security Advisor is to be the President's personal advisor while being absolutely fair to, and considerate of, the responsibilities and prerogatives of his Cabinet advisors.

The National Security Advisor and the NSC staff have a third function as well. That is to monitor the implementation of this President's decisions, to see that those decisions are carried out as the President intended.

Iran-Contra and The Tower Board

The Iran-Contra affair generated intense interest in, and investigations of, the NSC process. By Executive Order No. 12575 on December 1, 1986, the President appointed a Special Review Board, headed by former Senator John Tower, to "conduct a comprehensive study of the future role and procedures of the National Security Council (NSC) staff in the development, coordination, oversight, and conduct of foreign and national security policy; review the NSC staff's proper role in operational activities, especially extremely sensitive diplomatic, military, and intelligence missions; and provide recommendations to the President based upon its analysis of the manner in which foreign and national security policies established by the President have been implemented by the NSC staff."

It was a three-member board, which included a wealth of bipartisan expertise. Senator Tower was intimately familiar with national security issues from his role as Chairman of the Senate Armed Services Committee, and a stint in the Executive branch as arms control negotiator. Edmund Muskie was a distinguished Senator and Secretary of State. Brent Scowcroft was a retired Air Force Lieutenant General who had served in the White House and was President Ford's National Security Advisor.

The Tower Board issued its report on February 26, 1987, concluding that "the arms transfer to Iran and the activities of the NSC staff in support of the contras are case studies in the perils of policy pursued outside the constraints of orderly process."[3]

The Tower Board made several recommendations for changes, which I will discuss shortly. But it also declared its strong view

that tinkering with the system by new *statutory* directives was unwise. The Board specifically recommended that no substantive
change be made in the National Security Act of 1947 dealing
with the structure and operation of the NSC; it also recommended
that the Congress *not* require Senate confirmation of the National
Security Advisor, which some were urging. The Board proposed
specific changes that the President should make at the NSC that
would retain the 1947 Act's balance between a basic structure
in being and sufficient flexibility to allow each President to shape
the NSC system to his requirements. That flexibility, indeed,
has always been its strength. A President can use it or not use
it, as he sees fit. Every President's management style is different;
no rigid statutory specifications, no matter how well meant, will
necessarily suit. The Tower Board saw the seeds of Iran-Contra
in human error, not design failure.

The New NSC

The President appointed the Tower Board because he knew that
some changes needed to be made in the way his NSC system
operated. He wanted senior statesmen to review the NSC process and make recommendations. But he did not wait for their
recommendations before starting to fix his NSC system. The
President gave Frank Carlucci the mandate to make necessary
modifications when he took over as National Security Advisor
on January 2, 1987.

With this mandate, the new National Security Advisor oversaw
the rebuilding of the NSC staff and the tightening of management discipline. On the President's instruction, a directive was
issued to prohibit the NSC staff itself from undertaking covert
operations. The President ordered a comprehensive legal and
policy review, on an interagency basis, of all covert action programs; and he reaffirmed proper procedures for Congressional
notification of such programs.

President Reagan enthusiastically embraced the Tower Board
Report when it was issued on February 26. On March 4, in an
address to the American people, he promised to study its recommendations, make decisions on them by the end of March, and
report those decisions to Congress and the American people.
In National Security Decision Directive (NSDD) 266, dated
March 31, 1987, the President ordered that *all* of the Board's

recommended changes be made. He also proposed additional measures to ensure that the NSC process be put in the best possible working order. The current NSC is a product of the changes which the President ordered both prior to and by means of NSDD 266. It was a thorough reform.

NSDD 266 (the text of which was provided to Congress) spelled out the functions of NSC principals within the NSC process. It gave the Secretary of State responsibility for the formulation of foreign policy, subject to interagency review within the NSC process and the President's guidance, and for the execution of approved policy. The directive gave the same responsibility on defense and intelligence matters, respectively, to the Secretary of Defense and the Director of Central Intelligence. Yet, NSDD 266 recognized what has always been true of the NSC process: Department heads themselves sit only as advisors in connection with the President's exercise of his authority under the Constitution and laws of the United States.

NSDD 266 therefore gave the National Security Advisor explicit responsibility for day-to-day management of the interagency process, and noted his role as principal advisor on the President's staff for national security affairs. It strengthened his role within the White House by mandating that the National Security Advisor should report directly to the President. This marked a change from earlier practices in the Administration when the National Security Advisor reported to the President through the Chief of Staff or, at the start of the Administration, through the Counselor to the President. Yet even as the National Security Advisor has reported directly to the President in the last two years of the Reagan Administration, all decision memoranda for the President continued to go through the Chief of Staff. This highlighted the need for close cooperative relations—and the right personal chemistry—between the National Security Advisor and the Chief of Staff.

NSDD 266 also stipulated that the National Security Advisor should ensure the review within the NSC process of the full range of issues. He should also initiate periodic reassessments of policies and operations.

NSDD 266 also called for a restructuring of the NSC staff. It directed the NSC Executive Secretary to establish internal staff procedures for the most effective support of the NSC and the National Security Advisor in performing the responsibilities assigned by the President. The President envisaged a small, highly competent NSC staff with broad experience in the making of national security policy, a balanced staff drawn from the Executive departments and agencies, and from people outside of government. He envisaged a staff organization with clear vertical lines of control and accountability. It also empowered the Executive Secretary, through the National Security Advisor, to recommend to the President specific measures "to enhance the continuity of function at the NSC, including measures to ensure adequate institutional record-keeping from administration to administration."

For the record, it should be noted, again, that this reorganization of the NSC staff did not wait for the appearance of NSDD 266. When he became National Security Advisor, Frank Carlucci began to revamp the NSC staff organization. The Political-Military Affairs Directorate on the staff, which was involved in Iran-Contra, was dissolved. The NSC staff was streamlined and clear lines of authority and responsibility were drawn.

Frank Carlucci also added to the NSC staff a senior Legal Adviser. This position was created, as the President said, to ensure "greater sensitivity to matters of law" in the workings of the NSC. The Legal Adviser serves two distinct functions. The first, as NSDD 266 notes, is to "provide legal counsel to the National Security Advisor, the (NSC's) Executive Secretary, and the NSC staff with respect to the full range of their activities." To ensure the Legal Adviser's ability to perform this function, the President directed that "the NSC Legal Adviser shall be accorded access to all information and deliberations as may be required . . . and shall advise the National Security Advisor on all matters within his responsibility." It was recognized, in short, that counsel at the NSC has a compelling "need to know" if he is to advise his clients well, and this need can be accommodated without jeopardizing even the most sensitive programs and information. As a result, the passion for secrecy—if such there was—has given way to a habit of consultation that encompasses the agenda of the most senior interagency groups, which meet under NSC auspices to address regional conflicts, terrorism, covert action, economic relations, security assistance, pending legislation, and a host of other matters. At the President's specific direction, the NSC Legal Adviser also reviews all major decision documents, including, among others, National Security Decision Directives and intelligence findings.

The second function of the Legal Adviser is to "assist the National Security Advisor in ensuring that legal considerations are fully addressed in the NSC process and in interagency deliberations." A unique dimension of the lawyer's role on the NSC staff, this involves helping to marshal the learning and talents of legal counsel at other departments and agencies, and to coordinate the formulation of legal opinion on important national security matters, with a view to providing the President and other NSC principals the benefit of systematic legal analysis fully informed by department and agency concerns. This process is much the same as that undertaken by other NSC staff members, who are responsible for stimulating an effective interagency process on broad policy matters.

In this connection, the President directed the NSC Legal Adviser to "work cooperatively" with senior lawyers representing the President and the department and agency heads that participate in the National Security Council system. In practice, this has meant, in particular, the Counsel to the President, the State Department Legal Adviser, the Assistant Attorney General for the Office of Legal Counsel at Justice, the General Counsels at Defense and CIA, and the Legal Adviser to the Chairman of the Joint Chiefs of Staff.

At the start of his Administration, President Reagan had directed the establishment of Senior Interagency Groups (SIGs) and regional and functional Interagency Groups (IGs) to help NSC principals in fulfilling their responsibilities. NSDD 266 called on the National Security Advisor to institute an NSC review of these mechanisms to see if they were facilitating the deliberative process.

After a thorough review, the President issued NSDD 276 (the text of which was also provided to Congress). NSDD 276 reiterated that the NSC — the President in Council — remains the principal forum for considering national security issues requiring a presidential decision. It also reiterated the continuing role of the National Security Planning Group (NSPG) as a committee of the NSC. (The NSPG consists of the President, the Vice President, the Secretary of State, the Secretary of Defense, the Attorney General, the Secretary of the Treasury, the National Security Advisor, the Chief of Staff to the President, the Director of Central Intelligence, the Chairman of the Joint Chiefs of Staff, and the Director of the Office of Management and Budget.) The

NSPG meets, as circumstances warrant, to monitor and review the development and implementation of national security policy on behalf of the NSC.

An important innovation of NSDD 276 was to establish formally a new group — the Policy Review Group (PRG) — to serve as the senior sub-cabinet interagency group. Chaired by the Deputy National Security Advisor, the PRG is composed of Under or Assistant Secretaries or other senior officials of equivalent rank from the Departments of State and Defense, the CIA, the Organization of the Joint Chiefs of Staff, the Office of Management and Budget, and, as matters on the PRG agenda dictate, of the Executive Office of the President and other interested Executive departments and agencies. The PRG has become the principal interagency forum for review of issues and policies and recommendations to principals. It meets regularly as required by the urgency of the issues and the policy needs of the President and the relevant Cabinet officials. It has worked very effectively, bringing key policy-shapers and experts together to elucidate the issues and present them coherently to the President and other NSC principals.

The PRG has not replaced all SIGs and IGs. After the review of the interagency machinery, some were phased out and others continued. As required by the emergence of new issues, additional SIGs and IGs may still be formed. But all of these groups are subordinate to the PRG and regular meetings of the PRG have reduced the need for other interagency groups.

Frank Carlucci and I also made every effort to develop regular and thorough coordination and cooperation among the principals at the Cabinet level. Throughout the Reagan Administration, the Secretaries of State and Defense, the National Security Advisor, and their senior deputies have regularly met over breakfast once a week. As National Security Advisor, Frank Carlucci held occasional, other informal meetings with the Secretaries of State and Defense. During my tenure as National Security Advisor, these informal three-way meetings have occurred even more regularly.

Pursuant to NSDD 266, Frank Carlucci and I headed the NSC's Planning and Coordination Group (PCG) review of all covert action programs. We made sure that all covert programs were consistent with United States policy, law, and American values, and established a process by which all ongoing covert operations would be reviewed periodically. As the President put it in his address of March 4, 1987, "I expect a covert policy that if Americans saw it on the front page of their newspapers, they'd say, 'That makes sense.'"

We also instituted a procedure by which proposed covert actions would be coordinated with NSC principals including the Attorney General, and their collective recommendations would be communicated directly to the President; and all legal requirements for covert activities, including those involving Presidential authorization and Congressional notification, would be complied with fully and in a timely manner. Moreover, the use of private individuals and organization to conduct covert operations was appropriately limited and subject in each instance to close supervision by the appropriate Executive departments and agencies.

The Case of the Gulf

The changes we made in the NSC system were thoroughly tested in the Reagan administration's final two years by the constant demands of our national security responsibilities. Nowhere was the challenge more formidable than in the development of our policy in the Persian Gulf. Our new procedures, I believe, served the President and the country well.

The United States and its allies have long had vital interests in the energy resources of the Persian Gulf and in preventing hostile domination of the Gulf region. In early 1987, those interests were increasingly threatened. Iran had launched a major group offensive, and its forces had reached the gates of Basra, Iraq's second largest city. Iran had also stepped up its intimidation of the non-belligerent Gulf Arab states, particularly Kuwait, through terrorism and attacks on shipping. Meantime, the Iran-Contra affair had eroded Gulf Arab confidence in us, and the Soviets were eager to take advantage of doubts about our reliability and Arab anxiety about Iran. Responding to Iranian pressure, Kuwait sought protection for its shipping from both the U.S. and the U.S.S.R. In our case, it took the form of a request to put a number of its oil tankers under the U.S. flag in order to qualify for U.S. protection.

All of these developments prompted a review of our Gulf policy in January and February 1987. Gulf policy was the subject of some of the first Wednesday breakfasts that Frank Carlucci attended as National Security Advisor with Secretaries Shultz and Weinberger. At these breakfasts and in a series of PRG and NSPG meetings, we laid out a consistent, steady course in the Gulf, aimed at countering threats to our interests and rebuilding our position. The President decided on a policy that blended diplomatic efforts to seek a negotiated end to the Iran-Iraq war and build international pressure against Iranian aggression with security measures to help our non-belligerent Gulf Arab friends defend themselves and help safeguard freedom of navigation. It was a classic test of the NSC's 1947 mandate to assist the President in the integration of the military, diplomatic, and other elements of national security policy. Our diplomacy focused particularly on promoting U.N. Security Council action to end the war and on reinvigorating Operation Staunch, designed to deny Iran — the party which refused to negotiate peace — the weapons needed to continue fighting. On the security side, our approach involved a wide range of instruments, including Naval deployments, security assistance and technical advice for our Gulf Arab friends, and protection of U.S.-flag shipping. The consensus which emerged on our basic Gulf policy was reflected in strong Presidential statements issued on January 23 and February 27, 1987.

In early March, the President approved an interagency recommendation to extend U.S. Naval protection to eleven Kuwaiti tankers, which were re-registered in the United States. This move limited the Soviet Union's opportunities to expand its influence in the Gulf at our expense (the Kuwaitis had also approached the Soviets for protection); helped contain the Iranian threat to our friends and to freedom of navigation; helped restore Gulf Arab faith in our reliability; and stiffened their resolve in the face of Iranian intimidation. The decision to reflag and protect Kuwaiti vessels was not without risks, but at both PRG and NSPG discussions the risks of inaction were judged to be greater.

By mid-March, the State Department had informed key congressional staffers of the President's decision. Within two days of Kuwaiti final acceptance of our offer, the State Department had notified the staff directors of both Senate and House subcommittees on the Middle East and Europe and offered detailed briefings. Classified briefing materials were provided to staff members of the Senate Foreign Relations and House Foreign

Affairs committees. Assistant Secretary of State Richard W. Murphy briefed members of both the Senate and the House in closed session at the end of March.

It was in this formative period, therefore, that we established the pattern of thorough interagency coordination and frequent consultations with Congress that enabled us to sustain our policy in the face of the crises which later buffeted it. The first crisis was the accidental Iraqi attack on the USS *Stark*, May 17. At an NSPG meeting the next day, the President instructed us to redouble our efforts to explain our policy to the public and the Congress; the meeting also reviewed possible operational changes in our Gulf military posture. As the President stated in a May 19 speech, the Rules of Engagement (ROE) for U.S. forces in the Gulf would be changed to give them more leeway to protect themselves from military threats. We also decided at this time to increase our efforts at the U.N. Security Council to pass a resolution calling for an end to the Gulf War and withdrawal to international borders. Meantime, as another part of our integrated political/military strategy in the Gulf, the Administration won Congressional approval for several significant arms sales to help meet the self-defense needs of the Arab states of the Gulf Cooperation Council, including the sale of attrition F-15 aircraft to Saudi Arabia.

The weeks following the *Stark* incident saw frequent PRG meetings and another NSPG meeting convened by the President to monitor developments on the military, diplomatic, and Congressional fronts and to try to foresee further dangers that might emerge in the Gulf. Senior administration officials were also in regular contact with Congress to explain our policy. We successfully resisted efforts by some Congressmen to invoke the 1973 War Powers Resolution, maintaining the position of every administration since 1973 that that Resolution was unconstitutional, and noting that our reflagging decision in any case had not created a situation where the imminent involvement of U.S. forces in hostilities was clearly indicated. The objective of the reflagging, after all, was to deter, not provoke, attack. It is worth recalling that the Stark incident occurred before we had actually reflagged any Kuwaiti ships.

Following our reflagging offer and Kuwaiti acceptance, the Kuwaitis prepared the ships to meet all technical reflagging requirements. On our side, through the coordinated efforts of all agencies concerned, we were carefully implementing plans for a naval escort regime and gradually developing support for our action both at home and abroad. Once all military preparations were complete and we had quiet promises of cooperation from key Gulf states — and following consultations with Congress to ensure support at home — the President formally authorized commencement of reflagging.

The first two of eleven Kuwaiti tankers were reflagged on July 18, just outside the Gulf. Controversy again engulfed our policy when one ship in the first northbound convoy, the *Bridgeton*, struck a mine July 24. This incident spawned another round of PRG meetings and an NSPG meeting to consider how best to cope with the mine threat, and more consultations with Congress.

In August and September, our position in the Gulf strengthened as a number of our West European allies decided that it was in their interests — particularly in light of the Iranian mine threat and their own strategic and economic stake there — to support the effort to protect navigation and send a signal of support to moderate Gulf states. British, French, Dutch, Italian, and Belgian naval vessels — soon to outnumber those of the U.S. — were dispatched to the area. We were also receiving low-key but unprecedented support for our protection regime from Kuwait, Saudi Arabia, Bahrain, and other states in the area.

The broad support for this policy helped us weather another military incident in the fall. In mid-October, an Iranian SILK-WORM missile hit a reflagged tanker, the *Sea Isle City*, in Kuwaiti waters, despite several explicit warnings conveyed to Iran through diplomatic channels. Several PRG meetings and an NSPG meeting resulted in a Presidential decision to retaliate proportionally by destroying the Iranian oil platform at Rashadat, which had been used for surveillance of our convoys, for coordination of mine-laying, and as a staging base for small-boat attacks against neutral shipping. This act of measured firmness was applauded by the moderate Gulf states and quickly supported by our NATO allies. Our position gained additional support as the Arab Summit, meeting in Amman in November, called for the implementation of Security Council Resolution 598 and Iranian withdrawal from Iraqi territory and implicitly endorsed our reflagging and protection arrangement with Kuwait.

The next serious incident occurred in April 1988, when the USS *Roberts* hit a mine in the Gulf while returning from escort operations, again after several explicit warnings to Iran through diplomatic channels that we would respond to further acts of mining. Once more, the NSC system was called into operation to consider a suitable response. The NSPG convened, a series of PRG meetings developed options, and the President, after consultation with Congressional leaders, ordered our forces to undertake a limited strike at several carefully-selected Iranian targets. When the Iranian navy sought to challenge our actions, we destroyed or crippled several Iranian ships.

The steady, almost routine execution of convoy operations (nearly 70 convoys had been completed successfully by June 1988) demonstrated the degree to which the U.S. military, particularly the Navy, has been accomplishing its difficult mission in the Gulf. The tragic accidental downing of an Iran Air airliner, which did not answer repeated warnings and requests for identification, does not diminish the truth of the essential fact that our Navy has been carrying out the protective mission assigned to it. The quiet, ongoing cooperation with Gulf military establishments, the continued provision of security assistance to Gulf states, and frequent visits by the Chairman of the Joint Chiefs of Staff, commander of the Central Command and other senior military and civilian officials, have enhanced our military and political cooperation in a region still fraught with dangers.

We believe our Gulf policy has been an example of successful policy making. Close interagency coordination has allowed us to fashion a flexible, yet consistent course, applying our military and diplomatic resources to advance our national security interests. The effectiveness of our carefully integrated effort, as well as an increasing realization of the stakes involved, have helped win congressional and public support. With this essential support, we have helped contain Iranian expansionism, protect the sea lanes in the Gulf, limit the spread of Soviet influence, and strengthen the strategic position of the free world.

Conclusion

As our Gulf policy demonstrated, the changes we implemented in the NSC process have helped us to deal effectively with difficult issues. As I noted, these changes in the NSC process included, among other things, restoring the NSC staff to its proper role in the formation and implementation of national security policy.

It is not an accident that the process of reexamination of the NSC staff resulted in changes which strengthened its role even while ensuring its strict observance of its limits. The NSC system is indispensable for orderly policymaking, and the NSC staff is indispensable for orderly working of the NSC system. Writing about the national security process in 1961, Senator Henry Jackson observed:

> In the American system there is no satisfactory alternative to primary reliance on the great departments and their vast resources of experience and talent, as instruments for policy development and execution. At the same time, there is no satisfactory substitute for . . . the staff work of Presidential aides in pulling departmental programs together into a truly Presidential program, prodding the departments when necessary and checking on their performance.[4]

In short, while the NSC staff should stay out of certain functions — like implementation of covert operations — its role as keeper of the interagency process and as an advocate of the Presidential viewpoint remains crucial. History shows that the NSC system is and must be a flexible instrument that every President can adapt to his own needs. This flexibility is, as I said, its strength as an institution. It is why the Reagan Administration, like the Tower Board, has opposed legislation reorganizing the NSC system, even though such legislation might be well motivated by the desire to prevent abuses like those of Iran-Contra.

This President has reformed and reconstructed the NSC system to avoid such abuses, even as he preserved the flexibility so necessary to make the NSC system work for himself and future Presidents.

CHAPTER SEVENTEEN

Bipartisanship in the Nuclear Age

WILLIAM F. BURNS
DIRECTOR, UNITED STATES ARMS CONTROL AND
DISARMAMENT AGENCY

Introduction

One of the greatest strengths of our system is the peaceful transition of rule from one elected President to another. This stability, along with the unquestioned status of the President as commander in chief, provides the foundation for Presidential transition in the nuclear age. Our federal government has additional institutional entities that reinforce this smooth transition.

The permanent professional civil service, the cabinet system of government within the Executive Branch, and an established interagency process for review of policy and policymaking by the President provide, respectively, the institutional memory which is essential to maintaining continuity of purpose, unique points of view within the Executive Branch that serve as informal checks and balances to prevent extremism of any form, and a process of brokering of competing interests and positions that ultimately result, in the development and implementation of effective public policy.

The institutions described above may or may not produce bipartisan outcomes. Inevitably the relations between the President and the Congress largely determine the achievement or lack of a bipartisan consensus. Certainly the Senate Arms Control Observers Group which has visited Geneva frequently during negotiations has contributed to a spirit of bipartisan effort to negotiate effective treaties with the Soviet Union, as well as to support essential modernization of our strategic forces. US Arms Control and Disarmament Agency officials and others, representing the Executive Branch, regularly brief Congressional Committees, as well as staff, to keep them abreast of developments in negotiations as well as to consult with them.

The Role of the Arms Control and Disarmament Agency

The Congress itself, under the leadership of the late Senator Hubert Humphrey, deemed it desirable to create in 1961 legislation establishing the US Arms Control and Disarmament Agency (ACDA) as an independent agency of the Federal Government with prime responsibility for advising the President and the Secretary of State on all arms control and disarmament matters.

In brief, ACDA's Charter provides for the ACDA Director to:

• make recommendations to the President concerning US arms control and disarmament policy;
• conduct research on arms control and disarmament matters and coordinate all government research on that subject;
• manage arms control negotiations with other nations;
• report to Congress on the verifiability of arms control proposals as well as Soviet noncompliance with agreements; and,
• assess and analyze the impact of proposals for weapons research, development, testing, deployment or modernization programs on arms control and disarmament policies and negotiations.

None of these functions alone, even if properly conducted, can guarantee either an effective arms control policy or a favorable bipartisan approach to it. Conventional wisdom recognizes that the influence of any agency of government, including ACDA, will be no greater than that given to it by a President. An even greater constraint on what ACDA can contribute to nuclear arms control policy and process is the fact that arms control cannot, and should not, be an end in itself but an important element of a larger national security policy. It is only one means to an end, the end being the security of the United States. If equitable and effective arms control agreements result in lower levels of armaments and greater stability in a crisis, then they can help prevent war. However, it should be clear that weapons themselves do not cause wars; but instead, political tensions and differences cause conflict. These are premises on which the Reagan Administration has repeatedly based its policies and recommends as a realistic vision to future Presidents regardless of political party.

The uniqueness of ACDA and its greatest potential for contributing to the arms control process, when the conditions are propitious, is its specialized field of view permitting a concentration of resources, an institutional memory that contributes to continuity of policy and purpose, and a staff consisting of permanent civil servants as well as military officers, foreign service officers, academicians, and other government employees on temporary assignment which provide a blend of expertise not found elsewhere in government.

Bipartisanship and Arms Control

Bipartisanship is a concept that generally receives widespread endorsement in times of crisis or war. One of the great virtues of our democracy is the ability, despite the very partisan nature of the electoral system, to rally around the flag when much is at stake. Our President, regardless of party affiliation, is always the focus around which such unifying forces gather. The call for bipartisanship during an election year however, is often a more tenuous proposition. During these times, such a call and the system's response may necessarily be issue-specific. What this essentially political phenomenon has to do with the nuclear age, and specifically nuclear arms control, is the subject of this article.

Few dispute the fact that the issues of nuclear war and nuclear deterrence are high on the scale of national priorities, as issues not only of national, but also of human survival. For this reason, it seems to be a natural issue for a bipartisan approach. Unfortunately, the issues of nuclear deterrence and nuclear arms control are complex, involving numerous elements, competing interests, and sometimes outright contradictions.

The challenge we face in the nuclear age is to have the discipline — whether as politician, civil servant, soldier, member of Congress, or American voter — to draw the line between legitimate partisan positions and clear-cut bipartisan requirements of national security. This is easier said than done. Like other issues of national importance, effective nuclear arms control policy requires an informed citizenry that can provide the solid base of political support for decisions that may require difficult choices and sometimes sacrifices. This dilemma has become particularly acute during the present time of budgetary constraint. It requires national as well as local politicians to understand the issues and set aside parochial concerns, even at the risk of their political popularity in the interests of overriding issues of national security. Last, but not least, it requires Executive branch organization that promotes continuity of policy, while preserving the dual system of leadership through political appointment and loyal service by permanent civil servants.

There are some very concrete domestic and foreign policy reasons why bipartisanship in the nuclear age has become imperative. An effective nuclear arms and arms control policy requires a modern, effective, and credible nuclear deterrent. Without this, nuclear arms reductions through negotiation are more difficult because the chief adversary, the Soviet Union, has little incentive to negotiate seriously. In an era of competing economic priorities and budget deficits, maintaining credible deterrent forces will require difficult choices. Stop-and-start cycles of weapons research and development, hampered by continuous debate about the merits of deployment, can result in wasteful use of resources and ineffective systems. The choice of specific nuclear weapons force structures and nuclear weapons reduction policies must be pursued in an integral and farsighted fashion. Without a coherent national security policy that maintains a credible and effective nuclear deterrent, nuclear arms control policy will inevitably suffer.

We must assume that the Soviet Union well understands these considerations, which give it opportunities to weaken our hand in negotiations where and when possible — or alternatively — require it to negotiate seriously to mutual advantage where and when our posture is strong. The allies understand these considerations even more; our ability to manage nuclear arms procurement and negotiations in tandem has implications for allied unity and their ability to pursue effective deterrence and arms control with the East.

On one hand, realization by individual citizens in the West that their choices and their influence through the political system, in a collective manner, bear directly on the West's ability to deter and prevent nuclear war, can be profound. On the other, recognition of the complexity of the US political system that has become increasingly characterized by centrifugal tendencies, makes the task of true bipartisan unity a mind-boggling one. These tensions, felt at all levels, including the Executive Branch, define and direct our efforts to reconcile competing aims or, where imperative, to draw that line distinguishing partisan and bureaucratic interests from the "national interest".

In the remainder of this article, the arms control field will be surveyed with respect to past bipartisan successes at bipartisanship, past failures and lessons learned, and current and future bipartisan requirements in arms control and disarmament.

Successful Bipartisanship

Bipartisanship has been the norm rather than the exception since World War II. Indeed, that is why exceptions to, rather than examples of, bipartisanship receive publicity.

One of the most recent and noteworthy demonstrations of bipartisanship in foreign policy and arms control is the successful conclusion in December 1987, and ratification in June 1988, of the INF Treaty eliminating, on a worldwide basis, intermediate- and shorter-range ground-launched ballistic missiles (IRBMs) of the United States and the Soviet Union.

The unique military threat to Western Europe posed by Soviet deployment beginning in 1977 of mobile and highly accurate SS-20 IRBMs with multiple warheads was first recognized under a Democratic Administration. The NATO response to that threat — the dual track decision of 1979, calling for deployment of U.S. Pershing II and ground-launched cruise missiles in Western Europe and calling for negotiations with the Soviet Union to eliminate, if possible, the Soviet threat and thus obviate the need for US deployments — was also taken by the Carter Administration jointly with our Allies. Preliminary bilateral talks with the Soviet Union to consider negotiations were held in October-November 1980.

Following a broad review of Administration national security priorities and a specific review of INF issues, the Reagan Administration endorsed and proceeded to implement the 1979 NATO decision by proposing in mid-1981 new negotiations on INF systems. The Soviet Union finally accepted the offer and those talks got underway in November of that year. After two years of negotiations involving unacceptable demands by the Soviet side that the US abandon its deployment plan, which would have left the Soviet Union with a monopoly of INF missiles in Europe and Asia, the United States and its Allies proceeded with the planned deployments in 1983. We demonstrated strong bipartisan unity of purpose by going ahead with deployments, despite considerable propaganda and "warnings" of countermeasures from the Soviet Union, despite a considerable measure of public opposition in Western Europe as well as in the United States,

and despite the fact that the Soviet Union walked out of the negotiations in November 1983 in response to the initial deployments.

The Soviet miscalculation regarding the ultimate unity of the
West, and perhaps the US Government's capability to sustain
a bipartisan foreign policy objective, was proven by their return
to the negotiating table in 1985 under the rubric of an expanded
bilateral negotiation called the Nuclear and Space Talks. During
1985–1987, the INF negotiation proceeded and the US position
calling for elimination of US and Soviet INF missiles on a worldwide basis was ultimately accepted by the Soviet Union. The
signing of the INF Treaty, a Treaty that incorporates an extensive on-site inspection (OSI) regime for verification, the first of
its kind, represented a victory for bipartisanship. Moreover, the
final ratification vote by the Senate overwhelmingly in favor of
the Treaty is a herald of successful bipartisan arms control policy.

In the Strategic Arms Reduction Talks (START), there is much
work to be done and no clear promise of completing a Treaty
in 1988. Despite uncertainties, there are important agreed elements in the negotiation and areas of common ground. Although
achieved by the Reagan Administration, this progress addresses
concerns of the United States under several past administrations
of Democratic and Republican composition respectively.

The most obvious example is the Soviet Union's agreement
in principle in START to reduce its heavy missile force by one-
half. The SS-18 ICBM, the world's only heavy, highly MIRVed
ICBM, has been viewed as a threat to stability by the Administrations of Presidents Nixon, Ford, Carter, and Reagan. The
Soviet Union rejected US proposals to reduce heavy ICBMs in
SALT II and during much of the START negotiating period.
They have now agreed. Soviet ballistic missile throw-weight, a
measure of total ballistic missile force destructive capability, far
exceeds the US aggregate throw-weight, and represents a destabilizing imbalance which the United States has attempted to reduce both in SALT II and in START. Now, in START, the Soviet Union has agreed in principle to reduce its throw-weight
by fifty percent.

Finally, although the Soviets had rejected effective verification
measures for decades in various arms control negotiating fora,
they have agreed in principle for START to include many of the
same measures, including several kinds of OSI, that were agreed
in INF. US insistence on effective verification of arms control

agreements, including OSI, has now borne fruit in the current Administration, but it is a long-standing US position with solid bipartisan support, as demonstrated in numerous Congressional resolutions. These positions long advocated by the United States are excellent examples of the "payoff" to be gained by continuity of purpose in the arms control business through bipartisanship.

Another bipartisan success which involved more directly the Congress is the US-Soviet agreement to establish Nuclear Risk Reduction Centers (NRRCS) intended to improve communications, reduce the risk of miscalculations, and to serve as a vehicle for arms control notifications and exchange of data. The NRRCS concept originated as a result of proposals in the Senate advanced primarily by Senators Nunn and Warner.

Outside of the nuclear arms control arena, there are other indications of the value of bipartisan continuity of purpose — for example, in the area of conventional arms negotiations. Since the end of World War II, the Warsaw Pact has maintained numerical superiority in conventional forces in central Europe as a permanent military feature of the East-West Balance. This conventional threat to Western Europe has been offset to some extent by Western qualitative conventional advantages and by the deterrent value of tactical and strategic nuclear weapons. In recent years the U.S. and NATO have taken steps to strengthen the West's conventional force posture, to counter the massive military build-up by the Soviet Union. The Western approach to conventional arms control negotiations (i.e. the Mutual and Balanced Force Reductions, MBFR) since 1973, a negotiation involving again several U.S. administrations of different political parties, has been one seeking the objective of asymmetric Eastern reductions that would ultimately result in equal force levels at lower levels.

Although MBFR has not seen substantial Soviet movement, the basic approach taken by the West, coupled with Western efforts to improve conventional defenses, may now also be bearing fruit at this opportune time of potential change in Soviet views of the military balance in Europe. A new conventional arms stability negotiation has been agreed in principle that may better serve the original hopes for MBFR. Recent statements by Soviet leaders, including General Secretary Gorbachev, indicate that they may be prepared to begin serious negotiations on the basis of real rather than fictitious portrayals of the military balance in Europe. They have stated that the Soviet Union is prepared to reduce aysmmetries in the conventional balance where they exist. Moreover, the concept that the negotiations will address "stability", and not just numerical levels, supports the U.S. position that the destabilizing concentration of heavily armoured Soviet forces capable of surprise attack to take and hold territory must be addressed. These indications are tentative and without any guarantee, but they are positive indications that perhaps another long-standing bipartisan U.S. arms control policy for Europe is now paying off.

Past Failures and Lessons

One failure to achieve bipartisan consensus on arms and arms control policies has been most evident in the attempt to modernize the U.S. land-based ICBM force and do so in the context of negotiating arms reductions. As a case study it illustrates well the nexus of arms control and arms modernization considerations. The potential vulnerability of silo-based ICBMs has been recognized, studied, and addressed in the context of arms negotiations for two decades.

Steps were taken in the 1970s to increase Minuteman ICBM silo hardness but they only served as interim solutions. The increasing accuracy of Soviet ICBMs and the development of large, MIRVed Soviet missiles in large numbers made our Minuteman force increasingly vulnerable. U.S. SALT II proposals to address this problem through limitations on large Soviet MIRVed missiles were not accepted by the Soviet Union. Therefore, greater pressure was put on the United States to improve the survivability of its ICBMs through unilateral modernization.

The United States attempted to accomplish two ends at the same time in the 1970s and 80s: to field a new 10 warhead ICBM (the Peacekeeper) to offset a growing Soviet advantage in prompt, hard-target kill capability and, to deploy this missile in a more survivable (movable or mobile) basing mode. Numerous basing studies were conducted within the Department of Defense (DOD) but none of them were able to retain sufficient support to achieve a lasting consensus among the Executive and Legislative Branches on a basing mode. When President Reagan took office, his Administration undertook a thorough review and established a Bipartisan Commission on Strategic Forces, i.e., "the Scowcroft Commission", to make recommendations concerning the future of the U.S. land-based ICBM force, its place in overall U.S. strategic forces, and related arms control objectives.

The Scowcroft Commission recommendations of initial deployment of Peacekeeper in Minuteman silos, study of more survivable basing of additional Peacekeeper missiles, and research and development of a small, single-warhead mobile ICBM (SICBM), succeeded in establishing a consensus on the direction the United States should follow. The consensus in Congress concerning support of Peacekeeper and the SICBM was maintained until bipartisan budget reductions brought affordability into question.

Achieving a bipartisan consensus on this subject took place against the background of the negotiations in Geneva. Due to concerns about the verification of mobile ICBMs (i.e., the Soviet SS-25 and SS-24 mobile systems), the United States proposed a ban on such systems. Thus, there are difficult choices to make between verification considerations and our desire to enhance ICBM survivability. While the U.S. continues to insist that verification must be effective before it can consider allowing mobiles under START, we continue to pursue ICBM modernization programs that include deployment of Peacekeepers in silos and mobile basing options for a mobile version of the Peacekeeper and the small ICBM.

The lessons to be learned from this experience have been difficult and expensive. But there are positive things to report. The United States will have 50 Peacekeeper missiles in silos and on alert by the end of 1988, a significant enhancement of the land-based deterrent. Moreover, at the June Moscow Summit, some common ground regarding mobile ICBM verification was identified; but agreement on a complete, effective verification regime will be required before mobile ICBMs can be permitted in limited numbers in any START Treaty. Additionally, the President has also decided to proceed with full-scale development of a rail-garrison basing mode for 100 Peacekeeper missiles with initial deployment in late 1991.

DOD has been given clear direction with respect to the Small ICBM program, i.e., a recommendation that development be terminated principally due to affordability. However, in deference to preserving the strategic consensus that has supported the U.S. arms control negotiations in Geneva, and out of respect for alternative Congressional views regarding the merits of the Small ICBM, the Administration has retained the Small ICBM contractor structure at a minimum level of effort to provide a basis for the next Administration to continue the Small ICBM if it decides to do so. The Reagan Administration has determined, however, that the Peacekeeper in rail-garrison mode fully meets the requirements for a survivable and stabilizing land-based system, should mobile ICBMs be permitted in any future START Treaty.

Another area in which improved bipartisan consensus about U.S. national security priorities is needed is the Congress' approach to funding the Strategic Defense Initiative (SDI). Large budget reductions from the FY 1985, FY 1986, and FY 1987 Administration requested levels caused a reduction in the number of promising technologies being pursued in parallel and increased the difficulty of realizing adequate solutions to specific technical issues. Further significant reductions and restrictions made in FY 1988 placed the Strategic Defense Initiative Office in a position where simply scaling back alternatives is no longer viable. While the Congress has increased SDI funding each year, the difference between what the Administration has requested and what the Congress has appropriated is so large that it has had a substantial and increasingly detrimental impact on the Program. We are faced with either delaying the time when a decision on whether to deploy defenses could be made, or eliminating some technology efforts, thereby reducing the number of defense options that can support a decision.

If SDI funding continues to be limited and circumscribed, the United States will not only waste its greatest leverage — the innovation possible in a free society — but it cannot expect to do more than react belatedly to Soviet initiatives in strategic defense. The Soviets have a robust strategic defense program on which they have spent as much in the last 10 years as on their offensive forces. For example, they have the world's only deployed ABM system around Moscow. Also, as a result of budget cuts, Theater Missile Defense Architecture Studies will be delayed resulting in possible adverse impact on programs of interest to cooperative efforts shown by the Allies. If U.S. efforts to develop options for thoroughly reliable defenses are to be fulfilled, funding must be restored to levels that will allow the SDIO to effectively pursue options for strategic defense of the United States and its Allies.

Future Directions

The START negotiations have continued in session in the period leading up to this year's Presidential election. Our goal in the START negotiations remains unchanged: an equitable and effectively verifiable agreement for deep, stabilizing reductions in U.S. and Soviet strategic nuclear arsenals, resulting in force structures which reduce reliance on those systems that are most destabilizing—ballistic missiles, especially heavy ICBMs with multiple warheads. We have come a long way in the START negotiation toward achieving the promise of the ABM Treaty of 1972 which was signed on the premise that continued negotiations would result in stabilizing reductions in strategic offensive arms. The issues which remain to be resolved in the START negotiation are extemely difficult; working them out has been an enormous task and will remain so for the succeeding Administration should an agreement not be completed. It is the Reagan Administration's position — and hopefully the position of any future President — that we are not negotiating against a deadline. The United States should seek a good treaty, not a quick one.

Election year debate about defense issues, including arms control, is inevitable and is not necessarily unconstructive. Candidates have an obligation to convey to voters their position on key issues such as arms reductions; at the same time, they should consider carefully obligations which have the effect of undercutting any negotiations that are underway or which would likely resume at some point shortly after the Presidential transition. Undoubtedly, the strength of our democracy is that newly elected leaders can bring to the job new perspectives and new ideas, which in theory, reflect a point of view of the electorate that put them in office.

The above suggests that nuclear arms and arms control policies, although not divorced from politics by any means, should nevertheless be treated in politics with special care. The bipartisan approach to issues of survival does not prejudge the outcome of any particular debate. What it can do is add an extra degree of discipline to the actors in the system. There are issues and decisions that should transcend normal political processes and there are national security objectives which should transcend successive administrations as they have in the past.

Conclusion

Bipartisanship is a concept which assumes that certain exceptional issues of national security should be removed, when possible, from the day-to-day processes of brokerage politics. Nuclear deterrence and nuclear arms reductions are such national issues. Insightful and measured debate of nuclear arms issues in our system is, by all means, essential; but the concept of bipartisanship, like our system of majority rule, enjoins the participants to end responsible debate at some point, and agree on a consensus.

Clearly, in an election year, the bounds of responsible debate and consideration of alternative policies expand. Opportunities for change are present. However, the history of arms control, national security policy and our dealings with the Soviet Union strongly advise in favor of continuity of purpose and unity within this country and in the Alliance — the hallmarks of enlightened leadership and bipartisanship in the nuclear age.

CHAPTER EIGHTEEN

Defense Challenges for America and a New President

FRANK C. CARLUCCI
SECRETARY OF DEFENSE

This 1989 Presidential transition comes at the end of an unprecedented decade of progress toward greater security for America and its interests. Yet our nation faces major challenges if we are to preserve and build on that progress. The threats to our security have not abated, despite our improved dialogue with the Soviet Union, and the consequences of neglecting those threats are as great as ever. So at this juncture, it is appropriate for the American people and their newly elected and appointed political leaders to consider what is required for us to remain free and at peace.

The foundation for ensuring our nation's security must be an appreciation of the global nature of our task. America's long-term security entails safeguarding more than just our territory and citizens. Our national security interests extend well beyond our shores. We cannot endure in a world in which freedom, human rights, and other American values are in retreat. Moreover, U.S. prosperity depends on international trade, which requires that we help protect the free flow of resources we need and goods we sell.

For many Americans, isolationism retains great appeal—seemingly a reasonable defense posture for an island nation. It has great emotional attraction for a populace schooled in the dangers of foreign entanglements. But today, America is an island nation in geography only. In commerce, communications, and common ideals, we are a household within the community of nations—admittedly a wealthy and highly independent household—but still, one whose well-being cannot be isolated from the whole. The academic's term for it is global interdependence—the idea that America's destiny rests on more than the people and resources within her borders.

For America and other free nations in this interdependent

world, the major potential threat to our way of life will continue to be the Soviet Union. The basis of that threat is Soviet military power, whose forces and deployments have enabled Moscow to gain influence over other nations by its potential to dominate them militarily. Recently, Soviet leaders have claimed that theirs is a defensive military doctrine and that they seek nothing more than a "reasonable sufficiency" of weapons. Such a change in doctrine would be welcome, as is the greater dialogue we have with the Soviet military. But at present there is no hard evidence that the evolution in the USSR has resulted in a different and less offensively oriented force structure, or in any diminution of resources going into the military. Free nations must make their national security judgments on tangible evidence, not on assertions or changes in scripted exercises. The prudent course is to gear our military posture to Soviet *capabilities*. This is what we have done in the past. Such an approach has produced positive results and should not be abandoned.

With no tangible evidence of diminished threats to U.S. interests worldwide, our nation must meet a number of major challenges in order to ensure our future security. These challenges primarily concern the state of America's relative military strength, the continued cohesion of our alliances, and the efficiency of our defense preparations.

Preserving America's Military Strength

Regarding our military strength, our goal should be to pursue a stable U.S.-USSR balance, ideally at a much lower level of arms. The best route to this goal would be for Moscow to follow through on its recent declarations and adopt a less offensive military posture. The U.S. should do all it can to encourage such a shift. This includes continuing the vigorous dialogue between the U.S. and USSR defense sectors, which began during 1988. We should help Soviet leaders realize that the Soviet Union, and the rest of the world, would be enormously better off if the Kremlin would abandon its quest for military advantage and cut back on its military forces, now far in excess of its defense needs.

The U.S. should also pursue a better U.S.-USSR military balance through verifiable reductions in both nuclear and conventional arms. To succeed, we must be resolute and patient. We should conclude arms agreements only if they promote the security and interests of the U.S. and its allies, increase stability, constrain the Soviet threat, and add a measure of predictability to our military requirements.

Verification will remain essential for the success of any future agreements. As we enter into increasingly complex arms control negotiations, however, verification will become more difficult and the potential for undetected violations will likely increase. Mobile Soviet ICBMs, for example, which have been deployed only recently, are inherently more difficult to keep track of than their older silo-based ICBMs. We must realize that even with on-site inspections not every category of weapon systems can be made absolutely verifiable. Furthermore, as we negotiate agreements that reduce the number of systems on each side, the advantages of (and therefore the incentive for) cheating will increase. This is true because the advantage of having a given number of undetected systems will be greater as the number of permitted systems is reduced. Consequently, in cases where absolute verification is not attainable, we will have to make careful judgments about what for us is an acceptable degree of risk of undetected cheating. In some areas the risks may be such that we cannot accept unverifiable arms control constraints.

The essential requirement for ensuring a stable military balance is U.S. resolve to stay strong. For one thing, such resolve is necessary to convince Moscow to negotiate seriously toward significant arms reductions. If we unilaterally forego needed weapons modernization, Soviet leaders have no incentive to reduce their arms in order to obtain such restraint. For example, if NATO's resolve to deploy modernized intermediate nuclear forces (INF) missiles had broken down, what reason would Moscow have had to scrap its entire SS20 arsenal—as it has agreed to do? Our negotiations of recent years have taught us that the Kremlin will not offer to limit its existing, deployed systems in return solely for our promise not to deploy systems of our own.

In addition to providing the incentive for acceptable arms reduction agreements, U.S. resolve to stay strong also is essential to ensuring a stable U.S.-USSR military balance in the absence of such agreements. In particular, the U.S. must preserve a robust deterrent against a Soviet attack through our strategic nuclear triad—comprising a balanced mix of land- and sea-based ballistic missiles, and strategic bombers. Our triad provides deterrence in two ways. First, the triad is an important hedge against a single Soviet technology breakthrough that could threaten our overall deterrent. Second, the combined effects of the three legs of our triad complicates Soviet attack planning and its efforts to prevent U.S. retaliation. To deter all types of nuclear attack, our triad must possess various characteristics and capabilities — including survivability, prompt response, mission flexibility, adequate numbers and sufficient warhead accuracy and yield — to hold at risk those assets the Soviet leadership values most. No single weapons system incorporates all of these capabilities; hence, the importance of a proper strategic nuclear force mix.

To fulfill its purpose, our strategic nuclear triad must be modernized as required. We must continue to develop and deploy new systems that will ensure the credibility and effectiveness of our deterrent. We must resist the temptation to postpone modernization in hopes that arms agreements will obviate the need, or in hopes that we can safely reject currently available systems and wait for the next generation.

To deter *non*nuclear aggression, we must continue to rely on a mix of nuclear and conventional U.S. and allied forces. Our ability and declared intention to respond to a Soviet conventional attack with *nuclear* weapons — at a level of escalation of our choosing — constitutes the fundamental deterrent to Soviet aggression. At the same time, *conventional* forces are needed to make sufficiently stable and credible our deterrence of nonnuclear attack. Conventional forces are essential as a first defense against aggression. As such, they help nations — especially our allies in Europe — resist intimidation, which would be more threatening if our only recourse to Soviet conventional aggression were nuclear retaliation. Thus U.S. and allied security requires *both* nuclear and conventional forces, and our modernization should neglect neither.

Deterrence of nuclear attack against the U.S. and its allies could also be strengthened if we could destroy incoming ballistic missiles. Just as the diversity of our nuclear triad strengthens deterrence by complicating Soviet attack planning, so too would effective strategic defenses add to deterrence by undermining Soviet confidence in executing a nuclear attack successfully. Therefore we must sustain our efforts under the Strategic Defense Initiative (SDI) to investigate the possible contribution advanced antimissile systems can make toward strengthening deterrence.

SDI is one example of what we we have termed *competitive strategies* — ways to preserve a stable U.S.-USSR balance by identifying long-term Soviet weaknesses that can be exploited by directing our military competition into areas where the United States has a comparative advantage. Such an approach is consistent with our long-standing policy of relying on our qualitative edge in basic and applied technology to offset the Soviets' quantitative advantage in manpower and weapon systems. Apropos of that policy, it is revealing to note that the Soviets are as concerned about the SDI's development of advanced technologies — which may have many applications — as they are about its potential defensive systems.

There are two ways to maintain our technological advantage over the Soviets. First, we must continue to restrict Soviet access to Western technology by strengthening export controls. Second, we must widen this advantage by investing in our defense industrial and technology base to encourage research and development in advanced technologies.

Fulfilling America's Global Coalition Strategy

The proven formula for a safe America is collective security — a global strategy founded on forward defense and international partnerships, a strategy endorsed by Republicans and Democrats alike for the past forty years. Security alliances offer democratic nations the best means for defending their shared values. The deterrent value of our combined strength is far greater than the sum of each ally's defense capability. By our cohesion we warn adversaries that aggression against any alliance partner will be met with a response by the alliance as whole.

The future cohesion of America's security partnerships will depend heavily on how well we manage an issue commonly referred to as *burdensharing* — that is the distribution of security costs and responsibilities among allies. This has become a prominent political issue, mostly because our alliances have made possible a degree of economic prosperity sufficient to ensure that many of our allies now enjoy standards of living similar to our own. With this increased prosperity, however, comes an increased stake in — and responsibility for — the preservation of the system that created it. Given these realities, there is no question that America's allies should strive to shoulder more of the burden of their security and the security of allied interests outside their borders.

In the United States, however, we must resist turning our legitimate concerns about equitable burdensharing into a politically cathartic exercise in ally-bashing. U.S. allies contribute more to our common defense than is generally appreciated. Still, they can and should do better. The question is how best to encourage that. The key is for the United States to lead, not threaten. Toward that end, the Reagan administration began an intensive high-level dialogue with our allies both in NATO and in the Far East. This type of mutual undertaking can lead to a more fully equitable sharing of the roles, risks, and responsibilities of coalition defense.

To coax greater defense efforts by her allies, America must lead by example. We hardly can hope to persuade others to do more if we do less. How can we convince allies of the risks of neglect, if we are cutting our defense budget? Nor can we assume that if America cuts back, our allies will take up the slack. At least as likely a scenario is this: if we do less, our allies will assume that we believe the threat has diminished and will do less themselves. Should this occur, we would all be less secure.

The imperative for a new U.S. President and Congress will be to use burdensharing as a vehicle to *strengthen* our alliances, not as an excuse to reduce the U.S. defense budget. Imaginative, do-as-we-do American leadership is the key to achieving equitable allied burdensharing.

One security burden America must continue to bear is the overseas deployment of a significant portion of our military forces. The U.S. cannot deter or defeat aggression against our worldwide interests with U.S.-based units only. Forward-deployed forces increase our ability to respond quickly and effectively if need be. Such forces also reassure allies of America's commitment to the common defense and encourage them to resist intimidation.

By providing base rights for U.S. forces, our allies make a major contribution to shared security. The future, however, will see pressures for change in our base status, as occurred recently with Spain, or with actual changes in our base status, as will occur in Panama in 1999. In part, these pressures reflect concerns over national sovereignty, a reduced sense of danger, and feelings that the compensation we provide for base rights is inadequate. In some cases, pressures reflect a host nation's misguided belief that it can reap the benefits of collective security, without carrying a reasonable share of the burdens. Whatever the causes, we must plan for inevitable change in our basing arrangements. The United States does not want to maintain its forces where they are not welcome, or where they are not needed. Nor can we undertake defense roles on behalf of friends or allies who prove unwilling to contribute or cooperate in our effort. Most important, we do not want to find ourselves in a position where we must accept a reduced ability to meet our security commitments, while we search for alternatives to our current forward bases.

Complementing our forward deployments on behalf of collective defense is *security assistance* — a highly cost-effective tool to help friendly nations preserve their security, which thereby helps protect the U.S. and allied interests as well. Security assistance is an area in which our more prosperous allies can and should make greater contributions. However, to blend U.S. security assistance efforts with those of our allies, Congress must support an adequate foreign affairs budget and resist micro-managing the funds it does provide. At present, roughly 85% of our severely constrained military assistance funding is reserved for five countries — Egypt, Greece, Israel, Pakistan, and Turkey. Consequently, we do not have effective security assistance programs for many other deserving and strategically important nations. If this trend continues, it will mean that the United States cannot be counted on to aid friendly, developing nations in providing for their security. Our economically strong allies are not likely to share the burden of assistance programs, if we continue to cut our own. Nor can we plan effectively with our allies to gain the maximum efficiency through our combined security assistance program if Congress continues to earmark our already limited funds.

The key is to use our alliances, security assistance, and other forms of influence to maintain a global involvement to protect our global interests. We should also continue to encourage the active participation of our allies in the protection of their interests outside the formal boundaries and constraints of alliance commitments. We have seen evidence of this allied commitment to global interests in the efforts of the United States, Britain, France, Italy, the Netherlands, and Belgium to support the right of free navigation in the Persian Gulf. Other examples include Britain's support of our retaliatory strike on Libya; the combined efforts of several NATO members to clear mines from the Red Sea; U.S.

and French assistance to Chad; the Multinational Force and Observers in the Sinai; and the combined peacekeeping effort of the United States, France, and Italy in Lebanon.

The collective security of free peoples requires that we nurture the values that define us. In the future we must encourage the emerging democracies of the Third World and encourage those seeking freedom as they struggle against repressive, totalitarian regimes.

During the last decade, many Third World states embraced democracy, expanded individual liberties, and introduced market-oriented elements into their economies. Having encouraged such changes, we and our allies must assist these nations through their difficult periods of transition. This support requires a consistent, well-directed program of economic, security (including foreign military sales), and political assistance. Our aid must encourage the recipient country's implementation of market-based economic reforms aimed at strengthening that country's democratic roots. In some cases, as in El Salvador and the Philippines, our assistance will be required not only to help democracy flourish, but to ensure its survival.

Assistance to friendly Third World nations unquestionably serves Western security interests. Moreover, the costs of assistance are trivial compared to the costs of allowing these states to fall prey to the inherently destabilizing forces of poverty and repressive government, which our adversaries can exploit.

Similarly, when consistent with U.S. interests, we must support indigenous movements struggling against totalitarian oppression. Experience shows that, especially in the Third World, these movements can succeed when the conditions are right and when consistent support is provided. We must build a durable consensus in the United States, and among our allies and friends, to support anti-Marxist fighters whose goals are compatible with those of democratic states.

Getting the Most from our Defense Dollars

Because threats to our interests worldwide show no sign of diminishing, the United States must sustain a steady strengthening of our military forces, which will also provide incentives for arms agreements and stimulus for cohesive alliances. To achieve such a strengthening, our nation must muster the political will to sustain real growth in our defense budgets. And at least as important, we must ensure that our defense dollars are spent wisely and efficiently.

The most important determinant of efficiency in defense spending will continue to be *stability* — stability in the overall defense budget and stability in funding for specific weapons programs. When funding is always uncertain, planning and cost savings are nearly impossible, both in the Pentagon and in individual defense firms. With no assurance of future funding, there is no incentive for long-term investments aimed at productivity gains. Congress holds the key to greater stability. Progress is possible if it chooses to switch to biennial budgeting for defense and approves more of the Defense Department's requests for multiyear procurement plans.

Efficiency would also be served if Congress drastically reduced its micro-management of the Department of Defense and its purchasing. Our budgeting and acquisition system is already too complex, and badly needs to be streamlined. Congressional oversight should concentrate on broad policy issues and major procurement decisions — and leave implementation to the DoD. Defense officials should be given sufficient flexibility to manage the execution of U.S. defense policies and to improve the system, and then be held accountable for their performance.

Similarly, Congress should examine its vulnerability to pressure from specialized constituencies and defense firms — aimed at getting members to intervene in defense procurement decisions. What America buys for its security should be based on valid defense needs and the expected performance of competing contractors, not on political clout. Only by reducing politically motivated intervention and budget instability will acquisition officials and defense firms have a full opportunity to equip America's armed forces as effectively and efficiently as possible. For its part, the Executive Branch must ensure that high quality, experienced, and morally sound employees administer procurement programs and that wrong doers are quickly identified and vigorously punished.

With defense budgets likely to be squeezed in coming years, it is essential that a new President and Congress set wise priorities for military spending. In my view, the wise course is to continue to aim at the three priorities I directed for our Fiscal Year 1989 defense budget request:

• *Quality military people.* People are the most important factor affecting America's defense strength. During the 1980s, the quality of our military people rose dramatically. We now must sustain that achievement by providing our uniformed men and women adequate pay and support in recognition of their dedication and sacrifice.

• *Readiness.* We are better off accepting a smaller military if that is necessary to ensure the readiness of the forces overall. To preserve readiness, we must fund training and maintenance sufficiently, which in turn will help us retain quality professionals in our military ranks.

• *Efficient acquisition.* In addition to pursuing stability and other acquisition reforms, we must be prepared to terminate or defer lower priority programs to achieve economic production rates for higher priority ones.

Nurturing America's Defense Industrial Base

Future U.S. Presidents and Secretaries of Defense should recognize that America's military might will continue to depend on our economic strength. We must have a defense industrial base able to produce sophisticated weapons systems (from rifles to aircraft and ships) and their components (e.g., radars and engines), and to provide adequate logistics support (e.g., fuel, repair parts, and ammunition). We must have not only the capacity and capability to produce goods at an appropriate rate, but also the advanced technology from which our systems will derive their battlefield advantage. The crucial component of America's defense industrial base will remain people: the scientists, engineers, managers, technicians and others, whose skills ultimately will determine our nation's fate. To preserve that base, we must be certain that there are appropriate risk-reward ratios to stimulate investment in research and development, productivity improvements, and people, in an industry that depends substantially on one customer.

Conclusion

As in the past, America will face formidable challenges as it seeks to remain free and at peace in the years ahead. While we see hopeful signs of diminished danger — particularly the possibility that the Soviet Union may recognize internal and external realities and adopt a more moderate international policy—threats to U.S. interests and values remain as serious as ever. To meet its defense challenges, America must continue to be guided by these proven national security principles:

- *Realism.* We must deal with the world as it is, not as we wish it to be. Our posture and policies must be based on the actual capabilities and actions of our adversaries, not on their pronouncements of promises. Wishful thinking is no basis for defense decisions.

- *Strength.* There is no substitute for military strength to safeguard us against armed adversaries. Moreover, our resolve to stay strong can convince others to join us in reducing arms, enhancing stability, protecting human rights, and resolving regional conflicts.

- *Cohesion.* The unity of free nations is their best defense for their shared values. America's defense decisions must be made with an eye toward the critical goal of ensuring the cohesion of our alliances.

- *Consensus.* America's leadership in the world demands a steady course, which is only possible if we nurture a bipartisan consensus on our defense policies and posture. A new President and Congress must cooperate on national security matters, so that as a nation we speak to the rest of the world with one voice, united for the preservation of our republic.

Good fortune has thrust the United States into its role as leader of the world's democracies and champion of liberty around the globe. To this solemn responsibility, we Americans must bring wisdom and imagination. Above all we must exercise prudence, for our mistakes may well be irreversible and our neglect may deny millions the prospect of a free and comfortable life. If we proceed wisely, the 1990s will prove to be a decade in which the freedom we cherish will remain secure and will be shared by those who now wish for it.

CHAPTER NINETEEN

USIA in the 1990s: Building on a New Foundation

CHARLES Z. WICK
DIRECTOR, UNITED STATES INFORMATION AGENCY

Public diplomacy received full recognition as one of the national means available to achieve U.S. foreign policy goals and objectives in the early years of the Reagan Administration. The United States Information Agency (USIA) is the U.S. Government agency principally responsible for the conduct of public diplomacy programs abroad. Through its activities, USIA seeks to explain to foreign audiences U.S. government policies and actions in ways that are clear, credible, and likely to elicit support for U.S. interests.

As we approach the end of the Reagan Administration and the beginning of the 21st Century, USIA finds itself at a crossroads. Developments in information and communication technology, which have already had a major impact on the way USIA operates, will play an ever-increasing role in world affairs and in shaping foreign public perceptions of the U.S.

Developments over the past eight years, strongly supported by President Reagan, have positioned USIA to face the challenge effectively, provided that the next administration reaches consensus in support of *ongoing* foreign policy initiatives and makes a commitment to providing a consistent level of resources for public diplomacy programs.

Specifically, this Administration has sought to strengthen generally underfunded and undervalued public diplomacy programs in five ways by 1) expanding the role of public diplomacy in the conduct of U.S. foreign policy; 2) modernizing and expanding communications technologies; 3) expanding and creating new cultural, educational, and informational programs; 4) facilitating the growth of democracy around the world; and 5) expanding cooperation with the American private sector.

Public Diplomacy in U.S. Foreign Policy

From its inception, with one of the nation's premier political communicators as President, the Reagan Administration has appreciated the potential contribution of public diplomacy programs to explain and advocate U.S. policies, and build international understanding of American society and values. USIA had the central U.S. responsibility in planning such major international events as the annual seven-nation Economic Summits and the four Reagan-Gorbachev Summits between 1985 and 1988.

Public diplomacy programs have become much more comprehensive and vigorous, characterized by strong articulation of Administration positions on international issues bearing on U.S. interests. Public presentations on U.S. reaction to martial law in post-Solidarity Poland, and the continuing Soviet military presence in Afghanistan were designed to reach massive international audiences, as were presentations in support of action by the U.S. and neighboring Caribbean states in Grenada.

Of special importance and significance was the Agency's role in developing public diplomacy programs in support of the deployment of medium range missiles in Europe in the early 1980's and the INF Treaty in 1987. USIA programs played an important role in developing support for these NATO Alliance initiatives.

USIA has also been called upon to play a significant role in developing forceful and convincing arguments in support of U.S. positions on a wide range of political and economic issues. USIA products for overseas audiences — publications which are available for reprint in local foreign newspapers, international radio and television broadcasts, and briefings of foreign journalists both in the U.S. and overseas — have presented complex U.S. perspectives comprehensively and understandably in a number of languages. Our officers abroad have continuously addressed foreign concerns about U.S. policies in discussions with host country officials and foreign media often in local languages.

In addition, USIA has succeeded in engaging senior Administration officials, including the President, to communicate more frequently than ever before with foreign media in the kind of dialogue that has always existed domestically. This reflects a growing awareness that the consensus of U.S. allies and other nations is vital in the pursuit of U.S. foreign policy objectives.

The Administration also understood clearly both the obstacles to the free flow of information within and into the USSR, and the global challenge posed to U.S. national security interests by Soviet international "information" policy. The Administration called upon USIA to take the lead in engaging the Soviet Union in discussions aimed at ending their jamming of international radio broadcasts, particularly the Voice of America (VOA), which is a part of USIA, and in encouraging media reciprocity, including greater access to Soviet media for U.S. administration officials, equal to the access Soviet officials have to U.S. commercial media, and a range of opportunities for American private media to reach Soviet publics.

USIA has also played a prominent role in countering Soviet "disinformation," that is, the placement of false and misleading stories about the U.S. and its foreign policies in foreign media by Soviet agents. Despite increased Soviet sensitivity to U.S. concerns, and an apparent awareness of the damage that disinformation can inflict on U.S.-Soviet relations, the Soviets have not yet entirely halted their disinformation activities.

Soviet jamming of most VOA broadcasts ceased on May 23, 1987, but the Soviets continue to jam VOA's Dari and Pashto services to Afghanistan and Radio Free Europe and Radio Liberty broadcasts to the Soviet Union.

Also on May 20, 1985, the Voice of America Radio Marti program was created from a three-year bi-partisan effort to provide the Cuban people "news, commentary and other information events in Cuba and elsewhere to promote the cause of freedom in Cuba." Radio Marti is on the air seven days a week 17½ hours per day from 5:30 to 11 p.m.

Former Cuban political prisoner Armando Valladares told a congressional subcommittee in September, 1986 that Radio Marti has penetrated the "void" of information that exists in Castro's Cuba today. "Every exiled Cuban I have spoken to listened to Radio Marti when they were in Cuba," said Valladares, who spent 22 years in Cuban jails before his release in 1983 and whose book, *Against All Hope*, details his brutal treatment.

In that same congressional hearing in September, 1986, Radio Marti Director Ernesto Betancourt described the eloquent text of a letter to him from Ricardo Bofill, president of Cuba's underground Human Rights Commission, and former professor of Marxism at Havana University, who has been in prison numerous times for his defense of human rights in Cuba. Bofill's letter began: "It seems to me there will come a time, with respect to the problems existing in Cuba today, in which we will have to talk about the time before and after Radio Marti went on the air."

While the above confirms that the Reagan Administration has elevated public diplomacy to the status of a key element of national power, we hope the gains will be institutionalized in the future. For example public diplomacy programs can be even more effective if international public opinion is considered *before* policy options are chosen, and if program plans are developed *before* policy decisions are announced. Public diplomacy should be "present at the creation" if we are to avoid misunderstanding overseas of U.S. foreign policy goals and objectives. Therefore public diplomacy and the officials and organization responsible for it should be more systematically involved as advisors on the policy process before options are chosen, decisions made or actions taken.

Modernizing and Expanding Communications Technologies

Under the Reagan administration, USIA was able to transform television into one of the primary tools of public diplomacy. With the initiation of WORLDNET in November 1983, USIA could bring America's leaders directly to foreign media and into the homes of people around the globe. WORLDNET, broadcast via satellite, permits simultaneous interaction (largely two-way audio, one-way video, but occasionally two-way video) between administration spokespersons in USIA's Washington studio and multiple USIS facilities overseas for discussions of current U.S. policies and developments.

The President has used WORLDNET to address foreign audiences directly, and whenever officials such as Secretary Shultz, Secretary Carlucci, arms negotiator Nitze, or Assistant Secretary of State Ridgway appear — especially when important news is breaking — overseas print and electronic media give them extended coverage. WORLDNET is now being increasingly used to create links between scientific, cultural and educational communities, for example, between U.S. and Soviet cancer researchers, who met via WORLDNET last spring.

As of the fall of 1988, WORLDNET has placed over 130 of

a projected total of 150 TVRO dishes for the worldwide network expected to be in placed by October 1989. In addition, in Europe and the Near East, WORLDNET was being used by 156 cable systems, 260 hotels and 35 broadcast television stations.

In 1982, President Reagan announced a major long-term commitment to VOA modernization to restore U.S. government radio broadcasting as a first-rank global source of news and information. In earlier years, VOA's signal was being heard with increasing difficulty by its audience of 120 million listeners around the world as a result of increased competition in international short-wave broadcasting, deteriorating equipment, and Soviet jamming.

VOA now has agreements for new and high-powered transmitters in Antigua, Belize, Botswana, Costa Rica, the Federal Republic of Germany, Grenada, Israel, Morocco, Sri Lanka, and Thailand.

VOA now broadcasts a total of more than 1100 hours weekly in 44 languages (including Radio Marti which broadcasts in Spanish to Cuba and VOA Europe). Decreased levels of funding in recent years, however, if maintained by the new administration, could significantly curtail still needed modernization.

This administration's commitment to modernizing the tools of public diplomacy was demonstrated as early as 1981 when USIA's Wireless File, a daily compendium of accurate information on U.S. policies and the current American scene distributed via radio teletype to USIA posts overseas for use by countless local newspapers and government officials, made the transition to instantaneous communication via computer and satellite.

The File, which contains up to 50,000 words, now reaches USIA posts in just minutes via telephone modem, and a new Express File relays information directly into newsroom and offices abroad, ensuring that influential media and top foreign decision makers and opinion leaders have access to full texts of official U.S. foreign policy statements and authoritative interpretations of policy positions as stories break.

As we look to the future, USIA must retain its position at the cutting edge by investigating the latest breakthroughs in the communications revolution. For example, the Agency should be adequately funded to investigate the long-term prospects for employing Direct Broadcast Satellites (DBS) to transmit radio and TV signals directly to individual receivers abroad. A combination of technological advances, market conditions, and changes in international law, politics and regulation will ultimately determine whether and how soon the full potential of DBS is realized. U.S. public diplomacy programs, however, should not be left behind because of declining budgets.

Expanding Cultural, Educational, and Informational Programs

Exchange programs have been an essential aspect of public diplomacy. USIA has played a central role in their expansion over the past eight years. For example, the Agency significantly augmented the Fulbright international educational exchange program which, since its inception in 1946, has taken more than 56,000 U.S. students, teachers and scholars abroad, and brought more than 106,000 foreign academics to the U.S. In 1987, there was an increase in the Fulbright program to approximately 6,500 grants.

The President's Youth Exchange Initiative, announced at the Versailles Economic Summit in 1982, has already promoted some 22,000 additional exchanges beyond those taking part in traditional people-to-people exchanges facilitated by USIA and its network of civic and volunteer organizations.

Finally, the long-time USIA International Visitors program, which brings foreign leaders to the U.S. for thirty-day orientation visits, has been increased to 3,500 grants annually.

Such exchange programs merit continued increased funding to establish a cross-cultural dialogue with "successor generations" overseas in the last years of this century. There is simply no more effective way to develop understanding of U.S. foreign policy among the foreign leaders of tomorrow than to allow them to understand American society today.

Facilitating the Growth of Democracy

In his speech before the British Parliament in 1982, President Reagan called upon the free nations of the world to fund and support programs that would encourage the development of democracy and democratic institutions in nations where they did not then exist. An element in the U.S. contribution to the concept was creation of the National Endowment of Democracy. The

Endowment is organized to mobilize the energies and talents of private Americans and groups abroad who aspire to move their societies toward democracy.

USIA has long supported the growth of democracy abroad by providing information on U.S. political institutions, processes and values, and by making possible through grants and exchanges of persons a continuing dialogue and cooperative efforts. The Agency annual plan establishes democracy building as a major priority.

USIA efforts have concentrated in two areas, 1) public affairs — supporting ideas of democracy, constitutionalism, human rights and electoral participation; and 2) exchange and cultural activities focusing on international visitors, academic, campus program and youth exchange.

Foreign Press Center tours and briefings for foreign journalists, USIA's Wireless File, magazines, WORLDNET, VOA broadcasts, exhibits and paper shows, and US/USSR exchanges support these themes. Agency media resources, including the Voice of America, fully support and cover events of special importance to democratic institution building such as support for the Second Conference on Parliamentary Democracy, European Parliament in Strasbourg.

USIA has an active program to help convey democracy to special audiences in the Soviet Union and China. Nearly 2.3 million Soviet citizens saw how technology is revolutionizing American life through USIA's "Information USA" exhibit which toured nine Soviet cities during 1987–88. Computer displays, video terminals and multi-media centers complement the work of 24 Russian speaking American guides in demonstrating the creative benefits of a free and open society.

As the President has said repeatedly, support for the emergence of democratic values and processes and the growth of democratic institutions abroad is at the heart of U.S. human rights policy. Human dignity can be guaranteed only by limiting the powers of government, and basing government on the consent of the governed. Democracy is the only form of government that will ensure respect for human rights. The United States Government should continue to support democracy building and respect for human rights.

Expanding Cooperation with the American Private Sector

U.S. public diplomacy has gained immeasurably from the activities and contributions of the American private sector. Private initiative is, after all, the wellspring of American economic well-being, and private interests in foreign policy and nations abroad have resulted in a number of cooperative projects that have effectively supplemented official programs. One small, but significant current private sector project which dovetails nicely with official U.S. government public diplomacy programs is the MacMillan Corporation's production of "English by TV" which has been placed on TV around the world to introduce millions to our language or to improve their existing English-language skills.

In addition, private sector contributions have made it possible for major exhibitions such as "Three Generations of Wyeths" to tour internationally. USIA's travelling exhibitions in the Soviet Union have been significantly assisted by contributions from American private corporations.

Over $100 million in donations and in-kind contributions come from the private sector for support of Agency programs and initiatives. With the help of ten private sector advisory committees, USIA has more effectively carried out its mandate with the views and suggestions of world opinion leaders on ways the United States can improve its image abroad.

Volunteerism is one of the hallmarks of American democracy. USIA regularly calls upon the services of several hundred groups involving more than 700,000 American volunteers in order to organize the travel around the nation of more than 3,500 official participants the Agency's International Visitors program and an additional 2,400 foreigners who pay their own way to the U.S. under the Voluntary Visitors program. American volunteers have undertaken extraordinary efforts to create ties with other societies. We think it is essential to maintain a cooperative relationship between the government and the private sector in the future to generate improved understanding of our nation abroad.

The Need for Continuity and Commitment

American public diplomacy programs have contributed to the

advance of freedom and democracy around the world in recent years. USIA has fostered increased understanding of our nation and our policies while helping facilitate mutual understanding between Americans and peoples from other countries. The public diplomacy gains of the Reagan Administration must be consolidated, no matter which Party comes to power in the next U.S. elections. The nation must renew its commitment to continuing and enlarging U.S. public diplomacy programs abroad to respond both to the continuing Soviet information challenge and the demands of a volatile world, linked by modern telecommunications, but still divided by ideology and unresolved regional disputes.

In his inaugural address, President Reagan said, "Above all we must realize that no arsenal or no weapon in the world is so formidable as the will and moral courage of free men and women." We Americans can take great pride in having displayed such courage, and we must continue to communicate it and nurture it abroad.

PART FIVE

The Presidency and the Economy

CHAPTER TWENTY

The President's Council of Economic Advisers

CHARLES H. ZWICKER
ADJUNCT PROFESSOR OF BUSINESS ADMINISTRATION
POST COLLEGE (CT)

Founding the Council

The economic depression of the 1930s was not solved until the advent of World War II, but for almost two centuries before that most American Presidents had to concern themselves more with economics than with war. Thus when that war seemed to be coming to an end, and with it the huge expenditures and employment engendered by war, most economists feared a resultant depression and unemployment such as had occurred a quarter century before when World War I ended.

The civilian population, including members of Congress, still remembered with horror the insecurity, fear, starvation and despair which gripped the nation during the long years of the Great Depression. It was this economic catastrophe which brought about the election of Franklin Delano Roosevelt, creation of the New Deal and the ever increasing role of the federal government in our personal and business lives. This welcome or unwelcome intrusion reached its height during the war years, and it succeeded in bringing about a kind of unnatural prosperity.

Fear was constant that the sudden decline in the huge expenditures for armament, military personnel and other materiel associated with the conflagration would again plunge the country into an economic abyss. When *Fortune* magazine conducted a poll late in 1944, "Do you think the federal government should provide jobs for everyone able and willing to work but who cannot get a job in private employment?", 67.7% replied in the affirmative.[1] Many prominent economists predicted that by early 1946 there would be eight to ten million unemployed.[2] This was reasonably based on the fact that at the peak of the war over

11,500,000 men were in the armed services in addition to an even larger number in civilian war-related jobs.

Congress began attacking the problem as early as 1944, with the introduction of several bills which after much travail resulted in the passage of the Employment Act of 1946. Originally it was called the Full Employment Act, but because of doubt about the government's ability to fulfill such responsibility and efforts of opponents to dilute the concept of everyone's "right" to work, compromises were made.

The Act created in the Executive Office of the President a Council of Economic Advisers to be composed of three members appointed by the President, qualified to analyze and interpret economic developments, to appraise economic programs and activities of the government and to formulate and recommend material economic policies to promote employment, production and purchasing power under free competitive enterprise.[3]

The duties and functions of the Council are described in the Act:

1. To assist and advise the President in the Economic Report;
2. To gather timely and authoritative information concerning economic developments and economic trends . . . ;
3. To appraise the various programs and activities of the federal government designed to create and maintain employment;
4. To develop and recommend to the President national economic policies to foster and promote free competitive enterprise, to avoid economic fluctuations or to diminish the effects thereof, and maintain employment . . . ;
5. To make and furnish such studies, reports thereon, and recommendations with respect to federal economic policy and legislation as the President may request.

While as early as 1944 Harry Truman believed in a national policy which would bolster the civilian economy when it failed to produce a satisfactory level of employment, once the Act was finally passed he did not show any immediate enthusiasm for it. Perhaps he had what he considered more important things on his mind, but it was several months before he made the three initial appointments to the Council to get it under way. He selected as the first Chairman, Edwin G. Nourse, who had outstanding credentials as an economist at the prestigious Brookings Institution and had been president of the American Economic Association.

For vice chairman, he appointed Leon H. Keyserling, a Columbia trained economist and Harvard trained lawyer who had participated in the New Deal economic planning. He had a great enthusiasm for the Council, having in 1944 won a $10,000 prize for a competitive essay which called for "maximum standards of living depending upon full employment of manpower skills, plant and resources."

As the third member of this pioneer body, Truman selected John D. Clark whose background was both academic and business. Leaving a lucrative position as vice president of Standard Oil of Indiana at an early age, he earned a Ph.D. in Economics and after several years as a professor became dean of the School of Business at the University of Nebraska. His involvement in Democratic politics had led to several FDR administrative posts before his appointment by Truman to the Council.

These three were the trail blazers who it was hoped would find the means whereby the government would guarantee employment and thus provide greater economic security for those able and willing to work.

Precedent was set by the first Economic Report which was released by President Truman on January 8, 1947. The structure has been followed more or less by succeeding administrations, starting with an analysis of the previous year's economy, providing statistical tables including comparisons with the past, pointing out potential dangers, and making short and long-term recommendations. It emphasized the importance of cooperation in international economic relations and stressed the formation of an International Trade Organization.

The midyear report followed the same format but extended the period of coverage.

Unfortunately, the three Council members differed in personality, general attitude and methods of procedure, let alone economic convictions. At the same time, Truman had little economic knowledge and tended to dislike and distrust economists.[4] Also, Nourse's relationship with him was unsatisfactory, distant and tenuous. This lack of harmony did not serve to enhance the reputation and influence of the Council.

A sense of frustration caused Nourse to resign in November of 1949. He was succeeded as Chairman by Keyserling who served until January 1953. This period was marked by price inflation, a sluggish economy and the disruptions of the Korean War. The Keyserling Council guided the enactment of price and wage controls and the mobilization of manpower and industry. The efforts to combat inflation during the Korean War emphasized in the 1953 Economic Report earned for Keyserling considerable respect.

The Eisenhower Council

Upon his becoming President, Dwight Eisenhower confronted the Korean War, price and wage controls, and fiscal and monetary problems. The selection of Arthur Burns as CEA chairman was a fortuitous one. His broad background as a respected economist came from his association with Columbia University and as director of research of the National Bureau of Economic Research. His reputation stemmed from his prestigious study of business cycles and his anti-Keynesianism. He preferred the inductive method of analysis and he shied away from theoretical approaches. In an exposition of his economic viewpoint, he wrote, "Subtle understanding of economic change comes from a knowledge of history and large affairs, not from statistics or their processing alone . . . to which our age has turned so eagerly in its quest for certainty."[5]

President Eisenhower recognized the potential importance of the Council and felt that it did not, under Truman, have the status it should have had, and he intended to reinvigorate that body.[6] At the Senate confirmation hearings, Burns enunciated his concept of the role of the Chairman and the Council. "My own personal inclination would be to stay out of the limelight, make my recommendations to the President, indicate to him what the basis for the recommendation is . . . and then having done that remain eternally quiet."[7]

This was the first Republican administration in twenty years and a relatively conservative one. It was committed to a balanced budget, less interference on the part of government, tax reduction and the belief that the business cycle carries its own cure. Yet during his campaign for election, Eisenhower promised a policy of mobilizing the government's power to combat recession.[8]

The Council had fallen into such disfavor under Truman that Congress gave it only a nine-month budget for the 1953 fiscal year. Its future was placed in jeopardy, and even more so when a request for $75,000 for the non-appropriated remainder of the year was first reduced to $25,000 and then settled by Senate action at $50,000.

Burns rebuilt the Council, added excellent staff and enthusiasm, in time to meet an impending economic decline. The 1955 Economic Report, after reviewing the 1954 year, gave voluminous recommendations in the areas of Taxes, Business Regulation, the Public Debt, Unemployment, Pensions, Minimum Wage, Housing and International Economic Relations. Subsequent reports followed the same procedure as the physical size of the reports grew.

Burns' rapport with the President was generally excellent. There were weekly meetings, and situations and programs were discussed, with often divergent views from the Treasury. He had a good relationship with the press and when the recession of 1953–54 came, his suggested remedies of government interjection, while not in agreement with ingrained conservative philosophy, served to provide means to improve the economy.

When induced to return to Columbia and the National Bureau of Economic Research, Burns turned the chairmanship over to Raymond J. Saulnier in December 1956. Saulnier continued the work of strengthening the CEA's operations and furthering its influence. Eisenhower's second term was marked by a valiant battle against creeping inflation and recession, and the battle had principally been won by January 1961.

The Kennedy Council

John F. Kennedy came into office with the enthusiasm and optimism of youth. His own economic education was not broad at all, although he did spend some unspecified time at the London School of Economics and even sat in on some classes given by Harold Laski.

Walter W. Heller took leave from his position as chairman of the Economics department of the University of Minnesota to head and organize the Kennedy Council. In commissioning the Council, Kennedy enunciated his view of the importance of its work and the contributions it could make. "Under Dr. Heller's direction, I expect the CEA to take its place as a key element within the Presidential Office. I believe it can make a major contribution to the successful organization of the Presidency and by revitalizing the Council of Economic Advisers we shall fill a gap in the services available to the President."[9] Kennedy personally telegraphed Heller's selection of James Tobin and Kermit Gordon urging them to accept membership on the Council.

The swell of enthusiasm and drive emanating from the youthful administration's slogan of "getting the country moving again" infected the members of the Council. Ten days after taking office Kennedy proposed a "Program for Economic Recovery and Growth" which had been quickly drawn up for his use during several tiring, intensive all-night Council meetings.

The Council was steeped in Keynesian economic theory. Contrary to what followed twenty years later with Ronald Reagan and his supply-side economics, this Council perceived prosperity as coming from the demand side. It advocated increased government spending, lower taxes, lower interest rates and easier money. It stressed the concept of a balanced economy rather than a balanced budget. Here the Council came into conflict with the Treasury Department which strongly opposed deficit spending. By 1963 due to the Council's acceptance of over-optimistic predictions of revenue at a time of rising expenditures, the year ended with a sizable deficit. The disagreement with the Treasury dissolved, however, and it finally agreed to a lowering of tax rates to help the economy even at the expense of continuing deficits.

The continuous advocacy of tax reduction as a means to increase purchasing power and employment finally bore fruit in 1964. Despite a need for more revenue rather than less, Congress heeded economic advice and made a radical reduction of tax rate schedules for all individuals and also reduced the basic corporation tax rate. The Treasury Department originally opposed it but finally acquiesced.

The Heller Council had great impact on the workings of the Kennedy Administration. During the Kennedy years the Council may have achieved its greatest acceptance. One of the many reasons was the strength, ability and professionalism of members of the Council such as James Tobin, Kermit Gordon, John P. Lewis and Gardner Ackley. There was competition for different ideas and different approaches from the Treasury, the Federal Reserve and the Bureau of the Budget, but the CEA more than held its own. Heller and Secretary of the Treasury Dillon had important differing views on many of the day's problems but their mutual respect for each other prohibited acrimony and promoted harmony.

Economic actions evolved by Kennedy's economic team included a program of slum clearing, accelerated housing, extension of unemployment insurance benefits, aid to dependent children of the unemployed, area development programs, relief for farmers and accelerated expenditures of previously approved federal programs.

The Johnson Council

When assassination ended the Kennedy era, it brought to the White House an entirely different presidential personality and a very different perspective. Heller achieved fine working rapport with Lyndon Johnson and his "Great Society", but in 1964 he completed his term and went back to the University of Minnesota. Gardner Ackley who had served for two years under Heller was appointed Chairman and helped advance the ambitious economic aspirations of the new President for almost four years.

Johnson's vision was a challenge to economic policy. In a 1964 speech at the University of Michigan, he emphasized that economic policy must support human compassion in the attack on poverty, and that while economic policy cannot make men wise, sympathetic and cultured, it can find ways to finance their schools, libraries, museums and galleries.[10]

This invigorated declaration of aims was not new to the Council. In 1962 it opened its Annual Report as follows:

> The Report of the Council of Economic Advisers is a document directed towards economic problems and national economic policy. It is written in keen awareness that the ultimate goals of the Nation are human goals, and that economics is merely instrumental to the making of a better life for all Americans.[11]

In 1964, taxes were reduced to spur a declining expansion. By 1966 the Report proudly noted a rise in living standards, an unemployment rate of 4.1%, the lowest since the mid 1950s, and the price structure under control.

However, attention was given to the situation in Vietnam, the rising military requirements and the economic dangers emanating from them. Warning was given that the stimulative policies must now be moderated or restrained in order to avoid an inflationary wage/price spiral. Recommendations were made concerning excise taxes, timing of tax payments and an indication that fiscal and monetary policies might need to be utilized for this purpose.

The aims of the Great Society and the war on poverty, however, put great pressure on the American economy. The avowed belief that the country could have both guns and butter brought burgeoning deficits and a vast expansion of the money supply. As the Vietnam War escalated and expenditures for expanded domestic programs increased, there was tremendous strain on the nation's economic structure. The demand on the labor force to meet this surge of activity could not easily be met nor could the existing factories working at almost full capacity meet the requirements of the day. The inevitable result was a rapid rise in the price level for all goods and services.

Lyndon Johnson's energy, arm-twisting and determination of purpose had their way, and the years 1965–1968 saw increasing budget deficits, spiraling prices and wages and ever-mounting inflation. Such policies do create less unemployment but the price is a high one that has great implications for the future.

Back in 1962 the Council of Economic Advisers had created a system of wage/price guideposts which it hoped would maintain some degree of stability in the economy. They were complicated in that hourly wages would be tied in with average long-term gain in output per man-hour. There were many exceptions, more or less educational in nature, and they were actually voluntary, with no effort for governmental enforcement, except in some federal contracts. However, the pressures on the economy by the Johnson administration were such that it was recognized that this system of price and wage regulation was not working and by 1966 it succumbed to the deluge of inflationary pressures.

It is important to note that the chairman and the members of the CEA are not really their own men. Whatever their desire to do a good job, they are beholden to the President who appointed them and they are part of his team, aware of his policies and intent. While the Chairman has the advantage of direct access to the President, the latter has many other economic advisors who often are in a position to influence him. These come from the staffs of the Treasury, the OMB, the Departments of Agriculture, Interior, Commerce, Health, Education and Welfare and a myriad of other bureaus who see economic needs from their own varied, and often conflicting, points of view.

Theoretically the CEA stands above these narrow, segregated advocacies. It is supposed to advise the President independently and impartially, avoiding the pressure of these special, selfish interests, however important they may be to their champions. Politics often rears its ugly head, and what is advisable frequently must give way to what is practical. Then again there is the Federal Reserve Board with its vast powers, actually independent of the President, with the ability to act contrary to what is seemingly in the President's best political interest. The limitations of the Council of Economic Advisers must be kept in mind but they do not minimize its importance.

When Gardner Ackley resigned as chairman in February 1968 he was replaced by Arthur M. Okun who held the office until Johnson left the White House one year later. Incoming President Nixon appointed Paul W. McCracken of the University of Michigan as the new chairman.

Before leaving office, Johnson finally took steps to control the runaway economy. What was called a temporary tax increase was enacted and the Revenue and Expenditure Control Act of 1968 brought about a slight surplus for the 1969 fiscal year. The Federal Reserve Board also helped alleviate the situation by clamping down on monetary expansion. However, no wage/price controls were instituted, economists having noted that they had not accomplished their purpose very successfully in the past, other than during World War II when patriotism was the moving spirit.

The Nixon Council

The new President had as his inheritance the budget deficits, the emotional and financial drain of the unpopular Vietnam War, recently enacted expensive social programs which required sustenance, and a huge volume of money in circulation which was feeding the fourth year of rapid inflation. There was no apparent end to this inflationary cycle. Workers were demanding large pay increases to match the rise in the cost of living and to protect themselves against expected future increases. At the same time, industry, expecting costs to increase, tried to meet the impact of inflation by making plant investments now at high interest rates for borrowed money, hoping to make repayment in the future with cheaper money as the inflation took its toll. This certainly was not the scenario for a healthy economy.

The years 1969 and 1970 were years of trying to battle and restrain this relentless surge of higher prices, higher labor costs and budget deficits. Its success was analogous to the Dutch boy trying to hold back the flood by putting a finger into a hole in the dyke.

During 1971, the Council helped formulate and implement what was probably the most far reaching economic policy since FDR's New Deal. Working extensively not only behind the scenes but at public meetings with the Cost of Living Council, the Joint Economic Committee, the Treasury and the Office of Management and Budget, among others, the Council's activities resulted in the President announcing a New Economic Policy on August 15, 1971.

Its purpose, nothing new but much more extensive and direct, was to halt the rise in prices and wages, and while bolstering domestic economic activity also stimulating international economic activity. Prices, wages and rents were frozen for ninety days, after which there would be instituted a more flexible and comprehensive system of mandatory controls. At the same time the President suspended the convertibility of the dollar into gold, and placed a 10% surcharge on imported goods. As an aid domestically, a series of tax cuts were made. This was strong medicine for the Council and the President, but the New Economic Policy was adopted only after much consideration and consultation with a myriad of governmental and private agencies.

A revealing insight into the internal operations of the CEA is provided in a section of the Economic Report for 1971, entitled "Report to the President on the Activities of the Council of Economic Advisers During 1971."[12] The Council recognized that its major responsibilities were to "provide the President with information and analysis of economic conditions, to evaluate economic policy, and to make recommendations designed to foster the goals of the Employment Act of 1946 . . . , to promote maximum employment, production and purchasing power." This was a time of great activity for the Council. It rendered to the President formal opinions on over two hundred bills going through the Congressional mill, and examined the impact of political actions on such diverse areas as energy, international trade, transportation, the environment, research and development and the problems of communities suddenly bereft of defense contracts.

The Chairman of the CEA coordinated the activities of the newly formed Cabinet Committee on Economic Policy, and served on a multitude of committees covering a broad range of government activities, both foreign and domestic. Over 50,000 copies of the annual Economic Report were distributed, and its statistical office prepared the monthly Economic Indicators issued by the Joint Economic Committee. Public contact was made through meetings with academicians, business leaders and labor economists, and Council members and Senior Staff Economists gave speeches on economic matters in various parts of the country.

The Chairman was in direct personal contact with the President and represented the Council at Cabinet meetings. The other two members of the Council supervised and directed the work of the professional staff which at that time numbered fourteen senior staff economists, two statisticians, five junior economists, two research assistants, and an administrative and secretarial staff of twenty-three. In addition, a student intern program was maintained as was a list of consultants called on when needed.

President Nixon's New Economic Policy achieved moderate success for a short period of time. The rate of unemployment fell from 6% to a little under 5% and there was a substantial increase in the Gross National Product. However, this was accompanied by a resurgence of high inflation and by the end of 1974 unemployment reached its highest level since 1958, and the nation was in the throes of both inflation and recession. Herbert Stein, who replaced Paul McCracken in January 1972, served as Chairman of the Council during these tumultuous times and his work was made even more difficult by the Energy crisis.

The Ford Council

Gerald Ford succeeded Nixon in 1974 and in his pessimistic Economic Report to the Congress cited the difficult economic problems confronting the nation in 1975 as "reflecting years of misdirection". Alan Greenspan had taken over the Council chairmanship only a month before Nixon's resignation with the dilemma of coping with the effects of OPEC and keeping the recession from developing into a full-blown depression. Several decisive steps were taken: an investment tax credit to spur purchases of capital equipment, a windfall profits tax, extension of unemployment insurance benefits, and tax cuts to stimulate the economy. Fiscal restraints were adopted, and when he left the chairmanship in January 1977, inflation which had been 11%, had been cut in half and the economy was showing a strong recovery.

The Carter Council

When James Earl Carter, Jr. assumed the Presidency, despite growth in the economy, unemployment was close to 8% and creeping inflation was continuing to be a problem. Carter appointed Charles Schultze as chairman with the usual directives to improve the economy, reduce unemployment, institute an effective Energy program and solve inflation. At this point the nation was slowly recovering from the 1974–1975 recession, the worst in forty years. However, despite anti-inflation methods such as voluntary wage and price standards, attempts at fiscal and monetary restraints and the usual tired but unsuccessful efforts of the past, 1978 saw inflation soar. Consumer prices rose from a 6¾% rate in 1977 to 9% in 1978. Wages rose unhealthily and costs of production did likewise, and by the end of the year the nation saw inflation on its way to the highest level of modern times.

A doubling of world oil prices by OPEC in 1979, a decline in productivity, and prices still climbing caused the CEA to forecast a "mild" recession in 1980, and offered the usual panaceas.

The Reagan Council

The election of Ronald Reagan in 1980 marked the beginning of an economic revolution in the United States with changes that confused some and exhilarated others. The recession the Council predicted brought a rise in unemployment, a sharp drop in the GNP, high interest rates, and the Consumer Price Index which had risen to 13½% in 1980 falling to 10.4% in 1981. Murray L. Weidenbaum was selected chairman in February 1981 and was in the midst of the change bringing supply-side economics onto the American scene, but the CEA was not included in the inner loop of policymaking. After eighteen months he left. Succeeding him was Martin S. Feldstein, a highly regarded economist whose relationship with Reagan and his chief of staff Baker was probably the worst in the history of the CEA. The burgeoning budget deficits were anathema to the chairman and he permitted his feelings to go public, angering the administration no end.

Nevertheless, after a short but deep recession, the business scene changed dramatically with a great improvement in the economy. The Tax Reform Act of 1986 was passed which reduced taxes rates for the ostensible purpose of reinvigorating the American work ethic and inducing investment. The dollar was temporarily stabilized, interest rates fell, price controls were removed, deregulation of industry was pushed, employment rose to new record levels, unemployment was reduced to 5.5%, and inflation appeared less threatening. These accomplishments were achieved at a cost which caused consternation among orthodox economists. The national debt doubled to over $2.3 trillion and the nation went from being the world's largest creditor to the world's largest debtor.

After less than two years, Feldstein expressed his discontent and fears for the economy by resigning. For a time the Administration considered abolishing the Council altogether.[13] This was not the first time that there was sentiment to do away with the CEA. In March 1953, when there was no appropriation from Congress to carry on, the newly sworn Arthur Burns had serious problems until a supplemental budget was passed.

When Feldstein left, the Reagan White House waited seven months debating what to do with the CEA before a successor was appointed. Finally, Beryl W. Sprinkel was transferred from the Treasury Department where he was under secretary. A strict monetarist, he was against the abandonment of floating exchange rates and was not in agreement with the drastic tax changes being proposed. He found the influence of the Council very much restricted as to policy. The mandates of the Employment Act of 1946 were complied with: it gathered information regarding economic developments and trends, it made the necessary studies and analyses, it cooperated with other governmental agencies on interacting agendas, and worked on the President's Annual Report. But as a strong influence on the actions of the government relative to its supply-side economics theory, it had diminished in stature.

Conclusions

During its forty-two years of existence the Council of Economic Advisers has had its successes and failures, praise and criticism, and opposition from other governmental agencies engaged in exerting influence for actions beneficial to their specific areas of responsibility. Even within the White House bureaucracy there are different viewpoints and jealousies especially at those times when the relationship between the incumbent President and the Council chairman is close and cooperative. There is a need for this close relationship. With diverse and often selfish groups

tugging at the President's coattails, it is necessary that he have
his own appointed group of advisers whose loyalty is entirely to
him — not to labor unions, the National Association of Manufacturers, defense contractors, education lobbies, and others, most
of whom are sincere and devoted to their cause. Since he appoints the members of the Council and their purpose is to provide loyal, impartial advice, it should be a comfort to him to receive such advice and compare it with the self-centered pressures
of other economic advisory organizations, most of which, as
stated, have their own particular axe to grind.

There are too many conflicting economic pressures on the
President, who, regardless of his many admirable attributes, may
not be too knowledgeable as to the effects of economic forces.
One interesting suggestion[14] is that the Council of Economic Advisers as presently constituted be replaced by a new economic
council, the candidates to which would be nominated by the
American Economics Association in the same manner as the
American Bar Association recommends judicial appointments.
The composition of the new council, to provide diversity, would
have three economists selected by each major party and any third
party receiving over 5% of the electoral votes, with one candidate selected by the President.[15] The economic council would
be given an independent locale away from the White House to
give it the appearance of independence and bipartisanship. The
present staff would be retained, but the council's policy recommendations would presumably be given greater weight.

Change over the years is inevitable. There are many who accept the current workings of the CEA as being effective in an
area where uncertainty is endemic and solutions are often prob-
lematical. Also, the power of political necessity often offsets economic realism. The CEA, as presently constructed, has had its
good years and its bad years, but it did perform its function of
advising the President. If it can be improved in any way, fine
and good, but the intentions of the reformers should be evalu-
ated with care.

CHAPTER TWENTY-ONE

Managing Transitions at the Council of Economic Advisers

RAYMOND J. SAULNIER
FORMER CHAIRMAN
PRESIDENT'S COUNCIL OF ECONOMIC ADVISERS

In the 42-year history of the Council of Economic Advisers (CEA) the transfer of agency responsibilities from one presidential administration to another has presented no difficulties except in 1953. That transition was a special case, however, and one that has often been misunderstood.

As things stood in January of 1953 the preceding Congress (the last during the Truman administration, with both House and Senate under Democratic control) had passed an appropriations bill that provided the Council with funds only through March 31, 1953, and the bill was signed into law by President Truman. The result was that, in the absence of new legislation, the CEA would have gone out of business on the March 31 date. And it has been said more than once that that was what Congress had in mind for the Council when it passed the appropriations legislation in question, and that its wish to see the Council ended was a shared by the incoming President. Here indeed was a transition problem. Why did Congress do what it did? And how, in fact, did the new President respond to it?

On the first of these questions, it is plain that some in Congress and in the public at large, and doubtless also some within the new administration, were dissatisfied with how the Council had been operating and would have preferred some other arrangement for providing the President with the economic advisory services called for in the Employment Act of 1946. And it could be that some who voted for an appropriation that would carry the CEA only to March 31, 1953 did so to force either the agency's termination or reorganization. Indeed, giving an agency an appropriation that carries it only to a date short of the end of a full fiscal year is a tactic used now and then in Congress to bring about the victim's demise as quietly and unobtrusively as possible.

But termination was not the reason why the March 31, 1953 deadline was written into the CEA bill. The reason was that there was an economy move afoot in Congress in 1952, and, like the budget for a number of other Executive Branch agencies, the CEA budget had been cut back sharply in the House, roughly by twenty-five percent; and Leon Keyserling, who was Chairman of the Council at the time, reacted to this by managing, when the appropriations bill reached the Senate, to have it modified in a manner that left unchanged the amount of funds available to be spent but shortened the allowable expenditure period to nine months from the standard twelve. In short, it was a stratagem that deflected the economy ax, at least for nine months.

True, there was the possibility that the next Congress might not be willing to extend the Council's life beyond the March 31, 1953 deadline, but that was a risk that Keyserling and his supporters in the Senate were prepared to take. (The supporters included, among others, O'Mahoney of Wyoming on the Democratic side and, on the Republican side, Robert A. Taft of Ohio, the Minority Leader.) In any case, the effect was to put the ball in the White House court. What would the incoming President do about the future of the Council beyond the March 31, 1953 deadline, if it was to have a future?

Acting with the advice especially of Gabriel Hauge, at the time Special Assistant to the President with responsibilities for economic matters, Eisenhower's response was to engage Arthur F. Burns, Professor of Economics at Columbia University, and at the time Director of Research at the National Bureau of Economic Research, to study the CEA problem and make recommendations for its resolution. However, prior to the completion of these studies, which were carried out jointly with the Bureau of the Budget (now the Office of Management and Budget), the administration went to Congress with a request for funds to carry the Council to the end of fiscal 1953. The idea of replacing the CEA with a single Economic Adviser to the President was never adopted by Eisenhower, though interest in such an arrangement was sufficiently strong in Congress that a bill creating an Office of Economic Adviser to the President was passed before the administration made any recommendations of its own; and, as an interim arrangement, Dr. Burns was appointed by President

Eisenhower to that post. In the end, however, the continuance of the Council as a three-member agency was assured when the White House, following completion of its study of the question, requested that (i) the CEA be provided with funds for the full 1954 fiscal year, and (ii) the Employment Act be amended to assign exclusive responsibility for reporting to the President and for administering the Council's affairs to the Chairman (under the Employment Act as written in 1946 these duties were shared equally by all three Council members) and to terminate the office of Vice Chairman.

There was no need for such questions to be raised in 1961, when the transition took place between Presidents Eisenhower and Kennedy. There was a budget then in place that, in the normal manner, provided the Council with funds through the full 1961 fiscal year. And budget requests delivered to Congress by President Eisenhower in January 1961 had requested the same for the 1962 fiscal year.

Accordingly, as soon as I knew who the new CEA chairman would be, which was well in advance of the January 1961 inauguration date, I invited Walter Heller, the designee, to come to the Council's office to discuss transition business. Apart from a few housekeeping matters, there was little to talk about. There would be a few staff vacancies to be filled, as some economists who were at the Council on other than a permanent civil service basis returned to their academic posts or went elsewhere in government or into the private sector. But there were other economists at the Council at the time on a permanent civil service basis, and by their agreement and with the agreement of the new Council Chairman their employment continued at the Council without interruption. Likewise, the entire staff of the Council's statistical office continued with no change, as did others on the Council's support staff.

The new administration made certain changes in 1961 in the way the Council conducted its business: among other things it terminated the Advisory Board on Economic Growth and Stability and certain other standing groups, including the Cabinet Committee on Small Business. But every administration makes certain structural and procedural changes to suit its own taste and style and to facilitate the conduct of the programs it intends to install. In all basic organizational and administrative respects the CEA continued in 1961 in general unchanged.

And so it has been in all subsequent transitions, of which there have been five. And there is no reason to believe it will be otherwise in the sixth. Of course, it will not necessarily always be thus, but transitions at the CEA, where the function of the agency is advisory and not programmatic, should normally go smoothly.

Changing Markets

RICHARD ROSE

DIRECTOR, CENTRE FOR THE STUDY OF PUBLIC POLICY
UNIVERSITY OF STRATHCLYDE
GLASGOW, SCOTLAND

> No President can have an economic policy; all his policies
> must be political.
>
> Richard E. Neustadt

In the marketplace of politics, payday is the first Wednesday after
the first Tuesday in November, when two candidates who have
invested years campaigning for the White House learn which
has won the jackpot in a high-stakes competition for the
confidence of millions of voters. The winner does not abandon
the practice of politics just because he has won the election, but
the President-elect also faces new responsibilities where the outcomes are calculated in tens or hundreds of billions of dollars
in federal deficits, borrowing and interest payments, hundreds
of billions of dollars in taxes and appropriations, and trillions
of dollars of activity in the economy.

Being President requires a politician to change markets; although votes count, resources decide. Many things that a President would like to do, such as bolstering the nation's defense,
increasing social security benefits for the elderly and the sick,
and cutting taxes, require tens or hundreds of billions of dollars.
When the economy is buoyant, a President can enunciate policies without pain, financing the cost of additional spending or
tax cuts with the greater revenue brought in by the growth of
a boom economy. However, if the economy is in trouble, then
a President faces painful choices about cutting spending without
cutting taxes, or raising taxes without providing more benefits,
or raising taxes and cutting spending. If the economy is in a mess,
a President cannot expect to have his stock rate high in the electoral marketplace.[1]

In 1988 the concern of candidates with winning votes leads
them to avoid discussions of the economy or endorse vague gener-

alities, such as pledges to cut waste, as if waste were an easily
identified line in the budget, or stop tax evasion, as if people
who for years had escaped the IRS could easily be tracked down.
A candidate who becomes specific, for example, pledging new
spending benefits, invites embarrassing questions about his plans
to raise taxes to finance these benefits. A candidate promising
to cut taxes will be accused of wanting to weaken the nation's
defenses or cut social security benefits through consequential
budget reductions. A hopeful who announces that there is a need
to increase taxes, as Bruce Babbitt of Arizona did, may win the
plaudits of commentators, but very few votes in the primaries.

Changing markets must start before the election winner is inaugurated ten weeks after polling day, for bankers and businessmen from Frankfurt and Boston to New York and Tokyo will
begin to make decisions in the light of what they expect the new
President to do once in office.[2] Decisions taken from November
to January will influence the economy before the President's first
budget is due in February. The first thing a President-elect must
do is understand the state of the economy that he inherits, and
the resources that are at hand, both personal and institutional.
In a world in which economic interdependence means that
foreigners no longer give an uncritical vote of confidence in the
dollar, a President-elect must convince a watching world that
the measures that he takes not only make sense in vote-catching
terms, but also in terms of dollars, Deutsche Marks and Yen.

The Starting Point

There is widespread agreement among politicians about the goals
of economic policy. Economic growth is good, inflation is bad,
and unemployment and a big deficit in international trade are
also undesirable. Differences of opinion usually concern the priority to be given each of these goals. In the heyday of Keynesian
economics in the 1960s, there was a widespread belief in government and in universities that government could manage the
economy to produce success on all four counts. Today, there is
neither consensus nor confidence about the impact of government upon the economy.

The central political questions are both normative—What
should the President do about the economy?—and instrumental—
What can he do? The Constitution requires the federal govern-

ment to see that taxes are levied and collected for the common defence and general welfare of the United States. When the federal government spends more than 20 per cent of the national product, its role is far more than that of a passive nightwatchman in the American economy. A contemporary President is expected to give a lead to Congress on economic policy, and to the international economy, and his moves are scrutinized critically by those who watch the money markets on every continent.

Political calculations are central in determining what the President does, and this is as it should be. When the country cannot simultaneously enjoy growth, price stability, low unemployment and a trade surplus, deciding between these competing goals is a legitimate function of government. The dominance of politics can be demonstrated by comparing how a President and his economic advisers are likely to evaluate an issue. A President must view all economic proposals in terms of political implications. By contrast, an economist thinks first of the costs and benefits of putting a policy into effect. When the President and his economic advisers agree that a policy is desirable or both consider it undesirable, the President can follow his political instincts, and economic advisers will support his action with technical arguments. However, when economic advice points in a politically undesirable direction — for example, raising taxes — the President is likely to ignore such advice because it is politically undesirable. A President can endorse a politically attractive course of action even though economists regard the technical arguments as dubious, for example the supply-side advice to cut taxes offered to President Reagan in 1981. A President is predisposed to dismiss proposals that may be economically rational but politically undesirable.[3]

The state of the economy reflects what happens in markets in which political desires are not sufficient to produce what the White House wants. The state of the economy reflects the interaction between what government does, what happens in the national economy, and what happens in the international economy, including random and unpredictable events. Actions of business, unions, workers and consumers impose constraints upon the policies of a modern President. The international system is an increasingly important constraint too. A contemporary President cannot make the American economy boom in the midst of a world recession, or expect the rest of the world to finance the federal deficit without receiving something in return. Every time the President seeks an economic benefit, he must also pay a political cost.

In theory, managing the economy resembles managing a space ship. It is assumed that economics is a science like astrophysics, and that economists agree about where they want the economy to go, just as space crews agree about the destination of their mission. If these assumptions are accepted, it is a relatively straightforward task to manipulate the dials that steer the economy so that it will arrive at the desired destination. The basic problem with this theory is that it is a model for policymaking in outer space; it omits such earthlings as politicians. On earth, politicians must be incorporated as part of the process — if only as the joker in the pack.[4]

The first lesson that economic advisers teach a President-elect is: There is no such thing as a free lunch. While computer models of the American economy are today far more sophisticated than two decades ago, the actual outcomes are less attractive. Inflation and unemployment have at times risen together to produce "stagflation". Even when the economy has grown in the 1980s, deficits in the federal budget have risen to unprecedented heights. The United States has run up a mammoth trade deficit with the rest of the world, and the value of the dollar depends not only upon what Americans do but also upon what foreign central bankers and speculators do.

The second lesson is that there is neither agreement nor certainty among economists about what should be or can be done. Economists disagree in diagnosing the nature of the economic problems facing the United States, and in prescribing what the government should try to do. The President faces a choice between economic ideologies with contrasting assumptions about how the economy works. The choice ranges widely from the established views of the neo-Keynesians to the supply-side economics of Congressman Jack Kemp and economist Arthur Laffer. There is no consensus among economists about which perspective is most appropriate. Major universities award top posts to Keynesian and anti-Keynesian economists. The Swedes display their political neutrality by giving Nobel Prizes to economists of each faction.

As unexpected and puzzling problems arise in the economy, successive Chairmen of the President's Council of Economic Advisers (CEA) have been increasingly articulate about the fact that economics is not a science producing predictable results, like aeronautical engineering leading to flights in space. It is a social science, in which the relationship between abstract theories and actual events is a matter of probabilities. Consider the following comments[5] by former chairmen of the CEA:

> Models are bankrupt; they pay little attention to the real world. (Arthur Burns)
> We don't know as much as we used to think we knew. (Arthur Okun)
> Our experience really confirmed how little economists know, especially in the rather new conditions we face. (Herbert Stein)

The bottom line for politicians is: "Economists cannot deliver what politics requires".[6]

Resources of the Presidency

As long as votes are the medium of exchange, a new President is his own best asset, for election victory gives him a high credit rating in Congress, which can be used to secure legislation early in his term of office. When national economic indicators are the measure of success, the value of a President falls sharply, because a President knows little about how an economy works, or even about the institutions of economic policymaking. Presidential rhetoric (or gaffes) can influence confidence in the economy, but White House public relations efforts cannot hide hard evidence of a recession or inflation. Even if Americans are impressed by TV film clips of the President appearing presidential, there is little reason why foreign bankers should regard this as more important than evidence registered in America's balance of payments deficit, or by their own measures, whether expressed in dollars, Deutsche Marks or Yen.

Campaigning for the Presidency has a high opportunity cost for the President-elect. The time devoted to campaigning for the nomination, and then for the White House is time not available to learn about the business of government. By contrast, leaders of parliamentary systems such as Britain, France, Germany and Japan have normally spent years in government office, often in the ministry of finance, the central department dealing with economic issues. In France and Japan, before entering electoral politics many Premiers have also served in economic ministries as senior civil servants. Before becoming Prime Minister a European or Japanese politician will have participated in Cabinet decisions about reconciling spending and taxing totals, and trading off domestic goals against international pressures.[7]

No post-war candidate for the Presidency has ever had any hands-on experience in making national economic policy. State Governors deal with state budgets, but the scale and impact of state spending is less than the impact of federal spending within their state. A Governor has no influence over the national or international economy. He is accustomed to meeting members of the National Governors Association, and not Federal Reserve Board's governors. Nor does a state Governor have any experience of dealing with the interconnections between national economic concerns and international relations from Tokyo to Bonn to Moscow.

A Member of Congress who moves to the White House is likely to have some familiarity with the budget process, and the political significance of a single line-item for particular issues or Congressional districts. Until the adoption of the Gramm-Rudman-Hollings Act in 1985, Congress had virtually no concern with the "bottom line" figure that constituted the collective outcome of line-item choices. Even today, Congress and the White House often prefer to game the budget deficit, rather than treat hundreds of billions of borrowing and tens of billions of debt interest payments as serious business. A Vice President has the worst of both worlds, lacking the influence of Congressional committee members, and rarely being involved by the President or executive branch colleagues in serious discussions of the economy.

The President-elect can turn to four institutions at hand, collectively described as the Quadriad: the Council of Economic Advisers, concerned with such broad macro-economic issues as economic growth and inflation; the Office of Management and Budget, which prepares the federal budget on behalf of the President; the Treasury Department, particularly concerned with taxation and international economic policy; and the Federal Reserve Board, the government's central bank. As part of the Executive Office of the President, the CEA and OMB are closest to the Oval Office. But while they have the President's ear, they do not have their hands on the action. CEA's role is purely advisory, and OMB is principally concerned with making recommendations that Congress can accept or treat as dead on arrival. *Because* they are outside the White House, the Treasury and the Fed have their hands on important levers in the economy. Given four disparate institutions with inter-acting concerns, the challenge to the President is to see that the Quadriad is four horses pulling together rather than pulling apart.

Like most institutions in the Executive Office of the President, the Council of Economic Advisers depends for influence upon winning the confidence of the President, and this means providing the President with help in dealing with the political world as it is seen from the Oval Office. The CEA's primary technical concern is monitoring the state of the economy in order to see what problems are emerging that may require government action, and assessing the implications of policy proposals for the economy. It also prepares forecasts of economic trends, from which can be derived estimates of likely tax revenue, spending levels and the budget deficit, and these estimates are important constraints upon the making of the federal budget for the year ahead.

While CEA staff are highly regarded professional economists, their knowledge and ideas are only relevant insofar as the President is informed about their thinking, understands what they say, and regards CEA advice as helpful in addressing his problems. Since Walter Heller became prominent in fronting as well as formulating policies of the Kennedy and Johnson administrations, CEA chairmen have increasingly assumed a public political role as advocates of policies. This increases their potential for political influence, but it also increases their risk of rejection on political grounds.[8] For example, President Reagan's first two chairs of the CEA, Murray Weidenbaum and Martin Feldstein, each resigned the job because they disagreed with what they considered was the President's pre-logical approach to the economy.

The director of the Office of Management & Budget tries to add up numbers that do not add up, the departmental requests for money to spend on next year's programs, which normally are well in excess of total tax revenue plus whatever the White House considers an acceptable level of borrowing to finance the deficit at the bottom line of the budget. Budgeting is about politics as well as money, for it concerns the reconciliation of competing claims of spending departments for large but finite federal funds.[9] The staff of OMB constitutes the only sizeable pool of non-partisan expertise in the Executive Office of the President. Budget examiners have years of experience with particular agencies, programs and Congressional committees. If the White House wants to, it can make use of this collective knowledge to re-design or cut programs.

The separation of powers limits the influence of OMB, for unlike an equivalent agency in a parliamentary system, the budget that it recommends does not become law. It is no more and no less than a set of recommendations to Congress, which has the power to determine taxes and votes appropriations for programs. Upwards of 90 per cent of the money in the budget is "uncontrollable", that is, expenditure mandated by laws enacted long before a new President enters office, such as social security; by commitments of a previous administration, such as interest payments on the debt; or by defense procurement contracts and the salaries of career military personnel. The President's room for maneuver in budgeting may affect 5 or 10 per cent of federal spending, the equivalent to more than $50 or $100 billion. It leaves more than $900 billion in spending carried forward by the force of inertia.

In the government of most advanced industrial nations, being in charge of the Treasury is one of the top jobs of government, and it can be a stepping stone to becoming Prime Minister. For example, the British Chancellor of the Exchequer, the politician in charge of the Treasury there, is responsible for the macroeconomic forecasting policies of the CEA; decisions about spending in the budget undertaken by OMB; taxation and relations with other nations, a responsibility of the US Treasury; and can influence the Bank of England, which is less distant from the executive branch than is the Federal Reserve Board. Furthermore, he is normally a contender to be the next Prime Minister.

In Washington the Secretary of the Treasury has been seen as a buffer, protecting the White House from involvement in economic problems and interest group concerns. The Secretary has been the President's representative to the banking community and Wall Street. In a Democratic Administration this qualification may make an individual suspect to some liberals on the White House staff. A Treasury Secretary usually has no political credentials of his own, and holds no other job in Washington. The autonomy of the job makes it attractive to a banker but the independence of the Treasury from the White House also means that the Secretary of the Treasury is in danger of being ignored when he wants the President's ear.

The White House normally has no senior staff person interested in and well informed about the technical concerns of the Treasury with tax policies, and the international monetary system. White House staff are inclined to see economic issues as political problems. Technical studies by Treasury staff of taxation are not so relevant to pending legislation as are estimates by the President's Congressional liaison staff of what Members of Congress will endorse if the President puts it forward. CEA staff understand what the Treasury is about, but they have their own political position to consider. A CEA Chairman will be more concerned with "big picture" considerations of macro-economic policy than with the day-to-day operational anxieties of the Treasury. Nor will a CEA Chairman want to use his limited political influence with the President to fight another organization's battle. Technical tax issues of concern to interest groups and Congress can be resolved by Treasury officials within sub-governments at no cost to the President in time or political capital.

The Treasury has risen in importance with the decline of the dollar internationally, for the Secretary of the Treasury is the frontline defender of the dollar.[10] In 1971 John Connally achieved brief prominence by taking the dollar off gold and devaluing it. Connally's action reflected America's capacity to use its political power to impose economic outcomes abroad. In the 1980s James A. Baker, III has been in a different position, seeking cooperation from foreign governments, especially Germany and Japan, in actions intended to reduce America's trade deficit. When Baker has been asked by foreign governments to do something about the federal budget deficit, there is little he can say, for making the budget is not a responsibility of the Treasury.

Like it or not, every President has to live with a banker, namely, the Chairman of the Federal Reserve Board, which engages in financial activities on behalf of the government, and funds the government's operating deficits. While the Federal Reserve is involved in highly technical operations, its responsibility for the money supply and interest rates makes its actions have very visible political consequences affecting house prices, the cost of buying a car, economic growth and employment. While the Fed likes to treat its activities as technical and non-political, they also concern the political priorities of the President. Since academic theories about the impact of the Fed's monetary policies upon the economy have increasingly been subject to dispute, decision-making on monetary policy may be described as "an arena for resolving academic disputes by political means".[11]

The Federal Reserve Board is insulated from the White House, because the Chairman of the Fed is appointed for a four-year term of office, and invariably has several years to run on his term when a new President enters office. Moreover, the Fed is wide open to pressures from the marketplace. If the interest rate that it offers to purchasers of U.S. Treasury bonds is not high enough, it will have trouble financing public expenditure, and if its economic policies are deemed unsatisfactory internationally, this affects the value of the dollar in international trade. Because the Fed is concerned with foreign exchange, it is in regular communication with major foreign central banks, and its New York office is continuously monitoring exchange rates as they float up and down in international money markets.

While in theory the Fed is independent of both Congress and the President, it cannot carry out its responsibilities in isolation from other Washington institutions concerned with the sub-government of money, including the White House, Congress and the Treasury, and such non-government institutions as American and foreign banks, international investors and speculators, and free-floating economists with ideas. The President and the Chairman of the Federal Reserve normally try to accommodate their actions to each other and there are advantages for the White House in the Fed being seen as responsible for politically unpopular measures, such as increases in interest rates.

With experience, a President learns to juggle many problems with which the CEA, OMB, the Treasury and the Fed deal. Non-intervention is one way in which to respond to the complexities of economic policymaking. This allows individuals with strong personalities and political skills to exercise influence, and run political risks. If the results are successful, the President can share in the credit and if they are not, then others can take all the blame. A President can intervene selectively in the process of making economic policy, as President Reagan has done in vetoing tax increases favored by many economists and consistent with the Gramm-Rudman-Hollings Act. When a President does decide to intervene on an economic issue, he has typically "relied on a trusted adviser or group of advisers settling many issues bilaterally with the interested parties".[12]

The immediate problem of a President-elect is that he has yet to gain the experience necessary to understand how to work an economic policy process that is complex and unfamiliar. In time, this experience can be gained. But time is money, and the cost of a President's education can be substantial. This is particularly true when the economy is in transition, and decisions influencing it must be taken before a President-elect has been sworn in as President. Yet the President-elect cannot ignore what is happening in the economic marketplace, for if he does not exert influence, then others will, at home and abroad.

A Beginner in the Market Place

When a new President enters office he is a fresh face viewing old problems. The value of the dollar in international trade has been of concern for a decade, first because it was very high and then because it fell to a low point against the Japanese Yen and the German Deutsche Mark. Deficits are familiar in Washington, but it is new to have deficits run well above $100 billion a year, and especially to have a large portion of the deficit financed by foreign lenders. The trade concerns that will face the President the day after inauguration in January 1989 are a well publicized creation of the Reagan years. The alternatives for dealing with deficits, such as increasing taxes, cutting expenditure or both, are not novel.

Hitting the ground running is a difficult challenge for any new President and it is doubly difficult when the President is an absolute beginner, as is the case in dealing with the politics of the economy. As a prisoner of first-things-first, a President-elect must respond to action-forcing events and deadlines. A President-elect will have no shortage of things that must be done in the ten weeks between winning office and actually taking office on Inauguration Day. The quieter the economy is, the better it is for a politician intent on other priorities.[13]

Markets are open every day, and the internationalization of currency flows and stock dealings from New York to London and Tokyo means that the dollar can plummet or share values fall while Wall Street is literally asleep. Between the election of a new President and his inauguration, there are ten weeks of dealing, in which foreign banks can, if they want, sell America short in fear of the consequence for their pocketbooks of what our President does. In the same period, foreign investors can push share prices up or push the Dow-Jones average down, or even do both, depending upon the degree of their confidence in the economic policies to be adopted after Inauguration. While scholars of transition have devoted attention to considering problems facing the nation if a foreign policy crisis arose between election day and inauguration day,[14] virtually no attention has been given to how to handle a major economic crisis during this interregnum.

Even if stability in the market produces no pressure for prompt action, there is immediate need to concentrate upon the budget recommendations that the new President must put to Congress in February. Making a budget requires a series of inter-related steps that normally take twelve months to complete. A President-elect must compress the process into less than 16 weeks, and for most of that time neither he nor his staff are in command of the departments critically involved in the budget process. Yet a President-elect cannot let inertia determine the content of his first budget; doing so would make him simply a passenger on the ship of state, and he is likely to have ideas about ways in which spending and taxing priorities ought to be altered. But testing whether these ideas make sense in dollars-and-cents budget calculations is a challenging task. One of the first lessons that a President-elect learns about the budget is that pledges that sound good on the campaign trail often do not make sense in terms of budget arithmetic.

A President-elect must begin learning about the budget promptly, for the markets are watching closely for signals about the direction in which the budget will lean, and their expectations then influence what the President can do. What is it rational for the market to expect of a new President? The Reagan Administration leaves behind an ambiguous legacy. Budget-making was politically rational, for the White House and Congress were anxious to blame each other and avoid blame themselves for anything that might go wrong with the economy. Autumn, 1987 provides a precedent for a worst-case analysis. Congress had refused to enact a budget by the start of the financial year on October 1st, and federal agencies had to be financed by temporary appropriations. The estimated deficit exceeded the Gramm-Rudman ceiling for the year ahead, and threatened $23 billion in arbitrary spending cuts if Congress and the White House could not agree. Black Monday on Wall Street shook the world's confidence in the American economy, but the White House and Congress continued political business as usual. For example, a $29 million budget saving was claimed by requiring truth in frozen pizza marketing, on the grounds that federal cheese subsidies would fall in consequence of requiring frozen pizza manufacturers to label products as artificial cheese if they did not use real cheese. With the aid of continuing resolutions and by working over a weekend, when the government could not be in default because banks were closed, Congress finally enacted a budget at 4 a.m. on December 22.

In Washington, the ability of Congress and the President to agree upon the federal budget three months after the start of the financial year and a month after arbitrary cuts were meant to start was hailed as an achievement of the political process. One official told a journalist from abroad: "You Europeans just don't understand how a real democracy works". But one-liners that can stop criticism in the nation's capital are inadequate to answer the questions posed by international markets from London and Zurich to Tokyo and Hong Kong. The chief international economist of Goldman Sachs, an old line New York investment house, drew a different moral for people whose business is dealing in dollars:

> When it gets down to the nitty gritty, the bottom line is that America can't make major budget decisions. This may be democracy gone wrong. The nonsense of what is proposed is flashed across the screen and feeds sceptical markets each day. The markets are so unsure of what will go through that they are not going to give the dollar the benefit of the doubt.[15]

A President-elect can promise a watching world that there must be a better way than this to give direction to the world's largest economy, and in principle this is true. But a President-elect must move quickly, and there is neither time nor tolerance for mistakes. In little more than ten weeks a President must take four major steps in making economic policy. While the four can be analyzed separately, their interconnections are such that they all must be dealt with simultaneously, and dealt with while other matters are making pre-emptive claims for attention.

The first need of a President-elect is to gain an appreciation of the economic problems facing the country. It is particularly difficult to do so today because many features of the national and international economy are puzzling, and reputable economists often disagree. While a President-elect does not want to become engaged in academic controversies he does need to understand the immediate yet relatively abstract connections between different sectors of the economy—the budget, interest rates, trade, exchange rates, economic growth, inflation, and unemployment—and the interconnection between domestic and international measures in an increasingly interdependent world economy. A President-elect has no shortage of advisers and transition staff willing to tutor him in a subject to which he has previously devoted little time or thought. The difficulty is finding time to get to the bottom of a subject that is intrinsically complex. If a President-elect decides to ignore the economy, when the markets learn this they may react nervously in ways that compel his attention.

The good news for an incoming President is that there is scope for choice in economic policy. The bad news is that every policy has costs as well as benefits, and the price of dealing with the country's economic difficulties is rising all the time. The trillion dollars that have been added to the budget deficit during the Reagan Administration impose extra interest charges of $60 billion or more on the federal budget. Foreign borrowing to finance the budget deficit and the trade deficit imposes further costs. A trade deficit of the order of $150 billion a year can be reduced, but not overnight, and while money owed foreign banks can be repaid, this too takes time, given present levels of deficit.

As the President-elect gains understanding, his second priority becomes the development of a political strategy identifying the means and ends for dealing with the economic problems facing him. Is the new President to make economic growth his first target, or do something about the trade and budget deficit, or give first priority to fighting inflation or else unemployment? Whatever the desired goal, the President-elect must assess the political acceptability of the policy measures needed to advance toward his goal, and the costs of ignoring other concerns. The computerized design of an economic policy is simple by comparison with the development of a strategy that Congress, the Treasury and the Federal Reserve must implement, and that will also require the co-operation of national markets, foreign central banks and the international money market, and the support of American public opinion.

Appointing people to carry out an economic strategy is logically the third step in changing markets, but the transition pressures are such that appointing a Secretary of the Treasury, director of the Office of Management & Budget and Chairman of the CEA can be the decisions that force the President to express his strategy for dealing with the economy. There is nothing to stop a President-elect from viewing these appointments like conventional political plums to be distributed in ways that will best satisfy important political constituencies. For example, a Secretary of the Treasury may be appointed because he has the confidence of Wall Street, where the President tends to be friendless. The director of OMB may be appointed because of his knowledge of the budget and of Congress (David Stockman), or because of personal friendship with the President (Burt Lance, under Jimmy Carter).

The Chairman of the CEA is normally an academic economist with some political contacts. Appointing a Chairman who speaks for the Keynesian approach to the economy may make sense to a President concerned with balancing conflicting points of view — but not to Wall Streeters looking for monetarist policies. Appointing a monetarist from Chicago risks alienating neo-Keynesians, who remain influential in thinking about economic policy. If America were still a closed economy, the President could appoint people with conflicting views, using the clash of opinions between them to test the political attractiveness of different ideas. But disagreements that appear normal in Washington may appear abroad as evidence of confusion or indecisiveness to the disadvantage of the President and of the American economy.

Most Presidents have not thought it necessary to have in the west wing of the White House a trusted adviser to consult or advise about economic problems on a day to day basis, as the President's national security adviser does. The reason is simple: a President rarely wants to keep in day to day touch with the economy. The normal procedure is that the President receives frequent memoranda from his CEA Chairman, the budget director and the Treasury Secretary, but does not invest a large amount of time in face-to-face meetings, or in committee meetings to debate difficult technical issues. National security concerns are normally the first priority of the President, and there are enough of these to keep the President occupied for most of the week. As economic problems become of greater concern in relations with other nations, with Congress, and public opinion, then the President may well decide that it is desirable to give greater attention to economic matters, and this will either lead to a substantial change in the role of the Chairman of the CEA, or to the introduction to the west wing of an interagency coordinator of the President's economic policies.[16]

The 1980–81 Reagan transition illustrates the importance for policy of the sequence in which individuals are appointed. David Stockman, the new budget director, was in place and securing Presidential endorsement for budget cuts before many heads of spending departments were appointed. Given Ronald Reagan's political priorities, a strategy in which a champion of spending cuts was given the initiative made good sense.

The next President may choose different priorities, or be forced to do so by events. Insofar as the dollar's position in the world economy is defined as the central strategic question, then the appointment of a Secretary of the Treasury is the critical first step, for Treasury works with the Federal Reserve and with central banks and finance ministries abroad to maintain a viable position for the dollar. A President-elect may think it desirable to make the Chairman of the Council of Economic Advisers the point man of the economy, since he or she is within the Executive Office. But this is not practicable, for the Chairman's role is only advisory; he cannot give direction to the budget director or the Secretary of the Treasury, let alone to the Chairman of the Federal Reserve Board. A CEA chairman is most effective when advising the President or amplifying Oval Office views. If difficult decisions are anticipated, a President-elect may well want the Treasury Secretary and the Chairman of the Fed to be the lead people in a field in which unpopular decisions are likely to be frequent.

The ultimate challenge to the President is to win support for his goals and strategy from Congress, the American people, and internationally, three very different audiences that each need convincing by different means. Without the support of Congress, the President's budget recommendations will falter, and he will be seen to be weak in the Washington community. The support of public opinion is important electorally, and can be used to influence Congress to do what the White House wants. Public opinion is also important insofar as many activities in the market, from decisions about corporate investment to purchases by ordinary households and wage demands by workers, are influenced by their expectations of what is happening in the economy. People who do not have confidence in what the President is doing can vote with their feet and pocketbooks against his economic policies. Foreigners have an even wider range of options, for the American economy is only part of their sphere of business, and the dollar is not their prime concern. There are some foreign investors who hope to profit from America's difficulties, increasing imports to the United States if the dollar soars in value, or buying American companies and real estate if the dollar plummets in value. The less the intangible confidence generated by the White House, the greater the material concessions it must make.

Every politician making the transition from being a candidate to being President is vulnerable. Veteran Presidency-watcher Richard Neustadt characterizes an incoming President as full of "ignorance and hopefulness; the ignorance is tinged with ignorance, the hopefulness with arrogance".[17] The President's responsibilities for the economy do not involve risks as high as those for national security in a thermonuclear age. Economic mistakes can be costly, but not catastrophic. However, even seemingly small mistakes involve tens or hundreds of billions of dollars. Because markets are continuously active, a President who makes mistakes in his early days in office may recover once he has learned how to calculate in terms of the economic as well as the political marketplace. But because economic difficulties cost a President political support at home and confidence abroad, it is in his immediate political interest to keep the losses low.

To change markets to best effect a President-elect must find time to formulate a political strategy for directing the economy in the weeks between winning election and arriving in office to find that bills are now due for past borrowing as well as for campaign promises. To succeed in office a President must not only deliver an effective first budget message to Congress, but also be effective internationally, as the American economy that has increasingly become integrated in an interdependent international system.

PART SIX

Science Advice to the President

Presidential Science and Technology Advising: 1950–1988 Personal Reflections

WILLIAM T. GOLDEN
PRESIDENT, NEW YORK ACADEMY OF SCIENCES

The world was, or seemed to be, a simpler place in mid-1950, when, after the outbreak of the Korean War, President Truman, with strong encouragement from Congressional leaders, asked me to serve as a special consultant to advise him on the organization and utilization of the government's scientific research activities. Emphasis was to be on the military aspects. The study involved discussions with some 150 scientists, government officials, academic leaders, and industrialists. My recommendation, dated December 18, 1950, "for the appointment of an outstanding scientific leader as Scientific Advisor to the President,"[1,2] was promptly approved by President Truman.

The pace of change has quickened in the intervening years, and the prospect appears to be for continued acceleration. Among the well-recognized factors distinguishing the world from what it was at the end of World War II are faster communication, faster transportation, computerization, the opening of the new world of space, progress in biomedical science, the further internationalization of industry, commerce, and finance, the unequal growth of populations, the rise and decline of nations* and the ferment of the developing world, the overhanging danger of a nuclear holocaust, the expansion of armaments and the contagion of terrorism, the increasing industrialization of agriculture, growing concern for the environment, greater sense of societal responsibilities, and the increasing participation of women and minorities.

Yet human nature changes slowly and certain principles remain unchanged, even as scientific and technical factors increasingly influence virtually every aspect of life on Planet Earth. Thus,

---

* *"Many shall rise that now are fallen: and many shall fall that now are held in honor." Horace. Ars Poetica*

more and more, every level of our government (including states and municipalities) must take science and technology factors into account in policy formulation and in long-range and day-to-day decision-making.

Science and technology advising has experienced undulations of popularity and, like life itself, has responded in an evolutionary way to changing circumstances, adapting with more or less successful mutations to a varying environment.

Modifications will continue to occur, stimulated by changes in the personalities of the Presidents and in the competitive strengths of the several Departments of the Executive Branch and of their Secretaries. The Congress and the Judiciary will, of course, be affected by comparable factors. Also influential will be the progress of science and technology and their increasing involvement in virtually every aspect of human life, throughout the world; and the changing national and international political, military, societal, and economic environments.

Science and technology advising has a long history,[3] going back to Adam and Eve.[4] Adam and Eve were the first executives (and co-investigators). The serpent was, of course, the first Science Advisor. Were it not for that primordial research project, we would not be writing on this subject for a volume on Presidential Transitions. Original sin or initiation of scientific research, the outcome should not discourage the quest for knowledge. Indeed, the episode supports the need for a President's Science and Technology Advisory Committee (or Council [PSTAC]), of diverse experience and wisdom, to supplement and buffer a single full-time Science and Technology Advisor to the President.[5] For, however talented the Advisor may be, and however close the Advisor's rapport with the President, he or she cannot be omniscient and will also need a PSTAC, as PSAC served in the past, to provide scope, collegial discussion, and loyal opposition.*

All PSTAC members should be men and women of stature, ability, scope, independence, and patriotism. They would command the respect of the members of the Cabinet, notably the Secretaries of State, Defense, and Commerce: and the President's National Security Adviser, the Directors of the Office of Management and Budget and of the National Science Foundation. All

---

* *"Where no counsel is, the people fall: but in the multitude of counselors there is safety." Proverbs 11:14*

would be Presidential appointees and would be inspired by that distinction and responsibility. All would understand that they are chosen to represent the best interests of the United States as a whole, not any special interests of the scientific and engineering communities, or any political party, or geographic area, or ethnic group. They would be there to serve the President, and the President to serve the people.

All would realize that they are members of the President's staff, responsible to him: and that their effectiveness and survival depend on the President's confidence in them, both for wisdom and for discretion. Their advice will be sought and should also be volunteered. It will not always be taken. Presidential attitude and action will be the resultant of many forces, political and economic as well as scientific and technological. Realists will understand that. Much of the advice will be influential rather than decisive. Much of it will be of long-term value, long-term influence on policy issues that may involve no immediate decisions. Fire prevention may be more effective than fire-fighting.

There is a lesson for us in the Roman observation: "*Tempora mutantur, nos et mutamur in illis.*" ("The times are changing and we are changing in them.") Or, to paraphrase Charles Darwin, "Adapt or perish." Let us change course thoughtfully.

"To Promote the Progress of Science . . .": Considerations for the President

R. GORDON HOXIE

PRESIDENT, CENTER FOR THE STUDY OF THE PRESIDENCY

Historical Background

At this time of presidential transition we may well recall the mandate of the Constitutional Framers, "To promote the Progress of Science and useful Arts. . . ." The First Congress requested one of the Framers, Alexander Hamilton as Secretary of the Treasury, to advise them on the promotion of manufactures. His masterful response, his 1791 *Report on Manufactures*, provided a blueprint for a great industrial power. In it he wrote, recalling the 1775–1781 War for Independence:

> The extreme embarrassments of the United States during the late War, from an incapacity of supplying themselves, are still matters of keen recollection: A future war might be expected again to exemplify the mischiefs and dangers of a situation, to which that incapacity is still in too great a degree applicable, unless changed by timely and vigorous exertion. To effect this change as fast as shall be prudent, merits all the attention and all the zeal of our Public Councils; 'tis the next great work to be accomplished.[1]

National security was the primary engine which drove Hamilton to advance science and technology and to encourage invention, engineering, transportation, and trade policies. Lincoln in the midst of a great civil war in 1863 signed the charter of the National Academy of Sciences, an agency to advise the government on scientific and technical matters. Wilson, at the onset of World War I had authorized the creation of the National Research Council as an operating arm of the National Academy of Sciences. Wilson, the former president of Princeton University, was rallying the scientists and engineers in the universities to help design the instruments of modern warfare and to serve as advisers to the War and Navy Departments.

From Washington and Hamilton, who stressed the importance of science and technology, through Eisenhower, who in 1957 created a science adviser position on his White House staff, the linkage between science and technology and national security was fundamental. Then in 1962 Kennedy accepted legislation placing the science adviser in the Executive Office of the President with two masters, the Congress and the President. In turn in 1973 the position was banished to the National Science Foundation. The 1976 restoration of the President's Science Adviser in the Executive Office of the President had again given him two masters, the Congress and the President. The Congress gets science and technology advice from the General Accounting Office and also from its own Office of Technology Assessment. It does not need the President's science advisory system.

The Science Adviser, in reality the Science and Technology Adviser, should not have to serve two masters. Ideally the Science Adviser should be an Assistant to the President and the President should have his own science advisory committee. The science adviser's primary responsibility should be to advise the President. It should *not* be to serve the science community, nor, indeed the Congress. His primary area of advice should relate to national security affairs. He should be a statutory adviser to the National Security Council just as is the Chairman of the Joint Chiefs of Staff and the Director of the Central Intelligence Agency. In the Eisenhower years, with the cordial support of General Andrew Goodpaster (the staff secretary) and Gordon Gray, the special assistant for national security affairs, a close relationship had developed between the science adviser and the NSC. This relationship needs rebuilding and statutory recognition. Further, the relationship with the Office of Management and Budget also needs strengthening. In accordance with Public Law 94-282, the Science Adviser is directed by the President to participate in budget recommendations to OMB. Indeed, the Office of Science and Technology Policy could be mandated to review all R&D budgets before they go to OMB. This authority should be limited to *total* budgets; the parts should be negotiable. The prestige and the value of the science adviser could further be enhanced by an annual report. This could be a major policy document like the President's annual Economic Report to the Congress prepared by the Council of Economic Advisers. It would set the tone for science and technology policies.

While the science adviser's advice to the President should be multi-faceted, including agriculture, arms control, energy, environment, medicine, space, transportation, and societal matters, and in part, international in character in keeping with international agreements, the primary focus should be *national security*. Again this focus became confused in the mid 1960s as it came to relate to the Johnson's Great Society programs. Under Carter the science adviser was virtually cut off from national security affairs. This was, in part, due to the hostility of much of the science community to the Carter administration. This had been a hostility begun in the Johnson and Nixon years, abated briefly in the Ford Presidency; revived in the Carter years, it continues in the Reagan period, making, for example, the American Physical Society an unwitting ally of Common Cause in opposition to the Strategic Defense Initiative (SDI).

There has been some restoration of the primary security focus under Reagan. In keeping with this mandate the science adviser needs ready access to the President, the Cabinet and Cabinet Councils, the National Security Council, the Office of Management and Budget, the departments of State and Defense, and the President's Foreign Intelligence Advisory Board. Without losing this primary focus he needs effective liaison to other departments including Commerce, Education, Health and Human Services, and Interior and with the National Science Foundation, National Academy of Sciences, National Academy of Engineering, and National Research Council.

Clearly there is needed as science adviser a person of stature and breadth of vision, respected in the scientific community, but not that community's servant. Clearly science advice and politics, like oil and water, do not mix. Dr. Edward E. David, Jr., member of the present White House Science Council, who had been Nixon's Science Adviser, warns that the 1973 abolition of the old Kennedy created Office of Science and Technology had resulted from its strident advocacy. "From a purely operational viewpoint, offices with an advocacy rule and an outside constituency to serve can exist within the White House structure only so long as the cause is popular as perceived by the political arm of the White House." Dr. David concludes, "the Science Adviser's post must be filled by a statesman rather than an advocate, if it is to remain viable."[2] Dr. Franklin A. Long, who had served on the ideal President's Science Advisory Committee of the Eisenhower-Kennedy years, emphasizes the critical need for a science and technology "adviser that is close to the president and on whom he can have a special sort of reliance. Eisenhower," he concludes, "was the first president to face up to this."[3]

One of the great challenges of the remaining period of the Reagan administration and that of Reagan's successor will be a rebuilding of trust between the presidency and the science community. This is pointed out in the Op-Ed essay by Secretary of Defense, Caspar W. Weinberger, in *The New York Times,* August 21, 1987; therein Weinberger counters the American Physical Society's "pessimistic study of SDI . . . containing important technical errors," and asserts, "By making perfection the enemy of the good, critics consign themselves to a fantasy-land."[4] Clearly a common ground for the common good must be rediscovered between the Presidency and large segments of the scientific community.

By contrast with the scientific community's cordial support of the President in the Franklin Roosevelt, Truman, Eisenhower, and Kennedy administrations, in the Johnson, Nixon, Carter and Reagan administrations that community's cordiality was replaced by sharp criticisms. While seeking to better relations with the university scientific community, other constituencies must also be considered. In terms of research and development, industry plays a major role. Indeed where the U. S. government was in the past the largest R&D participant, today it is industry which expends 54% of all R&D funds. Dr. George A. Keyworth, II, and Dr. William R. Graham, as the Reagan's science advisers, have sought to emphasize the industry, university, and government joint roles in an effective triad. Progress has been substantial.

Periodically, over the past century, beginning with the Allison Commission in 1884, Congress has given consideration to establishing a department of science and technology. But as William Carey, Director of the American Association for the Advancement of Science, has observed, such a department would more likely end up a "Noah's Ark" than an effective national policy instrument. Fortunately many agencies like NASA and NSF cherish their independence to such an extreme that they would effectively block creating this conglomerate.

What is needed then is *not* a new department of science and technology but a better defining of the Office of Science and Technology Policy on the one hand and the President's Science Adviser on the other. The 1976 legislation had recognized that what had been created was not the final solution. It had encouraged additional study. But it had provided a long list of needs as Congress perceived them; beyond being the President's adviser, they would have him wearing several hats, advising the President, advising the Congress and coordinating the execution of policy.

The President's science adviser should *not* be the creation of Congress. Congress now has its own sources of science advice. The science adviser needs access to the President. His primary responsibility should be that of the President's science adviser. To do this effectively he should be in the White House as the Assistant to the President for Science and Technology. Essentially this had been one of the two principal 1950 recommendations of William T. Golden, the other being the President's Science Advisory Council. The two proposals had not set well with the White House staff in 1950, and they would probably arouse similar opposition today. As George Reedy, veteran of the Johnson presidency expressed it in 1970, "to bring more assistants into the White House . . . increases the amount of jostling; the amount of elbowing; it places the 'rite of the long knives' on continuous run. . . . Believe me, any White House assistant with any sensitivity could . . . write about the court of Paleologus in Byzantium; all he would have to do would be to . . . look up a few Greek names."[5]

Although White House staff resist all boarders as interlopers, there is something special in their resistance to science advisers. As Professor James Edward Katz has observed, "The chronic resistance of White House staff to Science Advisers and staffs is motivated by more than considerations involving power politics. The scientists are seen as being overspecialized and their advice as too esoteric and narrow for the Presidential level."[6] In 1957, seven years after Golden's recommendations, it had taken Sputnik and Eisenhower to get a science adviser on the White House staff and to constitute the President's Science Advisory Committee. Eisenhower was deeply grateful for the help of the science adviser and the PSAC in the last three, the most productive years, of his presidency. Reflecting on it he concluded, "Without such distinguished help, any President in our time would be, to a certain extent, disabled."[7]

President Kennedy, on the advice of Professor Richard E. Neu-stadt in 1962 had supported the legislation which moved both the adviser and the PSAC out of the White House and into the Executive Office of the President. There the adviser, no longer a member of the White House staff, was subject to Senate confirmation. There the Congress could call the adviser to appear before its committees. Senator Hubert H. Humphrey, chairing a subcommittee of the Government Operations Committee in 1958, had been miffed when Eisenhower's Special Assistant, James Killian, refused on grounds of executive privilege to testify.[8] Since then Humphrey had been determined to get the science adviser out of the protective position of the White House staff. In part, Neustadt and Kennedy had succumbed to these pressures. This had deeply troubled both Kennedy's science adviser, Professor Jerome Wiesner, and the committee. They recognized that the 1962 statute had both removed them from proximity to the President and had given them a second master, the Congress. The science adviser was no longer a member of the White House staff, being instead in the Executive Office of the President.

The real deterioration of the relationship of the science adviser and the PSAC with the President had set in under Johnson and climaxed under Nixon, with the discontinuance of the PSAC and the relegation of the science adviser to the National Science Foundation as an additional duty of the director. Reedy's 1970 warning about the 'rites of the long knives' had been fulfilled. However, the politicization of the PSAC after 1965, with open criticism of President Johnson's and then President Nixon's Vietnam policies had been a contributing factor. So also had been the leak to the press of PSAC criticism of the administration's plans for a supersonic commercial aircraft. The criticism had contributed to Congressional rejection of the proposal. Moreover, Office of Management and Budget Director Roy Ash had made a convincing case for OMB's own science advisory role and that of the Department of Defense.

Realizing the mistake that had been made, Gerald Ford only five days after he became President, instituted measures to restore a science advisory system in the Executive Office of the President. It was not, however, until May 11, 1976 that he could sign into law Public Law 94-282 establishing the present mechanism, the Office of Science and Technology Policy with a Director who would also serve as Science Adviser to the President. The fact that the adviser is not on the White House staff posed no problem in the Ford administration. In accordance with the President's desires, the Chief of Staff, Richard B. Cheney, gave him access to the President. However, accessibility became a problem in the Carter and Reagan administrations.

Recommendations

Although being on the White House staff is no guarantor of accessibility, it helps. Moreover, it would remove the adviser from the dilemma of serving two masters, the President and the Congress.

In essence the position of Assistant to the President for Science and Technology would be parallel to that of Assistant to the President for National Security Affairs. Further, his relationship to the Office of Science and Technology would be analogous to that of the Assistant for National Security Policy to the National Security Council. Just as the Assistant for National Security Affairs is the staff director of the President's National Security Council, the Assistant for Science and Technology would be the staff director of the Office of Science and Technology Policy. Reinforcing this relationship the Assistant for Science and Technology should be made a statutory adviser to the NSC like the Chairman of the Joint Chiefs of Staff and the Director of the Central Intelligence Agency. All of this would restore the primary focus of the science adviser to national security affairs. Other aspects of OSTP activities could be more effectively shared with the National Science Foundation. The President's science adviser should be relieved of peripheral time-consuming tasks such as chairing the Federal Coordinating Council for Science, Engineering and Technology and the Intergovernmental Science, Engineering and Technology Advisory Panel. With the support of the Office of Science and Technology Policy, the President's Assistant for Science and Technology should have a defined role in approving overall R&D budgets before they go to OMB. In point of fact it is OMB through the budget process which currently controls science policy. (To the credit of Keyworth, Reagan's Science Adviser 1981–85, and Graham since 1986, they did secure substantial R&D increases for science and technology.)

Essential to a better science advisory system is restoration of the President's Science Advisory Committee which the Assistant to the President for Science and Technology could chair. In its re-emergence it might more appropriately be re-designated as the President's Science and Technology Council. By its nature, like the NSC, it is only advisory. The term council is more prestigious than committee. Neither the Council nor the Assistant to the President for Science and Technology would require Congressional approval. However, the National Science and Technology Policy, Organization, and Priorities Act of 1976 should be amended, with decreased extraneous responsibilities for the OSTP Director and increased for the National Science Foundation.

As to the Chairmanship of the Science and Technology Council there are two schools of thought. When Eisenhower constituted it, as the PSAC, his old friend Professor Isidor Rabi had proposed an independent chairman, rather than the President's assistant. Nonetheless Rabi had graciously stepped down as chairman of the predecessor ODM Science Advisory Committee to make way for the Killian appointment. There is much to be said, however, for the independent chairman appointed by the President. Coincidental with the increasing problems of the PSAC in the Johnson Administration was the 1966 enactment of the Freedom of Information Act. In order to ensure the confidentiality of the deliberations of the proposed Council, a new Executive Order may be required.[9]

The proposed Council should be smaller than the original PSAC, perhaps no more than a dozen of the nation's most distinguished scientists. The present White House Science Council has done laudatory work, but it is the science adviser's council, not the President's. Among all of the former science advisers to the President there is agreement that, whatever the exact name, the President's Science Advisory Committee should be restored. William T. Golden, the person who originally proposed such a body 37 years ago, recently put the case for the restoration most eloquently when he wrote:

> . . . the President (and the Executive branch) needs the enrichment of novel, creative ideas and diversity of viewpoint on science and technology as aids to comprehensive consideration, policy formulation, and decision-making on a wide range of subjects relating to peaceful, to military, and to arms limitation and conflict-resolution issues. He does not now get much advice. What he gets is opinion from a Science Advisor who is limited by White House staff. The Science Advisor is served by his own small staff and by his self-selected

White House Council, which does not have the stature of Presidential appointments nor the inspiration and efffectiveness that would come from direct access to the President.

Mr. Golden concludes, "President Reagan, his successors, and the Congress should consider this salutary and relatively simple alternative to the illusory benefit and assured turbulence of a Department of Science and Technology."[10]

In the event President Reagan needs further counsel as to the wisdom of this recommendation, he might ask his good friend, Prime Minister Margaret Thatcher. She followed the Eisenhower (Golden) model with an advisory body of scientists and engineers appointed by and reporting directly to the "iron lady" herself. In addition, she has her Science Advisor, Dr. Robin Nicholson, who, together with the advisory body, is credited with much of the resurgence of British science, technology and industrial growth in the 1980s.

Here in the United States both the needs and the opportunities are unsurpassed, requiring the "bully pulpit" of Presidential leadership. The President needs his own assistant unfettered by the myriads of little detail currently encompassing his advisor in OSTP. The President needs his own council which can offer new vistas of leadership, restoring American competitiveness and American advance on new frontiers of science and technology.

The Nation's prosperity and security are inextricably related to its science and technology policies. In 1990 we shall be observing the centennial of Dwight D. Eisenhower's birth. Historians are increasingly recognizing his skillful crafting of the institutional presidency. He did so with the accumulated wisdom of many persons, including that of William T. Golden, when he created the White House staff position on science and technology and his own advisory committee on those subjects. A new administration and the Nation would profit enormously by the restoration of both.

This is something to ponder when we consider the words of the Constitutional Framers 200 years ago: "To promote the Progress of Science." As we begin this third century under the Constitution we shall either move ahead or move behind. Science and technology do not stand still. As Hamilton expressed it three years after the ratification of the Constitution, this "merits all the attention and all the zeal of our Public Councils; 'tis the next great work to be accomplished."[11]

PART SEVEN

Presidential Communication

Establishing an Administration: The Place of Communications

MARTHA JOYNT KUMAR
MICHAEL BARUCH GROSSMAN
PROFESSORS OF POLITICAL SCIENCE
TOWSON STATE UNIVERSITY

"Reagan Asks for a First Waltz and Wins Hearts in the Capital" declared *The New York Times* in a front page article the day after Ronald Reagan's initial post-election visit to Washington.[1] Jimmy Carter's first visit to the capital inspired a less favorable prediction from *The Times* about his relationships with Washington's most important inhabitants: "Carter's Program Will Face A More Assertive Congress: Legislators Viewed as More Intent on Challenging President and Exerting Bigger Influence on Policy."[2] These two headlines were typical of both events and press reaction to them during the eleven weeks separating the election from the inauguration of these two presidents. Whereas Reagan appeared to move into an atmosphere of warm relations, Carter appeared to be stepping into potential troubles.

The difference in approach between the Carter and Reagan transition teams reflected the approach of the two men to governing. Reagan and his staff used their transition to provide an image of the man who would become president to the national governing constituencies in Washington. They used the period to establish Reagan's priorities as the agenda they would have to respond to and thus reinforced the legitimacy of his claim to govern, already established in the election. Reagan and his staff members had a sense of what kinds of decisions had to be made and what the most fruitful timetable was for making and executing them. Carter and those around him did not seem to have this same sense, an important failing for them as the Washington political environment was not nearly as hospitable to President-elect Carter as it later would be to President-elect Reagan.

Reagan's initial Washington advantage stemmed in part from the power he demonstrated in his electoral victory. Reagan's victory brought Republican control of the Senate for the first time in 26 years. In his narrow popular and electoral college victory four years before, Carter had run ahead of only one Democratic Senator, James Sasser (Tennessee). Both men profited from the glow cast by their electoral victories, but Reagan maintained the glow for a longer period of time and used it as a governing resource through his more effective utilization of the transition. For both men, the period between their election and the first Easter Recess of Congress after their inauguration became a time that served as a precursor of the successes and failures their administrations were to experience.

Presidential communications policies played an important role in establishing those patterns of success and failure. Decisions made relating to communications demonstrate how the two administrations understood and dealt with the political and governmental needs of establishing those administrations.

Internal and Governmental Transitions

Although what is formally referred to as "the transition" begins the day after the election and ends with the inauguration, the analysis here extends it into the first two or three months of the new administration. The entire period involves the establishment of as well as the transition to the new administration. In the portion of the transition before the formal accession to power — November to January — the president elect and his team learn about the differences between campaigning and governing. During this period they have to transform the rhetoric of campaign expectations into an agenda deemed realistic by those with whom the president will share governing authority. The period from January to March is a period of transition for the government itself as it makes the break with one president and moves to another. Thus both phases of a transition are important for the success of the new president and his administration. Different considerations and actions are taken during the two phases but both are transitions.

Internal Transition

The two phases of the transition are the internal and the governmental transitions. The internal transition runs from November until the inauguration. It involves the changes that must be made within the internal environment in order for the president to govern. The considerations revolve around sifting through the staff and the ideas of the campaign. They are looking internally at those who worked for the campaign and sifting through the promises made during the campaign to decide who should join the governing team and which promises should be turned into governmental proposals. During this pre-presidential period, the incoming president is basically dealing with allies in an effort to harness his people to direct and staff the administration. Communications is important to the president elect in this period because his communications appointments are made as well as his image as president is developed.

Governmental Transition

While the period prior to the inauguration is basically an internal operation, the months following the inauguration find the incoming president and his staff fashioning the governmental transition. It is a period of development of external relations. The president is dealing with people with power bases and agendas of their own. It is a time when the integration of factors developed during the pre-inaugural days come together. Communications is important because it is during these days that the administration is presented with its elements tied together: personalities, programs, agenda. The early days of the pre-inauguration are days of development while those following it are days of exposition and presentation of what was developed. While the internal transition is usually one of decisions arrived at somewhat separately, the governmental transition is one of integration of elements of the administration.

Officials must get the attention of those in administrative and legislative positions and convince them of what they want to do and then get their support. All of the elements of the communications package — personalities, programs, agendas — must be integrated to get their full value for each one individually. The president, for example, presents himself to his best advantage when he can tie together his personality as seen in his leadership style with his agenda and program. The presentation of an agenda is a key item during this period whether it takes place implicitly or explicitly.

The governmental transition starts with the inauguration and continues until Congress leaves Washington for its Easter recess. It is a time when the president has the attention of the Congress in a way that he will not be able to count on again during ordinary times. He has them disposed towards supporting him and are eager to listen to what he has to say.

The Place of Communications

In an important way, communications is a key to the difference in the approaches of Jimmy Carter and Ronald Reagan to their job, their constituencies, and policy development and passage. Communications is a critical element in their transitions just as it is in all presidential transitions because it is at the heart of the process of shaping the images of the electoral winner as a sitting president. Few notions exist of how he will behave as president. The point during the transition during which these actions are taken is important for the later success of the administration. There are three areas in particular that are important in the establishment of the ways in which an administration will communicate its goals, strategies, and personalities. The three areas are communications appointments, policies, and strategies.

1. An administration gathers together the people who will be important in both creating and carrying out communications policies. While others may join the administration after it has begun, the people hired during these early days are the ones who will be a part of establishing the tone of the administration. The first line of appointments, such as Jody Powell, are made in the internal transition. In the Carter transition team, however, Powell was one of the few people at a high level position to keep his position once Carter was inaugurated. In the Reagan administration, however, the same people were prominent in the transition and the administration as senior advisers to the president.

2. A general communications policy will be established. A communications policy, whether or not it is an articulated one, will be established based on the views of the president of what he believes the public must know, how involved the public should be in administration decisions, and how he wants to project the ideas of his administration. He is the one who establishes the broad brush strokes of his communications policy, whether it is through his statements, his actions, or by a combination of them. How communications will be managed is also an impor-

tant aspect of a communications policy. The communications policies, while most often not enunciated as one policy, become evident in the early months a president is in office. The broad themes of the Reagan administration were established during the internal transition. Carter's failure to define themes in either the internal or the governmental transitions made the point that his would be a themeless administration.

3. The communications strategies used to establish the administration will be developed, or at least begun, during these early days. Plans used to frame the personalities and agenda of the administration will be put together at this point. During the internal transition period, Reagan was able to use the communications people he appointed, such as David Gergen, to work with the key designated senior advisers for the administration, Jim Baker, Edwin Meese, and Michael Deaver, to develop strategies to turn Reagan's key agenda items — budget and tax cuts — into law within the first year of the administration. They developed a 100 day plan for publicizing and coordinating their policy efforts.

These communications policies are indirectly established through the actions of the president-elect as well as through those of staff members. In order for a president to establish his administration, he must imprint an image in the public mind of a candidate as an official and of a platform as government policy.

Communications

Communications is an important aspect of appointments in two ways. First, there are appointments of people who are responsible for developing and carrying out communications for the White House. The press secretary is the most important of these officials. Second, there are officials appointed during the early period for whom communications is an important aspect of their work. The chief of staff, for example, works on strategies to enhance the standing of the president and his policies. The communications component needs to be taken into account when making staff selections. A president must decide what responsibilities he wants his staff members to assume.

Jimmy Carter was quick to appoint Jody Powell, his long time press secretary to the position of White House Press Secretary. Powell had served as his press secretary when he was governor of Georgia and when he campaigned for the governorship and for the presidency. It was almost a foregone conclusion that he would appoint Powell to the position. But that makes his appointment no less important for what it meant to how the president would communicate. Ronald Reagan chose James Brady as his press secretary, someone whom he hardly knew and who had no ties with Reagan as an officeholder, that too was an important decision as it related to the release of information about the president and his administration.

In selecting a press secretary, both presidents had to first decide what information they wanted to release from the White House and how they wanted to manage the release of information in their administrations, including the use of other communications people in the White House. While the press secretary is the most visible of the people in the communications area, he is not the only one. There are other communications staff people reporting to the president, such as the assistant to the president for communications, who are important in the release of information. Consideration must be given when appointing a press secretary, and others in the communications area, to how they will complement one another and how they will fit into the overall communications policy. There are three basic choices that a president chooses from among when he selects people in the communications area: spokesperson; manager; announcer. These three types of press secretaries and communications people combine certain characteristics as far as the release and control of information are concerned.

Spokesperson

The spokesperson is the person empowered to speak for the president on a formal as well as an informal basis. (Not all administrations have people who act on a formal basis as a spokesperson on a regular basis. There will always be people who know the mind of the president on a particular issue or issues but few will be able to speak on a routine and open basis for the president.)

Jody Powell could serve as a model for the spokesperson. Not only did he regularly speak for President Carter but he also was understood to know the president's response to various situations. "Through Jody Powell you had a direct pipeline to the President of the United States," remarked reporter Walter Rodgers, now with ABC News.[3] "In both the Ford and Reagan administrations you have a direct pipeline one step up the chain of command but not in any case to the president." As the administration got underway, James Brady had little knowledge of President Reagan's responses to congressional reactions nor was he empowered to discuss the president's thinking on legislation.[4] His role was that of an announcer of decisions and statements developed elsewhere. Larry Speakes was in somewhat of the same position for most of the administration's years in office.

Not all press secretaries are spokespersons in the true sense of the term. For the term spokesperson implies two attributes: authority to speak for the president and knowledge of what the president thinks. Few press secretaries display both attributes. Authority to speak for the president means that the person can provide information that the president wants released but in addition that he can answer questions in an informed fashion. To be of real value to the press, a spokesperson needs to know the mind of the president. He needs to be able to have a feel for what the president would say in a given situation and have the authority as well to speak for him as well. A spokesperson tends to be so absorbed in the job of providing information that there is little or no time for developing communications strategies, an important component of a communications policy. Thus a president must be sensitive to the need to choose others to manage the communications strategies for the administration. In the case of the Carter Administration, no managers were chosen in the early months, only a spokesperson.

Announcer

The announcer is someone who releases information rather than a person who can authoritatively answer spontaneous questions posed by reporters. While the announcer is usually the press secretary, in certain policy areas others may come forward. For example, in the Reagan administration, Robert McFarlane and his predecessor in the national security adviser's spot, Richard Allen, often briefed the press on national security issues. McFarlane gave an annual review of national security issues and problems. When he was serving as the director of the Office of Management and Budget, David Stockman regularly briefed the press on budgetary matters. While policy specialists would speak to reporters during the Carter Administration, it was rare for them to speak from the podium in the press room. Jody Powell spoke for the president whether the issues were domestic or national security.

While having the press secretary serve as an announcer rather than as a spokesperson causes dissatisfaction among reporters, it is a model that works well from the viewpoint of the White House. The only information that is released is that which the White House has determined needs to get out. When the press secretary serves only as an announcer, the White House has a greater possibility of determining what the White House story will be on the evening television news. The only authoritative information that is given out at the briefing is that which the president and his staff want to get out. They don't top their own lead. They have one story for the day or a combination of stories with the same theme. When a spokesperson handles the briefing and can answer questions on a broad range of topics, there is less chance that the White House will be able to control what gets on television or on the front page of the major newspapers. There are several stories that reporters can choose from among, which is not true when less information comes out of the briefing. When the press secretary is operating as an announcer, he is serving as a funnel for the messages that are developed elsewhere in the White House.

Manager

The manager is a person working in the communications area whose job it is to organize the release of information and to develop strategies in presenting the administration to its publics. While the press secretary had a management component to his job, beginning with the Nixon presidency, the managers in the communications area are not likely to be the press secretary. There are too many tasks of an immediate nature that prevent a press secretary from taking the role of a manager. Instead persons such as the director of communications and the head of the media liaison operation are involved in communications as managers who lay out what images the administration should be trying to achieve and what strategies they might use to reach their goals.

No matter whether the administration is a Democratic or Republican one, the persons who serve as the managers of communications are most likely to be the new crop of communications specialists who serve beyond the press room in offices removed from the press corps. Their role is not that of a spokesperson or announcer but as a strategist and planner. There is a basic difference, however, in how recent administrations have used managers. Republicans have viewed communications advisers as essential to have in place as the administrations begins. A Democratic White House, however, is not as likely to establish managerial communications positions until many months have gone by, if then.

There was no communications director in the Carter White House as there was in both the Ford and Reagan administrations. In fact, during the internal and governmental transitions no senior level managers were appointed who were involved with communications strategies. All of the communications duties were under Jody Powell's control. He was responsible for the operations of the Press Office, the Office of the Assistant for Media and Public Affairs, Media Liaison, the White House News Summary, the Photo Office, the speechwriters, and the press advance operation. Gerald Rafshoon, who worked as a senior level adviser specializing in communications coordination and strategies, did not come to the White House until July, 1978. It did become apparent that a press secretary cannot deal with the daily routines of the White House as well as long range planning and coordination. While Rafshoon was brought in to make sure that everyone spoke with one voice, he was not able to break the patterns that had already been establishedd in the early months. "No one ever sang the same song for four years," remarked Anne Wexler, who headed the Office of Public Liaison in the Carter White House.[5]

In the Reagan White House, however, senior level managers were appointed before a press secretary was chosen. Michael Deaver, one of the "troika" of senior advisers, and the one most closely involved with communications, Edwin Meese and James Baker being the other two, was responsible for scheduling the president. He had a particularly fine sense of what events suited Reagan's style and was able to choose ones where the president could effectively communicate the desired message.

If Brady was to serve as an announcer, a strategist had to be in place to develop, coordinate, and execute the communications strategies. David Gergen, Special Assistant to the President for Communications, was selected before the administration came into the White House. Gergen brought with him previous White House experience. His earlier communications work in the Nixon and Ford administrations allowed him to immediately be of value. "There is a cumulative quality to working in the White House . . . that enables you to work with a little more wisdom," said Gergen six months after the Reagan Administration took office.[6] "You learn a great deal about the rhythms of the press, you learn a great deal about the nature of White House reporting—the kinds of events that are likely to be communicated clearly to the public and events that are likely to incur criticism."

Communications Policy

At the same time that an incoming administration must make its communications appointments, it must do so on the basis of a communications policy. While most often an unarticulated one, a communications policy goes to the very core of an administration's relationship with the public. A communications policy involves the ordering of several relationships; most specifically, the president's relationship with the public and with the press. There are four types of communications policies that are decided at this point:

1. The president's public appearances. The use of the president himself to enunciate policy choices and to develop support for them is the key decision to be made early in the days following the election. While an extension of the policies adopted during the campaign, the president elect and his staff will consider how frequent or how sparingly the president himself is to be used. He is the most important resource an administration has and his value must be recognized during the internal transition. By Christmas, following the 1976 election, for example, Carter had held nine news conferences. They were so frequent that *The New York Times* stopped carrying the transcripts of them. Reagan, however, carefully timed his formal appearances before the press holding only one news conference, two days after the election, during the first month following the election.
2. White House organization of press policy. The extent to which the White House will centralize the release of information throughout the executive branch will be decided. It comes out through the policies established for the selection of public information officers for the departments (will they be chosen by

the departmental secretary or by the White House?) and through the coordination mechanisms put in place for departments to work with the White House on the release of information (regular meetings, frequent phone calls from the White House Press Office). In the Carter White House, it was basically each departmental secretary for himself. In the Reagan administration, more control was exercised by the White House staff.

3. The use of surrogates and spokespeople for the president. One could sense the differing use of spokespersons for the two newly elected presidents during the first month following the election. Two days after the election Reagan named Edwin Meese as the director of the transition and William Casey as the chairman of the transition's executive committee. Meese then regularly appeared as the spokesperson for the transition. When they got to the White House, the patterns continued. During their first nine weeks, Reagan held two news conferences while Carter held four as well as a town meeting and a telephone call-in program.

4. The president's relationship with the public. Involved is what that relationship implies concerning the information a president will release for public view. How much information does the president want to see released to the public. Does he believe that there should be a policy of sanctions for those releasing information that has unfavorable consequences for the administration. What policies will the president adopt to inhibit the unauthorized release of information. The Carter White House had leaks everywhere with no sanctions applied. In the Reagan White House, strong control was not exercised until the information leaked worked against the administration.

The same kinds of characteristics tend to shape the relationships with both the public and the press. An administration that is forthcoming in providing information to the public is going to do the same with the press. There are three basic models an administration can choose from in determining how they should provide information: open, closed, modified closed.

Open

An open administration is one in which there are few stated policies about the release of information by the president or by senior advisers to the president. Staff members are not told to limit their contacts with the press nor do they have to go through the press office to arrange press meetings. Press arrangements tend

to be loose with the initiative in contacts belonging to staff officials
and with reporters. There are no real disincentives for speaking
with reporters. In an administration with an open communications policy, there is little coordination of a lasting nature between the White House and the departments. In an open system
reporters can get to those in the White House responsible for
policy decisions and to those with information about the president. It is a system with little control exercised by the president
or by communications managers. Even if the Carter administration had wanted to exercise communications control, they did
not have the managers available to do it.

Closed

A closed communications policy is one in which staff members
are meant to coordinate their press activities. It is a system designed to further a White House message. Communications
strategies are developed at the higher rungs of the White House
staff ladder and the middle and lower level people are expected
to carry it out. The Press Office acts as a funnel for messages
developed in the inner offices of the White House. A closed communications policy makes a high cost for providing information
to reporters that the White House would rather not be divulged.
In a closed communications policy, the White House tries to keep
strong control over the departmental public information officers.
They seek to name them and coordinate their activities with those
of the president. A policy of establishing lie detector tests to ferret
out persons giving privileged information against the wishes of
the White House and the firing of those caught leaking are policies typical of a closed White House. The Nixon White House
was a closed one and the Reagan one came close to it, at least
on paper.

Modified Closed

The Reagan White House structured a closed system but in carrying it out, they never were able to make it stick. The difference between the policy designed by the White House and how
it was enforced rendered it a modified closed system. The intention to limit staff-reporter contacts was there but the ability to
enforce the limits was not. While many administrations want
a closed system, they are reluctant to establish it at the beginning of their White House tenure. They seek coordination in

publicity activities but do not encourage staff members to talk with reporters other than on specific issues and occasions.

Communications Strategies

An administration needs to act on its communications strategies before the president takes office. It is in the early period when the images of the president are established and his administration's agenda is articulated. The campaign is not governing. They are two very different periods as far as projecting an image and articulating a program are concerned. What is important during the campaign can practically disappear as an issue once an administration takes office.

During the transition two things are done as far as communications strategies are concerned: policy priorities are established and strategies are developed to create support for their adoption. The priorities must be established early in the transition because the public as well as government officials need time to accept and understand the agenda of the incoming administration. The Reagan Administration was able to both establish the priorities and develop strategies during the weeks prior to the inauguration. The Carter Administration did neither during the period before the inauguration or during the early months of the administration. In sharp contrast to President Reagan, Carter presented a full plate of high priorities including energy, the economy, and executive reorganization. In his first nine weeks, President Carter sent 26 communications to Congress, according to a total of weekly figures from *Presidential Documents*. Only seven of them dealt with his three priorities; the remaining 19 did not. In the same time period, Reagan had 16 messages that fell within the "Communications to Congress" category. Of the 16, 9 dealt with the economy. While the Reagan White House was focused in its dealings with the Congress, it was also careful to control how often the president appears in an open forum where the discussion could be diverted from a central point the administration wanted to make.

What Difference Does It Make?

A view of those early months and how the two incoming administrations dealt with the three communications areas—

appointments, policies, and strategies — gives an insight into the
readiness of the administrations to govern. An administration
that has an articulated communications plan has a much greater
chance of achieving its policy goals than one that does not. Coordination in the communications area is an indicator of a general
readiness to take office. Communications plans are among the
first to be developed thus if no plans have been put together in
that area, it is unlikely that they have been established in any
other area. Thus communications plans serve as a good barom-
eter of the general preparation of the administration.

Controlling Expectations

One of the benefits to be reaped from a coordinated communications effort is the ability to influence how people view the incoming administration. By being able to develop strategies in
reducing what the public expect from him, the president elect
can assume office without the public thinking that he is going
to have immediate achievements.

Ronald Reagan sought to lower expectations immediately after
the election. He announced that he would focus on one issue,
the economic issue, when he took office. The economic issue was
defined as cuts in federal spending levels and tax cuts to stimulate the economy. By having his appointments to top positions
named within two weeks of the election, including the chief of
staff and his other two senior staff members, Reagan was able
to use them to develop strategies in the early days following his
victory.

Focus Attention

By announcing the key goals of an administration early in the
internal transition, the president elect is able to get the attention
of the public at a time when people are focused on the presidency. He automatically has their attention with his victory and
he can use it to his benefit by giving the public an idea of where
his presidency will be headed. The campaign necessarily involves
discussion of many issues and positions. The public wants to know
where the president is going to spend his time and if he has developed his communications strategies, he can use these plans
to direct public attention. In his press conference two days after

his election, Reagan announced the important place of the economic issue on his agenda. He told reporters about his economic program, including tax cuts: "I think that it was the issue of the campaign; I think it is what the American people told us with their votes they wanted. And so we'll move instantly on that."[7]

Symbolic Achievements

An administration that has communications strategies that it can carry out when the president elect takes office can offer at least symbolic achievements early in his term. When he took office, Jimmy Carter announced his amnesty program. Rather than unite people at the beginning of his administration, it allowed divisions to develop over policy matters at an early date. Ronald Reagan put a freeze on the hiring of federal employees as a symbol of his administration's commitment to control government growth and spending. It turned out to be a popular action with few critics.

Presidential Image

At the time of his victory, the president elect has an image as a candidate but not as a president. If he can use the early months to establish the image he wants to build, he runs less of a risk of his critics defining him. That is why he must start early when the picture of him as a potential president is blurred. Seizing the initiative means having control over the image that is first established. Once an image is etched, it is somewhat hard to change.

Being able to get into operation shortly after the election means months of a positive image. Reagan developed an image of a decisive leader in the month after his victory. He came out with his priorities in the first two days following the election and then he worked on presenting himself to Washington. He traveled to Washington to make his round of meetings with governmental officials, including the members of the Supreme Court and congressional leaders. He went to their offices and charmed them on their ground. He followed his meetings with a party for several thousand of Washington's most influential residents. He wanted to communicate an image of someone who would meet them on their turf and make the special effort to come into agreement with those with whom he had to work whatever their party.

Jimmy Carter used his internal and governmental transitions as times to get a feel for how the government operated and to sift through the demands of his supporters as well as his campaign promises. While Reagan announced his agenda on November 7th, Carter did not have his in either the internal or governmental transition periods.

Gathering Support

After an agenda is put together, the president elect needs to pull his supporters together behind it. The task was made easier for Reagan by his being able to bring in a Republican Senate with him. In addition, many of his supporters, most noticeably conservatives, felt as if they had not been in power in a very long time and were willing to go along with an agenda established by him even if it did not include the social items they were especially concerned with. Jimmy Carter had the opposite problem, a set of supporters who let him know in the first week that they felt they had provided him with his win. Groups representing the interests of labor, urban areas, civil rights, and Democratic congressmen came out publicly reminding Carter of his debts to their interests. Instead of gathering support for his agenda, he was being forced to consider theirs.

Without a clearly articulated agenda of his own, it was difficult for Jimmy Carter to keep his supporters in line as the administration took office. He was not able to establish the initiative for his programs. He did not have a plan to establish strong control of the government and it showed in his communications plans. Ronald Reagan, on the other hand, was able to establish an agenda and communicate it through his appointments, policies, and strategies. While Carter was not able to get control over these three areas in either the internal or governmental transition, Reagan did in all three areas. Doing so gave him a margin to work with as his administration began. When doubts arose as to where he was going or how he was handling his job, the good will that he established during the transition worked to his benefit.

Transitions in the Press Office

WILLIAM C. SPRAGENS
PROFESSOR EMERITUS OF POLITICAL SCIENCE
BOWLING GREEN STATE UNIVERSITY

This essay will consider the development of the press office in the White House with particular attention to presidential transitions. First to be considered will be the development of the function and office of press secretary in the history of the presidency. Next will come a commentary on how the office of press secretary has been handled during presidential transitions from 1933 to 1981. The insights of two veterans of the press office in different presidencies will be presented: George Reedy's observations on his experience in the Kennedy and Johnson administrations and David Gergen's reflections about the Ford and Reagan presidencies.

Development of the Press Office

A vital White House staff function occurs in the Press Office where the impact of the communications revolution is striking. Earlier transitions provide some significant lessons for the 1989 transition. A brief review follows of the development of the White House information function.

Early administrations almost midway through the Nineteenth Century saw direct sponsorship of friendly newspapers by the administration in power and its opposition. Thus Federalist backers supported the *Gazette of the United States*, identified closely with Treasury Secretary Alexander Hamilton. Opposition Jeffersonian newpapers included Benjamin Franklin Bache's *Philadelphia General Advertiser* and Philip Freneau's *National Gazette*. This kind of sponsorship held true through the period of Amos Kendall's *Argus of the Western World* which played a key role in President Andrew Jackson's election.[1]

By the 1850s a rise of journalistic professionalism had resulted in early adherence to something resembling modern standards of objectivity and balanced reporting. This coincided with the development of press services such as the Associated Press, United Press and International News Service (the latter two forerunners of United Press International). Between 1860 and 1960 a gradual change occurred. Print media were dominant during the first 60 to 70 years of this period. Radio moved into dominance between the 1930s and the 1950s. Television took a prime position by the 1960s.

In early White House years, when the President's staff was small, his personal secretary handled press relations. Before the Press Secretary's position was clearly defined in the 1920s, such persons as James P. Tumulty on President Woodrow Wilson's staff acted in this capacity. Tumulty also was appointments secretary. The first President to conduct informal press conferences with Washington correspondents was President Theodore Roosevelt (1901–1909). After an early active beginning, President Woodrow Wilson almost discontinued his press conferences under the mounting pressures of World War I. Republican successors Warren G. Harding, Calvin Coolidge, and Herbert C. Hoover responded only to written questions subject to screening.

Origins of the modern White House Press Office may be traced to the Hoover Administration (1929–1933) when George Akerson and then Theodore Joslin held the title of Press Secretary (Akerson was the first officially designated thus). Also in the formative period the Franklin D. Roosevelt Administration (1933–1945) saw Stephen T. Early, a former Associated Press journalist, named as FDR's Press Secretary. FDR began holding press conferences twice a week; questions were oral rather than written.

Stephen Early, aided by North Carolina publisher Jonathan Daniels, was succeeded by Charles G. Ross, Joseph Short and Roger Tubby during the Truman Administration (1945–1953). While Truman continued FDR's practice of taking oral questions, Truman's press conferences were held somewhat less frequently, on the average about once a week. Reporters sometimes accompanied him to Key West, a vacation haunt.

James C. Hagerty's incumbency as President Dwight D. Eisenhower's Press Secretary (1953–1961) probably launched the modern growth of the office. One of Hagerty's many innovations was to film Eisenhower's news conferences, edited for television audiences. During and after Eisenhower's heart attack in September 1955 Hagerty oversaw unprecedented coverage of the

President's illness, with full disclosures of Eisenhower's condition until his recovery. Hagerty is generally regarded as the best press secretary. Eisenhower had fewer news conferences than Truman, spaced farther apart, but still about once a month.[2]

Press Office growth continued under Pierre Salinger as President John F. Kennedy's Press Secretary (1961–1963). Salinger introduced live television broadcasts of Kennedy's news conferences from the State Department auditorium in what is now the old Executive Office Building west of the White House. Kennedy became the first President to meet a small group of television correspondents for an annual interview. His last such session in December 1962 drew much attention; he had planned a similar interview for 1963 until the assassination intervened.

President Lyndon B. Johnson (1963–1969), who experimented with various press conference formats, never found a satisfactory one. He even walked around the White House grounds with his dogs, Him and Her, in tow with the press frantically following. Johnson briefly retained Pierre Salinger as Press Secretary, but on Salinger's departure in early 1964, George E. Reedy was named; then Reedy was succeeded in turn by Bill Moyers and George Christian. All three men were able, but some Washington correspondents found Christian most faithfully reflected Johnson's views.

President Richard M. Nixon (1969–1974) deliberately downgraded the Press Secretary's position and held infrequent news conferences, believing correspondents distorted his views. Nixon preferred live television for presidential addresses without the Washington correspondent corps' "filtering" influence. In Nixon's tenure his press relations were stormy. Nixon had an encounter with CBS' Dan Rather in a Houston news conference at a broadcasters convention, and at a famous news conference in 1973 in Orlando, Florida, Nixon made his pronouncement on Watergate: "I am not a crook." Ronald Ziegler, the former advertising agency copywriter who served as Nixon's Press Secretary, accused *The Washington Post* of printing lies and distortions about the Watergate scandal, and later was forced to admit that his statement was "inoperative." Ziegler's relations with the press deteriorated so badly that when Communications Director Herb Klein left the White House, Ziegler was moved into Klein's slot. Press conferences during Nixon's final months were conducted by Deputy Press Secretary Gerald Warren.

Gerald R. Ford (1974–1977) entered the White House with much good will from the press; he tried to conduct more open media relations than his predecessor. But Ford's first Press Secretary, Jerald R. ter Horst, former *Detroit News* Washington correspondent, resigned after only a month in September 1974 to protest the President's decision to pardon Richard M. Nixon. The pardon embarrassed ter Horst who was kept in the dark, and assured the press that no pardon was pending. Ter Horst's successor was an NBC Washington correspondent, Ron Nessen, who served out the remainder of Ford's term. Ford held more frequent news conferences than Nixon, but Nessen was not as popular with the journalists as Salinger and Hagerty had been.

With the arrival of the Jimmy Carter Administration (1977–1981), Jody Powell served as Press Secretary. Powell had been on the Governor's staff in Atlanta. His relations started out well but because of the decline in Carter's popularity after the Bert Lance resignation as OMB director in late 1977, never were quite the same after that. An exception was Carter's favorable coverage during and immediately after the Camp David Summit with Egyptian President Anwar Sadat and Israeli Prime Minister Menachem Begin. Powell was respected by the correspondents because they knew he had ready access to President Carter and was one of his close advisers.[3]

Powell's reminiscences in *The Other Side of the Story* gave credit to the Ford staff for its assistance in the transition. Powell expressed resentment toward the press over a number of issues, including the Lance controversy and press exposés dealing with Billy Carter's business dealings. (The President's brother had been involved in overseas transactions considered questionable.) Powell also felt the media made too great an effort to pinpoint and emphasize Israeli reservations about the Camp David accords and the ensuing 1979 peace treaty negotiations involving the President.

Another focus of White House resentment during this period was the investigation by a special prosecutor of allegations against Hamilton Jordan, the Carter chief of staff, concerning use of drugs. While the degree of bitterness did not parallel that of the Nixon years, a higher degree of friction with the press marked the latter half of Carter's term. Factional disputes with Senator Edward M. Kennedy (D-Mass) and coverage of the Iranian hostage crisis aggravated this friction and kept it alive.[4]

Ronald Reagan, inaugurated in 1981 and 1985, has been served by three de facto Press Secretaries, although officially that title has been retained by Jim Brady. Brady's background before his initial appointment in 1981 had been that of a Capitol Hill press aide to Senator William Roth (R-Delaware). The affable Brady was critically injured March 30, 1981, when would-be assassin John Hinckley Jr. shot the President and gravely wounded Brady, who almost failed to survive. After that, most of Brady's responsibilities were handled by Deputy Press Secretary Larry Speakes, a veteran of Senator James Eastland's staff who had previously served in the Ford White House and with the Hill and Knowlton public relations firm.

Speakes left the administration in 1987 to take a public relations post with the Merrill Lynch brokerage firm in New York, where he stayed until a controversy over his actions during the 1985 Geneva summit prompted him to resign and go on the lecture circuit in 1988. Speakes was succeeded by Marlin Fitzwater, previously Vice President George Bush's Press Secretary, who like Brady, had Capitol Hill experience as a press officer.

In *Speaking Out: Inside the Reagan White House*, Speakes comments: "One of the main sources of pressure on me was a fellow White House aide, David Gergen . . . (who) was in the speechwriting shop." Speakes charged in his book that Gergen had designs on the Brady post, stating: ". . . (W)hile Brady was lying at death's door in the hospital, Gergen went to (Jim) Baker and suggested that he be given the title of Press Secretary in place of Brady. . . . (Later) Gergen was named director of White House communications, with control over the speechwriting unit and the out-of-town press corps, while I was appointed deputy assistant to the President and prinicpal deputy press secretary. . . ."[5]

A controversy arose over the following comment in Speakes' memoirs (preceding Speakes' resignation from Merrill Lynch):

> Fearing that Reagan was losing the media version of Star Wars, I instructed Mark Weinberg to draft some quotes for the President. I polished the quotes and told the press that while the two leaders stood together at the end of one session, the President said to Gorbachev, "There is much that divides us, but I believe the world breathes easier because we are talking here together." . . . Another Reagan quote which we manufactured that received extensive play in the press was, "Our differences are serious, but so is our commitment to improving understanding."

In retrospect, it was clearly wrong to take such liberties. Certainly, Reagan would not have disavowed the words, but the Soviets could have said they never heard anything like that. . . .[6]

The ensuing controversy apparently did not arise from surprise that busy prinicpals must rely on such assistance from their aides, but from Speakes' indiscretion in admitting that he did not clear the statement with the President before issuing it.

> As the time approached for the Reagan team to move into the White House, I remembered from my own experience with Ford when we left in 1977 and the Carter crew came in what a rude shock it was, leaving and not knowing what you were going to do. . . . I was the one who had to inform the press three days before Reagan took office that more than two dozen accountants, secretaries, mail openers, and others in low-level White House jobs were being fired. Most of those employees had been hired under Jimmy Carter to replace staffers from the Ford days, and I pointedly remarked, "We're going to treat the employees of the Carter Administration with the same dignity and courtesy that President Carter accorded the staff of President Ford in 1977." . . .[7]

Speakes also recalls the note of confusion added to the transition by concluding phases of the Iranian hostage crisis, as well as his own difficulties in reaching his new office as a result of zealous security people during the inaugural parade.

During the period from Salinger through Powell's tenure, the Press Office grew in size substantially. Besides serving the Washington correspondent corps, the Office set up an operation to handle its business with the out-of-town press, and an office of public affairs was established. This office handled assignment of speakers and varied contacts with the public.

Categories of Transitions

Interparty transfers of power are exemplified by the experiences of 1933, 1953, 1969, 1977 and 1981. Each will be discussed briefly.

Bitter differences over economic policy characterized the 1933 transition from Hoover to Roosevelt. In the Press Office, this involved a transfer from Joslin representing Hoover to Early as Roosevelt's agent. The Hoover Administration desperately sought to get Governor Roosevelt's backing for steps to deal with the Depression. The President-elect, feeling he lacked power and could not act until after the inauguration, demurred. This situation exacerbated the normal bitterness which follows a hard-fought election campaign. All press relations were focused on the effort to avoid undermining the government's credibility on economic policy. Many of these issues were dealt within the New Deal's first hundred days.

The 1953 transition lacked the bitterness over economic policy, but it was strained by President Truman's view that General Eisenhower had engaged in demagoguery in announcing his plans for a trip to Korea. Resentment by Eisenhower toward Truman was fueled by orders from the outgoing President that Major John Eisenhower be returned to Washington for the inauguration. What Truman felt was a perfectly natural desire to have the son present at his father's inauguration was construed by Eisenhower as an attempt to embarrass the President-elect. In the Press Office, Hagerty was taking over from Tubby and had to deal with the strained relations between the two men. This animosity apparently had abated by the time of President Kennedy's funeral when his two immediate predecessors shook hands.

It was perhaps because of the strained relationships that occurred in 1953 that some movements toward institutionalization of transition procedures affecting the Press Office developed by 1961. Despite the difficulties of 1953, President Truman had instructed his subordinates to conduct briefings of the incoming Eisenhower team. The Eisenhower staff did the same for the incoming Kennedy team in 1961. Despite partisan differences, the movement toward institutionalization in 1961 was perhaps helped along by political realities. President Kennedy's election by a slender margin made it necessary for him to seek support from moderate Republicans. Salinger found it helpful to have the assistance of Hagerty and his staff in the takeover, and the situation just referred to was reflected in the conferences President Kennedy held with Eisenhower regarding the Bay of Pigs aftermath and his consultations with General Douglas MacArthur about the situation in Vietnam.

The 1969 transition from Johnson to Nixon (from Christian to Ziegler in the Press Office) followed a campaign which ended in another close election. The initial Nixon slogan of "Bring Us Together" at the time of that transition was now undergirded by the experience of several recent transitions, so that a routinization of transitions was beginning.

A special set of circumstances accompanied the 1977 transition from Ford to Carter (from Nessen to Powell in the Press Office). Not only had a very close election occurred in 1976, but also the outgoing President who had taken office under terms of the 25th Amendment was serving as the first unelected President (in the sense that unlike other succeeding Vice Presidents, he had been confirmed by Congress under 25th Amendment procedures rather than elected by the voters). By this time a strong precedent had been established for cooperation across party lines as this was the fifth takeover involving the procedures following the Truman precedent for the 1953 transition.

The 1981 transition from Carter to Reagan (from Powell to Brady initially in the Press Office) was complicated by the strained relations between Presidents Carter and Reagan. Although President Carter and President Ford later exchanged visits at their respective presidential libraries, Carter's attacks on Reagan in his negative campaign in 1980 had not endeared the Georgian to his successor. Although the Reagans attended the Carter Library dedication, Jimmy Carter like Harry Truman between 1953 and 1961 was the object of an official snub. However, precedent was by now overcoming some of the personal animosities involved in transitions.

Transitions in the Press Office may occur within the same administration, as occurred in the Press Office during the Lyndon Johnson Administration. In 1964 the Press Secretary's office was turned over by Pierre Salinger to George E. Reedy; in 1966 Reedy left the White House and Bill Moyers took over; a year later George Christian took over from Moyers when the latter went to *Newsday* as its publisher. Christian's experience was as press aide to Governor Price Daniel of Texas; Reedy had served with Johnson on Capitol Hill, and Moyers came to the White House from the Peace Corps and has since had a distinguished career with CBS News and the Public Broadcasting Service.

In these transitions there was no real change in power, only a change in the style of the Press Secretary who is working for the same President.

Three examples can illustrate a third type of transition. This finds an emergency bringing a change in the Presidency, but with a Vice President of the same party succeeding to the Oval Office.

The change that occurred in 1945 found Jonathan Daniels assisting Stephen Early in the shift in the Press Office which involved a takeover of duties by Charles G. Ross, previously a correspondent for the *St. Louis Post-Dispatch*. Image problems were difficult for Mr. Ross, whose principal had to face comparison with a President who was highly popular, had guided the nation through the Great Depression and most of World War II, and who had had a 12-year tenure.

The 1963–1964 transition differed from the 1945 transition as well as that of 1923 in that unlike Harding and FDR, President Kennedy was the first assassination victim since President William McKinley in 1901. The difficult circumstances surrounding the transition which began November 22, 1963, included previous animosity between Attorney General Robert F. Kennedy and President Lyndon Johnson going back to the 1960 Democratic convention at Los Angeles at which the former opposed putting LBJ on the ticket.

The Press Office during this time found Pierre Salinger transferring the operation to George E. Reedy, who served Lyndon Johnson as press aide during his vice presidency. The two had worked together harmoniously between 1961 and 1963.

Perhaps the most unusual transition involving emergency situations was that in the summer of 1974, when President Nixon resigned in August after a Supreme Court ruling went against him in making possible the disclosure of the White House tapes which came at the end of the Watergate crisis. Gerald Ford, as vice president, had been walking a tightrope between loyalty to the President who appointed him and the need to avoid involvement with the series of events labeled Watergate. After becoming President, Ford felt compelled to testify before a congressional committee investigating the Nixon pardon to give his word of honor that there was no prearrangement for a *quid pro quo* connected with the Nixon resignation. It was a difficult period for the Press Office, with Ron Ziegler's credibility called into question, deputy Gerald Warren acting on his behalf, ter Horst being first designated by Ford and then resigning a month later because he was not told about the pardon, and Ron Nessen finally being designated as Press Secretary. During 1974 a good deal of instability occurred in press relations; this appeared to be in contrast to 1945 although the factional frictions may have borne some resemblance to the 1963–1964 transition.

The 1963–1964 Transition

Professor George E. Reedy recalled the 1963–1964 transition in

correspondence with the author early in 1988. According to Mr.
Reedy, currently Nieman Professor of Journalism at Marquette
University:

> The Kennedy-Johnson transition had some unusual features and
> I doubt whether it would fit the pattern of most such changes. For
> one thing, Pierre Salinger and I had become fairly good friends and
> he frequently sought my advice while JFK was still in office. He
> also included me in his pre-Presidential Press Conference briefings
> with government information officers. As a result, I was familiar
> with the mechanics of the Press Office at the time I took over and
> needed no period of instruction.
>
> The more important factor, however, was President Johnson's de-
> termination to reassure the American people that a crackpot with
> a rifle could not kill the U.S. Government — that assassination would
> merely bring into the Oval room another man who would do the
> same things. Therefore, he went out of his way to maintain as much
> of the Kennedy staff as he could and to follow the Kennedy style
> to the greatest extent possible. In effect, our transition was merely
> putting into place a new cast of characters.

On his most vivid recollection of the assassination transition,
Reedy commented:

> My most vivid memories center around the series of meetings called
> by LBJ to bring together the two staffs. I soon came to realize that
> he and the Kennedy staffers were at cross purposes. He was looking
> to them for indications of what Kennedy would have done had he
> lived; they were looking to him for indications of what he wanted
> them to do. I will always believe that someone misread a signal during
> those meetings and started the course towards becoming bogged
> down in Viet Nam. I tried on one or two occasions to explain to
> him that the basic psychology at work with the JFK people was 'the
> King is dead; long live the King' but he did not understand me.
> I tried to explain his motivations to some of them but that didn't
> work either. They were too accustomed to a strong, self-willed LBJ
> to believe in one who would subordinate his ego just to reassure
> the country.

With respect to presidential transitions, Reedy observed:

> As for the Press Staff itself, it would be helpful if the incoming Press
> Secretary could spend at least a month [presumably between
> November of election year and the ensuing January] in the Press
> Office working with the old staff. Essentially, it is a simple job once

the mechanics are understood. The real problem does not lie with the process but with the President who eventually will come to regard journalists as his enemy.[8]

The 1981 Transition

The 1981 Carter-Reagan transition was quite different from the 1963–1964 transition described by Reedy. For one thing, the 1981 transition involved a partisan shift in the White House. It was described in a November 1987 interview with David Gergen. As a Nixon speechwriter prior to the Nixon resignation in 1974 and as director of communications from 1981 to 1984 in the Reagan Administration, David R. Gergen, currently editor of *U. S. News and World Report*, was in a position to contrast the 1974 transition (an intraparty one) with the 1981 transition. The Gergen recollections, offered "with particular reference to communications and the press," dealt with both the transition to Ford and that to Reagan.

The similarity to the Kennedy-Johnson transition can be seen in Gergen's remarks about the Nixon-Ford transition:

> Now with regard to Ford (in 1974), he of course came in with a small team from the vice presidency and with him on the Hill, and there hadn't been much time through the transition to think through that issue; they simply had to go in and take over on Day One.
>
> Most of the Nixon people had clearly resigned, and he came in with his own press aides, and he soon named his own Press Secretary, Jerry ter Horst, and ter Horst and his successor Ron Nessen appointed the rest of the staff.

Gergen, differentiating the 1981 transition from that of 1974, commented:

> First, the transitions were utterly different. One was a prepared transition, and the other was not. In the Reagan case, Jim Baker worked in the transition effort, and it was understood at the time that he would become chief of staff, so that you had someone who had a personal as well as a professional interest in the success of the transition. He knew what kind of players he was helping put into place.

In discussing the designing of the Reagan Press Office, Gergen provided a context for the personnel selection process:

There was a large office which we rented on M Street here in Washington, and we had mostly full-time staff. I was working at the time at the American Enterprise Institute, and I worked at the center a fair portion of that time — the end of November, December (1980), early January (1981). Organizationally, the idea at that point was to determine who was going to head each section of the new White House staff, and then allow them to work with Jim and his assistants in filling out that group. For example, Max Friedersdorf was asked to head up the legislative office, and he then went out and recruited everyone else. . . . He came back to Baker with a list of those he thought would be best for the legislative office.

Similarly, with regard to the Press Office, a good deal of time was spent thinking through who would be the best Press Secretary. We reviewed a large number of names, and as that office is so closely tied to the President himself, several of the potential appointees actually went to see Reagan for interviews. We sorted out the names with Baker talking to Reagan from time to time; it was a fairly prolonged exercise because we couldn't settle on any one individual who was necessarily the best. . . .

A problem which faces those selecting Press Secretaries is the choice between selecting the prospective one most compatible with the President and his staff ideologically, or the one most likely to have smooth relationships with the press as a whole.[9] Gergen explained the problem and its resolution by the Reagan transition team this way:

In that office in particular [the Press Office], especially during the transition, there is a good deal of interest on the part of the President's partisan supporters in who it's going to be [as Press Secretary]. With an ideological President such as Reagan, naturally the conservatives wanted someone who believed in their cause and was more conservative, so we did look at several conservatives.

There was a conflicting point of view which was that, while Pat Buchanan individually was certainly an outstanding individual, it would be better not to have too combative a Press Secretary at the opening gun. There were those who were veterans of Washington and also some within the original Reagan entourage from California, such as Mike Deaver, who thought it would be better to have someone who got along well through thick and thin and would not be ideological. The idea was that the President himself would carry the ideological burden, and the Press Secretary's role should be more neutral and not that of an adversary.

He should be someone who would provide information and would not have a bitter relationship with the press. It was also felt that there was no reason to pick a fight with the press. We should succeed far better by getting some legislative victories under our belts, and establish the respect they would have for the President, and enact his agenda over time and get his measures out of the box.

In any event, after a fair amount of discussion and a lot of looking, it was agreed that the man who had been acting as the Press Secretary during the transition, Jim Brady, would in fact make a very fine Press Secretary in his own right. That recommendation went forward to Reagan that he place Brady in the Press Secretary's position.

It was a concurrent recommendation that he also ask Karna Small to come with him as his deputy, and we were looking for a second deputy. Brady thought Larry Speakes would be an ideal one. Speakes of course went on to succeed Jim very ably.

Because of the structure of the speechwriting operation, dealings with the international press, handling requests for speakers and information from individuals outside the press, special needs of radio and television broadcasters, and special needs of the out-of-town press, it should not come as a surprise that the communications director had broader responsibilities. Gergen commented:

I might say one other thing: that there is far more than selecting the Press Office staff involved in the transition on the communications side. A good deal of time [in the Reagan transition] also went into the preparation of an agenda that he could pursue in the early months of his Presidency that would not only relate to legislation and his political activities but would also relate to the communications of his program to the country.

We spent an enormous amount of time studying the records of other Presidents, previous Presidents, what they had done in their first 100 days, and to determine what their mistakes were, what positive things they had done that had helped their Presidencies, and from that a group of us worked on what we called the 100-day plan. This was essentially a communications plan of how Reagan could get off to a fast start, and it was tied very closely to his legislative agenda, as the whole idea was to build public support, mobilize public support for his legislative agenda.[10]

And I must say a good deal of the genius in the success of Jim Baker as chief of staff [in explaining the significance of having an integrated and coordinated strategy] was that he was one of the few chiefs of staff in my knowledge who has successfully blended legislative, political, and communications activities in one plan, and to really work in that direction. He drew those reins, all three of those reins, into his hands, as chief of staff during the transition. And he was able to pull on all three at the same time in a way that we worked together as opposed to apart from each other, and I think that was one of the successes of that transition.

A further lesson was drawn by Gergen in assessing the wide range of ages and experiences in the Reagan camp, which the former communications director felt broadened the variety of viewpoints available to the President: "Another lesson, I think, for the success of the Reagan case is that his staff were older; he didn't restrict himself. One of the things that you find in the Presidency is that the average age of the staff is decreasing, from Kennedy through Carter, so that by Carter's time the average age of people in charge of the White House was mostly in their 30's. Reagan . . . for a variety of reasons, brought in some older people. Which was a good thing to do, not that 35-year-olds don't have a lot to contribute — they have an enormous amount to contribute — but you don't want your entire team relatively new to the job."

New technologies [introduced since the last interparty shift of power in 1977] have basically made the challenge more complicated. You see a bewildering variety now of communication techniques, so that any press operation is practically a 24-hour-a-day proposition. You have to deal not only with the so-called pencil press, the print press, but the electronic press is far larger, it's very demanding in its needs, and it's very, very immediate in the way that they communicate information.

News out of the White House now is almost instantaneous, so that the number of people who are involved has just grown by leaps and bounds; it's just gigantic in the number of people who cover the White House. All that makes it more complicated. It hasn't changed the nature of communications. The lessons and models that were set by Jim Hagerty apply as well today as they did then. It's simply the numbers that are different.

It may be a general rule that transitions prompt observers in and outside the press to look for efforts to overcome flaws and problems that plagued the preceding administration. In this context, Gergen's reaction to the problems of the 1981 transition was that

. . . the 1980–1981 transition was almost a model of what a transition should be like. We were able to learn — I must say that there were people in the Carter Administration who were extraordinarily helpful, primarily Jack Watson and Hamilton Jordan and Jody Powell — were extraordinarily helpful in recognizing that the Presidency is not simply a partisan institution — helpful to the Reagan people in how the system worked, how the lay of the land was, what they had done. That eased the transition a good deal. By that time there was also a lot of scholarship on the transition — there was a lot of lore on that issue. . . . Everyone took the transition seriously and I think it worked about as smoothly as I think one could.

I must say I think the Carter people were influenced to a degree by the Ford People as they left, who were quite gracious and it helped in easing the transition for the Carter people, and in turn I think that has become part of the tradition of transitions. I would expect that the Reagan Administration, whether or not it's a Democrat or a Republican who's elected in 1988, will be extremely helpful.

Someone like Ed Meese, for example, cared deeply about the transition. He was a very, very important player as the transition chief of staff. Baker essentially organized the White House; Ed Meese spent a good deal of his time helping to organize the departments, and he held daily meetings during the transition, to think through the problems of the transition, so that we had a lot of talent working through that transition. Bill Casey was the chairman.

People took it seriously, were dedicated to the idea of helping Ronald Reagan get off to a fast start. We had a very large team to work on substantive issues for the departments, and what ought to be the priorities of each department. I have to say . . . I do think the Reagan transition was about as well handled as any transition . . . There were very few special difficulties of which I am aware.[11]

Many observers feel that since James C. Hagerty's day the pattern of activity in the White House Press Office has been remarkably stable as to the general function of informing the public through the press, despite many technological changes. The White House Press Office pattern of operation in dissemination of information can perhaps only be understood against the background of a growing trend toward specialization. This along with the growth of the correspondent corps has multiplied the ways in which the basic functions continue to be performed.

The Washington correspondent corps is still served by the main part of the Press Office, as it has been for many years. But now a number of different tasks have been added. A special section of the Press Office deals with interview requests and other business from the out-of-town press. An office of public affairs deals with requests for speakers for community groups in and outside Washington. Specific needs of the out-of-town press are focused on by another part of the Press Office. Still another is concerned with equipment needs of radio correspondents. Different needs in terms of camera and other technical equipment have to be met for television correspondents. The Office of Public Liaison deals with out-of-town press and related needs while non-press public relations clear through the Office of Public Affairs.

Needs of the international press are dealt within this structure by press aides, just as information officers deal with the special needs of television and radio, as well as print media.

Further change will be likely as specialization grows and technology advances. Incoming administrations should keep abreast of these technologies while recognizing that the principal task of the Press Office remains that of achieving the goal of articulating clearly the President's policies and making them understandable to the public. Strong policy planning preceding the election, during the campaign, will make this task easier according to those who have served in the Press Office.

CHAPTER TWENTY-SEVEN

Presidential Communication: An Essential Leadership Tool

THOMAS C. GRISCOM*
PROFESSOR OF COMMUNICATIONS/PUBLIC AFFAIRS
UNIVERSITY OF TENNESSEE AT CHATTANOOGA

In his book, *Behind the Front Page*, "Washington Post" political correspondent David Broder describes President Reagan's communication strategy as "projecting his voice and his views far more widely than any other politician's. It has enhanced the power of the Communicator-in-Chief as against that of other institutions of government, particularly Congress and state and local elective officials. I would not strip any of these tools from the President, for communication is central to his leadership ability, and this system of government does not function well without strong presidential leadership."

A few pages earlier, in the chapter on "Reagan's Way—and a Better Way," he notes that "Ronald Reagan's relationship with the press evolved through almost six years of stunningly successful news management, followed by one of the most embarrassing and politically costly blowups in the modern presidency. . . . In only a few weeks, a man who seemed the master of presidential public relations saw his image begin to crumble . . . (and) cast into doubt Reagan's political effectiveness in his final two years as President."

Those excerpts from Broder present an accurate assessment of communication by this President. He commanded the media as the tool for getting his message out, but also became dependent on the searching, searing words of the media to interpret the power and impact of the first presidency in more than twenty years to span two full terms.

President Reagan built on an ever evolving presidential model to communicate important ideas to the American people using news conferences, addresses from the Oval Office, and regular

---

* *Professor Griscom served at the White House as Assistant to the President for Communications and Planning before his appointment in the Summer of 1988 at the University of Tennessee.*

Saturday radio addresses as a vehicle for policy dissemination. In doing so, he shaped and formed the public debate to produce a national consensus.

Unlike Congress, which on any given day has many differing voices on a particular point, a President, as an originator of information, is able to draw clear lines that influence national and international policy. For example, as Congress wrestled with the War Powers Act to determine whether it applied to a certain foreign policy initiative, the President was able to focus attention on and build public support for the placement of American military resources in a strategic area of the world. In large part, the support for his decision was based on the President succinctly communicating a single policy goal rather than having to gather differing voices for a concise objective.

President Reagan examined the array of communication outlets at his disposal and made sure that the focus framed his side of the argument and minimized his opponent's counterattacks.

During the campaign of 1980 when he defeated President Jimmy Carter, Ronald Reagan, recognizing the importance of television, maximized the visual opportunities that accompanied the message. The President and his aides decided the best time and the best format to lay out his message. Sometimes it might be in Hoboken with the Statue of Liberty looming in the background, or on the steps of the Capitol in Washington, but certainly in a setting where the visual complemented the line-of-the-day. Always it was with the understanding that while the word was important, so was the way it was pictured. Attention was also given to controlling his exposure to inquisitive reporters' questions so that it did not make him more vulnerable to conflicting messages on a particular day.

In most cases, President Reagan was successful. His ability to convince the American people, and thereby the Congress, to reverse 40 years of government policies was, by any measurement, a major achievement. Through the use of the media, primarily television, President Reagan generated the public support necessary to pressure a reluctant Congress to cut spending. On the tax side, his approach was to consistently refer to the last tax cuts, implemented by President Kennedy, and appeal to Democrats to embrace a policy they had overwhelmingly supported in the early 1960s. His early victories came, in part, by crafting and controlling public perception of change in the nation. The impact could still be seen at the Democratic debate in Washington in December 1987. Senator Albert Gore quizzed Senator Paul Simon on how he would pay for "new" federal programs. That question was a direct result of a President, of the opposite party, being able to reshape and refocus the public debate; to dominate the public airwaves.

What became apparent was that this President had an extraordinary ability to communicate his message in precise language: a positive tool for any President, but particularly for one who came into office with an established agenda. To reach his goals, domination of the message was essential.

For a President to be a leader, he must work with the news media and use his White House staff and Cabinet to reinforce his themes. The use of support staff as "the other voices" in a town that listens to repeated echoes is essential.

When the President decided to reform the tax code, his message had to drive and dominate the whole issue development process. It is not enough for the President to be perceived as merely a voice. Repetition by a wide range of people both inside and outside of government can turn an idea into a political reality. This President mastered that technique for almost six years — as Broder noted in his book. To win — in Washington where winning is everything — there was *his* voice drowning out all others.

Early in his first term, there was pressure on the President to spell out his entire legislative plan in 1981 and put on a full court press to achieve those objectives immediately. He and his staff realized that his strength was to draw public attention to a particular issue, and not to diffuse his message. That principle prompted him to push ahead in the first six months with his budget and tax changes, putting on hold, at least temporarily, some of the more emotional social issues.

Not that those were unimportant, but the opportunity to galvanize early public support for his economic program was critical. His message was finely tuned and coordinated to look at the mistakes of the past: double-digit inflation, 20 percent interest rates, rising unemployment. He counter-balanced those with his vision for a growing economy with low inflation, low interest rates, and greater job creation. The White House team spelled out the message, and the proposed revisions occurred. The President set the policy, set the direction, set the message, and an administration team followed his lead. The media was given a single voice with little deviation. The American people responded by sending letters and making phone calls to members of Congress, and the proposals became law.

The presidency was the offense. And it was carefully orchestrated using the media to create a positive change — leadership.

Compare that to the situation in late 1986.

Less attention had been given to his message since the re-election in 1984. President Reagan returned to an economy moving ahead and the determination to preserve those things that he achieved in 1981; but not the same dominant theme control that marked the first four years. The focus from 1985 onward shifted more to foreign policy, which is not as easy to manage through a day-to-day communication plan. For example, consider the relationship with the Soviet Union: four Soviet leaders, stalled arms control talks because of the proposal to ban inter-mediate range missiles and pressure for unilateral disarmament. Clearly, that is not the picture one would pitch to a client as a major communication strategy. There was less focus on objectives, allowing the media to select the items to be highlighted and communicated to the public at large.

The President and his new White House staff found a country and a press corps that was more skeptical of his policies and his ability to set the agenda.

The 1986 mid-year election found the Democrats regaining control of the Senate after six years out of power. This drastic political change raised questions about who would establish the legislative priorities for the final two years of the presidential term: Congress or the White House.

And then the Iran-Contra affair broke. The result was White House confusion. The President's staff became part of a growing communication problem. The media and public pressed for details and the communication control that had marked his administration was not there. For all the Reagan White House had done in the first four years to "produce" the news, this four-month period in late 1986 and early 1987 threatened to bring it all to a close.

A President who had been able to structure the political landscape was now being seen as out of touch and unable to handle the issues. The support role that had been played so well by some on the White House staff was now virtually non-existent. In other words, a well-oiled public relations machine sputtered and communication mistakes were made that fed a growing sense of trouble.

Why did it happen?

The strain brought on any organization during a time of pressure can result in certain actions being taken or not taken. No matter what the situation is, well-skilled communicators deal with the problems, set them straight, and then recapture control.

The President held a news conference in November in which he tried to answer many of the questions arising from the Iranian arms shipments. But the unfolding story did not go away. Each answer prompted more questions. Then in January, the President underwent surgery and his schedule was sharply curtailed, giving the impression of a leadership void. The White House press corps, deprived of access to the President and his key policy makers, took on the role of communicator and attempted to portray a White House in hiding. The image created was a disengaged presidency. The media, an ally in other times, became the harsh critic and controller of the public message from the White House.

Confidence in the President fell to an all time low, with pollmaster Dick Wirthlin showing that President Reagan's approval rating was in the high thirties. Even worse, the number of Americans who believed he was not telling the truth was twice as high as those who felt he was.

A scene in the Roosevelt Room at the White House on March 1, 1987, illustrates this lack of direction. Senior aides were struggling with a planned Presidential address to the nation and a follow-up press conference the next week. The dates were already on the calendar and announced. Finally, the focus turned to what to say. Something had fundamentally gone awry—the event drove the message rather than the message driving the event. Those early guidelines of coordination were lost. The plan was to put out the best weapon—the President—and see what happened. Dan Rather commented on the "CBS Evening News" that the March 1987 presidential press conference, the first in over five months, was going to "determine" whether this President could still govern. That raised the importance of the press conference to an all-time high.

Both events came and went. The President put some of the persistent, nagging questions in perspective; although others remained. At least, a plan was developed to recast and communicate the next eight months: the Reagan presidency was still viable, he had told the truth, and it was time to get on with the country's business while the investigation unfolded.

But the damage had been done. Political pundits continued to speculate that the country would be on hold until the presidential election in November 1988. They were wrong, misjudging the resiliency of the President and his ability to restore his communication skills, to once again capture public attention, not to diminish the investigations, but to make them part of the daily routine. While the news media focused mainly on the Tower Commission, appointed by the President, the American people were not so one-dimensional in their interests and concerns.

There was a realization at the White House that, regardless of the Iran-Contra hearings, it was better to have the President actively participating in government rather than sitting on the sidelines.

A President is the tone setter, the one person this nation turns to for leadership in a time of crisis. The failure to answer that call can be devastating and the results can flow into every area of his authority.

President Reagan, knowing that he could not erase the Iran-Contra affair, put it in context and moved on to other issues. He called for an Economic Bill of Rights, repackaging some of the fundamental Reagan economic planks of the line-item veto and a balanced budget amendment, that engaged the Congressional leadership in striking a budget compromise. His tenacity in pushing the Soviets for a verifiable INF treaty led to two successful summits that put his imprint on U.S.-Soviet relations. He commanded the stage and he spelled out the objectives—not afraid to face controversy in order to achieve his aims. Hugh Sidey wrote in TIME magazine in June 1988, the Administration was "steadied and nudged off again in the right direction." Those are some of the communication and message management techniques that the next President and the next will review in charting a course for presidential handling of the agenda.

Just as his predecessors tossed ideas into the air to determine the appropriate ways to nudge along policy decisions, so this President has added to that cadre of ideas.

The press conference was seen by this Administration as only one means to influence the decision-makers. Recognizing that he operated better in more controlled settings, the President set out to finely hone his message and to place it in a more structured format. There is nothing wrong with a President deciding how he wants to come across to the American people. President Reagan utilized the electronic media as his main source for communication with the public, and he used the Oval Office address effectively as an integral part of his communication strategy.

However, because it worked for this President does not mean that it will work for successive presidents. Each has to determine how best to get his voice, his hopes, into the public debate. To this end, the news media will remain the natural vehicle for such expression in a timely way.

The relationship that naturally exists between a President and those who depict him and his policies to a curious public audience will not be altered. Possibly, there will be a clearer acceptance of the responsibility the media has as the primary vehicle to communicate the leadership image of the President. There should be no illusions; it means dealing with the good as well as the bad. A complete communication strategy looks past today's events and plans for tomorrow's. But foremost, the public perception of the President and his ability to shape the discussion requires his direct, continual involvement. Americans look to a President as a calming figure in a sea of storms; if he is not there to demonstrate the skill to navigate treacherous times, then the void that exists will be filled and controlled by others.

PART EIGHT

The President and Congress

Notes to the Next Administration: Thoughts on Effective Congressional Relations and Legislative Liaison

KENNETH M. DUBERSTEIN
CHIEF OF STAFF TO THE PRESIDENT OF THE UNITED STATES

DAVID C. KOZAK
PROFESSOR OF POLITICAL SCIENCE
GANNON UNIVERSITY

Inevitably, the next president and his top assistants will soon come to realize — as all of their predecessors have — that relations with Congress must receive highest priority. They may think they understand this now, but the sheer weight of Congress must be felt first-hand before it is fully appreciated.

The U.S. political system is not a unitary one. The consent of a highly independent Congress is required before major presidential initiatives can be enacted. As Jeff Fishel has so succinctly stated, "Presidents control what they initiate; other institutions (especially the Congress) control what presidents achieve."[1] How well the President works with and influences Congress will strongly affect Presidential standing and prestige and the president's ability to determine public policy. In sum, presidents cannot overemphasize congressional liaison, especially at the outset of a new administration. Whomever we elect and inaugurate as President Reagan's successor is going to have to be able to get on with the formidable U.S. Congress. And one of the major criteria by which he and his administration surely will be judged is how well he can persuade the Congress on his programs.

The purpose of this essay is to offer the new administration of 1989 some recommendations on how to deal effectively with Congress, how to manage relations with "the Hill," and how to derive maximum gains from that relationship. The essay reflects the different vantage points of the two authors: Chief of Staff to the President Duberstein, who previously served as Assistant to the President for Legislative Affairs from 1982–83 and as Deputy Assistant for the House during the critical year 1981, provides recollections of strategic success and early planning. Kozak, who taught courses in legislative affairs and liaison in Washington, D.C. at a U.S. Government institute, has conducted an academic study based on interviews with more than twenty-five legislative liaison experts within the Reagan administration. Our hope is to blend these practitioner and academic perspectives.

Our essay unfolds in four parts: (1) general propositions about the U.S. political system, Congress as an institution, and doing business in a pluralistic democracy; (2) recommendations concerning congressional relations in the transition; (3) a strategy for maximizing Presidential influence; and (4) suggestions for continued effective interface between the administration and Congress.

1. General Propositions about the U.S. Political System, Congress as an Institution, and Doing Business in a Pluralistic Democracy

Effective relations with the Hill need to be conducted with the following general propositions in mind. Each needs to be part of the operational code of any President who hopes to succeed on the Hill.

Understand the System

The American system is predicated on a deliberate fragmentation of power that creates co-equal branches. To use Neustadt's famous phrase, the essence of the American political system is "separate institutions sharing power."[2] For Edward Corwin, the constitution is "an invitation to struggle between President and Congress" with regard to national priorities.[3] The result is a political system featuring adversarial rivalry and ceaseless agitation.

The framers of the U.S. Constitution were not interested in creating a neat, orderly, efficient government. They were driven by a desire to protect and preserve individual liberty. It was their hope that they could structurally prevent a constitutional dictatorship by creating multiple centers of power comprised of different institutions. Furthermore, each institution was to be constitutionally intruded into the business of the other in a scheme of checks and balances whereby power would countervail power and ambition would rival ambition. Such is the legacy of the American system, and the first step toward wisdom in effective relations with Congress is acknowledging Congress's legitimate responsibilities, powers, and functions in the policy process. Congress is the strongest legislative body in the world. Despite a worldwide decline of legislatures this century, the U.S. Congress has grown in its authority. Its powers of the purse and statutory and oversight policy tools are truly awesome.

Politics in a pluralistic system is best practiced with a sense of mutual respect

Adversarial relations do not require acrimony. Different positions and interests can and should be pursued in an atmosphere of comity and mutual respect. This doesn't mean you should run from a fight — it means that, as Sam Rayburn used to say, "you learn to disagree agreeably." As a result, the system will run much better and the chances of maximizing your goals over the long run will increase.

Understand Congress as a Unique Institution

Congress is a unique organization. Its members are independently elected. Within the Congress, therefore, there exist 535 separate political fiefdoms.

Four aspects of Congress's peculiar structure must be kept in mind. First, Congress is a political institution, driven by an electoral connection. Members get there through an election and want to get reelected. Of course, this means pursuing electoral and constituency interests. Second, there are many power centers on the Hill: two houses; subcommittees and committees in each for authorizations, appropriations and budgets; informal work groups; and staff, staff, staff. Third, although congressional leaders have the potential to centralize this diffuse structure, they are less influential than they used to be. And, finally, the congressional process has multiple stages, involving numerous successive decision points (e.g.: subcommittee, committee, floor, conference) each of which requires a separate strategy. Furthermore, each policy domain (agriculture, defense, education, etc.) constitutes a distinctive issue-network subsystem, replete with its indigenous power structure in Congress. Each must be worked separately.

From an administration's point of view, the consequence of

these characteristics is the creation of a policy process that moves slowly and incrementally and is strongly affected by constituency parochialism. All who work with Congress need to be ever mindful that it is more a conflict resolution body than a solutions-oriented body. This is key to understanding it.

'Bipartisanship' and 'Compromise' are the watchwords for dealing with Congress

In almost all votes on the Hill, victory comes as the result of bipartisan coalition-building. A President will, of course, start with a base afforded by his own party in Congress. But, because of inevitable defections, the administration must build beyond this by encouraging support from the opposition party. For this to happen, another Rayburnism must be observed: "always realize that today's adversary on a particular bill may be tomorrow's ally on other bills." In other words, keep the lines of communication open to the opposition. You'll need them.

Of course, give and take compromise is the lubricant of a pluralistic system. You can't have it all your way. You can hold out for the best deal but you've got to deal and at the right time. And, you need always keep in mind the famous LBJ dictum: "half a loaf is better than none." Always keep your principles and promises in mind, but a simple fact of life in a system of shared power is that effectiveness in policymaking requires bargaining, negotiation and eventual accommodation. This policy process responds best to consensus-building rather than cause-driven zealotry.

The President is expected to be a legislative leader; but that doesn't happen automatically

Presidents must provide legislative leadership. Even most members of Congress acknowledge the need for an activist President to lead the nation; but that leadership is something that must be won and then safeguarded through hard work and sophisticated power-wielding.

It is vital for the functioning of the American political system that the President be effective in leading Congress. As analysts from Hamilton to Neustadt have emphasized, the U.S. Presidency constitutes the unity and energy of the American system, the one true centripetal force in an otherwise fragmented structure. It is the one institution offering the potential for coordinated, integrated, and centralized policymaking. Harry Truman may have stated it best, "The President is the only official elected by all the people. He is the lobbyist for all of the people."[4] If the nation is to have policy coherence and direction, the president must be able to exercise influence on the Hill.

The nature of the American system is such that many factors combine to constrain and limit Presidential power, especially Presidential leadership of Congress. The President and the Congress reflect different time frames, policy roles and perspectives, and constituencies. Inevitably, this means that the President and the Congress may be at loggerheads. Members of Congress — though generally high-minded, nation and public interest oriented — are in the last analysis understandably driven by constituency and re-election interests that do not always coincide with "the national interest." Congress frequently reflects partisan, parochial, short-term, and segmented concerns. And, an assertive Congress incessantly attempts to impose its will on the administration in order to put its imprint on public policy.

To survive and prevail, presidents must carefully husband their limited stocks of power. Power cannot be squandered needlessly on agenda overload and fighting for impossible causes. When a President goes to the mat with the Congress he must go to win. Every potential conflict with Congress must be gauged for its impact on the President's prospective power — the ability to influence future events on the Hill.[5] Success will beget success; failure will foreordain more failure. Always, the President must have the perception if not the reality of being able to influence the Congress. He must be viewed as a winner, as a force to be dealt with, and as someone who plays to and frequently does in fact win. This does not come easily nor automatically. Some practical observations along these lines: Don't stake all your prestige unless you have a high probability of winning. If you make a deal stay with it. If you threaten the veto, use it, unless the threat has already accomplished the changes you seek.

Presidential prestige, public standing, and professional reputation in dealing with Congress are inextricably intertwined. The sophisticated exercise of power in dealing with Congress will stand a President well. Maladroit relations with the Hill will cause incalculable political difficulties on that and other fronts.

2. Recommendations Concerning Congressional Relations in the Transition

The approximately ten-week transition period between election and inauguration is a crucial one for establishing the proper relations with Congress. As Neustadt points out, there is great hazard as well as opportunity in the transition.[6] The outset of an administration involves a honeymoon period, a rare time of relative harmony between President and Congress and also a rare open window for Presidential leadership of Congress. Except under conditions of grave national crisis or emergency, the President will never have a greater opportunity to steer the ship of state. A smooth transition emphasizing congressional relations will provide a firm foundation for subsequent good relations. Awkward transition and early missteps will not only close the window and preclude Presidential leadership in this crucial early period in the life of an administration, but also create an image of ineptitude that will be exceedingly difficult to shake. In Washington, neutralizing and overcoming an image of political incompetence is almost impossible. It takes a long time to come back, and while recovering you lose the ability to influence.

The Reagan transition of 1980 established a strong base from which the administration was able to build and develop a successful strategy for dealing with Congress. Among some of the important lessons learned are the following.

Hit the ground running

An imperative in the transition is to organize for congressional relations as early as possible. A President will not have a better opportunity to exercise Presidential leadership than at the beginning of a new administration. Legislative liaison must take advantage of this and that means being organized at the outset. The beginning of a new administration is no time for awkwardness, false starts, and a rickety shake-down cruise. You never get a second chance to make a first impression. Congressional relations have to be organized from the start.

The Reagan transition team featured an office of congressional relations that well served the administration. It made early contact with members of Congress on behalf of the President-elect, signifying the priority President Reagan placed on having good working relations with Congress. Such early efforts are indispensable for effective liaison with Congress.

Keep the President's legislative agenda focused on a few crucial agenda items

To take maximum advantage of the honeymoon period, the administration's legislative agenda must be prepared early. Moreover, agenda overload must be avoided at all costs. The President is most likely to maximize legislative benefits with an initial highest priority agenda that entails no more than two or three items. These proposals should reflect major themes of the President's campaign platform, be ideas for which a mandate can be reasonably claimed, and be politically feasible on the Hill. Keeping it simple, not overcrowding the focus of the country nor of the Congress, and offering proposals embodying mandate ideas floated in the campaign that are likely to carry in the Congress will start any administration out on the right foot.

The Reagan administration's budget and tax proposals are a great case illustration. Both were campaign pledges, enjoyed early support and offered reasonable opportunity for success. A macro focus on only those two legislative priorities kept the calendar uncluttered and gave an all-so-important early impression of Presidential success.

Develop and cultivate a team concept with members of Congress as soon as possible

Some of the best relations Presidents develop with members of Congress grow out of a sense of teamwork. Two factors help produce a team concept. One is early and continued consultation between a President and congressional leadership — especially the leadership of his own party in House and Senate who will serve as loyal lieutenants in their respective chambers. Presidential candidates cannot begin this process too early. Consultation needs to be continued with regard to top Presidential appointments and devising the policy agenda.

A second factor contributing to teamwork begins even before the election as the Presidential candidate campaigns with his party's candidates for the House and Senate. Developing and continuing such a sense of "shared fates" helps enormously.

Recruit experienced Congressional operatives for Congressional Liaison staffs

An almost universally acknowledged, early, critical, misstep of the Carter administration was the appointment of the head of the White House Office of Congressional Affairs. A talented and subsequently successful liaison official, he was unfortunately hampered by his own lack of Hill experience. The hard lesson learned: staff liaison offices with people who know the Hill and, more importantly, people whom are known to the players — both members and staffers — themselves.

The choice of Max Friedersdorf and his staff of experienced congressional liaison specialists from both the Hill and the Nixon-Ford liaison apparatus was a deliberate effort by the Reagan administration to avoid this early problem on the Hill and enable President Reagan to hit the ground running.

Get the President's personal time for Congressional liaison

Presidents usually are most influential when they bring their own political skills to bear on powerful and key members of Congress. A number of rules of thumb must be observed in effectively exercising personal bargaining. First, the importance of time being allocated for this purpose must be impressed on the President and his scheduler. The President's personal time — that most crucial commodity of the Presidency — must be freed up in order for the President to make and take calls, to receive emissaries from the Hill, and to bargain. Next, the President must meet with not just the congressional leadership but the many bloc, issue-area and strategically located powers who make things go and stop in Congress. In early strategizing about initial programs, it is wise to give these players a stake in the outcome, perhaps by getting their advice and relying on their help. Last, although certainly all members are not equal, effective relations with Congress require an early reaching out to both the opposition and junior back-benchers. Coalition building is crucial. Good relations established early on can be energized on close votes vital for continuing a President's "magic" on the Hill.

The AWACS vote is a good case in point. In 1981, there was a good chance that a Presidential veto of legislation prohibiting the administration's sale of AWACS aircraft to Saudi Arabia would be overridden. The legislation would have dealt a major loss of face to the administration. To avoid that, it was imperative that the President personally lobby Congress as Commander in Chief and Head of State. President Reagan's involvement was significant. He put aside more than eight hours on the eve of the vote to make personal calls to wavering and undecided members. It worked, and a potentially embarrassing defeat was averted and turned into "magical" victory.[7]

3. A Strategy for Maximizing Presidential Influence

Moving legislation through Congress is a most uncertain process. Numerous hurdles and chokepoints exist to undermine even the most forcefully pressed of Presidential proposals. Legislation can be bottled up in subcommittee or committee, pigeonholed in the scheduling process, and scuttled on the floor or in conference committee. Congressional leadership — even those friendly to you — will sometimes be a barrier to working the administration's way. To cope, Presidents must have a sense of strategic thinking and timing in dealing with Congress. The following are offered as ingredients for successful strategy:

Package it

For the Congress, the more general a bill is, the more likely it is to be adopted. Of course, the reason for this is rooted in coalition-building. A broad bill that lumps together several items attracts more supporters, offers something to everyone, and becomes very difficult to oppose. The Reagan administration benefited enormously from the omnibus nature of the 1981 and 1982 reconciliation bills. This all encompassing character contributed significantly to the crucial budget victories. There are, however, limits to packaging. The trend over the last few sessions toward super legislation offered with a take it or leave it approach, especially in appropriations vehicles, substantially constrains Presidential power.

Give bills a catchy, politically appealing name

Bills with such tags as "the Economic Revitalization Act" or "the Fiscal Responsibility Resolution" become hard to oppose. To maximize the chances for success, legislative strategy sessions should devote some effort to naming bills.

Try to get proposed legislation assigned to the jurisdiction of a favorable committee

Because committee jurisdictions overlap, proponents of legislation have some say in how a bill will be assigned. Care should be taken to insure in drafting that a bill will go to a committee offering the best chances for a favorable hearing.

Work key members of Congress, giving them a stake in passing proposed legislation

Each bill requires a separate strategy. Key members on subcommittee, committee and in leadership need to be courted. Legislating is a lot easier when they are supportive, help carry the water, and have pride of ownership.

Know how and when to bargain

In a system of separated powers, government becomes a bargaining arena. Things are not done simply because the President says they should be done. They are done because a bargain has been struck for them to be done that way. A most important skill for moving legislation along is the ability to negotiate and strike a deal. Bargaining must be honed and developed to a finely tuned art form.

Occasionally, when necessary, threaten to "go over their heads"

When faced with a recalcitrant Congress, Presidents have an important trumpcard to play: go to the people. Put the heat on members by going to the people in public statements and press opportunities. The television-oriented bargaining arena in Washington provides incentives for this ploy.[8] An occasional, adroit direct appeal will yield substantial dividends. However, this is a ploy that should not be over-used. Going public too frequently can dissipate a valuable presidential resource.

Understand that there is no "sudden death" on the Hill

Legislative finality is rare. Issues and programs rarely die or fade away; things are hardly even brought to closure. Even when a bill is authorized, it must receive an appropriation. Even when you have succeeded with both authorization and appropriations, you still must worry about being derailed in the implementation phase. It never ends and you shouldn't expect it to. Things can come apart even after you think you've put them to bed. Conversely, never assume an item you have "killed" is truly dead. Accept this fact of legislative life readily and remain constantly vigilant.

4. Suggestions for Continued Effective Interface Between the Administration and Congress

Effective legislative liaison requires persistent, continuous inter-action. There are essentially two modes of congressional relations: fire-fighting and gardening. The first is ad hoc, reactive trouble-shooting, e.g. stopping a harmful amendment. The second, is an effort to cultivate ongoing and somewhat permanent relations. If gardening is well done, some of the fire-fighting will not be necessary.

A recent survey of twenty-five experts in legislative affairs provided many insights into what makes for good legislative liaison. The following are among the most frequently mentioned tips on legislative gardening for those representing the administration on the Hill. We have divided them into three categories: Congress as an institution, agency internal processes, and selling the agency's programs.

Congress as an institution

• The Hill is a small town. To be an effective representative of your office, you have to get to be a citizen of it. Personal relationships are the key.

• Know the members, their themes, priorities, concerns back home, and staff. Spend time on the Hill: talk, observe, listen. The key is being visible.

• Don't bypass staff. Any approach to a member should include staff.

• Develop an information network that includes members from both parties in both houses on major substantive committees, appropriations subcommittees, and in the leadership.

• Know where to go for information on what is happening in Congress. Follow *CQ Weekly Reports*, *National Journal*, *Roll-Call*, to name a few.

• Understand the differences between the House and Senate and adapt liaison strategies accordingly. The House—because it is larger—is more structured, more committee-oriented and more driven by rules and procedure. The smaller Senate is more flexible, less committee- and more floor-oriented, and driven by unanimous consent resolutions. Because of the possibilities of filibusters and non-germane amendments (riders), agencies must constantly monitor the Senate.

Agency internal processes

• Insure your agency speaks with one voice in legislative liaison. To do otherwise can be most harmful to agency interests.

• Remember in legislative affairs who you work for.

• Don't go to Congress with problems that can be solved within your own agency.

• Be responsive to inquiries about your agency from Congress. Insure your agency is responsive to the needs and inquiries of members. These are the jobs of a successful legislative liaison official.

• When responding to a congressional inquiry, if you don't know something, admit it and find out from someone who does.

• Never say "no" instinctively to a congressional request. Check back with your agency, then respond, explaining why the answer is as it is.

• Learn you sometimes must take "no" for an answer.

• Recognize that committee staffers often have comparable expertise in their area as those in the executive branch.

• As much as possible, keep continuity among personnel in legislative affairs.

Selling your programs

• Defend your positions programmatically and with reasons and arguments, but don't discount the political element. Don't assume that logic will prevail over politics; things don't happen merely because they are the right thing to do.

• Prepare yourself for congressional hearings and testimony by getting as much information as possible, anticipating questions, and understanding the theatrics of congressional questioning. Don't take it personally.

• Realize that you will win some and lose some. After the losses such as the refusal of the Senate to confirm Robert Bork — pick yourself up and get ready to fight another day.

A final thought for a new administration is to promote unity of effort in legislative affairs. Many individuals represent the administration on the Hill. To insure a unified front, we recommend two procedures that were employed with some success in the Reagan administration. First hold legislative strategy sessions with key operatives. The Legislative Strategy Group of the Reagan administration brought together all major players at the White House—White House Chief of Staff, Directors of OMB and Congressional Relations, lead cabinet officials—to strategize about legislation proposed or pending. Such groupings could also be employed successfully at the departmental and subdepartmental levels. The second procedure for promoting unity is to continue the practice of giving a say to the Director of White House Congressional Relations in the appointment of under or deputy and assistant secretaries in the various departments and agencies who will have jurisdiction over legislative liaison.

Conclusion

The government hammered out in Philadelphia that hot summer of 1787 features a system of separated power. For the Presidency, this means that power is shared with other institutions that can either facilitate or frustrate the president's agenda.

Making this separation of powers work toward coherent national purposes has been a major challenge to the American system. Political parties have been of some help but as Neustadt so perceptively states, "what the Constitution separates, our political parties do not combine."[9] Throughout American constitutional history, the task of making the system work has fallen more often than not on presidential leadership. Strong executive leadership is the force that has allowed our government to cope with the nation's problems.

In 1981, when President Reagan took office, commentary abounded concerning crises of legitimacy and competence and how the Presidency was an "impossible job" and a "no-win situation."[10] Due to the early legislative victories, talk of a "futile political system" vanished.

President Reagan's four predecessors experienced various degrees of failure and frustration in legislative affairs. As Charles O. Jones convincingly argues, each of the four pursued Congressional relations with an aberrant style: Johnson using the style of majority leader, Nixon acting as a foreign minister, Ford as minority leader, and Carter as a layman amateur.[11]

In contrast, President Reagan conducted legislative liaison in a more traditional manner, in the mode of Truman, Eisenhower and Kennedy—present a focused agenda to Congress and continuously work it in consultation with the leadership of the President's party in Congress. Such a style, we believe, allowed President Reagan to steer the ship of state well, to avoid being taken advantage of by the Congress and the media, and to put his imprint on legislation. Although, to be sure, Republican control of the U.S. Senate for the first six years was a significant benefit to the President—providing him with an advantage enjoyed by no other post-Eisenhower Republican President—still the nimbleness of the President and his chief advisers in legislative affairs can not be over valued. As James Pfiffner writes, "President Reagan's impressive victories in his first year in office demonstrated that a determined and popular president could, even with control of one house, have his way with Congress."[12] Reagan may not have had the best record nor the highest percent of legislative victories,[13] but he had the image of great success, and, in Washington, appearances are reality. As Steven Wayne writes,

> By almost any standard, Reagan's first year with Congress must be judged a success. He got the legislation he wanted: his initial budget requests and many of his second-round reductions, his tax bill with most of its major components intact, and a farm bill he could accept. The sale of AWACS planes to Saudi Arabia was not stymied by a legislative veto, nor was the confirmation of Sandra O'Connor to the Supreme Court derailed by conservative opposition. Moreover, Reagan prevented legislation he did not want from being seriously considered, and he created an atmosphere conducive to his future success.[14]

To this we need also to add that President Reagan was reelected by a landslide in 1984.

Making the system work is the challenge to all administrations and the generations they serve. The suggestions we list here served President Reagan well in his dealings with Congress. The interests of the nation will be served by their application in the new administration, no matter who is elected and regardless of the political alignment he faces in Congress.

Executive-Legislative Consultation in Foreign Policy: Impediments and Proposals for Change

CHRIS J. BRANTLEY
ATTORNEY
WASHINGTON, D.C.

DUNCAN L. CLARKE
PROFESSOR
SCHOOL OF INTERNATIONAL SERVICE
THE AMERICAN UNIVERSITY

"To study one branch of government in isolation from the others," says Louis Fisher, "is usually an exercise in make-believe."[1] Few significant actions of Congress and the executive branch are wholly independent. Initiatives by one trigger reactions by the other, whether of a conflictive or cooperative nature. The focus here is on a key factor in executive-legislative interactions: consultation. After delineating the issue, the article examines major impediments to effective consultation and assesses various proposals for change.[2]

The Issue

At the most general level the necessity for adequate consultation between the executive and legislative branches of government appears virtually self-evident. The American democratic system simply cannot effectively support major foreign and defense policies over the long-term without an acceptable degree of consensus between Congress and the President, and for this, some degree of consultation would seem essential. But there are conflicting views as to what, specifically, constitutes adequate consultation because judgments on this matter relate to preferences and choices in three overlapping areas:[3] substantive policy preferences, as-

sumptions about executive and legislative functions and responsibilities, and definitions of consultation.

Substantive Policy Preferences

The adequacy of consultation often inheres in substantive policy
preferences: consultative procedures are endorsed if they further
one's policy preferences. If the President articulates and supports
certain preferences, he (and congressmen sharing his preferences)
may be inclined to consider as obstructionists those legislators
having different policy stances — those who frequently then call
for "better" consultation.

While consultation sometimes facilitates acceptable compromises between Congress and the President, it cannot always
resolve fundamental policy differences. Some members of Congress, for instance, would have opposed President Reagan's Central American and Persian Gulf policies whatever the level of consultation. So consultation may help engender policy consensus,
but it is not always a sufficient condition for it.

Assumptions about Executive-Legislative
Functions/Responsibilities

Expectations about executive-legislative relations affect assessments. What we believe influences what we would like to see.
So if it is thought, especially in national security affairs, that the
President initiates and Congress merely reacts and ratifies, the
tendency is to grant the Chief Executive a broad mandate, institute relatively loose oversight of executive agencies, and be generally content with the level and quality of consultation that the
President offers Congress. However, if Congress and the President are deemed equals with coordinate powers, there will likely
be a disposition toward restricting the executive's freedom of action, vigorous oversight, and insistence upon a degree of consultation that *Congress* finds sufficient.[4]

Most observers hold that the congressional resurgence of the
1970s importantly and permanently influenced executive-legislative relations, for better or for worse, by greatly enlarging Congress' foreign policy role. This view is reenforced by the growing
linkage of domestic with foreign policy ("intermestic" policy) which
has compelled changes in modes of executive-legislative interaction.[5] Even Henry Kissinger, perhaps grudgingly, conceded that
the "struggle . . . over executive dominance in foreign affairs is

over. The recognition that Congress is a coequal branch of government is the dominant fact of national politics today . . . [F]oreign policy must be a shared enterprise."[6]

As Congress' foreign policy role grows, the importance of consultative exchanges increase correspondingly. Yet a common sentiment in Congress is that consultation between the two branches is seriously inadequate.[7] Instances of poor consultation or no consultation abound. The following are merely illustrative: the executive's continued avoidance of detailed consultation with Congress on even some major arms sales until the decision to sell is already made, despite various legally mandated reporting requirements; President Carter's 1978 announcement of the opening of diplomatic relations with the People's Republic of China, which took Congress by surprise; President Reagan's nonconsultation of Congress prior to his announced March 1983 decision concerning the Strategic Defense Initiative (SDI), which had profound defense, foreign policy, arms control, and budgetary implications; the Reagan administration's unilateral, revisionist reinterpretation of the ABM Treaty which prompted Senator Sam Nunn and others to vigorously reassert the traditional interpretation and contributed to funding cuts in SDI; and the President's controversial 1987 decision, taken without a full intelligence assessment of potential risks and without consulting Congress, to afford U.S. naval protection to reflagged Kuwaiti oil tankers in the Persian Gulf.[8]

Defining Consultation

Assessments of consultation are conditioned by perceptions of what it is and should be.

Definition in Reality. Presidents (and many in Congress) define "consultation" *in actual practice* simply as the exchange of various communications between the two branches. There is substantial difference of opinion, however, as to what *should be* the *purpose* of such communications. A typical presidential view was offered by President Reagan: "If there is something that *we* (the executive) feel that *we'd* have trouble with and, perhaps, have to find *ourselves* in a veto position, *we* see that *they* (Congress) are aware of that and what it is that puts *us* in that position . . ., and then keep in constant touch."[9] The President here defines consultation narrowly as legislative strategy, the avoidance of unsettling surprises so as to facilitate Congress' receptiveness to *his* policy proposals. Congress, however, while recognizing unique presidential prerogatives in foreign affairs, usually believes that the purpose of interbranch communications should be to enhance joint participation or codetermination in policymaking.

Presidential communications to Congress in a "consultative" context are of three sorts: notification, lobbying, and information gathering.

Notification.   The principal means of executive communication is notification — through reports, briefings, and telephone calls — to inform congressmen of policy proposals or decisions already made, rather than to solicit active congressional participation in an ongoing decisionmaking process.[10] Since the executive controls the timing of notification and crucial informational resources, a congressional policy input can often be foreclosed, at least in the short run.

Lobbying.   When substantial legislative opposition is anticipated and when simple notification is thought not to be the most assured route toward ultimately prevailing, the executive must persuade or lobby Congress for support.[11] Here it is usually important for the executive to allow for policy alterations in order to mollify powerful legislators or, if opposition is formidable, to engage in bargaining for purposes of damage limitation while still preserving the central thrust of the President's position.[12]

The executive enjoys distinct advantages when lobbying Congress. The President's standing as chief diplomat and commander in chief affords him considerable leeway in presenting and framing the issues. This was evident, for example, in the final weeks of the debate over the sale of AWACS to Saudi Arabia in 1981 where the Reagan administration shifted the focus of debate from the merits of the arms transfer itself to a test of the stature and integrity of the President in foreign policy: the supposed harm that a legislative veto would cause to U.S. credibility and the impropriety of foreign influence in America's affairs inherent in the slogan (that did not originate in the executive branch) —"Reagan or Begin."[13] The executive is further aided by its frequent monopoly of vital informational and analytical resources. Legislators are also often susceptible to favors or services, flattery, and appeals to personal loyalty or the national interest. But enlisting support from wavering congressmen comes at a cost, whether in time and energy expended or special favors.

And all lobbying efforts may fail if the presidential request contravenes a legislator's principles or his constituents' interests.[14]

Information Gathering. Collecting information about congressional attitudes may constitute consultation, at least from the President's perspective. Executive branch congressional liaison staffs count prospective votes and test the water for receptiveness to policy initiatives; congressional allies are singled out for consultation to assist in planning joint strategy for steering the President's policy proposals through Congress; and the executive assesses the actions, concerns, and public statements of individual members.[15]

Congress also initiates communications of a consultative nature. Members use executive branch liaison staffs and key administration officials to express their views, request information, seek support, or circumvent bureaucratic barriers. While many congressional hearings are devoted primarily to oversight, they also provide a formal mechanism for communicating views to the executive. Indeed, augmented congressional research and analytical capabilities have made hearings an increasingly significant vehicle for addressing emerging issues, weighing options, and recommending courses of action.[16] Some of the most effective consultations, however, occur in private meetings, not in public hearings.

Congress's Preferred Definition. While the above usually constitutes interbranch consultation in practice, most members of Congress hold that effective consultation should be defined as: the timely and active involvement of an appropriate spectrum of members in the joint making of significant defense and foreign policy decisions. This definition has four components: spectrum or range of members consulted, timing, significance of the issue, and (implicitly) the attitudes of involved parties.[17]

Spectrum of Members Consulted. Consultation may occur at four levels: congressional leadership, committees, subcommittees, or with informal networks of interested individuals or groups.[18] A decision on where to consult is largely one of executive strategy: to determine what range of consultation is necessary for incorporating the concerns of a sufficient number of pertinent legislators in order to design a policy that Congress will support.

There are advantages and disadvantages to consultation at each level. Consulting the leadership allows the executive to tap their

THE PRESIDENCY IN TRANSITION

political influence and intuition. But the leadership may lack the specialized knowledge and interests of individual members or committees. Accordingly, the frequent practice is to focus on the chairmen and ranking minority members of key authorizing committees, especially the House and Senate Armed Service Committees, the House Foreign Affairs Committee, and the Senate Foreign Relations Committee.[19] But this, too, generates difficulties partly because of overlapping committee jurisdictions, a problem that is magnified by the proliferation of subcommittees, several of which may have interests in particular issues. Moreover, the executive often overestimates the power of authorizing committees. The executive branch confronts a dilemma: expanding the scope of consultation takes time and strains executive staff resources, yet restricting consultation to key committees may, among other things, alienate excluded legislators and overlook the concerns of potentially consequential members.

The executive, therefore, must often consult with other interested members, caucuses and/or key congressional staffers. Consultations with interested legislators — particularly those thought likely to organize opposition or introduce unwelcome floor amendments — are invariably designed to secure support or at least deflect opposition. Such individuals must be identified and their interests determined. Close consultation with caucuses, however, is often avoided particularly when their generally pronounced policy orientation and connection to special interest groups runs counter to the mainstream of executive policy preferences. But the influence and accessibility of congressional staffers make them targets of consultative efforts, although the executive can not presume that they can deliver the support of their congressmen and committees.[20]

Timing. Timing communication is critical. When to include Congress in decisionmaking depends upon the role it is expected to play. Three possibilities include: consultation when issues first emerge, when policy options are considered but before decisions are made, and after the executive branch decision phase.

The executive usually communicates with Congress only after policy options are developed. While Congress recognizes a need to defer to the executive on certain time and security sensitive matters, the general consensus on the Hill is that consultation should occur as early as feasible but certainly as soon as possible after options are formulated.[21]

Obstacles to consultation at the issue genesis stage are often formidable, especially when the subject concerns what Robert Lockwood calls "threat policy"—the process of identifying emerging threats to national security. Lockwood finds that consultation on threat policy issues has regularly proven difficult or unworkable partly because of the problem of establishing timely contact with a diffuse Congress, many of whose members might legitimately demand a right of consultation, and because Congress lacks "real time" intelligence.[22] Even if such impediments are overcome, the desirability of congressional involvement at this stage is questionable. Executive branch information and analysis is likely to be incomplete, particularly when international events are changing daily or even hourly, and congressional involvement at this point could hamper ongoing internal deliberations among executive branch actors.

The policy option stage is another matter. Approaching Congress after issues are identified and alternative courses of action are weighed preserves presidential leadership and bureaucratic discipline and is generally sufficient to establish the executive's good faith. Consultation at this still relatively early phase of the policy process, instead of after a decision is made, may facilitate consensus by giving Congress a stake in the outcome. There is certainly broad-based congressional agreement in, for instance, the arms sales area (where timely consultation is required by the Arms Export Control Act), that contemplated transactions be discussed with legislators long before a potential recipient government concludes that it has received a commitment to sell from Washington.[23]

Significance of the Issue. For purposes of effective consultation, any issue or action requiring the support of Congress is significant. This clearly includes, among other things, appropriations, a wide range of legislation, treaties, presidential nominations and major, sustained overseas commitments of the armed forces. Since the ideal goal of consultation is policy consensus—which goal is very often a practical necessity as well—the executive may be well-advised to consult on any issue that arouses substantial congressional interest.

Attitudes. An essential element of effective consultation is a forthcoming attitude toward the other branch. Ideally, this is manifested by the executive when it solicits congressional views, candidly discusses policy options, and furnishes adequate and timely information. Conversely—again, ideally—congressional behavior should be such as to avoid creating understandable grounds for mistrust. At a minimum, effective consultation requires mutual recognition of the problems and responsibilities of the respective branches and an acknowledgement that each has a legitimate role in the foreign policy process.

Impediments to Effective Consultation

Seven broad categories of factors may impede consultation: attitudes, conflicting political and institutional interests, lack of knowledge and understanding of the other branch, personalities, time pressures, structural problems, and interest groups.[24]

Attitudes

Throughout the national security bureaucracy, and certainly the Department of State, a common sentiment is that Congress' role in defense and foreign policy should be minimal. Two former Assistant Secretaries of State for Congressional Relations— Frederick Dutton (1961–64) and Marshall Wright (1973–74)— respectively described State's attitude toward Congress as "enemy territory" and "fearful."[25] Patsy Mink, former member of Congress and Assistant Secretary of State for Oceans, International Environment and Scientific Affairs in the Carter administration, states that Foreign Service officers find Congress "amateurish, uninterested, unschooled, mildly xenophobic . . . (and believing) that State regularly plots to give away what rightfully belongs to the American people."[26]

Widely held executive branch attitudes that hinder consultation include the following:

- minimal consultation worked reasonably well in the past and, at any rate, Congress lacks the information, organization and usually the responsibility to do what only professionals are capable of doing: formulate coherent, consistent national security policy.[27]
- the President is the most legitimate representative of the public— Congress reflects only the sum of its constituent parts; and, despite legislation mandating consultation such as the War Powers Resolution, there is no constitutional obligation to do so.[28]
- politics should stop at the water's edge: foreign policy should be a game of follow the leader, or ideally, follow the leaders ("bipartisanship"). Congress can not lead since it is too parochial, incapable

of keeping secrets, excessively swayed by public opinion (members are obsessed with reelection), and prone to sacrifice national interests to the appeals of special interest groups.[29]
- subculture attitudes of career personnel in the State Department, especially the Foreign Service, encourage an "elitism" that makes cooperation with a "lesser" congressional partner difficult and dulls sensitivity to the importance of domestic politics.[30]

Rear Admiral John Poindexter, President Reagan's fourth National Security Assistant, misled Congress and excluded it from crucial policy matters. Explaining his circumvention of established congressional oversight procedures and mechanisms in the Iran/Contra affair, Poindexter stated: "I simply didn't want any outside interferences."[31] The sharp, immediate response this elicited from conservative and liberal legislators alike reveals some of the severe resulting costs when such an openly hostile attitude is operationalized. Poindexter's view, said Democratic Congressman Lee Hamilton, chairman of the House Iran-Contra investigating committee, "reflects an attitude which makes . . . our constitutional system of checks and balances unworkable. . . . You cannot gain and sustain the support of Congress . . . and the American people for significant foreign policy decisions when they are uninformed."[32] Two Republican legislators supportive of Reagan's general policy toward Nicaragua were equally critical. "The reason for not misleading the Congress is a very practical one," said Congressman Dick Cheney, "It's stupid. It's self-defeating. Because, while it may . . . allow you to prevail in the problem of the moment, eventually you destroy the president's credibility."[33] And Congressman Henry Hyde lectured Poindexter: "The problem with deceiving Congress is that your friends get deceived and they go out and talk to the media . . . and insist that what you have told us is true, and it can be very embarrassing. And it affects our credibility."[34]

Congress has its own, often self-imposed sets of attitudes (only two of which are mentioned here) that can hamper cooperation. Many members defer to the executive because they believe that: Congress lacks expertise, the Constitution gives the President primacy, Congress cannot speak with one voice, and/or Congress exceeded its proper foreign policy role in the 1970s and restoration of presidential prerogatives is therefore necessary.[35] Conversely, other members avoid consultation in order to prevent co-option by the executive and to preserve Congress' essential role as an independent body which must often be critical of executive policies.[36]

Conflicting Political and Institutional Interests

Negative attitudes toward consultation are reenforced by tensions between the two branches' institutional and political interests, processes, and behavioral patterns. Career enhancement and job security in Congress is rooted in constituent support. Legislators who neglect the political and economic interests of constituents risk their offices. The imperative of reelection — which, some assert, may take precedence over foreign policy substance or even national interest — instills at least three types of behavioral activities in congressmen: advertising one's name, credit claiming, and position-taking on those issues of particular concern to constituent interests.[37] The reelection imperative combined with the importance and accessibility of the media may invite grandstanding, gratuitous promises, excessive attention to matters of minimal significance to national needs but of exceptional importance to special interests, and "micromanagement" of, for example, defense programs. Such behavior is common when, for instance, the Pentagon proposes closing a military base or weighs decisions that affect other income-producing activities and jobs in a home state or district.[38]

Other distinctive features of policy processes may hinder effective consultation. While most congressmen are, and must be, "quick study generalists" who focus only sporadically on defense or foreign policy, the executive rewards expertise and discretion in the daily management of national security policy. Moreover, the legislative process emphasizes political compromise, open debate, access to information, and (often) lengthy deliberations.[39] In contrast, although political compromise is common in executive branch processes, compromise with Congress somehow appears inappropriate to executive officials when national security is at stake, especially when a presidential decision has already been made. Likewise, the notion of public give-and-take debate with Congress is alien to executive officials who know the importance of confidentiality in the conduct of diplomacy and, for these officials, *control* of information is thought necessary for security reasons and because information is a key to their power and influence. Finally, while the executive has been somewhat more receptive to a congressional role in broad policy matters since the mid-1970s, it zealously guards its prerogative to design the tactics of policy. Congressional actions or legislation that jeopardize tactical freedom of action are consistently criticized as unwarranted "micro-management."[40]

Lack of Understanding and Experience

Tension between the institutional interests of the two branches is sometimes heightened by a lack of experience with or understanding of the interests of the other branch. This problem is exacerbated in the executive branch by the continual turnover of personnel, especially political appointees. For example, four Secretaries of State and eight Assistant Secretaries for Congressional Relations served beteen 1978 and 1983.[41] Similarly, career Foreign Service officers who rotate tours of duty every two or three years have little opportunity or incentive to acquire experience in legislative relations. On the congressional side, demands on members' time usually means that their staffs engage in much of the essential contact with the executive. Many (by no means all) staffers lack an understanding of the executive branch's milieu and practices. Also, some legislatively imposed restrictions in the foreign policy area suggest insensitivity to or unawareness of the real world of executive branch officials.[42]

Personality

The personalities of actors can, of course, be a decisive factor, and the President's personality affects the overall executive-legislative relationship. The President's standing with Congress and his ability to nurture congressional support through personal contacts, private briefings, and ceremonial gatherings set the parameters within which White House and departmental congressional liaison staffs work. A Chief Executive who gives this function skillful priority sends a powerful signal throughout government that working interpersonal relationships are crucial to successful consultations.[43]

Sometimes the personality of one official can cloud executive-legislative relations. Henry Kissinger, already criticized for his condescending attitude toward Congress, lectured freshman Democratic congressmen in 1974 as if they were graduate students. Frank Moore, President Carter's personal assistant for congressional liaison, was considered disdainful of and unresponsive to Congress.[44] But there have been very successful personalities. Lawrence O'Brien built bridges between the two branches in the Kennedy and Johnson years. Likewise, the cooperative personal styles of Special Trade Representatives William Eberle, Robert Straus and William Brock facilitated congressional support for foreign trade policies.[45]

Positive personal chemistry, while vital, is substantially a matter of chance. Even the most engaging President or Secretary of State will not charm all 535 hearty individualists in Congress. But if the President emphasizes personal consultations and if the executive provides incentives to build quality and continuity into liaison staffs, personal discord might be minimized.

Time Pressures

Time pressures impede effective consultation. Crises pose special problems, especially when consultation is mandated by legislation such as the War Powers Resolution. Fast-breaking events in a fluid situation where information is imperfect combine with security concerns to disincline a President from consulting fully with Congress. Even if he wishes to consult, his own policy options may not be formulated in time to elicit a reasoned congressional response, nor are there developed crisis consultation mechanisms for sharing information with legislators.[46]

The daily demands on legislators and executive officials also affect consultation. In addition to constituent services and re-election efforts, by 1984 the average Senator served on eleven committees and subcommittees. The total number of committee and subcommittee meetings in the House rose from 3210 in the 84th Congress to 6179 in the 97th Congress. Moreover, Congress is in session longer than it was in the 1950s.[47] Legislators, then, have little time to think systematically about most issues or to function in a sustained, active process of policy codetermination.

Congressional activism and the proliferation of committees also burdens the time of executive officials. The Secretaries of State and Defense commonly spend twenty-five percent or more of their time preparing for and testifying before Congress, often delivering identical testimony to different committees. This detracts from their principal responsibilities and engenders resentment toward the consultative process.[48]

Structural Problems

Consultation is complicated by the structural diffusion of decisionmaking authority in both branches. The executive is hesitant to consult Congress until there is internal consensus on the direction of policy and, even then, achieving consensus among several executive branch actors is often so arduous — and, when obtained, tenuous — that policymakers are reluctant to expose it to congressional scrutiny. When the executive does elect to consult, internal differences are generally not divulged and certain policy options are deemphasized.[49]

The dispersion of decisionmaking authority within the executive branch creates many opportunities for confusing or misleading Congress. State Department communications to Congress may be seriously defective if State were excluded from, say, a White House-Defense Department decision. Moreover, breakdowns in intra-executive branch communications and coordination can result in miscommunication to Capitol Hill. The dispersion of executive liaison offices and the frequently inadequate coordination among them also contributes to the problem, one that is often further exacerbated by insufficient numbers of foreign policy specialists on liaison staffs and a tendency for these staffs to develop special relationships with "their" congressional committees which encourages "end runs" of administration policy in pursuit of parochial, departmental interests.[50]

The lack of hierarchical authority in Congress makes the diffusion of power even more pronounced in the legislative branch. This condition was intensified after the structural and procedural reforms of the 1970s which, inter alia, made seniority less decisive in committee assignments, limited the powers of committee chairmen, and reduced committee control over subcommittees while dispersing power among individual members at the expense of party leadership and committee chairmen. As a result, the executive must grope to ascertain the will of Congress and to know where and with whom to consult. There is no longer any assurance that the perceptions of a few key legislators will reflect a congressional consensus. The executive's dilemma, then, is to limit lines of communication to a manageable scale without excluding vital congressional actors.[51]

More than 100 committees and subcommittees regularly address bills on some aspect of national security policy. The prospect of consulting such an array of entities (many with overlapping jurisdictions)—much less individual members and their staffs—has a chilling effect on executive attitudes.[52] In 1987, for example, Secretary of Defense Caspar Weinberger had to appeal to the Speaker of the House to settle a heated jurisdictional dispute betwen the House Armed Services Committee and a subcommittee of the House Energy and Commerce Committee over which unit had the right to receive a Pentagon report.[53] Consultation is further complicated by the increasingly blurred jurisdiction between authorizing and appropriating committees. Authorizing committees are constraining appropriations, while appropriating committees are including substantive legislative provisions in appropriations bills. In 1984, for instance, appropriations committees appropriated $3 billion in defense programs that were not authorized by prior legislation. Hence authorizing and appropriating procedures are becoming competitive, rather than complementary.[54] In addition to impeding effective consultation and engendering turf fights among committees and subcommittees, Congress' structural fragmentation and the blurring of jurisdictional authority makes coherent, well-integrated legislation difficult or impossible and contributes to sparse committee attendance.[55]

Interest Groups

The reluctance of the executive to consult with a legislature that plays an active role in foreign policy is partly attributable to the role of special interest lobbies in Congress and the supposed inclination of some legislation to compromise the national interest in return for the political and financial support of such groups. But these lobbies also often provide useful advocate information to Congress and are sometimes indirect channels of communication between the two branches.

It appears, on balance, that when an influential interest group seeks to steer foreign policy in a direction opposed by the executive, early and forthcoming consultation with Congress is advisable. The executive can thereby seek to offset the political benefits of supporting that group with political promises (or threats) of its own. Early consultation also affords Congress a broader range of information on the issues which may dilute the influence of a single powerful lobby and, additionally, permit less well-organized groups to contribute to the debate.[56]

Proposals for Reform

However formidable the impediments, sound foreign policy requires a working consultative framework that accommodates inevitable interbranch differences. Three areas deserve particular attention: congressional access to timely and accurate information, attitudinal changes that evince a willingness to cooperate and recognizing the other branch's concerns, and better organization for managing consultation.

Strengthening Congressional Information Sources and Assessment

Information is the currency of decisionmakers. Although Congress acquires information from many sources, it is substantially dependent on the executive for much current defense and foreign policy information and assessment. And some of the information that inundates Congress is ill-suited to effective decision-making.[57] What is required for responsible congressional deliberations is full, accurate, timely information as well as assessment and analytical capabilities to process and filter out unnecessary information. Toward these ends, several measures have been proposed to augment access to executive information sources, develop independent sources, facilitate crisis consultation, and strengthen information filtering and assessment resources.

Informal Briefings. Regular informal briefings of members (including bipartisan groups of congressional leaders) by senior administration officials might reduce reliance on time-consuming hearings, provide an opportunity for candid discussion of policy options, and afford a forum for crisis consultation. But legislators are sometimes dissatisfied with such informal sessions either because of the executive's lack of candor or because they are used to garner political support for administration policies. These meetings will have restricted value for Congress unless the quality of information exchanged improves. Consideration might be given to occasionally shifting the focus from a one-way to a two-way discussion which, in turn, might be encouraged if the State Department provided members with a weekly, written "foreign policy bulletin" on significant international developments and U.S. policy responses.[58]

Tightening Reporting Mechanisms.   By 1984 Congress had required the President to submit annually 225 foreign policy and national security reports in addition to the 65 and 460 reports issued respectively by the Departments of State and Defense.[59] Such reports serve a variety of useful functions, including: supplying otherwise inaccessible information, such as details of executive agreements; providing a public record and focus for national debate; and sometimes avoiding divisive conflict by the timely submission of information on potentially controversial issues.[60]

But some required reports are used ineffectively by Congress and their sheer numbers burdens the executive. These problems have prompted several comprehensive reviews of reporting requirements by congressional committees. The Goldwater-Nichols Department of Defense Reorganization Act of 1986 reduced the number of defense reports required by Congress from the President and the Defense Department by about two-thirds of the total. There is a need to eliminate obsolete and duplicative reports in other areas. Consideration should also be given, on a case by case basis, to lengthening the reporting period in order to reduce the burden on the executive branch. Some observers have also recommended that Congress hold more oversight hearings devoted to considering issues raised in the reports.[61]

Annual Report by the President or Secretary of State.   Some have suggested that an annual "state of the world" report by the President or Secretary of State similar to one issued by the first Nixon administration could be a useful basis for congressional debate on the overall objectives and assumptions of U.S. foreign policy.[62] But the utility of such an exercise is questionable: it would consume considerable executive branch time and effort (the last report issued by the Nixon administration was 743 pages long); unless someone with unique authority directs its drafting, it is likely to consist of uninformative generalizations (when National Security Assistant Henry Kissinger directed the report's preparation it received some attention, but when this responsibility passed to Secretary of State William Rogers it went unread); and if, as is probable, it does not assess alternative policy options, Congress may see it as a self-serving exercise.[63]

Access to Classified Information. Congress' ability to address national security issues effectively may be impaired by limitations on its access to security sensitive information. This was an acute problem prior to the mid-1970s. But President Ford and, especially, President Carter were reasonably forthcoming with classified information and passage of the Intelligence Oversight Act of 1980 gave Congress a statutory right to be fully and currently informed of all intelligence activities. Therefore, until the Reagan administration, most members of Congress and key committees were generally content with the quantity and quality of classified information received.[64]

This changed. In the Iran/Contra affair, and at least one other Reagan Administration covert action, Congress was uninformed, not informed in a clear and timely manner, and/or knowingly misled by senior officials like Admiral Poindexter and Director of Central Intelligence William Casey. In some instances the Intelligence Oversight Act and other legislation was either violated or, at the very least, interpreted by administration officials in a dubious fashion. The Iran-Contra Committees made 26 recommendations in 1987 for upgrading congressional and executive oversight of covert actions. Bills were introduced to institute some of these recommendations.[65]

Information is often classified for reasons of administrative convenience or to avoid political embarrassment, and some Presidents (like President Reagan) sharply expanded the amount of information classified—to the real or perceived detriment of Congress. But Congress has traditionally deferred to the President's practice of establishing the national security classification system by the executive order. The Murphy Commission (1975) recommended creation of a statutory classification system explicitly designating the types of information subject to classification. Bills have been introduced to this effect, but none has ever been enacted into law.[66]

New Links to the National Security Council (NSC). In 1979 Senator Edward Zorinsky introduced legislation to make the appointment of the Assistant to the President for National Security Affairs subject to Senate confirmation. Senator Zorinsky's proposal, which never became law, had two objectives: to subject the National Security Assistant (NSA) to congressional oversight and to eliminate a gap that sometimes exists between what the Secretary of State tells Congress and what the NSC, in fact, decides.

Implicit in the propsal was the assumption that the NSA would
have to testify before Congress. In hearings on the bill, the Carter
administration, former NSA Brent Scowcroft, and all other witnesses spoke in opposition. Witnesses agreed that, among other
things, it would jeopardize the NSA's role as facilitator and coordinator of national security policy, restrict the President's necessary flexibility in formulating policy, and increase tension between the NSA and the Secretary of State.[67] This was also the
position of President Reagan's Tower Commission despite its
finding that NSA John Poindexter and other NSC staffers had
improperly participated in the covert sale of arms to Iran and
diversion of funds to the Nicaraguan Contras. Likewise, the Iran-
Contra Committees rejected the Senate confirmation option, although they did recommend legislation "requiring that the President report to Congress periodically on the organization, size,
function, and procedures of the NSC staff."[68]

It appears that substantive policy communications to Congress
from the NSA will, and should continue to be informal and at
the President's discretion. The example of NSA Frank Carlucci
(1987) might serve as a useful model. Carlucci fostered extensive personal contacts with legislators, a practice that was well-
received in Congress.[69]

A Question Hour. It has been suggested that the British
parliamentary system may offer a device that could improve
executive-legislation consultation — a "question hour" in which
Cabinet officers and/or the President appear before the full Congress (or alternate their appearances between the two chambers)
to engage in a question and answer exchange on foreign policy.
But whatever benefits might accrue from such a practice seem
clearly outweighed by the drawbacks: it is unlikely to be a productive source of new information, the time expenditure would be
substantial, and it would invite partisan attacks on policy and
grandstanding in full view of the media. The need for such a
procedure in the British Parliament, where members are heavily
dependent on the question hour for foreign policy information,
is far greater than it is for the U.S. Congress, and several congressional committees might view a question hour as threatening
their competence and integrity.[70]

Congressional Travel Abroad. Congressional travel abroad retains
its negative public image ("junket"), sometimes strains embassy
resources, confers rather mixed benefits on members who serve

as advisors at international conferences, and occasionally embarrasses the administration. Still, there is wide agreement in Congress that foreign travel is beneficial. It exposes members to foreign policy problems, provides a conduit for information flow to Congress (through reports filed by returning members), and enhances Congress' ability to pinpoint areas of concern to the executive.[71]

Congressional Crisis Center. Although Congress' role in crisis consultation is ill-defined, members are vocal in demanding full and timely information on evolving crisis policy events. Yet even when the executive is well-disposed toward this demand (which is infrequent), it is difficult to disseminate useful, discriminately selected information to a widely dispersed Congress in a timely fashion. One solution would be to create a Congressional Crisis Information Center.

A central problem is defining the Center's exact role. One proposal has it staffed with former executive branch officials, placed as a congressional support agency, answerable to the congressional leadership, and performing the following functions:

> Communicate with the staffs of executive branch crisis centers; receive selected and critical messages which the executive branch believes should be brought to the attention of Congress; seek and receive crisis information from a range of nonexecutive branch sources; compile chronologies of events to aid decision-making and to facilitate the later evaluation of the crisis management experience, draft and discuss policy options for the Congress, as well as for the executive branch; prepare the congressional leadership for meetings with executive branch crisis managers; draft and circulate situation reports to the general congressional leadership; and alert the congressional leadership to breaking crises which may require their attention.[72]

This is a formidable mission. Under the best of circumstances it is likely to cause unease in the executive branch, especially if the Center conducts crisis *analyses*. It may be advisable, then, for such a Center (which probably should be directed by the leadership — the President's historically preferred contact group) to serve exclusively as a focal point and facilitator of interbranch crisis communications. The Center's analytical functions, if any, should be modest and directed solely at serving Congress' needs.

There is a danger that a Crisis Center might become just another organizational layer, one that actually slows communications, sparks controversy, and itself attempts to influence policy. And what would the Center's staff do between crises to justify their existence? Because of these concerns, consideration might be given to having the congressional leadership's own staff act as an ad hoc crisis committee. That is, add a function, not a structure.

Strengthening Assessment. Since the mid-1970s Congress has greatly expanded its institutional capability to assess, evaluate and monitor the constant flow of information on national security policy. Staff resources have increased and support agencies — the Congressional Research Service, General Accounting Office, Congressional Budget Office, and Office of Technology Assessment — provide objective, balanced information and analyses. Excepting crisis assessment, support agencies now meet most of Congress' internal analytical needs.[73]

Alton Frye proposed creating a congressional "foreign policy auditor" to monitor the analytic output of the NSC, intelligence community, and other executive bodies.[74] But most Presidents would surely oppose or otherwise thwart such "meddling" in executive branch affairs.

Affecting Attitudes and Building Confidence

A competitive tension between the two branches is rooted in the Constitution. But negative attitudes toward consultation and cooperation are often exacerbated by a lack of empathy for the concerns of the other branch, misunderstandings, and communications breakdowns. Several measures might be explored with an eye toward building an acceptable level of mutual confidence.

A Congressional Code of Conduct. Congress could take various steps to build executive confidence that, collectively, might constitute an informal code of conduct. Some practices, like safeguarding classified information (where Congress' record since 1976 is better than the executive's), are obvious. Others, such as the executive's insistent call for a halt to "overly intrusive" legislation in areas like human rights and nuclear nonproliferation, are unlikely as long as policy differences exist — which will be a very long time indeed.

Congress is largely known for the quality of laws that it passes, yet the frequent use of nongermane amendments in the Senate to outflank executive (and sometimes legislative) opposition creates tension. Since the President is unlikely to veto annual defense or foreign affairs authorization or appropriations bills, they become convenient vehicles for forcing through often ill-considered, uncoordinated legislative proposals — many only remotely germane to the primary legislation — that might not otherwise be favorably received by the President. This occurs because the leadership lets it occur. Stricter enforcement of rules prohibiting nongermane amendments to appropriations bills would help avoid the use of continuing resolutions and government by deadlock. The Senate might similarly consider adopting the recurrent proposal under which a two-thirds majority of those Senators present and voting would be required to overturn a nongermane ruling from the chair.[75]

The Senate should also exercise more discretion in confirming presidential nominees. There are instances when the confirmation process rightly evolves into a public and contentious debate and Senators will at times seek to extract policy promises from nominees. But a price is often paid in executive branch confidence. This is certainly so when a single legislator, like Senator Jesse Helms, repeatedly holds up the confirmation of numerous Reagan administration nominees. Because of the costs to executive-legislative relations and expenditure of Senators' time, the Senate might consider either reducing the number of foreign affairs nominations required by law (currently averaging 1400 annually) or limiting the number of full committee confirmation hearings.[76]

Finally, Congress can reduce the workload of both branches by enforcing existing rules limiting the number of committee assignments a member can hold and reducing the number of subcommittees. This would also improve committee attendance and consolidate overlapping subcommittee jurisdictions.[77]

Policy Directives. Secretary of State Cyrus Vance's 1978 directive to his department is often cited as a turning point in State's relations with Congress in the Carter administration. That directive could serve as a useful model for other administrations and department heads. It did the following: authorized and encouraged consultation, designated classes of information to be provided, set forth specific guidelines for withholding limited types of information and for creating review procedures to evaluate questionable material, and specified officials responsible for consultative duties.[78]

An Undersecretary for Congressional Relations. The Assistant Secretary of State for Congressional Relations might be upgraded to an undersecretaryship on the assumption that this would symbolize State's commitment to consultation, provide a more prestigious route to Congress, and enhance those intradepartmental forces favoring closer consultative ties to Congress.[79] While this measure might succeed if the new undersecretary had the full confidence of the Secretary, it is not very promising. An official's actual authority and staff resources matter more than his title and it is questionable whether this new undersecretary would retain effective control over the Bureau of Congressional Relations. Indeed, State Department undersecretaries typically do not have direct bureau responsibilities. Moreover, State's regional and functional bureaus have long resisted efforts to centralize liaison activities. Finally, for liaison purposes, a Secretary can just as effectively place confidence in an assistant secretary as in an undersecretary.[80]

Appointing Members of Congress to the Executive Branch. A perennial proposal for improving mutual understanding is to appoint legislators to executive branch positions. The proposal takes various forms, each designed to tap the perceived benefits of a parliamentary system of government. One noteworthy variation calls for the inclusion of House and Senate leaders from the President's party to sit as members of the executive cabinet in pursuit of a more collegial decisionmaking process.[81]

There are numerous specific problems with these proposals but the chief concerns are their implications fo the constitutional system of checks and balances. In addition to requiring a constitutional amendment (Art. I, Sec. 6 of the Constitution prohibits Members of Congress from serving as "officers" of the United States), they raise the real prospect that these two-hatted legislators serving in the executive branch would be impaired from functioning either as effective "checks and balances" of the executive or as loyal administration officials. These problems can, of course, be circumvented if the President appoints former legislators to executive posts. Secretaries of State John Foster Dulles, Christian Herter, and Edmund Muskie; Secretary of Defense Melvin Laird; White House Chief of Staff Howard Baker; and Trade Representative William Brock are among the many in this category.

Personnel Exchanges and Training. Stereotypes that color each branch's perceptions of the other can be partly ameliorated through sustained programs of personnel exchange and effective training. Some mid-level career officers in the Departments of State and Defense are assigned to Congress for one year under established programs. These programs, that might usefully be expanded, have been highly praised for affecting basic attitudes and establishing working relationships that continue for many years.[82] Misunderstandings might be reduced further by various training programs and workshops currently available to executive and legislative officials through, for instance, the Foreign Service Institute, State's Congressional seminar program, the Congressional Research Service, and university foreign affairs centers.[83]

Organizational Reforms

Major structural changes commonly evoke formidable resistance and, by themselves, rarely resolve the central issues of executive-legislative consultation. Nevertheless, some recommendations for organizational alterations merit attention.

Improving Intra-Executive Branch Coordination. The quality of executive-legislative constultative processes relates importantly to a subject too vast to be addressed here: the overall effectiveness of executive branch coordination and integration of the many strands of national security policy. Beyond this, however, the creation of a vigorous legislative liaison/strategy function within the White House, like President Reagan's Legislative Strategy Group, seems important for coordinating the liaison efforts of executive departments and for sustaining priority attention to consultation. Within the State and Defense Departments there may also be a need to clarify liaison responsibilities among various offices.[84]

Reforming the Budget Process. No serious reform of the congressional budget process is easy because it alters existing power/authority arrangements among members and committees and, on occasion, between Congress and the executive. An acute sensitivity to the need for equity is therefore mandatory in any proposed redistribution of authority.

The present congressional budget process complicates the executive's consultative task by requiring liaison at three levels of review: budget committees, authorizing committees, and appropriations committees. Eliminating one level — perhaps by consolidating the authorization and appropriations functions into a new "program" committee — would simplify the process. It would also give Congress much needed time for considering budgetary and other matters. But this sensible proposal has a decisive shortcoming—its political feasibility. Committee consolidation is a euphemism for taking power from some committees and giving it to others. Legislators who stand to lose will resist.[85]

Two changes in the defense sector may be advisable. There is recurrent congressional interest in establishing a biennial budget for the Defense Department (which has obvious implications for the entire federal budget). In the first year of a new Congress, the administration would submit a two year authorization and appropriation that would be debated, amended, and approved by Congress. In the second year, committees would concentrate on reviewing, evaluating and overseeing existing programs, with authorizing committees addressing broad defense policy questions and appropriating committees paying particular attention to efficient program management. This procedurally (if not politically) simple step could ease the burden on both branches, assure more attention to budgetary and oversight issues, bring greater stability to the defense planning process, and permit more reflection on long-term security terms.[86]

In compliance with a provision of the Defense Authorization Act of 1986, the Pentagon submitted a two year budget to Congress in 1987. The authorizing committees were generally receptive but the appropriations committees continued to insist upon annual appropriations. Consequently, by 1988 the proposal for a biennial defense budget appeared to be dead or rapidly dying.

If a biennial budget is impossible to achieve, Congress might consider shifting from annual reviews of major weapons programs to a process whereby funds for such programs are authorized and appropriated only when the development cycle reaches a major decision milestone. The process would resemble the Pentagon's internal procedure and work much like authorizations for new ships do now. Specifically:

> Congress [would] authorize and appropriate multi-year funds for each major weapons system at four milestone decision points: (1) initial development, (2) full-scale development, (3) initial production, and (4) full production. As a weapon neared each milestone, the administration would request sufficient funds in the next year's budget to pay for the complete upcoming segment of the weapon's development or production, even though the funds would actually be obligated and expended over a several year period.[87]

Although the presumption is that annual reviews would no longer be required, Congress could still review controversial systems yearly. Explicit Defense Department reporting procedures for each milestone would also be required. This reform could bring greater program stability, more effective long-term policy, and better program management by conforming the congressional process more closely to the Pentagon's and by moving Congress away from its current tendency to review some decisions several times each year.[88]

New Consultative Bodies. Some have suggested Congress consider new institutional arrangements to facilitate consultation: new permanent committees, ad hoc committees, or joint executive-legislative commissions. But there is little congressional support for various proposals to create ad hoc consultative committees or a new National Security Committee.[89] In 1987, the House Foreign Affairs Committee and the Senator Richard Lugar, former chairman of Senate Foreign Relations Committee, did propose creation of an executive-legislative consultative group that would hold informal but regular meetings on major foreign policy initiatives. President Reagan, however, had no interest in the proposal.[90] Nor is there enthusiasm in either branch for joint executive-legislative commissions. The output of these commissions cannot be controlled. Therefore, their recommendations generally receive scant attention and are seldomly implemented. A joint commission might serve a useful role, but only if three conditions are met: it addresses issues ripe for decision, membership is balanced and bipartisan, and its findings reflect a politically sustainable compromise between both branches and both political parties.[91]

Strengthening the Congressional System. The task of consultation would be eased if a traditional focus for executive consultation, the leadership, is reenforced. This is easier said than done. The congressional reforms of the 1970s reduced the leaders' influence. Still, given the requisite will to use them, the leadership retains various tools to encourage support for its initiatives, including the power to schedule debate on legislation and the authority to appoint members of the key budget and rules committees.[92]

The jurisdictional scope of the two committees on foreign affairs has expanded somewhat since the 1970s. They might be further strengthened to enable them to serve as focal points for foreign policy consultations. But several factors probably preclude this:

other committees will continue to deal with some foreign policy issues, the foreign affairs committees' supposed liberal orientation may preclude them from being able to assure general congressional support for their positions, and they may lack the political base to prevail in Congress since they are often not linked as closely as other committees to powerful domestic interests.[93]

Perhaps the most promising option is the increased use of joint hearings among committees and subcommittees with overlapping jurisdictions. Joint hearings between House and Senate committees are rare, but such hearings within one chamber are now a more common occurrence. Joint hearings do raise certain procedural questions and might at times threaten a committee's traditional turf, but they do save time for both legislators and those executive officials called to testify. They also afford an opportunity to share expertise and staff resources.[94]

Conclusion

In one sense, this subject has no readily identifiable conclusion. The broad parameters for interplay and discourse between Congress and the President are substantially set by the Constitution. There will always be contrasting views about the adequacy of executive-legislative consultations on various defense and foreign policy matters.

However, it seems clear that mere after-the-fact notification to Congress of significant executive decisions is an increasingly unacceptable form of "consultation." Congress generally insists upon full, timely, accurate, and (often) reciprocal information flow. Of course, this congressional standard for "acceptable consultation" will not invariably bring harmony between the branches. But without something reasonably close to it, the kind of broad-based policy consensus that must accompany any successful, long-term foreign policy is unlikely to be developed and sustained. The President moves toward securing the foundations of the nation's foreign policy when he consults actively with Congress.

There is room for enhancing the quality of the consultative process. Some proposals for improving consultations are neither desirable nor doable, others are attractive yet unworkable, but some are both positive and feasible. There is no single "answer." However, the national interest, by anyone's definition, requires constant sensitivity and attention to this issue. Former Senator Charles McC. Mathias, Jr., touched the essence of the matter: "[W]e're losing track of a very essential word in the whole federal system, which is coordinate: the separate, equal, *coordinate* branches of government. . . . There's a lack of that spirit of coordination that is really the heart of the whole constitutional scheme. . . ."[95]

PART NINE

The Vice Presidency

CHAPTER THIRTY

The Institutional Vice Presidency

RONALD C. MOE
CONGRESSIONAL RESEARCH SERVICE
LIBRARY OF CONGRESS

Today, the Office of the Vice President of the United States has a distinct institutional identity. This fact, however, is of relatively recent origin. Until the Vice Presidency of Richard Nixon under President Eisenhower (1953–1961), the Vice Presidency was often viewed with some disdain, an office occasionally declined when offered and, if accepted, frequently the road to political obscurity. Jokes about the office and its occupants were abundant and pundits and scholars would write learned essays suggesting duties to be assigned in order that the Vice President might have "something to do" befitting his formal status. More than one serious observer recommended the outright abolition of the office. Lucius Wilmerding, for instance, writing in 1953, stated:

> That the office is unnecessary is not however the only or even the principal reason for abolishing it. Its mere existence presents a danger. For the President may die and who will succeed him? Not, as originally contemplated, the man who was honored by the second largest number of votes of the people for the same office, and who in consequence would probably be worthy of the place and competent to its duties, but a man who, from the nature of the choice, is probably unqualified to fill the office of the president and in whom the people of the United States would have no confidence as such.[1]

The importance President Eisenhower attached to the Vice Presidency as well as Eisenhower's two heart attacks highlighted the political importance of the Vice Presidency and generally ended the remarks about its alleged superfluity.

Evolution of the Office

Beginning in 1961, the institutional elements of the Office began to assume a character to support the newly acknowledged political importance of the second office in the land. Prior to the Vice

Presidency of Lyndon Johnson in 1961, the Office of the Vice President was located on the Hill with "outposts" at several other locations. When President John Kennedy moved Johnson "downtown" to the old Executive Office Building (EOB) (reputedly to keep closer tabs on his irrepressible Vice President), he was really beginning a process of institutionalization of the Office that continues to this day.

The growth process of the Vice President's Office in the 1970s is ably described by Paul Light:

> From an office with too many payrolls, too many locations, and not enough staff, the Office of the Vice President of the United States now has a distinct institutional identity. It is now very much a part of the Executive Office of the President (EOP). From an office with fewer than twenty staff members in 1960, the Vice President's office now has its own line with an annual budget of two million. From an office with five or six different locations, the Vice President's staff is now consolidated on the second floor of the Old Executive Office Building, with outposts on Capitol Hill and in the West Wing [of the White House].[2]

The Vice President's top aides are selected principally for their political rather than their managerial skills. These aids, in concert with the staff personnel with substantive knowledge and experience, constitute a major resource for the Vice President in performing his myriad advisory functions. The Vice President's staff is in many respects a mirror image of the President's staff. Frequently the two staffs become functionally integrated with counterparts working together.

A major, although rarely articulated, function of the Vice President's staff is to provide a "shadow" Presidential staff in the event of a Presidential emergency or death. A Vice President, upon becoming President, can have at his disposal some loyal and trained aides to immediately move into key positions.

The institutionalization of the Office is, arguably, the principal reason why the Vice President has emerged as a major actor within the White House structure. With a competent staff, the Vice President can be represented at a number of meetings at once, schedules can be tight, speeches well-written, and background briefings of a quality equal to that of the President. Even the spouses of Vice Presidents today have need for a staff.

Inauguration of the Vice President

A rich heritage is associated with the inaugurations of Vice Presidents. Stephen Stathis and Ronald Moe, students of this heritage, have chronicled the history of these inaugurations:

> Historically, the most salient characteristic of Vice Presidential inaugurations has been their diversity of character and format. The oath of office has been administered to Vice Presidents at different times than that of the President; at different locations, once even in a foreign land; and by persons occupying a number of different offices. On only three occasions have the President and Vice President taken their respective oaths of office on the same day, at the same place, and from the same officer. Even then, they took different oaths.[3]

The oath required of the President is set forth in Article II of the Constitution. The oath for the Vice President is determined by statute (15 Stat. 85; 5 U.S.C. 3331) and is the same oath as that required of all officers of the United States. The timing of the Vice Presidential oath-taking has frequently been different from that of the President although in recent years the Vice Presidential oath has been timed to immediately follow the administration of the oath to the President. In 1985, January 20, the day set aside in the Constitution for the beginning of the new Administration, fell on a Sunday and thus the formal ceremony was scheduled for Monday, January 21. Both President Ronald Reagan and Vice President George Bush had the oath of office administered to them privately in the White House on Sunday. The public ceremony took place the next day in the rotunda of the Capitol.[4]

Transition Phase

The transition of office from one President to another is a major event in American political history. It is a complex endeavor involving literally thousands of persons. It is a process difficult to describe and even more difficult to manage.[5] The Vice President's role in the transition process is largely determined by the President.

Apart from any responsibilities that may be assigned by the President, the Vice President must make some personal and institutional decisions. The Vice President first must resolve questions related to moving into the official residence of the Vice President on Massachusetts Avenue in the District of Columbia.[6] Then, the Vice President must decide which one residence, other than the official residence, shall be considered his home of residence. This decision, besides determining the state residence for tax purposes, assists the Secret Service in protecting the Vice President and his family. On an institutional level, the Vice President must appoint key staff personnel to assist in the transition process.

Prior to 1963, most funding of transitions between Presidents was covered by private donations or, as the twentieth century progressed, by the national party organization of the winning candidate. After considerable Congressional debate, the Presidential Transition Act of 1963 (78 Stat. 153) was passed and remains on the books today. The Act, as amended, provides financial support for Presidential and Vice Presidential transitions from one Administration to the next. This Act authorizes the General Services Administration to provide office space, compensation for staff personnel, travel expenses, and other services to both the incoming President-elect and Vice President-elect and the departing President and Vice President.[7]

Assistance to former Presidents is authorized by the Former Presidents Act of 1958 (72 Stat. 838). Under this law, a pension is authorized the President immediately upon leaving office. Staff, office facilities, and services are provided by the General Services Administration to a former President for the first six months by the Presidential Transition Act and thereafter by the Former Presidents Act.[8]

The most recent transition was in 1981 when the Carter Administration was replaced by the Reagan Administration. The bulk of the $1.7 million in funding made available for the Reagan-Bush transition was allocated for personnel compensation. Like the Carter-Mondale transition in 1977, the Reagan-Bush organization determined to use its Federal transition funding jointly between President Reagan and Vice President Bush. It is not possible, therefore, to provide an exact figure on the amount Mr. Bush received for costs related to the Vice Presidential transition process. The Reagan-Bush transition effort was also supported through funds raised by two private foundations, a practice that was, and remains, controversial.[9]

In 1987 and 1988, the Senate Governmental Affairs Committee and the House Government Operations Committee held hearings and issued reports on the Presidential Transition Act with the intent to amend the Act so as to authorize an amount sufficient to cover the 1989 presidential and vice presidential transitions.[10] Additionally, the Committees seek to make such legislative changes as will enhance the working of the transition and the reporting of any outside funding and personnel used during the transition. For instance, H.R. 3932 ("The Presidential Transition Effectiveness Act") would extend until 30 days after the inauguration the time during which transition funds might be obligated for the incoming President and Vice President. It also allows the outgoing President's transition team to begin obligating funds 30 days before his term of office expires, and for a period of seven months thereafter, at which time the Former Presidents Act of 1958 would take over. The vote on H.R. 3932 is expected to occur in the Summer of 1988.

Vice Presidential Pay and Allowances

The compensation and allowances for the Vice President are to be found under various authorities and cover both the functions of the Vice President in the executive branch and those as President of the Senate. As Vice President of the United States, the Vice President's compensation is set by law at $115,000 (3 U.S.C. 104; as amended). In addition, the Vice President receives an expense allowance of $10,000 per annum, a sum that is not reported as income (3 U.S.C. 111; as amended).[11] The Vice President is provided a residence with furnishings in the District of Columbia (3 U.S.C. 111). Civil Service benefits have been extended to cover the Vice President (5 U.S.C. 8331–8348).

The staff assistance provided the Vice President pursuant to his executive duties are provided in law and include, among others, five employees to be paid at the Level II rate of the Executive Schedule; three employees at Level III, three employees at the GS-18 rate and such number of other employees as may be determined appropriate at rates not to exceed the base pay of GS-16 of the General Schedule (3 U.S.C. 106(a) (b)). The Vice President is entitled to protection by the Uniformed Division of the Secret Service (3 U.S.C. 202).[12]

In the Budget for Fiscal 1988, the budget account titled, "Special Assistance to the President" provides the funding for the Office of the Vice President. A total of $2.25 million was appropriated permitting 24 full-time permanent positions.

The Vice President, while serving as President of the Senate, receives no additional compensation. For fiscal year 1988, the Vice President received $1,145,000 for administrative and clerical staff expenses in running his office on Capitol Hill. The annual rate of compensation for any one employee is limited to the annual rate of basic pay for position in Level V of the Executive Schedule. Various administrative expenses, e.g., stationery allowance, are separately provided for in the Budget.

Duties as President of the Senate

Presiding Officer: Article I, section 3 of the Constitution provides that "The Vice President shall be President of the Senate but shall have no vote unless they be equally divided."

The powers of the President of the Senate consist largely of presiding over the Senate. These responsibilities are determined by statute and by the standing Rules of the Senate but these have been severely limited by the Senate's traditions and practices, including the right to appeal rulings of the Chair to the full Senate and the expectation that the Chair consult the party floor leaders before taking any action. In addition, the responsibilities of the presiding officer are eased by the Parliamentarian of the Senate, who sits to the immediate right below the Chair, and who informs the Chair when it has the duty to speak and advises the Chair of the proper parliamentary response it needs to make.

The Vice President is not the only official with the authority to preside over the Senate. The same function is more often carried out by a senior Senator who holds the office of President pro tempore of the Senate, a position also provided for in the Constitution, or any Senator temporarily called upon to preside in the Chair. As a result of these varied limitations, the Vice President as presiding officer of the Senate is more the agent who administers the rules and precedents of the Senate than their master or even a participant in their creation. Modern Vice Presidents, therefore, have chosen to preside only in rare instances, such as on ceremonial occasions, or when it is expected that their vote may be required to break a tie, or when party leaders anticipate that an unusual parliamentary situation will require the

Chair to issue a precedential ruling. Vice President Bush, for example, spent 35 hours and 46 minutes in the presiding officer's chair during the 97th Congress, or only 1.7% of the 2160 hours the Senate was in session during the two-year period.

Illustrative of the duties and powers of the Vice President as presiding officer of the Senate are facilitation of routine parliamentary procedure and rulings on points of order (various Senate Rules); the administration of oaths of office to newly elected Senators (2 U.S.C. 21); the signing of enrolled bills to be presented to the President for his approval or disapproval (Senate Rule XIV); and the appointment of Senators to some special committees, commissions and boards (various statutes). Although a few of the duties of the Senate's presiding officer are assigned specifically to the President of the Senate, most of these may be administered by any presiding officer of the Senate.[13]

Casting Tie-Breaking Votes: Article I, section 3 of the Constitution provides that the Vice President of the Senate, "shall have no vote unless they be equally divided." From the first tie-breaking vote cast by John Adams in 1789, to one cast by George Bush in 1987, the record indicates that Vice Presidents cast some 223 tie-breaking votes. The most recent tie-breaking vote occurred on September 22, 1987, when Vice President Bush cast the deciding vote on a Department of Defense Authorization Amendment involving research on the Strategic Defense Initiative. During his years as presiding officer of the Senate, Mr. Bush cast seven tie-breaking votes.

Duties in Counting Electoral Votes: The Vice President, as President of the Senate, has the duty of receiving Certificates of States' Electors regarding their votes for President and Vice President (Constitution, Article II, section I, clause 3; Amendment XXI). The Vice President presides at the Joint Session of Congress convened to count the Electoral College vote (3 U.S.C. 15). The Vice President opens the Certificates of Electors at such Joint Sessions (Constitution, Amendment XII).

Power to Make Appointments to Various Bodies: The Vice President has the power to make appointments to various bodies. In practice, when the Vice President is required to appoint Senators to various bodies, the appointees are generally designated by the party floor leaders.

Illustrative of the appointments the Vice President must make are to name five cadets for each of the Service Academies. He appoints eight Senators to the Joint Economic Committee; two Senators to the Migratory Bird Conservation Commission; two Senators to the Harry S. Truman Scholarship Foundation; and three Senators to the Advisory Commission on Intergovernmental Relations.

The Vice President and Executive Responsibilities

Organization of the Office: Until the 1950s, the Vice President's Office consisted of several aides and clerical support in an Office on Capitol Hill. Today, as has been mentioned, the Vice President has an impressive staff (estimated to be around seventy persons including detailees) located for the most part in the Old Executive Office Building (OEOB), but with outposts in the White House and on Capitol Hill. Vice President George Bush had an office in the West Wing of the White House (so did Walter Mondale) and an elegant office in the OEOB. Mr. Bush, reportedly, divided his time about equally between the offices. His West Wing office provided direct access to the President and the President's top aides, but separated him from most of his staff. The well appointed Vice Presidential office in the OEOB was personally enjoyed by Mr. Bush as it permitted him to have direct contact with his staff and to reinforce the notion of a separate institutional identity.[14]

The Vice President's Office in the executive branch under George Bush was broken down into several sections. First there was the staff of the immediate Office of the Vice President in the West Wing of the White House. There the Executive Assistant and 2 staff assistants worked. In the OEOB, there was the Vice President's Chief of Staff with his three member staff. There was a Scheduling and Advance Office, Domestic Policy Staff Office, Legal Counsel Office, National Security Office, and Press Office. In the latter Office was located the Vice President's speech writers. As spouse to the Vice President, Mrs. Bush had the assistance of a five member staff. Finally, the Vice President enjoyed administrative support from the Office of Administration in the White House.

The Vice President as a person, and the office's considerable staff, have become an important source of advisory support to Presidents but this situation is always subject to change. A future President may actively dislike or distrust a Vice President and reassign the Vice President to function solely within the confines of the OEOB. All of which suggests that the key to Vice Presidential influence remains what it has always been, the desire of the President to include the Vice President in a small inner-circle of advisers.

Executive Duties: The duties of the Vice President are, for the most part, assigned by the President. In two hundred years, there have been few statutory responsibilities devolved upon the Vice President. The *U.S. Code* currently indicates but two formal assignments: (1) membership on the National Security Council and (2) membership on the Board of Regents of the Smithsonian Institution.

The Vice President presently sits in on Cabinet meetings and presides in the President's absence. But this is a twentieth century phenomenon. President Warren Harding invited Calvin Coolidge to attend Cabinet meetings, an invitation that Coolidge repeated to his Vice President, Charles Dawes. Dawes, however, declined to attend. Presidents since Franklin Roosevelt have routinely invited their Vice Presidents to attend and Dwight Eisenhower requested that Richard Nixon preside in his absence, a request that resulted in Mr. Nixon chairing some 19 Cabinet meetings.[15] The fact is, however, that neither the statutory requirements of the office nor the assigned Cabinet related duties add appreciably to the Vice President's political powers.

Ceremonial Responsibilities: The Vice President has numerous ceremonial responsibilities. Usually the Vice President is the surrogate for the President. This may be a "stand-in" role at the annual Memorial Day observance at Arlington Cemetery or it may be an extensive foreign tour. Foreign tours may be to head delegations to funerals of heads of state, or to conferences where substantive matters are discussed. The Vice President, however, negotiates only in the name of the President and then only upon explicit and detailed instructions from the President and appropriate executive officers.

Chairing Commissions: The contemporary Vice President, typically, chairs a number of commissions. Some of the assignments by the President are merely symbolic while other assignments reflect considerable trust and commitment by the President. In some cases, the assignments carry political clout for the Vice President, as was the case with President Kennedy assigning Vice President Lyndon Johnson the chairmanship of the Space

Council, while other assignments may involve political risks for the Vice President. One of the more important recent commissions was the Task Force on Regulatory Relief chaired by Vice President George Bush. In reflecting upon Bush's response to this and other commission duties, Paul Light says:

> Though Bush accepted two new assignments at the start of the Reagan term — the Task Force on Regulatory Relief and titular control of White House crisis management — both commitments were downplayed within the Vice President's office. Bush gave most of the responsibility for regulatory relief to his chief counsel, [Boyden Gray], while avoiding public discussion of his crisis management assignment.[16]

Partisan Political Responsibilities: The Vice President is expected to fill numerous political and particularly partisan political responsibilities. Campaigns, both for the general and mid-term elections, are a major demand upon the Vice President's time. Vice Presidents must expect to be party fund raisers. They must be prepared to be the liaison with various institutional groups, e.g., National Governors Association, and with political interest groups. In these endeavors they are expected to defend the President and Administration policies. Indeed, to criticize the President or his Administration would itself be a major news event and would threaten whatever credibility the Vice President might have with the President and the White House staff.

Advising the President: Considered historically, the role of the Vice President as policy advisor to the President is comparatively new. In many instances, Presidents and Vice Presidents have not been friends, indeed some have been enemies. And even when respect or friendship was present, they have often entertained such divergent opinions on critical issues as to make an advisory role for the Vice President untenable. This latter situation was certainly the case with two of Franklin Roosevelt's Vice Presidents; John Nance Garner and Henry Wallace.

In recent decades, however, the Vice President has emerged as one of the players in the game to provide the President both with policy and political advice. The position of the Vice President vis-a-vis other players is enhanced by physical proximity, staff back-up, and the fact that the public has come to expect the Vice President to be ready to be the "acting" President, a role reinforced by provisions of the 25th Amendment. Presidents now feel obligated to keep their Vice Presidents informed, or at least the obligation to appear to keep them informed. In turn, Vice Presidents are expected by the public to either have, or quickly obtain, experience and expertise in foreign affairs.

The pattern now is for Presidents to regularly, and publicly, meet with their Vice Presidents and presumably solicit their advice on issues. In turn, Vice Presidents are expected to retain their counsel on advice proffered and publicly support the President's position. When support of the President's position runs counter to the views of the Vice President's natural constituency, the Vice President can expect to suffer erosion in popularity. Recent Vice Presidents, particularly Hubert Humphrey and George Bush, have found themselves in a conflict between their loyalty to the man who chose them to be Vice President and their own personal ambitions to succeed the incumbent.

Even when the relations between the President and the Vice President are personally strong and their political perspectives in harmony, the nature of the Vice Presidency is such that it is a job with institutional limitations. One limitation is that the Vice President cannot attempt to replace or undercut the President's immediate staff for when staff are required to choose between loyalty to the President or to the Vice President, they will choose the President. Vice President Nelson Rockefeller, always in favor with President Gerald Ford and always the consummate "policy leader," found that he could not institutionalize his policy advisory role. His effort to operationally manage the Domestic Policy staff in the White House was by his own account, and that of others, a failure and he voluntarily, if unhappily, stepped aside.[17] Each Vice President must simultaneously learn from his predecessors and stake out new territory. There are a few rules of thumb, but otherwise the situation is marked by fluidity.

Leaving Office

At some point, all Vice Presidents leave office. Sometimes the leaving is to step into the Oval Office. In most cases, however, it is to return to private life. When they leave office, they have a few prerequisites. They are provided from transition funding sufficient monies to move household belongings, books and papers, and staff assistance to close and move their office. Although they are not automatically entitled to Secret Service protection, they can be assigned such protection on an individual basis for six months after leaving office as was the case with Vice Presidents Nelson Rockefeller and Walter Mondale. Unlike former Presidents, however, who enjoy certain permanent prerequisites, e.g., permission to stay in government quarters on Jackson Place when visiting Washington on public business, former Vice Presidents become private citizens in the full sense of the word.

"The Elected Crown Prince"

It should not be forgotten that the principal responsibility of the Vice President is to be the "elected crown prince." The Presidency of the United States is an extraordinary institution in that it combines in one person the twin office and authorities of the chief of state and the chief of government. In most nations, these offices and authorities are divided between two persons, as in Great Britain where the Queen is the chief of state and the Prime Minister is the chief of government. By combining these offices and authorities, the Constitution established for the United States a Presidency which resembled, in its essentials, an elected classical monarch.

An understanding of this basic intent of the Founding Fathers with regard to the office of the President is necessary if one is to understand the fundamental nature of the office of the Vice President. If the President is our elected monarch, this suggests that the Vice President is our elected crown prince.

Succession to power is one of the oldest problems to face the body politic. In most nations, at most times, this problem has been the root cause of civil strife and conflict. If anything, the problem is more acute in our contemporary age than in the past. America has been fortunate during its first two centuries to have avoided the turmoil often associated with the transfer of power and authority.

During the 1970s, the United States underwent a series of unprecedented crises involving both the Presidential and Vice Presidential institutions. Although a concerned citizenry and an interested world followed the events which saw Americans inaugurate three Vice Presidents and two Presidents within a period of less than two years, few, if any, doubted that the transfer in power would come about in an orderly fashion. The legitimacy of these transitions was never an issue.

The role of the Vice President is to be ready to be President. The history of crown princes is a history of frustration. There can be only one monarch at a time. One day the crown prince has no authority, the next day he has all authority. It is a fact to be understood rather than a problem to be solved.

The Vice Presidency in the Third Century

MARIE D. NATOLI
PROFESSOR OF POLITICAL SCIENCE
EMMANUEL COLLEGE (MA)

While the Vice President himself is involved in the periodic administrative transitions following the election of a new presidential team, the second office during the period of the modern Presidency has been involved in its own perpetual transition and evolution. This "changing" Vice Presidency has been in many facets of the office: the selection process and the criteria desirable for selection; the administrative, policy, legislative and political roles to be played by the Vice President; the preparation for the Presidency and the succession process; the national stature of the second office; and the use of the Vice Presidency as a stepping stone to the presidential office itself. As the Vice Presidency enters the third century, it is the beneficiary of the very many significant turning points it enjoyed in the second century of this Republic's experience. This essay will discuss this very different Vice Presidency than that which the Framers of the Constitution had anticipated.

Historical Note: What the Framers Envisioned

The experience of the modern Vice Presidency has demonstrated that this office can indeed serve more of a function than merely its Constitutional one of presiding over the Senate or breaking a tie. Contemporary Vice Presidents spend relatively little time in the Senate performing either of these functions, in fact. But a more important, although informal, legislative role has developed for the Vice Presidency. This new role is partly due to changes in the backgrounds of the incumbents of the office. Much as has been true of presidential candidates, many a recent Vice President and vice presidential candidate have been former members of the prestigious "upper chamber," the Senate — Harry S.

Truman and John Bricker in 1944; Alben Barkley in 1948; John Sparkman and Richard M. Nixon in 1952; Estes Kefauver in 1956; Lyndon B. Johnson in 1960; Hubert H. Humphrey in 1964; Edmund S. Muskie in 1968; Thomas Eagleton in 1972 (Eagleton had been George McGovern's initial vice presidential running mate but was removed from the Democratic ticket following disclosure of a history of mental illness); Walter F. Mondale and Robert Dole in 1976.

How extensive a legislative role any Vice President can play will depend upon a delicate balance of forces: the desire of the President; the issues at a given moment; the experience of the Vice President; and, crucially, the Vice President's understanding that the Senate is a very proud legislative body which does not welcome interference from outsiders. The most successful Vice Presidents in this legislative capacity have been not only those with Senate experience of their own, but those who knew, too, just how carefully to walk a very difficult tightrope. A Vice President *can* have influence in the Senate, but must do so quietly, unobtrusively, behind-the-scenes, selectively, and not too often, lest the Senate take offense at "executive infiltration" and lest the President take umbrage at a perhaps seemingly too ambitious Vice President.

In the period of the modern Vice Presidency, some Vice Presidents have fared far better, legislatively, than have others. Vice President Lyndon Johnson, for example, might have been far more legislatively useful than he turned out to be. For a number of reasons, Johnson's potential was never fully realized. The Kennedy people's dislike for the Vice President and their unwillingness to let it appear that the President had to depend upon the former Majority Leader combined with Johnson's own inability to submerge his ego to the personality and ego of the Senate resulted in a relatively inactive role for one formerly so powerful in the legislature.[1]

Johnson's own Vice President, Hubert Humphrey, did not suffer the problem of an insatiable ego and knew full well how his former colleagues in the Senate would perceive overt vice presidential interference in the legislative process; Humphrey also knew how the President would react should Humphrey appear to be too successful in the legislature. According to Humphrey's own observations, he was legislatively successful because he knew when and how to assert his influence.

Vice President Spiro Agnew, who had never enjoyed legislative experience of any kind, did not fare as well as had Humphrey. In fact, Agnew early suffered a legislative humiliation at the hands of fellow Republicans because the Vice President did not know a simple, basic rule of when to attempt to influence and when to steer clear.[2]

Lack of legislative background alone need not preordain vice presidential failure in the legislature. Nelson Rockefeller, for example, demonstrated the political implications of the procedural role played by the Vice President as Presiding Officer when he issued a parliamentary ruling making it easier for reformers to change the continually controversial Rule 22 (dealing with the numerical requirement for a cloture vote which would end filibustering). And President Ford used Rockefeller occasionally to influence Senators, such as on the issue of aid to Turkey.[3]

Walter Mondale could and did play a crucial liaison role for President Carter, and this as a result not only of Mondale's own legislative background but because of Carter's lack of understanding of Capitol Hill. Perhaps Hubert Humphrey's 1977 observation best sums up the delicate forces working to make Mondale so important.

> You see, part of Carter's problem is that he really doesn't know the little characteristics of our colleagues up here. You've got to know what makes 'em tick, you've got to know their backgrounds. You know, I used to say Johnson was a personal FBI. The son of a gun was incredible, but so was Kennedy, and so in a sense was Ford. All of the last four Presidents were creatures of Congress. Kennedy, Johnson, Nixon, Ford—when they went to the White House, they had connections up here, buddy-buddy connections.[4]

Much as George Bush's overall Vice Presidency benefited from Mondale's, so, too, was this the case with regard to his role as legislative liaison. Bush has served as a "point man"[5] for the President, and an early account of the Bush legislative Vice Presidency understood what came to be Bush's legislative style throughout his incumbency—"meet[ing] individually with . . . Senators . . . mak[ing] it a point to keep in touch with his many acquaintances on the House side . . . [and doing] a lot of listen[ing] and collect[ing] political intelligence of value to the White House."[6]

In its capacity in the legislature, the future of the Vice Presidency as it moves into the third century will undoubtedly play less and less of the role which had been provided by the Framers and more of what evolving political necessity warrants. As presidential candidates increasingly face the fact that a running mate must be someone with whom he/she can work closely, and as the President's legislative agenda becomes more varied and burdened, the individual who has "one foot in the legislature" will undoubtedly become more crucial as a liaison. How effective that individual will be, however, will continue to depend upon his or her own personality and ability to balance the needs of the administration, the nature of the Senate, and the political realities of the moment.

The Vice Presidential Selection Process: The Evolving Criteria

While the 1984 selection of Congresswoman Geraldine Ferraro as Walter Mondale's Democratic vice presidential running mate received a great deal of media and public attention, it must be remembered that the gender balancing of that ticket is but a part of the evolving criteria the vice presidential selection process has experienced in the contemporary era. As the Vice Presidency enters the third century, it is likely that additional criteria will emerge, just as they have within the last forty years.

The pattern which has developed in this evolutionary process is an interesting one. The criteria necessary in a given election year vary, depending upon a number of factors: the presidential candidate's own strengths and weaknesses — personally, demographically, ideologically, geographically; the national and international issues warranting attention at the time; the forces and tensions within the particular political party. A desirable combination of criteria in one election year may not be considered so valuable in another. Yet another force working in this evolutionary process is the continual political empowerment of different ethnic, racial, religious, and gender groups. Prior to the period of the modern Presidency, it would have been unheard of to consider anyone but a white, AngloSaxon Protestant male (indeed, Al Smith's disasterous presidential bid reinforced the conventional wisdom that only a WASP male could possibly win). But even just a cursory glance over the presidential and vice presidential candidates of this period reveals a radically different picture. Beginning with the successful Kennedy presidential bid in

1960, the anathema of a Catholic on the ticket was eradicated. Indeed, political analysts talked about "the Catholic vote," and in some election years a Catholic was intentionally sought for inclusion on the ticket. Certainly, this was one of Lyndon Johnson's considerations in 1964, as he struggled to deal with the Kennedy shadow. And so, even though Johnson eventually decided upon Hubert Humphrey of Minnesota, a Protestant, as his vice presidential running mate, he also seriously considered Eugene McCarthy, a Catholic, of the same state. Johnson's Republican opponent, Senator Barry Goldwater, did indeed select a Catholic running mate, Congressman William Miller of New York. Four years later, when Humphrey himself was the presidential candidate, his running mate was Senator Edmund Muskie, of Maine, who happened to be a Catholic. In 1972, when George McGovern triumphed in his bid for the presidential nomination, he first selected Senator Thomas Eagleton of Missouri as his running mate; Eagleton is a Catholic. Then, following Eagleton's rather hasty removal from the ticket following revelations of treatment for mental illness, McGovern's search for a replacement engendered a long list of possibilities, primarily Catholics, until he asked Sargent Shriver, a Kennedy brother-in-law and a Catholic, to run with him. And, of course, Geraldine Ferraro is also a Catholic. The continuing evolution in this area suggests that as the Presidency and Vice Presidency move into the third century, other religious groups may find their place on the ticket. Indeed, Abe Ribicoff, a Jew, was considered by McGovern in 1972, and a Jewish woman, Diane Feinstein, former Mayor of San Francisco, was considered by Mondale in 1984.

The empowerment of ethnic groups is also reflected in the evolving selection criteria one sees in the vice presidential nomination during the modern era of that office. Both running mates in 1968, Spiro Agnew on the Republican side and Edmund Muskie on the Democratic, came from ethnic groups formerly considered "ineligible" for inclusion on the ticket. Agnew was of Greek extraction and Muskie of Polish. During Walter Mondale's extensive search for a running mate in 1984, Hispanic empowerment in the United States was reflected in the fact that Mondale interviewed San Antonio Mayor Henry Cisneros. In the 1988 election year, the name of California Governor George Deukmajian, a man of Armenian background, reflects the growing acceptability of a plethora of ethnic backgrounds on the national ticket. Indeed, the Democratic nominee in 1988, Massachusetts Governor Michael Dukakis, is himself of Greek extraction.

The presidential and vice presidential nominations in the third century will undoubtedly witness the inclusion of other racial groups. Indeed, even though defeated for the nomination, the Reverend Jesse Jackson's unprecedented (in the degree of its success and its appeal to both white and black Americans) race for the Presidency in 1988 is clear evidence of both black empowerment and the increasing acceptance of and enthusiasm for black candidates by white Americans. These forces suggest that a black will be on the national ticket within the next several electoral years.

Thus, as we move towards the third century of this great American experiment of our unique form of democracy, there is no reason to expect that there will be anything but an increased understanding of the assets required by leaders to serve the people and to serve them well.[7]

Vice Presidential Preparation for the Presidency

The Presidency is such a unique institution that it can justifiably be argued that the only training ground for it is the Presidency itself. Nonetheless, the Vice Presidency is the closest we can come to having someone waiting in the wings should the need arise. To this extent, the second half of the twentieth century has been very beneficial to the Vice Presidency. A crucial turning point in vice presidential preparation came with the Truman Presidency. Having suffered his own dismal lack of preparation to assume the burdens of the highest office in the land, Truman vowed that no Vice President would ever come to the Presidency as ill-prepared as he had been.

Truman took steps to expand the Vice President's access to information. He invited the Vice President to meet with the Cabinet and submitted legislation to Congress which statutorily made the Vice President a member of the National Security Council. And in 1952, Harry Truman was the first President to initiate an extensive briefing process of the presidential and vice presidential candidates during the course of the campaign, a practice which has continued to date.

During the 1950s and Eisenhower's Presidency, several forces contributed to continuing the expansion of vice presidential preparation. Eisenhower's own personality and nature were comfortable enough to include his Vice President in the flow of information. And the pace of Nixon's activity, in both domestic and foreign affairs, helped in his preparation for the Presidency. As Sidney Warren observed, "As a roving representative of the President on numerous assignments abroad, he was constantly in the public eye. . . . Numerous meetings with foreign leaders and regular attendance at sessions of the National Security Council afforded Nixon an unusual opportunity for 'on the job' training in foreign policy and national security problems."[8] For all these reasons, Nixon's incumbency is the second turning point.

One force contributing to the increased preparation of the Vice President is the fact that individuals of considerable stature and background began to be attracted to the office. Certainly, it can be said that in 1960 Lyndon Johnson was at least as qualified — if not more so — than was John Kennedy. Hubert Humphrey, Nelson Rockefeller, Walter Mondale, George Bush all brought considerably diverse and well-versed backgrounds to the second office.

Another force underscoring the importance of vice presidential preparation is the series of events during the period of the modern Presidency and Vice Presidency which focused attention upon the likelihood of succession: FDR's death; assassination attempts upon the lives of Truman, Ford, and Reagan; the Kennedy assassination; the Nixon resignation.[9]

To a great extent, vice presidential preparation has been evolutionary *and* cumulative. Each administration adds to what the previous had done and does not subtract, at least not from the flow of information, even if the Vice President is not particularly regarded or treated as an "insider," as was the case with Vice President Lyndon Johnson under Kennedy or Vice President Spiro Agnew under Nixon.

A third crucial turning point in vice presidential preparation came with the Mondale Vice Presidency. Going well beyond the symbolic — yet important — moving of the vice presidential office into the White House, President Carter gave Walter Mondale extremely free reign in being fully prepared. This turning point came partially as a result of Carter's personality and style and partially from Mondale's own very astute understanding of how to best benefit from his position. Mondale wisely chose to be a general adviser to the President, thus placing himself in the full flow of the White House information loop. Moreover, the

Vice President had full access and invitation to any of the meetings in which Carter was involved, a policy followed by the Reagan-Bush team. Carter himself described the extensive degree of his interaction with Mondale. At a 1977 press conference, the President said, "I see Fritz four to five hours a day. There is not a single aspect of my own responsibilities in which Fritz is not intimately associated. He is the only person that I have with both the substantive knowledge and political stature to whom I can turn over a major assignment."[10] And by the end of his incumbency, Vice President Mondale could observe, "I have been closer to a President . . . than any Vice President in history."[11] And just as Carter regularly met with his Vice President for substantive business meetings, so, too, does Reagan meet with Bush. Thus, the Bush Vice Presidency has been the beneficiary of the Mondale experience.

Given the necessity of a Vice President to remain publicly loyal—which translates into agreeing with the President in public—these private one-on-one meetings become a crucial avenue for vice presidential input. As George Bush put it, "In the Vice President's role, sometimes it is better to quietly express your differences to the President rather than to command attention at the Cabinet meeting or an NSC meeting. It is a question of style, because you don't want to be putting the President on the spot or make him choose between the Vice President and the Cabinet officers."[12]

Unlike their predecessors in the Vice Presidency, both Mondale and Bush were privy to full and complete information contained in the Presidential Daily Briefing (PDB), a crucial source of data on foreign policy. Again, we see the evolution of more clear-cut and definitive briefing of the second office, since prior to this Vice Presidents only received summaries of the PDB. To the extent that contemporary Vice Presidents are briefed as extensively as they are, the Vice Presidency in the third century should promise the nation the leadership ready to assume the Presidency should the need arise.

Unscheduled Transitions: Disability, Succession, and the Twenty-Fifth Amendment

The odds that a Vice President will succeed to the Presidency are approximately one in four. Besides this, there have been many instances of presidential disability. What these two crisis areas suggest for the Vice Presidency in the third century are thus well worth examining.

During the period of the modern Presidency and Vice Presidency alone there have been three unscheduled transfers of power: from Franklin D. Roosevelt to Harry S. Truman in 1945, from John F. Kennedy to Lyndon B. Johnson in 1963, and from Richard M. Nixon to Gerald R. Ford in 1974.

Each of these crises of succession tells us what to expect should another unhappily occur; they also tell a Vice President how he/she must behave during such a transition. Truman, Johnson, and Ford knew full well that the nation needed to be reassured. Indeed, this is a key advantage to the office of the Vice Presidency—at all times, the nation and the world clearly know the line of succession. It is perhaps the American equivalent to the kind of stability the British enjoy in having an heir to the throne. This stability is in itself a reassurance. But the successor to the American throne needs to reassure the nation and the world in actions and words as well. This was done by Truman, Johnson, and Ford alike. In the cases of Truman and Johnson, reassurance had to be along the lines of continuity of the system and of policy, and, for awhile, at least, of personnel. In the case of Ford, reassurance had to come in terms of continuity of the system, but not continuity of Nixon's policy and personnel in all areas. The unusual circumstances of the Nixon resignation and the Ford succession warranted a very different approach than Ford's predecessors had to take. Nonetheless, in each of these unscheduled transitions, the successor had to act swiftly, with determination, and with confidence.

The Twenty-Fifth Amendment, the need for which became apparent following just this question after the Kennedy assassination, attempted to resolve just what a Vice President should do in the case of temporary presidential disability. In brief, the amendment provides that a Vice President may temporarily assume the Presidency until such time as the President is recovered. The amendment also provides for circumstances in which a President is either unable—or unwilling—to declare himself/herself disabled. In either of these cases, the Vice President, along with a majority of the Cabinet, may declare the President temporarily disabled. Should there be a disagreement between the President and the Vice President and the Cabinet, either regarding initial disability or the termination of a disability, Congress shall resolve the dispute by a ⅔ vote within a three week period of time.

This part of the amendment has several flaws. In brief, is it likely that a Vice President would run the political risk inherent in declaring a President disabled—unless the President is unconscious and unable to do so? Are Cabinet members—who are beholden to the President for their jobs—likely to take such a political risk unless the President is unconscious and unable to do so? Perhaps the reality is that this clause of the Twenty-Fifth Amendment will be invoked only in limited and clear-cut cases of presidential disability, and only physical disabilities, at that. The gray area of mental disability would be far too politically dangerous for a Vice President or the Cabinet to hazard.

Besides this, circumstances have already passed during which the Twenty-Fifth Amendment might have been invoked, but wasn't. The Reagan Administration did not take advantage of two opportunities during which it could have set a very important precedent regarding use of this amendment. The assassination attempt upon the President and the surgery necessary as a result of it as well as Reagan's cancer surgery were both instances during which the President should have declared himself disabled and asked Vice President Bush to serve as President. If this had been the case, the nation and the world would have had demonstrated the smooth temporary transfer of power; moreover, future administrations would have had a model by which to act. Because President Reagan forfeited these opportunities, the setting of this model will have to be left for the last part of the second or the early part of the third century of this nation's experience.

Beyond this, the third century might also demonstrate some of the other potential flaws of this clause of the Twenty-Fifth Amendment. What if the President and Vice President do indeed disagree? What happens to the nation during the three week period of Congressional determination? What level of confidence will the nation and the world have in the leadership of either the President or the Vice President in such a case? What if either the President or the Vice President barely "wins" or "loses" the Congressional vote? The Twenty-Fifth Amendment was well-intentioned; but in solving some problems, it may have left our heirs with more difficult ones.[13]

As an afterthought, the framers of the Twenty-Fifth Amendment decided to include a solution for instances of vice presidential vacancy. The process, at least on paper, is a relatively simple one. The President nominates a replacement, who must then be approved by the Congress. Ironically, filling the vacancy in the Vice Presidency is the only part of the Twenty-Fifth Amendment which has thus far been utilized — in 1973 with the selection of Gerald Ford to replace Vice President Spiro Agnew who had resigned, and in 1974, with the selection of Nelson A. Rockefeller to replace Gerald R. Ford who had succeeded to the Presidency following Nixon's resignation. The Congressional hearings in the Rockefeller nomination in particular suggest potential problems with the utilization of this clause of the amendment. During the four months that the Congress met, the nation went without a Vice President, thus defeating the original purpose of the Amendment. The unlimited time frame in which Congress may act may prove problematic in the third century.

Evolving Vice Presidential Roles and Relations with Presidential Staff

While the Constitutional job description for the Vice President has not changed, the growth in real terms has been extraordinary. To a great extent, this growth has been a corollary of the expansion of the duties and burdens of the Presidency. As demands on the Chief Executive have exploded, this explosion could not help but affect the only other constitutionally elected officer of the executive branch. Within this vice presidential job growth have been both several key turning points (Truman, Nixon, Mondale) coupled with steady, incremental expansion of the office.

Truman's succession from the Vice Presidency to the Presidency can be considered a turning point. Truman's determination to keep future Vice Presidents better prepared to assume the Presidency set the stage for the growth that was to follow. Truman's inclusion of the Vice President in the Cabinet symbolically underscored the beginning of the changing Vice Presidency, as did legislation to make the Vice President a statutory member of the National Security Council. Despite these measures, Truman's own Vice President, Alben Barkley, did not have a particularly active Vice Presidency. In addition to presiding over the Senate, Barkley's role was largely a ceremonial one.[14]

Extensive vice presidential activity would have to wait for the next and perhaps the most dramatic turning point, the Nixon Vice Presidency.

It is almost axiomatic of the Vice President's roles that once the institution is given a task it is very difficult, although not impossible, for the next administration to remove it. Not that Eisenhower wanted to backtrack, but there was no question that his Vice President, too, would continue to meet with the Cabinet (indeed, during Eisenhower's illnesses, Nixon had even presided over the Cabinet's meetings).[15] And, of course, the Vice President remained statutorily a member of the National Security Council. Beyond this, Eisenhower established the President's Committee on Government Contracts; Nixon was appointed Chair. Eisenhower's Vice President also served as Chair of the Cabinet Committee on Price Stability, designed to find ways to keep inflation under control. By Nixon's own estimation, he spent more than 90 percent of his time on executive duties overall.[16]

Clearly, however, Nixon's greatest role was a political one. During Nixon's incumbency in the second office, in fact, the political potential of the Vice Presidency became strikingly apparent. The Nixon Vice Presidency is a crucial case study demonstrating just how important presidential character and personality are in determining the level of vice presidential activity. Eisenhower's apparent dislike for party politicking, combined with what would be any President's uncomfortable necessity of having to juggle being President of all the people at the same time his party members expect him to be their leader, afforded his young Vice President with an extraordinary opportunity. It was Nixon who assumed the bulk of party activities during the eight years of the Eisenhower Administration. In this regard, Nixon's Vice Presidency is a clear-cut case of a major contemporary vice presidential role, that of Administration spokesperson. It is no wonder that by the time the Eisenhower Administration came to a close, Nixon, who had built up a plethora of party IOUs from his range of party activities over the years, was the obvious party nominee for President. (The irony may be that while this had given Nixon an edge towards the party nomination, Eisenhower's failure to more actively convert his own popularity into a party popularity may have contributed to Nixon's defeat in the general election.) And when the antics of Wisconsin Senator Joseph McCarthy began to be a danger to the nation and an embarrassment to both the President and the party, it was the Vice President — his own anti-communist credentials impeccably well-established — who took on Eisenhower's enemy.

This Administration Spokesperson role was not limited to party activities. Indeed, Nixon, in the words of one journalist of the time who had covered his activities, had become a veritable "roving ambassador" abroad for the Administration.[17] Nixon travelled to all reaches of the globe, and in doing so was widely covered, attracting both domestic and world attention. Besides giving him a very active Vice Presidency, this role immersed him in foreign affairs, clearly helping to prepare him for one day assuming the Presidency. It is no wonder that when Nixon eventually did become President his foreign policy achievements were so extraordinary.

Although Nixon's was an active Vice Presidency, the Vice President's relationship with the people surrounding the President was a continual source of unease. This has tended to be a difficult area for many a Vice President, although it might appear that Walter Mondale and George Bush fared better. Eisenhower's "team" made sure that the Vice President did not become too ambitious, especially during Eisenhower's several illnesses, and the Vice President was acutely aware of "keeping his place." It makes perfect sense that staff tensions largely began with this Vice Presidency, since the Eisenhower Administration can accurately be said to be the first full-fledged "institutionalized" Presidency, consisting of a large staff. Similarly, Nixon's was the first full-fledged vice presidential staff, especially during his second term as he looked ahead to the 1960 presidential nomination.[18]

When Lyndon Johnson assumed the Vice Presidency, the titular assignments largely remained intact. Kennedy revised the President's Committee on Government Contracts to give it a more vital role by combining it with another committee, the President's Committee on Government Employment Opportunity; Johnson chaired this new creature, which was quite effective in working against racial bias in government employment. Since Nixon had headed the Committee's predecessor, it was not politically feasible for Kennedy to take this away from his Vice President. Kennedy initially received criticism for having placed a Southerner in charge of such a sensitive task; ironically, the very fact that Johnson was a Southerner made him and the committee all the more effective.[19] This particular task suggests another role to be played by a Vice President: a President can emphasize his concern for a policy area precisely by having the only other nationally elected official serve as his stand-in. Kennedy similarly did so in placing Johnson in charge of America's space program (Johnson chaired the National Aeronautics and Space Council) and by sending the Vice President off to Berlin as his plenipotentiary when trouble plagued that divided city.

Much as the Eisenhower-Nixon relationship affected the role to be played by the Vice President, so, too, did the Kennedy-Johnson relationship. Although Kennedy was certainly cordial to his Vice President, often taking great care in making sure the rather sensitive Texan was not offended in any way, the two were never intimates. Moreover, the Kennedy staff largely despised Johnson, many never having forgiven him for the bitter primary battles in which Kennedy and Johnson had engaged in pursuit of the presidential nomination. Importantly, the President's brother, Robert, had a disdain for the former Majority Leader. Oftentimes, apparently unknown to the President himself, Johnson found himself the butt of White House abuse and derision. Besides these tensions between the Kennedy people and the Vice President, Kennedy and Johnson themselves found their new roles difficult. As a Senator, Kennedy had been Johnson's subordinate; now, roles were reversed. Indeed, some of the Kennedy people delighted in the fact that the former Majority Leader — who had once been so powerful — now had to come to them for assistance and access to the President.[20]

One might imagine that two former Vice Presidents such as Nixon and Johnson might have learned some very important lessons from having served in the second office, and that they might have treated their own Vice Presidents differently. Certainly, Hubert Humphrey would not say Lyndon Johnson had learned sufficiently to improve Humphrey's lot.[21] Humphrey's role in the second office, too, was the creature of the interaction of the President's and Vice President's personalities. Johnson was a hard task master, and demanded unswerving loyalty; Humphrey was willing to give it. Indeed, as Humphrey himself pointed out, being subordinate to Johnson was something to which he had become accustomed while serving in the Senate. Humphrey was fully aware, too, that he owed much in the way of his political advancement to Johnson, who had taken Humphrey under his wing in the Senate.[22]

Several of Humphrey's roles as Vice President logically followed from assets he had brought to Johnson's 1964 campaign. As a long-established liberal, Humphrey had helped Johnson establish linkage to that ideological sector of the party and the nation. Moreover, Humphrey had always had interests in the problems of youth and the cities (he had served as a mayor himself). Thus, Humphrey provided linkage between the Administration and the nation's mayors; similarly, Humphrey actively worked to have jobs for youth materialize, both privately and governmentally.

Despite this activity, Johnson's dominating personality and demand for loyalty, combined with White House staff-vice presidential tensions, set the scene for the Humphrey Vice Presidency. A role early removed from Humphrey was one that Nixon had somewhat played and Johnson had played more vigorously, and that was in the area of civil rights. Humphrey's liberal and strong civil rights credentials would have made him a natural for this role.[23] But apparently, even though the public announcement was that Humphrey himself thought the President's Council on Equal Employment Opportunity was no longer necessary and should be disbanded, this was actually a position maintained by Johnson advisers.[24] In an interview with this author in 1974, Humphrey recalled the difficulties he had encountered at the hands of the Johnson staff.

> If one became too popular or too effective, whoever the Vice President, the President says, "What's he up to?" Not so much the President — his staff. One of the things that happens to a President and a Vice President is that the presidential staff looks upon a Vice President as an extra wheel that ought not to be on the vehicle of government — it's a fifth wheel, so to speak. And as far as that staff is concerned, it never needs a spare, you know. To them, a spare is extraneous; it's surplus baggage. And that staff will cut you out time after time — almost without malice. It's just sort of subconscious. They just say, "Well, he isn't really needed." I remember Johnson, from time to time, exploding to his staff, saying, "Why didn't you have Hubert over here?" "Oh, I didn't know you wanted him, Mr. President." "Well, I want him around here," he'd say. And I used to wonder, is he doing that as an act or what? In fact I found out that sometimes they'd just plain forget.[25]

Whereas Nixon as Vice President had seemed to welcome the role of serving as Administration Spokesperson, Humphrey seemed to have had it forced upon him. Both because he had early opposed Johnson's bombing of North Vietnam (a position Humphrey had taken in the privacy of a National Security Council meeting, but one for which Johnson had not forgiven him and for which Humphrey was severely punished for a full year; during that year, Johnson not only gave Humphrey little to do — he also took opportunity to humiliate the Vice President when possible) and because of his strong liberal credentials, Humphrey was given the increasingly unpopular task of serving as a spokesperson and defender of Johnson's Vietnam policy. This role was given to Humphrey despite the fact that Humphrey rarely participated in Johnson's weekly "Tuesday luncheon," during which Vietnam policy was discussed. Humphrey's Vice Presidency clearly demonstrates a crucial dimension of the presidential-vice presidential relationship: the President can make or break a Vice President. For Humphrey, Lyndon Johnson had done both.

Humphrey's successor in the Vice Presidency, Spiro Agnew, maintained most of the institutionalized roles which had by this time devolved to the office; additionally, Nixon created the Office of Intergovernmental Relations, and Agnew was to be in charge. As a former Baltimore County Executive and later Governor of Maryland, this seemed like a natural service to be provided by the Vice President, particularly since he had had no foreign affairs experience; besides, foreign affairs was to be the President's domain. But the linkage that might have been provided by Agnew to the cities and states via this new office never fully materialized; in 1972, the Office of Intergovernmental Relations was abolished — shortly after the Nixon-Agnew landslide.

Much as had Humphrey, Agnew played the role of Administration Spokesperson. It took little time to realize that Agnew was becoming a critic of those perceived as "enemies" by the Nixon White House. In this capacity, the Vice President fulfilled his 1968 campaign promise of becoming "a household word." But although he played this role, Agnew, as had been Humphrey, was largely kept out of the policymaking process.[26]

Gerald Ford's relatively short incumbency in the Vice Presidency was a unique one, insofar as he had come on board in the midst of the growing Watergate controversy which was engulfing the White House. Unlike his predecessors, who would have welcomed greater access to the inner White House, Ford found it politic to steer clear, lest he too become tainted. For Nixon's part, Ford was considerably ignored as an adviser, much as had been Agnew. And perhaps in no other White House was it clearer that this Vice President could very well assume the President's job and take his own staff along with him, to the detriment of the tainted President's staff.

One of the most interesting Vice Presidencies is that of Nelson A. Rockefeller. Usually, it is the President who is the more nationally and internationally known figure in the Administration, with the Vice President as somewhat of a tag along. Not so in the Ford-Rockefeller White House. So initially it seemed that the prestigious Rockefeller would play a much more dominant role than had his predecessors. But many forces combined to not have this be the case. The presidential dominance was one of those forces—and this particular force suggests that perhaps there is an inevitability to the presidential-vice presidential relationship: no matter who the individuals, the Vice President MUST be subordinate and the President shall always prevail.

A second force which shortened the shadow that Rockefeller might have cast was the White House staff. By the time Rockefeller was confirmed by the Congress (following the procedures established by the Twenty-Fifth Amendment regarding a vice presidential vacancy), the Ford White House had been operating for some four months—long enough for the staff to get along quite well without having a Vice President with which to contend, thank you very much. Ford had initially promised a much more dominant role, especially in domestic policy making, but Rockefeller's expectations in this area never fully materialized, even though Rockefeller served as Vice Chair of the Domestic Council until his last year as Vice President.[27] But the Vice President, thanks to his own determination to be active and to the President's willingness to have him be so, was nonetheless able to play an ongoing advisory role. Insisting upon weekly meetings with Ford was quite astute on Rockefeller's part; in this way, he was able to openly and regularly discuss issues of interest to him and on the President's agenda, as well as make recommendations. But the Ford staff did not make Rockefeller's role an easy one, looking to cut the Vice President out wherever possible, particularly since Rockefeller had early on so candidly referred to seeing his own role as a "staff assistant."[28]

The Mondale Vice Presidency became the third key turning

point in the history of the contemporary institution. Partially because he came to the Vice Presidency with a keen understanding of the nature and potential pitfalls of the institution, Mondale carved out a role for himself unlike anything his predecessors had ever experienced. After having received advice from his political mentor and friend, Hubert Humphrey, as well as from Nelson Rockefeller, Mondale wisely chose to avoid line assignments. Rather, he chose to serve as a "general adviser" to Carter, thus placing himself in the full loop of information and policymaking in the White House. Besides Mondale's own wisdom, Carter was fully comfortable with, willing to, and interested in having his Vice President play a full role. Moreover, Carter needed Mondale's insights and experience. Carter symbolically underscored this new role by moving the Vice President's office from the Executive Office Building directly into the White House. Crucially, too, both Carter and Mondale were well aware of the staff tensions which were likely to develop unless they consciously addressed this problem area. Beginning with the 1976 campaign itself, in fact, there was a considerable merging of staffs, a practice carried over into the White House. For all of these reasons, Mondale became the most active Vice President to that point in the history of the office, in both domestic and foreign affairs.[29]

The Bush Vice Presidency became the benefactor of the very successful Mondale Vice Presidency. Much of what had made Carter-Mondale successful was the warm, close working relationship between the two men. Mondale fully understood that a Vice President must have the President's trust and confidence. Mondale also understood that a Vice President must be loyal and must not publicly voice disagreement, lest he lose the President's trust. Although Ronald Reagan and George Bush did not begin this partnership based upon such trust and confidence, George Bush worked hard to earn it. Loyal, self-effacing and hard-working, Bush time and again demonstrated his ability to work as a "team player," something which Reagan valued quite highly, and which earned Bush the respect of the Reagan staff. Importantly, too, particularly in the first term, was the fact that Reagan brought some Bush people onto his own staff; especially important was James Baker, who became part of the troika of Meese, Deaver, and Baker surrounding the President. In a 1982 letter to this author, Vice President George Bush wrote, "One area that needs exploring is the relationship of the Vice President to President's staff. This is a major thing. For me, it's working well."

Bush inherited not only the institutionalized roles which the Vice Presidency had accumulated to this point in time. The President also rewarded Bush's team spirit by naming the Vice President as head of Reagan's "crisis management team," this coming, ironically, just shortly before the assassination attempt on the President.[30] Vice President Bush also served in the capacity of Administration spokesperson, consistently and vociferously presenting and defending Reagan domestic programs across the board; he has also travelled quite extensively for Reagan, bringing the Reagan message across the globe.[31]

As the Vice Presidency moves into the third century, the lessons of the latter half of the second century suggest that its roles will continue to grow as the President's roles and responsibilities do. What is also clear is that a strong, working relationship must exist between the President and the Vice President to make these roles work effectively. Suggestions to formalize a vice presidential role (such as to make the Vice President the Secretary of State or the Secretary of Defense — the latter of which was suggested during the 1988 vice presidential considerations with regard to Democratic Georgia Senator and Foreign Relations Chair Sam Nunn) do not take into consideration that the President has to have flexibility to best utilize — or to get rid of, if necessary — those around him/her. In this sense, only when the President has established a working relationship with the Vice President can an ongoing role based upon that Vice President's strengths and weaknesses be ascertained. Besides this, while a President can get rid of staff and Cabinet members, not so easily does a Vice President exit. The third century should look towards making the burdens of the Presidency easier; it should not attempt to bridle the President's options.

The Vice Presidency as a Steppingstone to the Presidency

Some very interesting observations can be made by looking at the potential of the contemporary Vice Presidency as a route to the Presidency via the nominating process rather than through succession. In the period of the post-FDR Presidency and Vice Presidency, the second office has become a far more attractive commodity because of its increased political role. Vice Presidents during this period of time have been delegated a good deal of the party politicking that can help garner political IOUs which can be redeemed once the incumbent President is no longer eligible to run for another term.

Look briefly at the record. Had Vice President Alben Barkley not been of advanced age in 1952 he undoubtedly would have been considered as a possible successor to Truman; Richard Nixon's very extensive political activity during eight years of the Eisenhower Administration gave him the decided advantage as he approached the 1960 Republican presidential nomination; once Lyndon Johnson removed himself from the competition in 1968, his Vice President, Hubert Humphrey, was logically viewed by many as the heir apparent, despite the very serious competition from both Senator Eugene McCarthy and Senator Robert Kennedy; following Richard Nixon's landslide reelection in 1972 and prior to the revelation of Spiro Agnew's embarrassing and potentially criminal past, the Vice President had virtually immediately emerged as the heir apparent for 1976 (indeed, some even began to coin the phrase — to coincide with the Bicentennial of 1976 — the "Spiro of '76"); despite Jimmy Carter's defeat at the polls in 1980, his running mate and first term Vice President Walter Mondale had built up sufficient party IOUs and organization to assure him of the clear-cut advantage in the next presidential election; and Vice President George Bush's services for Ronald Reagan for eight years afforded him the opportunity to build a successful organization and campaign chest to give him the party's nomination in 1988.

All of this is on the plus side. On the down side has been the picture of one crown prince after another struggling with the legacy of an administrative record to defend during the course of his own presidential campaign. As Vice President, Richard Nixon had enjoyed eight years of a highly successful presidential administration. Indeed, were it not for the Twenty-Second Amendment, had Eisenhower been interested in a third term he quite likely may have met with success. But even in the most popular and successful of administrations there are bound to have been mistakes made. So, in 1960, Vice President Nixon found himself in the uncomfortable position of having to fend off opponent John F. Kennedy's criticisms regarding the developing economic recession, the embarrassment of the U-2 spying incident over the Soviet Union, the seeming administration inaction regarding Castro's Cuba, problems surrounding the islands of Quemoy and Matsu, and an alleged missile gap.

Hubert Humphrey's presidential nomination in 1968 was a hollow victory in light of the albatross of the very controversial Johnson record abroad, particularly in Southeast Asia. While the Vice Presidency had given Humphrey the arena of national and international prominence he had not been able to gain while he had been a Senator, that very arena had become one filled with lions. Perhaps the Humphrey experience best captures the interesting paradox of the Vice Presidency as a steppingstone. Humphrey was a Vice President who had very early but privately disagreed with the Johnson Vietnam policy; his own policy would have been very different. But as the incumbent Vice President *cum* presidential candidate, Humphrey was not entirely free to lay out for the nation just what his policy would be.

Four years after their reelection bid at the polls, Jimmy Carter's Vice President, Walter Mondale, went on to claim his party's presidential nomination. But despite the passage of four years, the American people and the American media did not allow Mondale the luxury of being completely his own man. Instead, Mondale found himself time and again being linked to the very unpopular and troubled Carter Administration. Despite Mondale's efforts to extricate himself, he had to live with the Carter legacy.

Vice President George Bush in 1988 was in the same position as had been his predecessors. To a great extent, Bush's position most nearly paralleled Richard Nixon's in 1960. Bush, too, had been the Vice President under two terms of a very popular and charismatic President. Despite the rather positive administrative record, nonetheless there were problem areas: the national deficit; the less than consistent Reagan foreign policy; the continuously unfolding Iran-Contra affair; and the Administration's relationship with General Noriega of Panama. These made more headlines than Vice President Bush's quiet accomplishments ranging from his role in the Euromissile deployment and the related INF treaty, the South Florida Task Force combatting drugs, and the Task Force on Regulatory Relief which spurred-on the economy. Thus the Vice Presidency, while a steppingstone to the presidential nomination, may ironically be a stumbling block to election.[32]

CHAPTER THIRTY-TWO

The Coordinating Role of The Vice Presidency

C. BOYDEN GRAY

COUNSELLOR TO THE VICE PRESIDENT

OF THE UNITED STATES

Vice President George Bush has continued and indeed strengthened the Office of the Vice President as a strong and integral part of the Executive Branch. It is, of course, much too early to tell whether his achievements and his handling of the office will translate into a permanent expansion of the role of the Vice Presidency. However, a review of both the Vice President's record and the ever-increasing demands of the Presidency strongly suggest that the nature of the Vice Presidency has been permanently altered.

Before discussing the Vice President's individual record, it is important to outline briefly the circumstances that had developed prior to 1981 to provide both the need for a vigorously functioning Vice President and the opportunity to make more out of the office than merely a waiting room for the expiration of two terms, resignation, impeachment or death.

One of the biggest problems in modern government is the increasing difficulty of coordinating the overlapping and sometimes competing policy roles of the great bureaucracies, both foreign and domestic, and the greater difficulty of coordinating between domestic and foreign policy. There is, of course, nothing new about bureaucratic turf wars. The problem is that an explosion of Congressional committee and subcommittee fragmentation and micromanagement in the 1970s has greatly augmented both the tunnel vision and single-mindedness of bureaucracies as well as helped increase their number. For example, the Office of the Special Trade Representative, initially designed to be a staff function in the Executive Office of the President, has grown to achieve national cabinet status in its own right, subject to its own specialized Congressional oversight. The NSC operation has also grown as a policymaker, rather than coordinator. As a result, there are few people available to coordinate the coordinators who were supposed themselves to work out the conflicts between the more senior bureaucratic baronies.

At the risk of oversimplification, the problem is, given all of these competing bureaucracies, who among them can call a meeting that all can comfortably attend without a loss of face? The answer is, very few. And since the President does not have time, the system does, by the process of elimination, put considerable pressure on the Vice President to resolve disputes (subject always, of course, to final decision by the President). This bureaucratic proliferation also has secondary effects on the Vice Presidency, stemming from increasing Congressional assertion of fragmented power over the day-to-day operations of foreign and defense policy. In many cases today, the State Department alone can no longer satisfy the lobbying and protocol demands of foreign visitors, who increasingly have to augment visits there with visits to any number of congressional committees. As a result, these visitors often look to the Vice President for help, again, in resolving conflicts.

The demands and opportunities, however, go well beyond protocol, and explain why the Vice President was able to play such a major contributing role in what many see as President Reagan's most important foreign policy achievement, namely the Euromissile deployment and the subsequent INF Treaty that it made possible. By now, the Vice President's successful whistle-stop tour of Western European capitals in February 1983 to persuade European governments to accept the Pershings and cruise missiles, is history. The Vice President has been an integral part of the day-to-day conduct of foreign policy. But its significance at the time was well recorded—perhaps best by the congratulatory *Washington Post* editorial, the headline of which read "George Did It."

It is doubtful in today's circumstances that a Secretary of State or Defense could have achieved the results that Vice President Bush did. This is because, given the fragmentation of power, it is unlikely that any Cabinet officer, or any Congressional official for that matter, can achieve the dominant stature necessary to command the ultimate result. This, of course, does not guarantee that a Vice President can do so himself. But it does help create the opportunity, which Vice President Bush exploited. Similar successes may elude his successor, but the opportunity will very likely be there.

The need to coordinate intractable bureaucracies also led to the Vice President's appointment as head of the South Florida Task Force, an effort to restore a measure of law and order to the Miami community that was rapidly losing its grip to the drug traffic in the early 1980s. The oversight bodies recognized the importance of the Vice President's success at the time, and more recently Senator Cranston and the Los Angeles Chief of Police have asked for the creation of an effort in Los Angeles modelled after the Florida project — a request that underscores the effort's success at least as far as the law enforcement community is concerned. Again the Vice President's diplomatic skills served him well in getting bureaucracies to cooperate with each other, but there will almost certainly be similar coordination requirements calling for involvement by future Vice Presidents.

The success of the South Florida Task Force in turn, led to its expansion all across the southern border as the National Border Interdiction System (NNBIS), and OCDETF, The Organized Crime Drug Enforcement Task Force established in six regions around the country. This expanded interdiction and enforcement program captured ever increasing amounts of marijuana and cocaine, virtually stopping the former and keeping the price of the latter higher by one-third, in the estimate of one recent independent study (Rand). It could not and did not, however, prohibit drug imports or curtail domestic drug use and demand.

Two other foreign policy examples of the use of the Vice President's effective management and diplomatic skills are worth mentioning. The first was his trip to sub-Saharan Africa in February of 1983. Although a decade-long drought was the major reason for the terrible famine in that part of Africa, many of the difficulties were man-made, resulting from the often uncoordinated government polices of AID, the State Department itself, and the World Bank (where our representatives answer to the Treasury, not either one of the above). The Vice President was able to coordinate their efforts well enough to help implement the Administration's free market policy that has already shown results — helped along, to be sure, by the recurrence of rain.

The second was the Terrorism Task Force. Although it is difficult to trace cause and effect, the issuance of the Report coincided with a drop in terrorist incidents that have continued to this day. The key, again, was success in getting bureaucracies to work more closely together. Much of the credit belongs to Admiral Holloway, the retired former Chief of Naval Operations, who served as the Task Force's Executive Director. His appointment illustrates one part of the Vice President's success — his ability to identify and attract first rate talent from the private sector for as long as it takes to finish an important task.

On the domestic front, the Vice President's chairmanship of the Presidential Task Force on Regulatory Relief is another example of successfully filling the need for supra-cabinet coordination of cabinet-level activities. Although space does not permit a thorough discussion of the Task Force's accomplishments, a couple of observations can illuminate what it did. The Vice President designed and implemented an oversight mechanism over the regulatory bureaucracies that no President had been able to put in place for nearly two decades. However one may judge the results, the Vice President was exercising oversight responsibility and power that no President had ever exercised before.

With respect to results, the President himself attributes what Europeans call "the American Miracle" of America's creation of 17-1/2 million new jobs since 1982 to regulatory relief, tax reform and return of authority to state and local governments (which was achieved primarily by deregulation). If the President is considered a biased observer, it might be useful to cite Lord Young, Margaret Thatcher's Minister of Trade and Industry, for the same proposition. Moreover, the current export boom owes an important part of its vitality to high manufacturing productivity growth, which has recently been running better than Japan's or West Germany's (and four times the level of the 1970s) and which is very much related to the elimination and avoidance of senseless burden on commerce (including the free flow of capital).

The American experiment with regulatory reform has now become a model for other industrialized countries — imitation again being the sincerest form of flattery. As with other efforts, the Vice President's success stems, in part, from his choice of Executive Directors (James Miller, Chris DeMuth, and Wendy Gramm, each of whom have gone to bigger jobs as OMB Director, President of AEI, and CFTC Chairman respectively). The success also reflects the Vice President's own experience as the pioneer of a high-technology industry and his first-hand understanding of how unnecessary red tape can stifle innovation. Future Vice Presidents should have similar opportunities in the future even if they don't have the same prior experience.

As indicated at the outset, there is also a crying need to provide a policy link between foreign and domestic policy. There can be no better illustration of this than the Vice President's role in the trade area. Again, space does not permit a detailed recitation of the Vice President's efforts abroad, particularly in Japan and Western Europe, to knock down barriers to American products. Nor is there time to explain in detail how, in the Republican primaries, the Vice President played a major role in defeating the Gephardt amendment, which by closing off American borders could have equalled the Smoot-Hawley legislation of 1930 and triggered another depression. Suffice to say here that his sweeping victory in the southern primaries on a free trade platform in the face of explicitly protectionist opposition, combined with Gephardt's primary loss, led to the AFL-CIO's withdrawal of support for the Gephardt Amendment. But the results are clear: it is no coincidence that the Japanese opened their markets for citrus and beef this summer just as the Congress cleaned up — though not nearly enough for some — the current trade legislation of much of its protectionist baggage. Although these recent actions by Japan and the Congress are far from all that ideally could or should be done, they reflect a certain balance which should keep world economic growth on an upward curve. And they both bear the imprint of the Vice President, who has been in a unique position to see clearly the critical relationship of foreign and domestic policy as it plays out in the trade arena. Indeed, because of the enormous threat the Gephardt amendment posed to the world trading order, it may be that the Vice President's contribution to its defeat may rate higher in the history books than his role in persuading Europe to deploy the cruise and the Pershing missiles.

These examples do not exhaust the Vice President's activities in his 7½ years as Vice President. Other achievements, such as his rescue of the Falashas from Ethiopia, his curbing of the death squads in El Salvador, and his initiation of the current debate on the War Powers Resolution and Congressional foreign policy micromanagement deserve study. They are not included here because they were not related in any important way to the coordination aspects of the Vice Presidency which will probably play the most critical role in the development of that office over the balance of this century.

PART TEN

Continuing Issues

Presidential Disability, Succession and the Twenty-fifth Amendment

KENNETH W. THOMPSON
DIRECTOR, MILLER CENTER OF PUBLIC AFFAIRS
UNIVERSITY OF VIRGINIA

Three factors combined in the final two years of the Reagan administration to inspire consideration of the question of presidential disability and the twenty-fifth amendment. Earlier, one overarching concern had made the subject legitimate to study.

From 1980, friends and critics alike had called attention to that overall concern. President Ronald Reagan will leave office as the oldest American president in history. However remarkable his health for a man of his age, nearly everyone recognizes the threat imposed by the realities of the actuarial tables. Yet studies of disability undertaken within the government would have been subject to misinterpretation. For that reason, officials in the Justice Department with ties to the University of Virginia let it be known that a review of the Twenty-fifth Amendment would be welcome. Their approach led to the organization of a Miller Center Commission co-chaired by former Senator Birch Bayh and Eisenhower administration attorney general Herbert Brownell.

In the final years of the Reagan administration, three other factors came together to heighten interest in the problem. February 10, 1987 was the twentieth anniversary of the ratification of the Twenty-fifth Amendment. It seemed appropriate to look back and review the historical experience of the Amendment. What was its intent? When and how had it been used? What were the perceptions of the Amendment by the public and by professional politicians? What changes if any could be suggested in constitutional provisions and political usage? How fully were its procedures understood by past and present leaders? Which aspects of the Amendment were clear and which subject to varying interpretations, perhaps because of ambiguities? What was needed to assure that future presidents would feel comfortable in invoking it? What about the public's acceptance of its use as a normal and rational course of action to take when presidents were temporarily or otherwise disabled?

A second factor embodied two critical life-threatening events that focused the spotlight of public attention on presidential disability. The first occurred on March 31, 1981, less than three months after the president's inauguration. A would be assassin, John Hinkley, seriously wounded the president. Dr. Daniel Ruge, who was the first-term presidential physician in the Reagan administration, responded to a question about the Amendment posed by the Commission saying:

> There is a big difference between Dan Ruge on March 30, 1981, after a shooting when he'd only been on the job two months for one thing and what Dan Ruge would have been like four years later [at the time of Reagan's colon cancer operation] when he would have actually had time from April 1981 to July 1985 to think about it. I think very honestly in 1981 because of the speed of everything and the fact that we had a very sick president that the 25th Amendment would never have entered my mind even though I probably had it in my little black bag. I carried it with me. The 25th Amendment never occurred to me.[1]

The second event followed some four and a third years later with President Reagan's hospitalization for cancer surgery. Fred Fielding, who was then counsel to the president, testified before the Miller Center Commission that serious thought was given to the use of the Twenty-fifth Amendment. He explained:

> Let's go back to the week before the operation. We knew—some of us knew—and I forget when it became public, that the President was going to have his physical. We knew at the time that he was going to have a form of anesthesia, to have the procedure that occurred on Friday, if I recall my dates correctly. He was operated on Saturday, got a procedure on Friday. What was going to happen was that there was a possibility that if something was found that they would have to instantly put the President under. I used that as an opportunity the preceding week to schedule a meeting with the President and the Vice President and Don Regan (then chief of staff). We sat in the Oval Office and we discussed the whole situation: the National Command Authority plus the President's desires on passage of power temporarily if he were suddenly temporarily incapacitated. . . .[2]

Mr. Fielding went on explaining that when the use of the amendment was first discussed he drafted an initial letter for the President's signature that followed Section 3 of the amendment to the letter. If the President had been willing to sign the first Fielding draft, the provisions laid down in Section 3 requiring that the powers and duties temporarily pass to the vice president would have automatically gone into effect. However, the President demurred and Mr. Fielding then drafted a second optional letter that allowed the President essentially to follow the procedures of Section 3 while maintaining he was not invoking the Amendment. The President did not want to set a precedent for future presidents. This left the media and the public confused about whether or not the President had actually employed the Amendment and that confusion was reflected in early discussions within the Commission. The majority believed the President had used the procedures while denying he was doing so but a minority took him at his word and concluded the Amendment had not been used. Whatever his reasons, President Reagan's hesitancy had nothing to do with any fear that the Vice President might engineer a *coup d'etat* of a Latin American variety. In other words, the President's reluctance was not based on political reasons.

What then were his reasons? Apparently he had honest worries that he might be setting a legally binding precedent. It may also be true that he anticipated strong public reactions at home and abroad approaching crisis proportions. It is also true that except for President Jimmy Carter who had been faced with the prospect of hemorrhoid surgery under anesthesia until his physicians decided on another treatment, no president has been confronted by the choice President Reagan had to make. He had to make his way alone.

However, the Commission concluded "that Section 3 of the 25th Amendment should have been used by Reagan and other presidents where anesthesia was involved. The Commission believes that the best course is to make routine the use of this mechanism so that its invocation carries no implications of instability or crisis."

Two points deserve emphasis because they are central to the Report. The first centers on the use of anesthesia which the Commission singled out as illustrating a disability producing action that fits the use of Section 3 of the Amendment much as a hand fits a glove. Virtually all physicians who appeared before the Commission spoke of the drastic nature of anesthesia comparing it to being hit by a ten ton truck. They showed impatience with the views of the surgeon whom Reagan and Fielding had consulted and who agreed that if the President was lucid enough to read and understand a letter they asked him to sign, he was ready to resume exercising the powers and duties of the office. It seems clear that the two aides were aware they were taking a calculated risk and Fielding told the Commission: "The worst thing in the world would have been to have him transfer . . . the power to the Vice President, take it back, and then later have to transfer it back again." Any premature restoring of responsibility to the President could backfire.

Anesthesia is only one, but a particularly obvious circumstance that the Commission recommended as probable cause for bringing Section 3 into play. It reasoned further: "Because anyone under anesthetic is unable to function both during the period of unconsciousness and afterwards while disoriented, presidents should accept the inevitability of a temporary transfer of power to the vice president that would extend beyond the immediate hours in the operating room, or even in the hospital, perhaps 24 to 48 hours." Not only a general anesthetic, however, but narcotics or other drugs that alter cerebral function should be viewed in the same light, as should any similarly debilitating disease or physical malfunction. The Commission urged that such circumstances be identified in advance and an understanding reached, say, between the president, vice president, attorney general, chief of staff and the president's spouse that Section 3 would more or less automatically be invoked when certain conditions prevailed. It seems clear this was not done effectively in the case of the Reagan presidency even though Mr. Fielding prepared an emergency book which he was frank to say was not available at the time of the assassination attempt.

The existence of such a book or a set of detailed contingency plans might help to reconcile differences such as those that existed between Don Regan and Nancy Reagan. In a highly critical book on the Reagan presidency, Mr. Regan charged that the first lady had sought to shield the President from White House duties after his 1985 hospitalization for prostate surgery. He alleged that she had consulted an astrologer about the timing of presidential travel and statements. He implied that the president's absence may have had harmful political consequences.

Privately and in an address on June 9, 1988 to members of a gas industry conference, Mrs. Reagan responded to the former chief of staff's criticisms. A president, she said, has many advisers. "But no one among all those experts is there to look after him as an individual with human needs, as a flesh-and-blood person who must deal with the pressures of holding the most powerful position on earth."[3] Referring to her responsibility to protect her husband she declared that's "one thing on which any first lady must be a stone wall." Donald T. Regan had sought to portray Mrs. Reagan as responsible for there being a "shadowy distaff presidency" and ruthlessly controlling the president's schedule. "Yes, there are demands of government, but there are also basic personal rights every president should not be denied," Mrs. Reagan replied to this remark and, for purposes of the Commission study, a key sentence followed: "as a wife, I believe my husband has as much right to a normal recuperation as any other husband."[4]

It is the gravamen of the Commission's report that the president is indeed a normal, flesh-and-blood person and, as with any other normal person, he is likely at some time or other to be hospitalized and even face surgery. During and immediately following surgery, the president's ability to make the discriminating judgments necessary to wise decision making is likely to be impaired. In calling for at least a 24 to 48 hour waiting period after surgery, the Commission recommended:

> It would be wise for a president to state this publicly so that the nation and the world is reassured, and importantly so that the pressure is lessened on those White House officials fearful of some loss of power.[5]

A third factor that came to the fore preceding and during the work of the Commission was discussion of the role of the presidential physician. At the time of the legislation, we have the word of one of the draftsmen that the place of the presidential physician was not given much attention. President Reagan's first term presidential physician came to see his position as "a blue collar job." From testimony before the Commission, it was clear that the White House physician was not consulted by the White House staff before the emergency surgery following the assassination attempt even though he was inside the hospital. The physician met Vice President Bush for the first time the day following the assassination attempt as well as members of the Cabinet. When the physician briefed the Cabinet, he sensed that their eyes glazed over at the mention of the Twenty-fifth Amendment. When the cancer surgery was performed, it was the surgeon and not the presidential physician whom the two aides consulted about the President's condition — a choice which all the physicians appearing before the Commission concluded was unwise from a medical standpoint. As one of them observed, a surgeon feels his work has been a success if he completes his task and the patient is still breathing. However parochial this view, it is clear that post-surgical and recovery decisions require different skills and competence than surgery itself.

One point that invariably comes to the fore in any discussion of the presidential physician is presidential preference. A president can be expected to pick a presidential physician in whom he has confidence. Nancy Reagan's stepfather, Royall Davis, recommended Dr. Ruge as presidential physician. He was a senior medical person in whom the President and First Lady understandably had confidence. Dr. William Lukash, who had been a navy medical doctor, was presidential physician for Presidents Nixon, Ford and Carter. The question was debated whether a service medical background was an advantage or disadvantage for a presidential physician with Dr. Lukash in particular pointing up some of the advantages.

We learned in the course of our discussions that the presidential physician not only serves the president but is the head of a White House medical office whose services are available to the White House staff as a whole. Thus the presidential physician has certain overall responsibilities that extend beyond the care and treatment of the president. He (she) has fifteen hundred constituents in the White House with a second medical office in the adjoining Executive Office Building and two assistant physicians who join the travelling groups which include, besides the president's Secret Service aides, the press, the military and communications personnel.

The Commission found it was easier to recognize that the physician's job should be upgraded than to know how to do it. The 1981 Congressional Directory contains a staff listing of fifty-five names for the Executive Office. The list is headed by the coun-selor to the president, the chief of staff and his (her) deputy, var-ious assistants to the president and the deputy assistants and spe-cial assistant. The last three names on the list in that order are the curator of White House artifacts, physician to the president and chief usher. Is it any wonder that the presidential physician met the Vice President for the first time or Cabinet members when he briefed them the day after the assassination?

The hard question for the presidential physician is the locus and extent of his (her) loyalty. The Commission listened to tes-timony in which it was asserted that past physicians had sought to hide from the public serious medical facts regarding *their* presi-dent. Making use of the Freedom of Information Act, Dr. Ken-neth Crispell has uncovered evidence that President Franklin D. Roosevelt, from early 1943 to March of 1944, was admitted to Bethesda Hospital twenty-eight times under such assumed names as Joe Franklin, Joe Delano, etc. Dr. Crispell writes: "By the time of the Yalta Conference, FDR could sit up only two hours a day. He was exceedingly short of breath and he already had what we in the medical profession call 'chronic heart failure' and severe high blood pressure."[6] Yet his physician, Admiral McIntire, reported in the press that FDR was fine for his age, considering his polio, much as Admiral Grayson persisted in saying that Woodrow Wilson's health was satisfactory even though Mrs. Wilson and Senator Carter Glass of Virginia "ran the government for eighteen months."[7] Lord Moran in his book on Churchill acknowledges that on December 22, 1941, the night before an important wartime conference planning the invasion of Europe, the British prime minister had a severe heart attack. When Dr. Crispell asked Lord Moran why he had not disclosed the extent of the illness even to his patient and whether he did not have a responsibility to the country, Lord Moran replied: "I have a responsibility only to my patient."[8]

Lord Moran's view was disputed by almost all the physicians who appeared before the Commission. They agreed with Dr. William Lukash who affirmed that presidential physicians cannot escape "accepting a dual loyalty to their own patients but also to the public." What if the presidential physician should discover that the president was physically incapable of performing the responsibilities and duties of the office? He should go to the vice president or the attorney general and perhaps also the presidential spouse and report his finding. "He or she must consider that he or she, and all those physicians who assist from time to time, are responsible not only for the care of the chief executive but also for the 'care of the country,'" the Commission asserted in an Annex on the president's physician attached to its Report.[9] It made reference to the American Medical Association Council on Medical Ethics extension of the idea of patient-doctor confidentiality to exceptions where it can be abridged in the national or community interest. However the Commission stopped short of recommending a statute calling for the presidential physician to accept a positive duty to communicate details about the president's condition if it jeopardized the national interest. It concluded such a statute could be self-defeating in practice and was not necessary if procedures were in place for communicating within the government.

In this area as in others, the Commission put the emphasis on an early meeting, sometime during the transition period, of the president-elect, vice president-elect, the prospective chief of staff, attorney general and perhaps the legal counsel. The president's spouse might be included. The purpose would be to work out contingency plans under the Twenty-fifth Amendment and, if possible, prepare a written protocol or emergency book on the steps to be taken if disability occurred.

The living history of the Twenty-fifth Amendment is concentrated almost exclusively on the voluntary transfer of powers and duties. If the president should challenge the transfer, he will prevail unless two-thirds of both houses of the Congress declare him incapable of serving. It is Section 4 of the Twenty-fifth Amendment which deals with involuntary cases. The first two sections are relatively simple and straight forward. Section 1 states that in the event of "the removal of the President from office or his death or resignation, the Vice President shall become President." Because "death" and "resignation" are indisputable acts and because Article II, Section I, Clause 5 of the Constitution is unambiguous in its language, some eight cases, beginning with the succession of John Tyler on the death of William Henry Harrison, have been covered by the Constitution.

Section 2 fills the void when there is no vice president. It provides for nomination by the president and confirmation by the Congress. It has been used twice. On October 12, 1973, President Nixon nominated Congressman Gerald Ford to fill the vacancy caused by the resignation of Spiro T. Agnew and on August 20, 1974, President Ford, who became president on Nixon's resignation, nominated Nelson A. Rockefeller to be vice president. Whereas the succession of a president under Section 1 is immediate, the requirements of a majority vote for confirmation of a vice president by both the House and the Senate is likely to cause delay. Ford's confirmation came fifty-four days after Nixon nominated him and Rockefeller's confirmation took 121 days.

Another delay is possible in the timing of the presidential nomination, which in Ford's case was 3 days and Rockefeller's 11 days. The question is raised, what if the president is killed before confirmation of a vice president occurs or what if, following confirmation, both the president and vice president should be killed in an airplane crash? In the latter eventuality, the Presidential Succession Act of 1947 would govern, except that some of its provisions are in conflict with the superseding Twenty-fifth Amendment, thus requiring adjustment by Congress. Section 3 has been the focus of the presentation of the present paper in all of the preceding discussion.

Section 4 remains the one section of the Twenty-fifth Amendment which has never been used. Looking back historically, it is the type of provision which theoretically might have been used in the last months of the Wilson and the Franklin D. Roosevelt presidencies. Its purpose is to provide a mechanism for confronting problems raised by a president who is disabled but not prepared to step aside. The Commission addressed this question saying:

> Prior to the 25th Amendment, other than impeachment, there was no mechanism for dealing with an unfit president who would not resign, or who was not mentally capable of resigning his office. Impeachment, however, was designed to deal with high crimes and misdemeanors, not health problems. In contrast, Section 4 has inspired much criticism and many scenarios for endless mischief. The effect of modern medicine on human life certainly has increased the imaginable scenarios. For reasons such as these Congress deliberated at great length before approving Section 4 in order to erect what might be called a large enough constitutional tent, with plenty of room inside to accommodate all possible cases, whether foreseen, completely unforeseen or simply imagined.[10]

The activation of Section 4 would be a drama in two acts. First, the vice president and a majority of the president's Cabinet can declare that the president is no longer able to carry out the powers and duties of the office. Or if a president, seeking to recover his powers following their temporary transfer as provided for in Section 3, is deemed unable to do so by the vice president and a majority of the Cabinet, they may seek to prevent the restoration of his powers.

Section 4 also leaves open the possibility of some other "body" being substituted for the Cabinet who would either take the initiative or concur with the vice president on the president's disability. If such other "body" were to be created, it would have to be established by statute by the Congress. The other "body" if created might be comprised of the chief justice, the speaker of the house, the president pro tempore of the Senate and the minority leaders of both houses, or of a medical group appointed for a term of years or designated by office, such as the surgeon general. The latter group would presumably be more objective than Cabinet members in evaluating the health of a president. Objections to each of the two groups have been raised. Inserting the Chief Justice or other members of the Court in the process could violate the separation of powers. At some point, the Supreme Court might have to rule on the application of some aspect of the Twenty-fifth Amendment. A "body" made up of medical authorities would raise other problems, particularly the intrusion of an "unelected" group who are unlikely to be politically acceptable. The inclusion of provision for another "body" is salutary because should the Cabinet fail to act when it is clear the president has suffered disability, the Congress is empowered to create another "body" to take action.

Second, a time frame is established for those who seek to question the president's ability to carry out the powers and duties of the office. If the vice president and a majority of the Cabinet or the other "body" wish to question the president's capacity, they must transmit within four days to the president pro tempore of the Senate and the Speaker of the House a written declaration to this effect. Upon receiving the declaration, the Congress must assemble within forty-eight hours to consider the question. The Congress, if it is in session, within twenty-one days after receiving the declaration or, if not in session, within twenty-one days after it is required to assemble, makes a determination by two-thirds vote of both Houses. It decides either that the president is unable to discharge the powers and duties and the vice president shall continue to discharge them or that the president is able to resume the powers and duties of the office.

What is clear is that compared with the relative simplicity of procedures under Section 3, those under Section 4 are more open to contention. The Commission noted that "scenarios for endless mischief have been constructed and widely printed as both fact and fiction, horror stories of what the 25th might produce."[11] Because the Amendment deals with unpredictable human frailties, it is not a perfect solution, but few exist in constitutional history. The task is to make the most of what the Amendment encompasses. Success depends on the good judgment and good sense of our leaders and the citizenry.

The source of good judgment is a greater understanding by the public and the press of the purpose and the procedures of the Amendment. In the words of the Commission: "there must be greater public recognition that presidents, like the rest of us, are subject to periodic illnesses and disabilities and that the 25th Amendment, among other things, offers excellent standard operating procedures for times of temporary presidential disability, a simple method to get through such contingencies without disruption of government or public alarm."[12]

If the public grows more accustomed to the normality of invoking these procedures, the president will be more confident about declaring he is using the Twenty-fifth Amendment.

But as in all matters human and political, wise policies are not self-executing. They require prudence and foresight by responsible leaders. In this case, prompt contingency planning must be set in train by the president and his closest associates immediately after the election. The presidential physician must be part of the team from the outset and must understand his dual role: "first, the traditional one of confidential doctor-patient relationship, and second and equally important in the uniquely presidential case, a role as a representative, in strictly nonpolitical terms, of the interests of the nation which elected the president."[13] The president, vice president and the Cabinet must understand from the beginning that the eventualities which the Amendment confronts are not some remote and theoretical possibility. Eight of the thirty-five men (some re-elected) who have occupied the White House have died in office, four cut down by assassins. Several suffered from serious illnesses that were hidden not only from the public but from other governmental leaders.

The Commission concluded its work with a sense of urgency rather than a "damned if I know" spirit. (Former deputy attorney general and later attorney general William P. Rogers tells of the confusion that beset him and Vice President Nixon. In Herbert Brownell's absence, Rogers was called on to advise Nixon and the government about possible courses of action when President Eisenhower fell ill. In casting about for direction about issues of succession, the two leaders said to one another "damned if I know." They went in search of a copy of the Constitution, could not find one but, finally, Mr. Rogers remembered his father's advice: Look in the *Farmer's Almanac* and there reprinted was the Constitution.) By contrast, the Commission urged in a concluding statement: "We must be better prepared to cope with the frailties of man in this nuclear age; the national interest demands it; the 25th Amendment can help."[14]

CHAPTER THIRTY-FOUR

Long Range Planning and the Presidency

PERRY M. SMITH
FORMER COMMANDANT
NATIONAL WAR COLLEGE

As the American political and economic system faces the serious challenges and the considerable opportunities of the post industrial era, visionary leadership on the part of our Presidents becomes increasingly important. The purpose of this chapter is to outline the need for long range planning in the White House and in all the major departments and agencies and to spell out in rather specific terms how a coherent long range planning system can be created and nurtured under the leadership of the Presidents in the years ahead.

As some wag said, "the future is not what it used to be". This is particularly true in the United States in the post World War II era. Harry Truman, George Marshall, George Kennan, Paul Nitze and others realized this in the late 1940's. They understood that the simple years when we could hide behind the Atlantic and Pacific Oceans were gone forever and that some systematic planning was needed. They created, particularly in the State Department and the Department of Defense, a system whereby coordinated long range planning could take place. Unfortunately, this nascent system did not survive the 1950s, and although a lot of lip service was paid to long range planning and visionary leadership very little was done in the 1960s, 70s and 80s. That which was done within our government was badly flawed. For instance, the long range planning done during the Carter presidency, particularly in the Department of Defense, State and Energy, was not only faulty (much too much gloom and doom based on unsophisticated trend analysis and a failure to understand the opportunities that technology and innovation could provide), but it also gave long range planning in our federal government a bad name.

As America moves rapidly into the techno-information age,

as the world becomes dramatically more interdependent, as the burdens of American world leadership, heavy defense expenditures and the so called "imperial overreach" come under closer public scrutiny, it is imperative that our historical and cultural bias against government planning be reevaluated. During the first hundred and forty years of American history (up to about World War I), pragmatism and muddling through worked reasonably well for our Presidents. Although, in retrospect, more systematic planning might have helped this country to do better in handling our problems with slavery prior to the Civil War, our economic problems during the periodic depressions after the Civil War and our foreign affairs throughout our pre World War I history, it was not until we came dramatically onto the scene as the most powerful nation in the world in 1917 that the need for long range planning became evident. Woodrow Wilson, who was a visionary of the first order, did not create a long range planning system. If he had done so and if he had included the Congress in that system, he might have won the great battle over the League of Nations.

Franklin Roosevelt did some long range planning, particularly in the economic area, and the work that George Marshall and his staff did prior to World War II to prepare the country for a multidimensional war is notable. However, it wasn't until Marshall became the Secretary of State that a long range planning system for national security was formulated. However, there has never been a system in the American federal government that pulls together political, economic, military, scientific and technological planning in a way that permits the coherent formulation and implementation of public policy with a long term emphasis. If Departments and major agencies of the federal government had a small group of long range planners, who had direct and regular access to their Secretary and if these planners worked closely with the long range planners in the other Departments, an important start could be made. In addition, if there was a small group of long range planners in the White House who had regular access to the President and who had the charter to coordinate long range planning across the government, this nation could begin to accomplish the kind of systematic long range planning that could help sustain the United States as the leader of the Western World and the beacon of freedom and hope for oppressed people everywhere.

Long range planning is also needed in the Congress so that coordination between the two branches of government could take place on a regular basis. Rather than create new committees of the Congress, an informal mechanism could be formed that could be modeled after the Military Reform Caucus which would include those members of the Congress who were interested in long range planning. Because this nation had the great good fortune of a vital and entrepreneurial population, enormous natural resources and no significant enemy for most of its history, it could avoid the hard work of systematic planning and still succeed in most of its goals. In our case the past is not prologue and the time has come to establish a system of long range planning that will sustain itself from one administration to the next.

What follows is a description of what long range planning is, how to think about the long term future and why there is a tendency for leaders to avoid long range planning. I will then cover the fifteen laws of long range planning which I developed after long experience in planning jobs in government and considerable research in the subject. It is my great hope that one day a president will take the lead in the development of an institutionalized long range planning system that will be so successful that it will be passed on to subsequent administrations. If this chapter contributes in some way to this goal, I would be extremely pleased.

There are many useful techniques which can help force any institution to reach out beyond today's issues, problems, policies, and mind sets and to think seriously about the long-term future. By long-term, I mean 10 years or more into the future. The most productive timeframe for serious consideration by long-range planners is the 10- to 25-year period. Any time short of 10 years is so near term that it is hard to conceive of significant changes or approaches that might move an institution in new directions. In addition, most innovative short to mid-term planning tends to be threatening to many who are committed to present policies. A timeframe beyond 25 years is so difficult to deal with intellectually that it is probably not worth much time and effort. Exceptions to this 25-year rule would be appropriate in certain technical and research and development areas where it is clear that something revolutionary and important could be accomplished, but not within the next 25 years. Examples are space exploration, medicine, or certain defense technologies. Other areas also worthy of consideration beyond the 25-year point would be long-term trends and opportunities in demography, mineral exploration, and use of seabeds.

1.   How to Think About the Long-Range Future

Some Useful Approaches.

The use of an alternative futures approach has been helpful to many long-term planners, for it forces the mind out of the "let's plan for the most likely future" technique which is so common yet so intellectually restrictive in most planning systems. By considering a world beyond the year 2000 when the Soviet Union might no longer be a superpower or when the United States might be facing one or more high-technology military threats or when the international economic system has collapsed or when a significant number of terrorist groups possess suitcase-sized nuclear weapons, the planner might find avenues of creative inquiry. The use of the alternative futures approach is both a sobering and a mindstretching exercise highly recommended for both long-range planners and decisionmakers.

Another useful approach to the future is the writing of prospective history. The idea is to pick a year, such as the year 2010, and then attempt to write a history from now to then. In this narrow context, the planner might ask these questions: what would the Department of Defense look like in the year 2010; what weapons systems will be deployed; what will the base structure — both overseas and stateside — look like; how will we be organized; what missions will we have retained; what new ones will have been incorporated; and what ones will we have given up and why? Once such questions are answered, an examination of the timing of both divestiture and research and development activities can lead to decisions in the near-term that would release money, manpower, and other basics through divestiture, for use in more productive areas.

How to Choose Long-Term Planners.

Only a small percentage of any professional group generally make good long-range planners. Identifying long-range planners and carefully selecting the best are very important responsibilities of the leader and his chief planner. There are some useful methods to identify, select, motivate, and reward long-term planners. The Kirtin psychological test measures a continuum of psychological preferences from highly adaptive to highly innovative. Those who are more than one standard deviation above the norm as innovators can be considered as potentially effective long-range planners because they tend to be very creative and they like to deal with new ideas and new approaches to issues. The Myers-Briggs Psychological Type Indicator is also useful in identifying individuals who are comfortable with long-range planning. Individuals who score high in the "judging" category tend to make good planners. At the National Defense University in Washington, DC, and other institutions, a great deal of research has been done with the psychological testing of executive-level people.

Interviews can be very helpful to see how widely read a potential long-range planner is. Those individuals with a deep understanding of history tend to make good planners because they can identify trends that may continue into the future. They also tend to be skillful in identifying those new developments that may have lasting impact of some importance on the future. Interviews can also identify those individuals who are uncomfortable with present policies and programs and who are willing to take risks to chart new courses for the future.

Long-range Planning Across the Government.

I hope that one day each of the major departments in our Government, each of the military services, and each of our Government agencies will have a small long-range planning division manned with carefully chosen, creative and energetic individuals with solid operational backgrounds. The President should take two hours each month to address a long-range issue, and he should provide comments to his long-range planners in reaction to their ideas and recommendations. I hope that the Secretary of Defense, Secretary of State, our top military officers, the chiefs and secretaries of military services, the directors of the CIA and DIA, and the national security advisor to the President will also meet with their long-range planners on a monthly basis and provide feedback to them. Once every six months, the long-range planners from these agencies should meet to present papers, give briefings on their most recent studies, and trade ideas. Once a year, the top planners from each of the alliance nations should meet to share ideas and insights.

It is my hope that a long-range national security plan will be prepared and signed out by each new President, preferably within nine months of taking office, which would create a strategic vision for the nation and a strategic challenge to the national security communities. This short, 8- to 10-page plan would establish goals and priorities, would be updated annually, and would be presented to the President each year for discussion, modification, and approval. The annual presentation could be held each July, timed to have the maximum impact on the planning of the departments, agencies, and military services involved in the development of national security plans, programs, and budgets. This approach would create the proper framework for decisionmaking.

When decisions are made within the context of a strategic vision and with a full consideration of the long-term consequences of each decision, greater coherency in planning and policymaking results. However, most leaders of governmental organizations are caught up in daily responsibilities and spend little time in creating a strategic plan for their agency or Service. In addition, they often fail to encourage the establishment of a long-range planning process that would allow them to deal with various long-range issues on a systematic and a regular basis. Leaders who are captives of an overly full daily schedule fail to plan systematically; they tend to rely on ad hoc long-range studies. Although these can be quite useful, I very strongly believe that an occasional ad hoc long-range study is not enough to ensure that opportunities are seized to take advantage of changes in technology and the international environment, economic factors, threat realities and perceptions, demographic factors, and other areas. A systematic long-range planning process is essential for creating and maintaining a strategic vision and for building a strategic program.

2.   Why Managers and Leaders Avoid Systematic Long-Range Planning

From my experience as a leader, a planner, an operator, a researcher, and a teacher, I have come to a number of conclusions that may help explain why there is so much resistance to an institutionalized long-range planning process.

Determinism.

A number of senior leaders in our Government have a basically deterministic view of the future, which is manifested in various ways. Some believe that the course of the future is already largely predetermined by forces outside their control. In their judgment, the best they can do as leaders is to adjust to an already predetermined future and make the best of what is bound to happen anyway. In fairness to these determinists, it is clear that certain things that will happen in the future are not controllable by men or women at any level or in any place. For example, Brazil will remain, for many years, a large country with enormous natural resources, vast areas of jungle, and a population largely concentrated along its coastline; Sweden will not count as much in world politics, economics, or military capability as will the United States, France, Germany, or the Soviet Union; nations will be largely stuck with their present climate, population, natural resources, topographical features, and periodic natural disasters for the foreseeable future.

What planners maintain, and determinists deny, is that man can make a difference, that strong, aggressive, and decisive leadership by leaders of major governmental and business organizations can, in fact, change the course of the future. The planners argue that the Roosevelts, Churchills, Ho Chi Minhs, de Gaulles, Nakasones, Reagans, Gorbachevs (and the planners who support them) can and do make a difference in the course of human history. Dedicated long-range planners also maintain that these leaders can make much more of a difference in shaping the future if they create a strategic vision and combine this vision with a systematic planning process that includes an element of long-range planning.

A significant impediment to the establishment of a regular long-range planning process is the fear by leaders that they will be "locked in" by a long-range plan. A long-range plan that is not reviewed and updated (at least every two years) becomes quickly outdated, evolves into rigid dogma for the institution itself, and might be misused by external forces. All long-range plans should be written in such a way that they remain useful guides for present and future decisions. "Sunset" clauses (provisions that phase out or cancel the plan at a specified date in the

future), scheduled reviews and updates, and flexible language
in the plans are all useful techniques to avoid overly rigid long-
range plans.

Long-Range Plans as Threat to the Authority of Certain Leaders.

Long-range plans, by their very nature, tend to be viewed as
threats to some leaders and staff directors. To not plan at all is
often a safer and more comfortable approach for leaders than
actions that lead to plans that appear to reduce the authority
of various leaders within an organization. This is especially true
when one organization is trying to develop long-range plans for
other organizations. For instance, major commanders in the field
sometimes are reluctant to allow a military service staff at the
highest level to develop force-structure master plans. The commanders in the field sometimes fear that the development of these
plans in Washington, as well as their modification over time, will
wrest a certain amount of power and prestige away from these
field commanders.

The Short Tenure of Leaders.

Most governmental officials hold their positions for relatively short
periods of time and tend to have "planning horizons" that generally correspond to the amount of time they expect to hold their
present jobs. Heads of departments and agencies and chiefs of
staff of the military services commonly can look forward to four
years or less in office before they retire, resign, or are ousted because of a change in administration. Helmut Schmidt, Margaret
Thatcher, Charles de Gaulle, George Marshall, and Dean Rusk,
with their long tenure in top positions, are very much the exceptions to the rule as far as leaders of large organizations are concerned. Many business leaders also face relatively short tenures,
as well as the requirement to report progress annually. People
who need to look effective in the short term seldom develop the
mentality or the apparatus for strategic planning.

The Ideological Bias Against Planning.

Planning has a bad reputation in this country. Planning, to many
citizens, has the appearance of heavy governmental direction or
control as well as governmental inefficiency and waste. Much
of this skepticism about planning in government is well founded

especially in the socialist countries where enormous bureaucracies in combination with ideological blinders make for terrible plans and programs. It is almost an article of faith particularly among those in this country on the right wing of the political spectrum that all planning is bad. Yet excellent planning can and is done in a number of democratic and capitalistic nations. Any future president who may wish to implement a long range planning system must understand this ideological bias and be willing and able to deal with it.

3. The Fifteen Laws of Long-Range Planning

As a result of my experiences with plans in the Air Force, the Office of the Secretary of Defense, and a major NATO headquarters, as well as my research in long-range planning at Columbia University, the Air University, and the National War College, I have developed 15 laws of long-range planning that should be helpful to anyone seriously considering the implementation of the long-range planning process. Although it is rather presumptuous of me to label these points "laws," it is my firm view that if long-range planning is going to be effective in the decision calculus of leaders in Government, most, if not all, of these laws must be followed. Many long-range planning efforts fail because one or many of these laws are violated or ignored. I recommend that these laws not only be used when establishing a long-range planning process, but also be used as a checklist for long-range planners at all levels to ensure that planners and leaders do not drift away from important fundamentals.

Before I outline my 15 laws, let me discuss in greater detail the monthly interactive sessions that should be held between the long-range planners and the top leaders of the organization. The chief planner of the organization (in the military, normally a two-star general or admiral) should introduce each of these monthly briefings and should remind the top leader or leaders that they are about to hear an "uncoordinated" briefing that addresses the long-range future. The briefings by the long-range planners should be short (20 to 30 minutes), should use a small number of visual aids, and should address one specific subject.

At the end of the briefing, alternative strategies or options should be outlined and the top leaders should be asked to react to these objectives and alternative strategies. The approach should be, "Which approach, strategy or option do you *like?*" (rather than, "Which approach, strategy or option do you *choose?*"). The long-range planners should not seek *decisions*; they should seek reactions and general guidance from the top boss. It is also important that the top leaders understand these ground rules. Because these are uncoordinated briefings that the rest of the leaders, staff, and field agencies have not seen, it is not fair to press for a decision at these long-range interactive sessions.

After the briefing is completed and the candidate strategies are covered, the rest of the two-hour period should be spent in a "no holds barred" discussion. The participating long-range planners must be willing to challenge policy, procedures, systems, organizations, and doctrine as they would or would not apply to a world 10 or 25 years hence. The chief planner must be willing to take the heat from his superiors if they react very negatively to "radical" briefings or recommendations.

Whether the leaders like or do not like any of the options outlined, the long-range planners must press the leaders for their reactions and general preferences among the options. Sometimes the leaders prefer a combination of two options or a less radical variant of one of the options. As the interactive session draws to an end, the chief planner should review the discussion to ensure he and his long-range planners understand fully the comments and feedback they have received and to remind everyone in attendance that no initiative will be taken without full coordination with staff and field agencies.

If the chief planner abuses his access and his mandate and uses the long-range planning process to "run around the system," top staff officers and field agency leaders will join together and try to shut down the access of the long-range planning division to the top leaders. Clearly, the chief planner has an important but delicate responsibility. He must encourage his long-range planners to be innovative and creative, to challenge present policy and to develop issues, briefings, and options that stretch the minds of the top leaders. In addition, he must be willing to take radical ideas, strategies, and doctrines to the decisionmaker. On the other hand, the planner must be fair to his staff colleagues in operations, finance, logistics, personnel, and research and development. He must convince them that he will not abuse his access by pushing for decisions on uncoordinated issues. He must also be fair to subordinate decisionmakers. In other words, the chief planner must be somewhat schizophrenic. He must support present policy and at the same time challenge that same policy as it might apply in the long-term. A planner who merely projects policy into the future is not a planner but is simply a caretaker or gatekeeper, while a planner who undermines present policy makers damages the coherence and legitimacy of the organization that he serves. Here lies the great challenge and the great opportunity; this is what makes long-range planning so rewarding.

1. Long-range planners must answer the "What's in it for me?" question.

It's important that long-range planners must be able to convince their bosses, themselves, and other planners throughout the entire organization that long-range planning, in fact, accomplishes something that is worthwhile not only to the institution but also to all the individuals in the process. The most important person to convince, of course, is the top decisionmaker himself. Unlike Secretary Stetson, who asked incisive planning questions, many decisionmakers may not seriously consider long-range planning requirements until it is too late to provide coherence to the series of day-to-day decisions they have already taken. The challenge, then, is to convince the leader very early in his tenure, when his mind is open and his energies are at their peak, that it is worthwhile to spend two hours every month dealing with a long-range planning issue. It is also important to convince him to reserve his valuable time for this endeavor, to engage the long-range planners in a serious dialogue, and, most important, to make day-to-day decisions in the context of a strategic vision and a strategic plan.

It is also important for the major staff chiefs and the major field agency leaders to understand and support the value of long-range planning, both at their level and at the very top of the organization. Their support, either active or tacit, for an institutionalized long-range planning system in which the decisionmaker gets to deal with radical ideas on a regular basis is important. By bringing up interesting ideas, insights, and alternative strategies to help solve some difficult long-range problems, the long-range planners can help the decisionmaker immeasurably. Over time, the decisionmaker will look forward to these sessions, for they can be opportunities for him, in a freewheeling environment, to be challenged by new ideas, new approaches and new insights, and most important, to articulate his objectives. He can also use the long-range planners as a sounding board for his ideas. In sum, if the decisionmaker sees no direct benefit to himself, then the long-range planning effort is doomed to fail.

2. Long-range planners must get and maintain the support of the top decisionmaker.

The top decisionmaker must be willing to tell his executive officer or his secretary that he wants to see the planners on a regular basis. This point is an adjunct to the first law, but it needs further development and clarification. There must be enough priority in his interest in these sessions that pressing issues of the moment do not cause the meetings to be postponed again and again. The long-range planners must make a contribution in this regard in that they must work out a schedule for each year. The subjects chosen for each session must be of high interest to the decisionmaker so that he will agree to these sessions on a monthly basis and stick with this schedule throughout the year.

It is also important that the decisionmaker be willing to allow approximately two hours for each session. Normally, anything less than two hours does not give justice to the issue nor does it give the decisionmaker the opportunity to really get away from his in-box and think about the long-term issue. Short sessions do not leave enough time for good discussion, dialogue, and feedback after the briefing is given. The decisionmaker must occasionally discuss the value of long-range planning in his staff meetings, in his decision meetings, and in his normal day-to-day activities with his staff and with the major commanders and leaders of the various field agencies. If he does not encourage long-range planning and if he doesn't ask the occasional question, "How does this decision which I am about to make fit into our long-range plan?" the long-range planners will have a great deal of trouble getting support as they try to fold long-range planning options and approaches into the normal planning, programming, and budgeting process. One useful technique is to schedule a long-range planning session shortly before the leader is about to travel overseas (for instance, holding a "Latin America in the 21st Century" session just before a Latin American trip), or before the leader is to make an important speech or to testify before the national legislature.

3.   Long-range planners must have direct access to the top decisionmaker.

It seems to be quite clear after the examination of long-range planning efforts in business and government that unless the long-range planners work directly for the decisionmaker or, at a minimum, have direct access to him, the long-range planning effort will not be successful. Most of the best run agencies or business companies in the United States have long-range planners working directly for the chief executive officer; the United States Navy has that system within the Defense Department. This is the ideal arrangement because the planners are protected by the boss. They remain close to the boss by being a part of the immediate staff. Another option is to have the long-range planners work for the chief planner but with direct access to the top decisionmaker on a regular basis. In this arrangement, the role of the chief planner becomes critical, as he must be committed to allow his long-range planners to develop radical ideas. He must not remove some of the best ideas on the way to the decisionmaker. If he filters the information and recommendations, the impact of the long-range planners on the thinking of the decisionmaker is reduced.

4.   Briefings by the long-range planners to the top decisionmaker must not go through the normal coordination process.

This is a delicate but very important point. If the long-range planners have to coordinate their briefings with all the agencies within the staff and with all the field agencies, many of their best ideas will be filtered out and much of the impact of their briefing on the decisionmaker will be lost. The tendency is that anything that seems to bring into question present policy, doctrine, tactics, or organization will be objected to by one or more staff agencies. The planners would then have to compromise their briefing and their recommendations to accommodate these concerns. This tendency inhibits an innovative and creative long-range planning system. Full coordination generally leads to a bland briefing and predictable recommendations that probably will not interest the decisionmaker. Over time he will lose interest in seeing the long-range planners.

5. *The long-range planning process must lead to some decisions in the present.*

The long-range planning process can be useful even if it does not lead to decisions in the present. However, to establish and maintain legitimacy and support for a continuous long-range planning effort, it is essential that an occasional decision be made for early implementation of an idea relating to a long-range issue or a long-range plan. So often the question is asked by critics of long-range planning, "But what does this all lead to?" Critics argue that unless the long-range planning process leads to some decisions in the present, it is just an intellectual exercise of little value. To gain legitimacy for the long-range planning process, it is helpful for the decisionmaker to take a good look, on occasion, at a long-range issue with the idea of early implementation. Making decisions in the near terms on long-range issues is a wonderful way to legitimize the long-range planning process.

6. *The process must be institutionalized.*

Having an institutionalized long-range planning process is very important. Ad hoc studies are useful and may play an important role in bringing a large number of people into the long-range planning process for a period of time and focusing attention on an issue or issues relating to the longer term, but ad hoc studies are not enough. If there is no institutionalized process to encourage the leaders at the top of the organization to consider long-range issues on a regular basis, many opportunities will be lost. Employing a combination of both ad hoc studies and an institutionalized, regularized, month-by-month long-range planning process is the best way to ensure that the advantages of long-range planning are maximized in an organization.

7. *Within the framework of an institutionalized process, long-range planning must remain flexible.*

The institutionalized planning process can become rigid and can lead to plans that are so inflexible that they become dysfunctional. In order to ensure that long-range plans remain flexible, all of the plans should be reviewed periodically so that they don't become too rigid or too out of date. There should be an established "sunset clause" of one to two years after publication of a plan, at which time the plan no longer has legitimacy and credibility as long-range policy. (Ad hoc studies should normally remain as studies and not become formal plans.) This expiration date should be stated specifically on the cover letter of each plan. What is stated in the cover letter about how the plan is to be used is very important. The decisionmaker should *not* sign most long-range *studies*, but he should sign most, if not all, long-range *plans*.

8.   In addition to the institutionalized process, periodic ad hoc studies are needed.

Ad hoc studies are the norm in most organizations and often lead to decisions that are innovative and useful. The ad hoc studies often get the visibility and support that the institutionalized process does not get. Some examples of excellent ad hoc studies accomplished in recent years by the military services of the United States are Seaplan 2000, AirLand Battle 2000, Army 21, Air Force 2000, and the Air Force Project Forecast II. One of the auxiliary benefits of ad hoc studies is that they often expose large numbers of bright people to long-range problems and issues. These people often become life-long advocates of long-range planning, and for the rest of their professional lives, they ask the big, long-term questions as they work on issues from staff and leadership positions. However, no matter how profitable a study or group of studies may be, the ad hoc approach is no substitute for an institutionalized planning process.

9.   Long-range plans must be readable and short.

There have been many long-range plans and studies that are of such length (often in multiple volumes) that few people ever read them. It is important that all long-range plans be short, readable, and as free of jargon and acronyms as possible. These plans should be packaged well — with many diagrams, charts, and the highlighting of words — to make them interesting enough for busy people to pick up and read through. Ad hoc studies should be no longer than 300 pages. The annual long-range plan should be even shorter — no more than 10 or 12 pages long, with a 1- to 2-page executive summary — so that it can be read quickly and have real impact.

10. *Planners must develop implementation strategies.*

The long-range planners should develop general implementation strategies to give the planners, programmers, and budget people ideas on how to carry out and implement the policies established in these plans. Decisionmaking is only one part of the overall planning process. Implementation strategies are as important as the decision itself. The long-range planning divisions, which should always remain small, can help the rest of the staff by providing some implementation ideas and avenues of approach. They should not be the implementers themselves, but they should assist the implementers as they move from plans to programs to budget to reality.

11. *Planners must avoid constraining the innovation and divestiture process.*

There is a general tendency in developing long-range plans to put constraints on plans related to budget, technology, and time, for example. Although these constraints can help make the plan look more realistic, they also tend to restrict the vision of the planners and, in turn, the vision of the decisionmaker. For instance, one of my big mistakes, in the development of the Air Force 2000 Plan was the rather severe fiscal constraints (1 percent real growth each year in the Air Force budget from 1987 to 2000) that I established before the planning began. As a result of these fiscal constraints, some interesting opportunities were rejected out of hand because they could not be funded within these boundaries. Long-range planners should avoid this kind of constraining activity, both from the point of view of innovation and creativity and also from the point of view of divestiture. There should be no scared cows; planners should be willing to recommend the divestiture of organizations, major weapon systems, and major R&D programs, for example. If planners constrain themselves by not allowing the full consideration of divestiture opportunities, they are doing a disservice to the institutionalized long-range planning process and to their boss.

12. *Planners must avoid single-factor causality.*

There are many people in pivotal institutions in this country who believe in single-factor causality. Basically they think that only one thing really counts, whether it be economics, technology, political factors, or another factor. However, single-factor causality is usually erroneous and is too simplistic. Those who accept it readily in their thinking develop a mindset that does not take into account other factors. Long-range planners must be broadly scoped people; they must take into account many factors in doing their planning. When a leader tends to focus on a single factor, it is the responsibility of the long-range planners to try to break him out of that mindset. They must try to convince the leader that, in fact, there are multiple factors that play roles in the development of future courses of action.

13.   Planners must avoid determinism — economic, political, technological, and others.

Anybody in the long-range planning business who thinks that the future of the world is determined largely by events outside the control of the institution in which he works should not be a long-range planner. Long-range planners must assume that their plans, ideas, innovations, creativity, and issues really count. They must feel confident that if the decisionmaker makes a decision based on their ideas, that decision can have an impact on the future courses of events. Planners must assume that people in key positions can and do make a difference. Those involved in developing long-range plans should be careful that no determinism creeps into the calculus of decisionmaking, the briefing, or the plan itself.

14.   Planners must stay in close contact with the operational, doctrinal, policy, R&D, communications, logistics, and manpower communities.

One of the lessons from the corporate world is that the long-range planners working directly for the chief executive officer sometimes get isolated over time from the issues, problems, concerns, and pragmatic considerations that really exist. This is one of the key reasons that the new chief executive officer of General Electric decided in 1984 to restructure and reduce the planning staff drastically at the corporate headquarters of General Electric. Long-range planners at the highest level must get out to the field and talk to the scientists in the laboratories, to field commanders and leaders, to the operators and maintainers, and to other staff agencies at all levels. Only by staying in close contact with these disparate groups can the long-range planners ensure that what they recommend to the decisionmaker is relevant, useful, and helpful in the pursuit of the goals of the institution. By getting out into the field and talking to people at all levels, the planners can try out their ideas informally to see how practical these innovative alternatives are. Moving about the organization also enables them to collect some of the better ideas, innovations, and creative thoughts of people at all levels that will help them develop better long-range issues, options, and plans.

15. *Incentives must be provided if innovation is to be maximized.*

It is rare when governmental organizations provide good incentives and rewards for the people who can think conceptually, broadly, and in the long term. Incentives must be established and publicized to encourage the person with ideas to come forward and present them. There should be awards to laboratories for creating new ideas in technology, awards to long-range planners for developing new concepts, and awards to manpower experts for developing better organizations, for example. When it is time to hand out awards, the decisionmaker should be involved and the ceremony should be widely publicized. Alternatively, if a large ceremony would create undue friction, personal notes or brief meetings can be substituted.

Those people who go into long-range planning should fully understand that they are taking risks; if they are going to do the job well, they are going to have to question present policy, procedures, organizations, doctrines, weapon systems, resources, and so forth. Creative and innovative planners are going to make people angry on occasion. If they are not self-confident people or if they are ambitious, risk-avoidance careerists they will have little to contribute to the process of long-range planning.

Long-range planning will never anticipate and solve all of the problems and dilemmas that we will confront in the future, but it can certainly help us to be prepared for some of them. Perhaps, even more important, a long-range planning process can keep us alert to new possibilities, new insights that will help us in decisionmaking, and new ways of meeting the future's challenges.

Conclusion

Future Presidents could learn a great deal from the examples of coherent long range planning that the Japanese, Chinese and

British have provided in recent years. Much of the value of long range planning is questioning the assumptions, the policies and the doctrines of the day. Margaret Thatcher did that in the mid 1970s and when she became the Prime Minister she had a plan for the restructuring of the British political and economic system. The fact that she stuck with her general plan despite much opposition and many setbacks is quite admirable. Her model might be the best one available to a future president. In any case a plan, an institutionalized process, an implementation strategy and a stick-to-itiveness over several terms is what is needed. Perhaps this is too much to expect in the American political culture, yet one day a person of vision who understands the need for planning will accede to the presidency. Perhaps he or she will come from the business world where there is already some excellent long range planning being done. Perhaps he or she will come from an experience in State government where long range planning has been the norm. Perhaps he or she will come from the Department of Defense or Energy where long range planning has at times been excellent. In any case let us hope that a start is made soon to build a long range planning system in our federal government that will provide the vision, the plan and the implementation strategies that are so necessary.

CHAPTER THIRTY-FIVE

Eleven Points for the Next President

WALTER F. MONDALE
FORMER VICE PRESIDENT OF THE UNITED STATES

In 1976, when I began to feel I could aspire to the Vice Presidency, I went to my old friend Hubert Humphrey and asked him whether he would recommend it. To my surprise he strongly urged me to take it. This is not the only time he misled me. I joke when I say that because I don't regret that decision for a moment. Hubert said it would broaden me, acquaint me with the world and its leaders, and give me a national view unobtainable elsewhere, even in the Senate. He said he didn't regret it, despite Vietnam, and neither do I. Had I been elected President I have no doubt at all that I would have been much better prepared for the Presidency.

This is especially true, since I was the first Vice President to be located in the White House and the first to work intensively with the President for four years with no restrictions whatsoever.

I saw daily, indeed hourly, up close, the enormous pressures and frustrations under which a President labors. I saw the miracle man from Plains, Georgia, begin with great hope and confidence, and then watched him slowly ground down until he left office four years later looking ten years older. I watched the confidence and optimism he brought with him slowly drain away. And I watched a tense, beaten and dispirited man leave the White House devoid of the self-confidence which was once his hallmark.

In different ways, in recent years, we have seen the repeat of this phenomenon until many now question whether we will ever again see a confident Presidency from start to finish. John Steinbeck once said, "We give the President more work than a man can do, more responsibility than a man should take, more pressure than a man can bear. We abuse him often and rarely praise him. We wear him out, use him up, eat him up. And with all this, Americans have a love for the President that goes beyond loyalty or party nationality; he is ours and we exercise the right to destroy him."

Perhaps it has always been much this way; the martyred

Abraham Lincoln was magnificent in his statesmanship, and the nation will ever mourn his loss.

I watched one President long enough to know I don't have the answer and long enough to doubt that there really is a complete answer. But I did see enough to have some observations that might be of some help to the next President.

I would like to address some of my suggestions in a form directed to the next President.

Here they are:

1. Mr. President, your most important decisions are made before you take office in the selection of your Cabinet and key personnel and especially your White House staff. You can ruin yourself before you start. You will make mistakes, but you must be terribly careful to make the best possible choices. Mediocrity, vanity, disloyalty, self-promotion, emotional problems and much else, including dishonesty, can hound you every day. The wrong choice, like a flat railroad wheel, gets worse with wear. A subpoint here: You cannot work around a mistake in a high position; you can only remove him quickly and try to find someone better.

2. Mr. President, you are not superhuman. Hard work, Yes; 18 hour days with no respite, No. You can't do it. It is a question of balance. You must be in touch and you must be in command and you must be informed. But you cannot run the United States all by yourself. If you try, you will lose perspective, miss the big picture, and they will drown you. That's what Carter did.

3. My next point is the opposite and my example is President Reagan. A President simply must be sufficiently informed to lead. Instincts and values are important up to a point. But most tough decisions, like economic management, arms control, national defense, the budget, and many more, require the President's decision. Almost every problem that's plunked on the President's desk is horrible, or someone else would have decided it. Your advisors are split, often in many directions. Only by knowing enough can you make a choice and lead. And only by knowing enough can you develop and hold to priorities.

4. Beware of the childishness factor among your key officials. Brains do not guarantee maturity. I have often watched grown men of great ability descend to the emotional level of second graders when they believe their turf or status are being threatened. Most disputes cross agency lines and unless your key

management is mature; unless they debate issues on the merits, your Administration will be ground up in petty disputes almost all of which becomes publicly known.

5. Mr. President, you must never, ever abandon your oath of office to faithfully execute the laws of the land. Your job will be horribly frustrating: the Congress; the press; the courts; your own Cabinet; our allies and our adversaries — practically everything will frustrate you. At some point you will be tempted to break out of these constraints by resorting to private government outside the law, and usually in foreign affairs. You will be told that you can achieve by covert and extra-legal means what cannot be done openly and legally. The thought, I believe, occurs to all Presidents. Mr. President, don't do it. You can't keep it secret if it's significant. If what you're doing would offend public opinion, its disclosure will be doubly offensive. Once you're caught, if you are like most, you will start trying to fib or cover up and that is the end. When you feel like taking this fateful step, please go fishing or go have more than enough with some friends. You won't get arrested; you have a driver, and the Secret Service will keep its mouth shut. You need your friends sometimes more than a good night's sleep.

6. Of course, try to capitalize on your opportunities, but expect some bad luck; it happens to every President and it will happen to you. You must deal with it, but don't break your back blaming yourself. You can't carry every load. I watched Carter burdened by the hostage crises and the quadrupling of oil prices, neither his fault, and both serious. He let it get the best of him, and it showed.

7. You must trust the American people. Let them in on things. Explain what you're doing. If they are not buying your direction, don't question them; question the direction or your explanation of them. One of the saddest days in the Carter Administration was when some people tried to persuade Carter that Americans were suffering from malaise. The party that was elected on the platform that we needed a government as good as the people nearly argued that what we really needed was a people as good as the government.

8. Don't let Congress tramp on your office, for they will surely try. Congress will test you early; they will try to cow you into submission, and then they will attack you for being weak. If you relent they will not respect you. You have many tools to hold

them in line—the veto, appointments, the control of the public dialogue, and your ability to campaign against them. Use all of them. I remember once telling Carter that the Congress was laughing at him and recommended that he veto something. He did, and you could feel the difference the next day. Once they know that you won't be pushed around, they will start to work with you.

9. Don't ever let yourself get isolated in the White House. Don't circle the wagons; stay out with the people. In a great book by George Reedy, Johnson's news secretary, called *The Twilight of the Presidency*, Needy recounted how Presidents become increasingly isolated, paranoid, and out of touch. Finally, only the sycophants can see him. It's disaster. Have friends in. See your Congressional opponents. Get out to speak. Go see a ballgame—anything to stay in touch. Beware of flatterers. Remember that in the Oval Office, even your worst critics sound like your best supporters. Don't believe it. Read the papers, watch television. Keep the flatterers away. They are poison. You are not God. You are only a normal mortal, as James Polk once said, occupying the White House for a limited period of time. Someone once said that politicians either grow or they swell. Be sure you grow. You can't do it alone.

10. Don't expect too much help from the press, but don't get paranoid either. Most of them are able, many brilliant. Their job is to question you and your government. You will not like their questions, but remember, there are no bad questions, only bad answers. If you decide the press is out to get you, you are probably done. Hold repeated news conferences. Be available. You will stay in shape and conquer them. By hiding, it only gets worse.

11. Keep your mental health and good judgment. Remember that there are worse things than defeat. Not much, to be sure, but nevertheless, defeat is not as bad as breaking your health, losing your self-confidence, destroying your dignity, composure and good sense. Most truly silly and damaging mistakes occur when a President, confronted with a fiendish and unanswerable crisis, does something really ridiculous in a bizarre attempt to rescue himself.

Mr. President, it was 200 years ago that our first President, George Washington, was inaugurated. You are his bicentennial successor. Washington proposed for "posterity" the reading of

The Federalist "because in it are candidly and ably discussed the principles of freedom and topics of government, which will be always interesting to mankind so long as they shall be connected in Civil Society." May I commend their reading to you and wish you Godspeed.

Notes

NOTES FOR INTRODUCTION

1. For the definitive work on presidential transitions from 1912 to 1953, see Laurin Henry, *Presidential Transitions* (Washington: Brookings, 1960).
2. Public Law 88-277, 78 Stat. 153.
3. Arthur Schlesinger, Jr., *A Thousand Days* (Greenwich, Conn.: Fawcett Publications, 1967), pp. 118.
4. Interview with Jack Watson, June 17, 1983, Atlanta.
5. *The Washington Post*, December 15, 1980.
6. Interview with the author, Washington, D.C., July 15, 1983.
7. For details and precedents see James P. Pfiffner, *The Strategic Presidency: Hitting the Ground Running* (Chicago: Dorsey Press, 1988), Chapter Six.
8. See Cary Covington, "Mobilizing Congressional Support for the President: Insights from the 1960s," *Legislative Studies Quarterly* Vol. XII, No. 1 (February 1987), pp. 91-92. See also James P. Pfiffner, "The President's Legislative Agenda," *The Annals* of the American Academy of Political and Social Science (September 1988).
9. Ben Heineman, Jr., "Some Rules of the Game: Prescriptions for Organizing the Domestic Presidency," in this volume.
10. See Stephen Hess, "A New Presidential Selection Timetable," in this volume; and Arthur M. Schlesinger, Jr., *The Cycles of American History* (Boston: Houghton Mifflin, 1986), pp. 322-325.
11. *Cycles of American History*, p. 324.
12. See Hugh Heclo, "The Changing Presidential Office," in *Politics and the Oval Office* edited by Arnold J. Meltsner (San Francisco: Institute for Contemporary Studies, 1981).
13. *The Washington Post* (July 16, 1987), p. 1.
14. See Linda Fisher, "Fifty Years of Presidential Appointments," in *The In-And-Outers* edited by G. Calvin Mackenzie (Baltimore: Johns Hopkins University Press, 1987.
15. See Patricia Ingraham, "Building Bridges or Burning Them?: The President, the Appointees, and the Bureaucracy," *Public Administration Review* (September/October 1987), p. 427.
16. *Ibid.*, p. 425.
17. For details see James P. Pfiffner, "Nine Enemies and one Ingrate: Political Appointments during Presidential Transitions," in *The In-And-Outers*, edited by G. Calvin Mackenzie (Baltimore: Johns Hopkins University Press, 1987).

18. Richard Nixon, *RN: The Memoirs of Richard Nixon* (New York: Grosset & Dunlap, 1978), p. 355.

19. For a critique of this approach to public management see James P. Pfiffner, "Political Public Administration" *Public Adminstration Review* (March/April 1985), pp. 352–356.

20. See James P. Pfiffner, "Political Appointees and Career Executives: The Democracy-Bureaucracy Nexus in the Third Century," *Public Administration Review* (January/February 1987), pp. 57–65.

CHAPTER FOUR NOTES

1. Fred Greenstein ed., *Leadership in the Modern Presidency* (Cambridge: Harvard University Press, 1988), p. 352.

2. Ben W. Heineman, Jr. and Curtis A. Hessler, *Memorandum for the President: A Strategic Approach to Domestic Affairs in the 1980s* (New York: Random House, 1980).

3. Ben W. Heineman, Jr., "Marrying Politics and Policy," in Lester M. Salamon and Michael S. Lund eds., *The Reagan Presidency and the Governing of America* (Washington, D.C.: Urban Institute Press, 1984).

CHAPTER SIX NOTES

1. U. S. CONST. amend. XXV (certified February 23, 1967), § 2: "Whenever there is a vacancy in the Office of the Vice President, the President shall nominate a Vice President who shall take office upon confirmation by a majority vote of both Houses of Congress." Section 1 of this amendment provides for succession of the Vice President to the Presidency on the death or resignation of the President. The other two sections deal with the matter of Presidential disability.

2. *The New York Times*, October 11, 1973. John C. Calhoun had been the only other Vice President to resign his office. He did so December 1832, after having broken with President Jackson over the issue of nullification, in order to become elected to the U.S. Senate from South Carolina.

3. House Comm. on the Judiciary, *Confirmation of Gerald R. Ford as Vice President of the United States*, H. R. Rep. No. 695, 93rd Cong., 1st Sess. 1 (1973) [hereinafter H. R. Rep. 695]; Gerald R. Ford, *A Time to Heal* (New York: Harper & Row, 1979) 104–111 where the author points out that the Senate vote for confirmation was 92 to 3 and the House vote 387 to 35.

4. Bob Woodward and Carl Bernstein, *The Final Days* (New York: Simon and Schuster, 1976) 426ff, 451.

5. Ford, *op. cit.*, 85.

6. Senate Comm. on Rules and Administration, *Nomination of Gerald R. Ford of Michigan to be Vice President of the United States*, Exec. Rept. 26, 93rd Cong., 1st Sess. 3–7 (1973) [hereinafter Exec. Rept. 26]; H. R. Rep. 695, 3.

7. 3. U. S. C. § 19, entitled "Vacancy in offices of both President and Vice President; officers eligible to act." enacted pursuant to U. S. CONST. art II, § 1, cl. 6. For a discussion of Presidential succession under both this statute and the Twenty-fifth Amendment see Brown and Cinquegrana, "The Realities of Presidential Succession: The Emperor Has No Clones," 75 *The Georgetown Law Journal* 1389–1453 (1987). Inasmuch as Speaker Albert was a leading Democrat, it is unlikely that Republican President Nixon would have resigned his office during those 58 days when it would have meant turning his administration over to a partisan Democrat for the remainder of the term until January 20, 1977. That such a transfer of the Presidency from one party to the other would nevertheless have occurred if President Nixon had died during that period appears to be a flaw in the statute, which could be corrected by putting the President's own cabinet members first in the line of succession, starting with the Secretary of State.

8. *The Washington Post* November 28, 1982. This belated news story concerns 58 days in 1973, but the record of a 19-page "comprehensive contingency plan" prepared by Theodore C. Sorensen to deal with an Albert transition to the Presidency remained secret for nine years. Not until then did the former Speaker agree, along with the plan's author (a veteran of the Kennedy transition to succeed President Eisenhower) to give *The Post* a copy "as a footnote to history." The news account also discloses that the Speaker had selected "his inner circle of advisers" for his Presidency (all Democrats to be sure) and that he had received during that period Secret Service protection and regular briefings on affairs of state by the Central Intelligence Agency.

9. Exec. Rept. 26, 17–18.

10. Robert T. Hartmann, *Palace Politics: An Inside Account of the Ford Years* (New York: McGraw-Hill, 1980) 75.

11. Woodward and Bernstein, *op. cit.* 174–175; but for a view of the situation at that time from inside the Vice President's office, see Hartmann, *op. cit.* 100–113.

12. On this topic, I wrote previously: "A vibrant chief executive is not apt to welcome from the Vice President and his staff any signs that they anticipate an abrupt end to the President's term in office. Mr. Martin Dooley, who knew 'ivrything' about 'ivrybody', observed of our nation's Vice President that he must never show in

the slightest way how heavyhearted he is whenever the President gives assurance that he remains in good health." Kenneth W. Thompson, ed. *Papers on Presidential Transitions in Foreign Policy* (Lanham, MD.: University Press of America 1986) Vol. II, 31. The reference to Mr. Dooley is from a collection of Finley Peter Dunne's political humor columns, Robert Hutchinson ed. (New York: Dover 1963), 216, 218.

13. Both the Vice President and Robert Hartmann, in answer to reporters' questions, had assured the press that "nobody on Ford's staff was doing any takeover planning." Hartmann, *op. cit.* 155.

14. Public Papers of President Gerald R. Ford, 1974 (Washington: Gov't Printing Office, 1975) 60. Each of the two later Vice Presidents has been assigned an office in the West Wing of the White House, close to the Oval Office, and has also been close to the President in his decision-making.

15. Unscheduled transitions have been Roosevelt/McKinley (1901), Coolidge/Harding (1923), Truman/Roosevelt (1945), Johnson/Kennedy (1963), Ford/Nixon (1974). The country barely escaped having another in this century when President Reagan was struck by a would-be assassin's bullet early in his first term.

16. Pursuant to the Presidential Transition Act of 1963, 3 U. S. C. §102 note, the Congress provides for Presidents-elect and Vice Presidents-elect facilities and funds to obtain transition services between election day and inauguration. During the transition from President Carter to President Reagan in 1980, 450 persons became assigned officially to work on transition planning, 10% of them on salary, at an estimated cost of $2.3 million to $3 million, 38 *Congressional Quarterly Weekly Report* December 27, 1980, 3657.

17. *Public Papers of President Gerald R. Ford, 1974* (Washington: Gov't Printing Office, 1975) 2.

18. Ford, *op. cit.* 24.

19. Ford, *op. cit.* 28.

20. Hartmann, *op. cit.* 157.

21. William J. Stewart, Acting Director of the Gerald R. Ford Library in Ann Arbor, Michigan, located a copy of this report in the files which I had compiled while serving in the Ford White House. The files also include material used on August 8, 1974, which represent the work of the 40-hour transition group to aid in the change of Presidents the next day. Nothing appears in the files concerning the deliberations of the earlier secret transition team.

22. Hartmann, *op. cit.* 167, 202.

23. Roger B. Porter, formerly on the staff of the Ford White House and now Professor of Government and Business at Harvard's

Kennedy School of Government, makes the same point, along with others, in his favorable appraisal of the Ford Presidency, *The New York Times*, May 15, 1988.

24. *The New York Times*, August 11, 1974.

CHAPTER SEVEN NOTES

* This paper was prepared with the assistance of a grant from Gerald R. Ford Library which the Center for the Study of the Presidency had recommended.

1. Richard E. Neustadt, *Presidential Power* (New York: John Wiley and Sons, 1980), 217.

2. Laurin L. Henry, "The Transition: The New Administration" in *The Presidential Reaction and Transition 1960–61*, ed. Paul T. David (Washington, D.C.: The Brookings Institution, 1961), 235–267.

3. D. H. Haider, "Presidential Transitions: Critical If Not Decisive," *Public Administration Review* 41 (Spring, 1981), 207–211.

4. Wallace Walker and Michael Reopel, "Strategies for Governance: Transitions and Domestic Policy-Making in the Reagan Administration," *Presidential Studies Quarterly* 16 (Fall, 1986), 734.

5. For example, as a result of a staff oversight Representative Olin E. Teague of Texas was not invited to the swearing in of President Ford. Teague Letter, 8/3/74, folder "Congressional Relations," Box 2, Timmons File, Gerald R. Ford Library.

6. Jones informs the White House staff that some handwritten envelopes had been arriving at the mail room to be sent out, but that all correspondence on White House stationary should be typed. Memo, Jones to White House staff, 9/4/74, folder "Congressional Relations," Box 2, Timmons File, Gerald R. Ford Library.

7. Listing of "Problem Areas," folder "Congressional Relations," Box 2, Timmons File, Gerald R. Ford Library.

8. Memo, Timmons to Haig, 8/10/74, folder "Congressional Relations," Box 2, Timmons File, Gerald R. Ford Library.

9. Laurin L. Henry, "The Transition: Transfer of Presidential Responsibility" in *The Presidential Election and Transition 1960–61*, ed. Paul T. David (Washington, D.C.: The Brookings Institution, 1961), 205–233.

10. Louis W. Koenig, *The Chief Executive* 5th ed. (New York: Harcourt, Brace, Jovanovich, 1986), 86.

11. "Move is Surprise", *The New York Times*, October 13, 1973.

12. Marjorie Hunter, "Vice President Shuns Transition Talk, But Says He's Ready," *The New York Times*, August 8, 1974, 7.

13. Clifton Daniel, "Ford's Aides Say He Seeks Decentralization of Power," *The New York Times*, August 15, 1974, 1.

14. The following account is drawn heavily from an article by James M. Naughton, "The Change in Presidents: Plans Began Months Ago," *The New York Times*, August 26, 1974, 1.

15. Daily Diary of President Gerald R. Ford, August 9, 1974, Box 72, Staff Secretary Daily Diary, Gerald R. Ford Library.

16. Richard Harwood and Haynes Johnson, "The Solemnity of Change," *Washington Post*, August 9, 1974, 1.

17. "The Transfer of Power," *The Washington Post*, August 10, 1974, 22.

18. "The Power Passes," *The New York Times*, August 11, 1974, 1.

19. Memorandum for the Vice President, 8/8/74, folder "Transition," Box 168, Seidman File, Gerald R. Ford Library.

20. Memo for the Vice President, p. 2.

21. Memo for the Vice President, p. 2.

22. Memo, Warren Rustand to the President, folder "Warren Rustand File," Box 2, Office of White House Operations, Alexander Haig, 1973–74, Gerald R. Ford Library.

23. John Herbers, "Four Named to Help Ford's Transition," *The New York Times*, August 10, 1974, 1. For further discussion see President Ford's First Hundred Days, 11/14/74, folder "Congressional Relations," Box 2, Timmons File, Gerald R. Ford Library.

24. Memo for the Vice President, p. 3.

25. Memo for the Vice President, p. 3.

26. Memo, White House Press Secretary to White House Staff, 8/9/74, folder "Transition," Box 168, Seidman File, Gerald R. Ford Library.

27. Memo to the Vice President, p. 4.

28. John Herbers, "Four Named to Help Ford's Transition," *The New York Times*, August 10, 1974, 1.

29. Memo, White House Press Secretary to White House Staff, 8/9/74, folder "Transition," Box 168, Seidman File, Gerald R. Ford Library.

30. Memo, Meeting with the Cabinet, 8/10/74, folder "Transition," Box 168, Seidman File, Gerald R. Ford Library.

31. *Ibid.*

32. List of Problem Areas, folder, "Congressional Relations," Box 2, Timmons File, Gerald R. Ford Library.

33. Remarks of President Gerald R. Ford, 8/13/74, folder "Transition To Incoming Administration FG3", Box 19, WHCF, Gerald R. Ford Library.

34. Transition Team Report, Draft No. 2, folder "Transition Team Report," Box 169, Seidman File, Gerald R. Ford Library.

35. *Ibid.*

36. *Ibid.*

37. James Reston, "Ford's Noble Beginning," *The New York Times*, August 11, 1974, 17.

38. "The Transfer of Power," *The Washington Post*, August 10, 1974, 22.

39. Remarks on Taking the Oath of Office," August 9, 1974 in *Public*

Papers of the President: Gerald R. Ford 1974 (Washington, D.C.: U.S. Government Printing Office, 1975), 1–2.

40. Oath of Office, p. 1.
41. Oath of Office, p. 2.
42. Memo, J. F. ter Horst to White House Staff, 8/29/74, folder "Congressional Relations," Box 2, Timmons File, Gerald R. Ford Library.
43. Douglas E. Kneeland, "New White House Mood Emerges," *The New York Times*, August 15, 1974, 1.
44. Clifton Daniel, "Ford's Aides Say He Seeks Decentralization of Power," *The New York Times*, August 15, 1974, 1.
45. Transition Team Report, Draft No. 2, folder "Transition Team Report," Box 169, Seidman File, Gerald R. Ford Library.
46. "Mr. Ford Changes the Atmosphere," *The New York Times*, August 18, 1974, 1.

CHAPTER EIGHT NOTES

1. In addition to *Presidential Studies Quarterly*, the Center's *Organizing and Staffing the Presidency (1980)* written by Bradley D. Nash with Milton S. Eisenhower, R. Gordon Hoxie, and William C. Spragens is very insightful and helpful in thinking about presidential organization.
2. In addition to the general literature on the Presidency, an excellent starting point in the review of literature on presidential transitions is James P. Pfiffner's superb work, *The Strategic Presidency: Hitting the Ground Running* (Chicago: Dorsey Press, 1988). Other important examples include the collection of papers, especially Laurin Henry's "The Transition: From Nomination to Inauguration," in Paul T. David (ed), *The Presidential Election and Transition 1960–1961* (Washington, D.C.: Brookings Institution, 1961), Frederick C. Mosher, *Presidential Transitions and Foreign Affairs* (Baton Rouge, LA: Louisiana State University Press, 1987), and James P. Pfiffner, "The Carter-Reagan Transition: Hitting the Ground Running," *Presidential Studies Quarterly* (Fall, 1983).
3. Edwin Meese III and Jack Watson, Jr. agreed to collaborate on the project to leave a written record of the transition.

CHAPTER NINE NOTES

1. "The Turnout Problem" in A. James Reichley, ed., *Elections American Style* (Brookings, 1987), p. 113.
2. See Curtis B. Gans, "Non-Voting," a paper prepared for the Brookings Conference on Party & Electoral Renewal," April 6–7, 1987.

3. This information comes from *The New York Times*, and covers the last 5 elections (1984, 1980, 1976, 1972, 1968), unless otherwise noted. The averaged high/low temperatures for these cities on present and proposed election days were Anchorage 32/23 (Nov.) and 57/40 (May, based on 4 days); Albuquerque 64/34 (Nov.) and 84/51 (May); Atlanta 61/47 (Nov.) and 79/59 (May); Cleveland 51/41 (Nov.) and 68/53 (May); Detroit 53/39 (Nov.) and 70/52 (May); Jacksonville 74/55 (Nov.) and 87/66 (May, based on 4 days); Little Rock 64/49 (Nov.) and 85/68 (May); Memphis 64/46 (Nov.) and 80/66 (May); Norfolk 63/47 (Nov., based on 4 days) and 82/65 (May, based on 3 days); Pittsburgh 52/38 (Nov.) and 71/52 (May); Portland, Me. 47/34 (Nov.) and 69/46 (May).

4. Technically there are no national holidays. Each state has jurisdiction over its own holidays. The President and Congress can only designate holidays for the District of Columbia and federal workers. In 1987, Alabama, Louisiana, and Mississippi did not observe Memorial Day, and it was observed on May 30 in Delaware, Illinois, Maryland, New Hampshire, New Mexico, South Dakota, and Vermont.

5. *Hearing before the Subcommittee on the Constitution*, Committee on the Judiciary, U.S. Senate, 98th Congress, 2nd Session, on S.J. Res. 71, "Commencement of Terms of Office of the President and Members of Congress," p. 7; also see "Recent Lame-Duck Sessions," *CQ Almanac 1982*, p. 6.

6. See Edward S. Corwin, *The Constitution* (14th edition, Princeton University Press, 1978), p. 149.

7. The high/low temperature readings for January 20: 38/33 (1969); 46/38 (1973, midnight through 6 p.m.); 33/20 (1977); 56/38 (1981); 15/3 (1985). The high/low temperature readings for July 4: 81/67 (1968); 81/68 (1972); 84/65 (1976); 90/73 (1980); 90/71 (1984).

8. *Presidential Transitions* (Brookings, 1960), p. 5.

9. Frederick C. Mosher in "Mosher, Bundy, Buchen Speaks on Transitions," *Newsletter of the White Burkett Miller Center of Public Affairs*, University of Virginia, Vol. 1, No. 9, Spring 1985, p. 1.

10. The following post-election transitions were within the same political party: T. Roosevelt-Taft (1904) and Coolidge-Hoover (1928); the inter-party transitions have been Taft-Wilson (1912), Wilson-Harding (1920), Hoover-F. Roosevelt (1932), Truman-Eisenhower (1952), Eisenhower-Kennedy (1960), Johnson-Nixon (1968), Ford-Carter (1976), and Carter-Reagan (1980).

11. During the transition of 1960–61, I was on the outgoing White House staff; in 1968–69, I was on the incoming White House staff; 1976, I was an adviser to the President-elect; 1980, at the behest of the Republican National Chairman, I prepared a plan for tran-

sition operations, which was presented to the party's nominee, who subsequently became President-elect.

12. Carl M. Brauer, *Presidential Transitions* (Oxford University Press, 1986), pp. 226 and 228.

13. See Contra, James P. Pfiffner, "The Carter-Reagan Transition: Hitting the Ground Running," *Presidential Studies Quarterly*, vol. 13, Fall 1983, pp. 623–645.

14. "What's Wrong With Transitions," *Foreign Policy*, no. 55, Summer 1984, p. 32.

15. In testimony before the Governmental Affairs Committee, U.S. Senate, September 17, 1987, I take a much more modest approach to this problem by merely suggesting a change of inauguration date from January 20 to December 30.

CHAPTER TEN NOTES

1. Richard E. Neustadt and Ernest R. May, *Thinking in Time* (New York: The Free Press, 1986), p. 32.

2. On reorganization in general, see Harvey C. Mansfield, "Reorganizing the Federal Executive Branch: The Limits of Institutionalization," 35 (Summer 1970) *Law and Contemporary Problems*, 465–495; Peri E. Arnold, *Making the Managerial Presidency* (Princeton: Princeton University Press, 1986); and James Garnett, "Operationalizing the Constitution via Administrative Reorganization," 47 (Jan./Feb. 1987), *Public Administration Review*, 35–42.

3. For the broadest treatments of presidential transitions see, Laurin Henry, *Presidential Transitions* (Washington, D.C.: Brookings, 1960), and James P. Pfiffner, *The Strategic Presidency* (Chicago: Dorsey, 1988).

4. James Pfiffner, p. 3.

5. Harold Seidman and Robert Gilmour, *Politics, Position and Power: The Dynamics of Federal Organization*, 4th ed. (New York: Oxford, 1986).

6. For a study of a presidential transition (1960/61) focused at the department level, see David T. Stanley, *Changing Administrations* (Washington, D.C.: Brookings, 1965).

7. Colin Campbell, *Managing the Presidency* (Pittsburgh, PA: University of Pittsburgh Press, 1986), p. 5. On this point, also see Erwin C. Hargrove and Michael Nelson, *Presidents, Politics, and Policy* (New York: Knopf, 1984), chaps. 6 and 8.

8. For a critical perspective on "grand" reorganization planning as practiced, for example, in the Nixon and Carter administrations, see Seidman and Gilmour, *Politics, Position and Power*, chaps. 1, 5, and 6. For a group of essays that investigate the limitations of large-

scale reorganization planning, see Peter Szanton (ed.), *Federal Reorganization* (Chatham, N.J.: Chatham House, 1981).

9. The most detailed description of the 1952–53 transition can be found in Laurin Henry, pp. 455–703. Also see Carl M. Brauer, *Presidential Transitions* (New York: Oxford, 1986), chap. 1.

10. Memorandum on duties of the committee, January 13, 1953, 10-3 A-2, Official File, White House Central File, Dwight D. Eisenhower Library, Abilene, KS.

11. For a detailed description of the first Hoover Commission and its recommendations, see Ronald Moe, *The Hoover Commissions Revisited* (Boulder, Co. Westview, 1982).

12. Arthur Flemming, interviewed by author, April 24, 1981.

13. Memorandum, n.d. file 24, PACGO, Eisenhower Library.

14. Memorandum, Advisory Committee to Eisenhower, December 21, 1952, Rockefeller (6), Administration Series, Papers of DDE as President, Eisenhower Library.

15. Preface to recommendations, memorandum, n.d., file 24, PACGO, Eisenhower Library.

16. *Ibid.*, p. 4.

17. Executive Order no. 10, 432, January 24, 1953.

18. See Arnold, chaps. 6 & 7.

19. Richard M. Nixon, *Memoirs* (New York: Grosset & Dunlop, 1978), p. 352. See Richard Nathan's discussion of the New Federalism, in Nathan, *The Plot That Failed* (New York: Wiley, 1975), chap. 2.

20. John Osborne, *The Nixon Watch* (New York: Liveright, 1970), p. 28. For a very personal perspective on transition staff building, see William Safire, *Before the Fall* (Garden City, N.Y.: Doubleday, 1975), chap. 2.

21. *The New York Times*, November 22, 1968.

22. Larry Berman, *The Office of Management and Budget* (Princeton: Princeton University Press, 1979), p. 105.

23. This preference for structure contrasts with Nixon's apparent preference for a more personalized system for handing high level foreign policy issues. See Stephen Hess, *Organizing the Presidency* (Washington: Brookings Institution, 1976), p. 112.

24. *New York Times*, December 5, 1968.

25. Larry Berman, pp. 105–6.

26. See Richard Rose, *Managing Presidential Objectives* (New York: Free Press, 1976), pp. 1–30. Also see Joel D. Aberbach and Bert A. Rockman, "Clashing Beliefs Within the Executive Branch," *American Political Science Review* LXX (July 1976), 456–468.

27. Frederick Malek, *Washington's Hidden Tragedy* (New York: Free Press, 1978), p. 15.

28. Richard Nathan, *The Plot that Failed*, p. 62.

29. *Weekly Companion of Presidential Documents*, Vol. 5, no. 15 (April 14, 1969), 530.

30. This sketch of Ash's views is derived through the perspective of Andrew Rouse, the council's assistant director and later executive director, interviewed by author, August 26, 1981.

31. *Public Papers of the Presidents, Richard M. Nixon, 1969*, "Special Message to the Congress Requesting New Authority to Reorganize the Executive Branch," January 20, 1969, pp. 32–33.

32. At its peak size in mid-1970, the council's staff included forty-seven persons. Testimony of Roy Ash, U.S. Congress, House, Committee on Government Operations, *Hearings, Reorganization of Executive Departments*, 92nd Cong., 1st Sess., 1971, p. 184.

33. The retention of "budget" in OMB was a sop to Representative George Mahon (Dem., Texas), chairman of the House Appropriations Committee. The original recommendation to the president had renamed the bureau, the Office of Management.

    Murray Comarow (first executive director of Ash Council), interviewed by author, April 24, 1981.

34. *Public Papers of the Presidents, Richard Nixon, 1970*, "Message . . . ," March 12, 1970.

35. *Public Papers of the Presidents, Richard Nixon, 1971*, p. 51.

36. Richard Nathan, chap. 4.

37. A very good discussion of "outsiders" and the changing selection process can be found in Samuel Kernell, *Going Public* (Washington: Congressional Quarterly Press, 1986), pp. 35–41.

38. Interview with Jimmy Carter, *National Journal* (July 17, 1976), 999.

39. On Carter's Georgia experience, see Gary Fink, *Prelude to the Presidency* (Westport, CT: Greenwood, 1980).

40. For Carter's account of himself, see Jimmy Carter, *Why Not the Best?* (Nashville, TN: Boardman, 1975); and Carter, *A Government as Good as Its People* (New York: Simon and Schuster, 1977).

41. Dom Bonafede, "Carter Staff is Getting Itch . . . ," *National Journal* (October 30, 1976), 1, 1547. See James Pfiffner, pp. 14 & 15.

42. *National Journal* (September 25, 1976), 1,361.

43. *National Journal* (April 23, 1977), 625.

44. Presidential reorganization authority had lapsed in 1973 and not been renewed. On the reorganization authority, see Louis Fisher and Ronald C. Moe, "Delegating With Ambivalence: The Legislative Veto and Reorganization Authority," in *Studies on the Legislative Veto*, prepared by the Congressional Research Service for the Subcommittee on Rules of the House of the Committee on Rules, 96th Cong., 2d Sess., 1980. Committee Print.

45. Public Law 95–17, approved April 6, 1977.

46. The administration's approach to reorganization planning is out-

lined in, President's Reorganization Project, "Plan for Conducting Federal Government Reorganization and Management Improvement Program" (Washington: Executive Office of the President, March 1977).

47. For a view of Carter's approach to organization and policy consistent with this, see Jack Knott and Aaron Wildavsky, "Jimmy Carter's Theory of Governing," *Wilson Quarterly*, 1 (1977), 49–67.

48. This point is evident particularly in Schlesinger's congressional testimony. U.S. Congress, Senate, Committee on Governmental Affairs, *Hearings, Department of Energy Organization Act*, 95th Cong., 1st Sess, 1977, p. 121.

49. These figures come from Ronald C. Moe, "The Carter Reorganization Effort," Report No. 80–172 GOV (Washington: Congressional Research Service, 1980).

50. Richard P. Nathan, *The Plot That Failed* (New York: John Wiley, 1975), chaps. 3–4.

51. Neustadt and May, *Thinking in Time*, chap. 12.

CHAPTER ELEVEN NOTES

1. See the essay by William T. Golden and that by R. Gordon Hoxie for a careful discussion of the President's scientific advisory system.

2. Arthur M. Schlesinger, Jr., *A Thousand Days* (Greenwich, Connecticut: Fawcett Crest Books, 1965), pp. 631–632.

3. Daniel J. Elazar, "The Evolving Federal System," *The Power to Govern*, Richard M. Pious, editor (New York: Proceedings of the Academy of Political Science, 1981), p. 12.

4. Hugh Heclo, "One Executive Branch or Many," *Both Ends of the Avenue*, Anthony King, editor (Washington, D.C.: American Enterprise Institute, 1983), p. 32.

5. Francis E. Rourke, *Bureaucratic Power in National Politics*, third edition (Boston: Little Brown and Company, 1978), p. ix.

6. Richard M. Pious, *The American Presidency*, p. 238.

7. Francis E. Rourke, *Bureaucratic Power in National Politics*, p. 159.

8. Roger Porter, *Presidential Decision Making* (Cambridge, England: Cambridge University Press, 1980), p. 236.

9. William D. Carey, "Presidential Staffing in the Sixties and Seventies," *Public Administration Review*, Volume 24, September/October 1969, p. 457. Richard Fenno similarly refers to the "plural political universe" in public policy decisions. See "President-Cabinet Relations," *American Political Science Review*, Volume 3, June 1958, p. 388.

10. Graham Allison and Peter Szanton note that the White House staff "has no purpose but to serve its single superior, (they) bring to that service no counter pressure from statutory responsibili-

ties, bureaucratic loyalties, professional identification, or Congressional supervision." "Organizing for the Decade Ahead," *Setting National Priorities: The Next Ten Years* (Washington, D.C.: The Brookings Institution, 1976), page 256. See also Lewis D. Dexter, "Court Politics," *Administration and Society*, Volume 9, November 1977, p. 276.

11. Don K. Price and Rocco C. Siciliano, *A Presidency for the 1980's* (Washington, D.C.: National Academy of Public Administration, 1980), p. 32.

12. Jack Valenti, *A Very Human President* (New York: W.W. Norton and Company, Inc., 1975), p. 62.

13. Francis Rourke, "The Presidency and the Bureaucracy," *The Presidency and the Political System*, Michael Nelson, editor (Washington, D.C.: Congressional Quarterly, Inc. 1984), p. 356.

14. Rexford G. Tugwell and Thomas E. Cronin, *The Presidency Reappraised* (New York: Praeger Publishers, 1974), p. 9.

15. Theodore H. White, *The Making of the President 1968* (New York: Atheneum, 1969), p. 171.

16. "Executive Office Staff Expanding Despite Decentralization Pledge," *National Journal*, Volume 2, April 25, 1970, p. 858.

17. *Ibid.*, p. 860.

18. Thomas E. Cronin, "The Swelling of the Presidency," *Saturday Review of the Society*, Volume 1, January 20, 1973, p. 33.

19. Joel Havemann, "The Cabinet Band—Trying to Follow Carter's Baton," *National Journal*, July 16, 1977, p. 1104.

20. *Ibid.*, p. 1104.

21. Dom Bonafede, "Carter Staff is Getting Itchy to Make the Move to Washington," *National Journal*, October 30, 1976, p. 1544. Jack Watson was appointed by Carter in June 1976 as the director of the campaign's transition team. Part of Watson's responsibilities as transition coordinator was to develop an organizational structure which fostered Cabinet Government. Once in office, Carter used Watson's plan for a Cabinet cluster system of policy development to implement Cabinet Government.

22. Joseph A. Califano, Jr., *Governing America* (New York: Simon and Schuster, 1981), p. 16.

23. Jimmy Carter, *Why Not the Best?* (New York: Bantam Books, 1976), p. 169.

24. Jimmy Carter, *Keeping Faith* (New York: Bantam Books, 1982), p. 66.

25. Jimmy Carter, *Why Not the Best?*, p. 171.

26. David Broder, "Shaping the Administration's Policy," *Washington Post*, February 12, 1978, p. A14.

27. *Ibid.*, p. A14.

28. Steven Weisman, "The President as Chairman of the Board," *New York Times Magazine*, January 10, 1982, p. 1.

29. Ronald Brownstein, "Jobs are the Currency of Politics, and the White House is on a Spending Spree," *National Journal*, December 15, 1984.

30. Barbara Kellerman, *The Political Presidency* (New York: Oxford University Press, 1984), p. 246ff.

31. Colin Campbell, *Managing the Presidency* (Pittsburgh: University of Pittsburgh Press, 1986), pp. 266–267.

32. R. Gordon Hoxie, "Staffing the Ford and Carter Presidencies," in Bradley D. Nash, et al., *Organizing and Staffing the Presidency* (New York: Center for the Study of the Presidency, 1980), pp. 44–85.

CHAPTER TWELVE NOTES

1. Samuel Lindsay observed over 50 years ago that "No single act of the President transcends in importance the appointment of his cabinet. The country forms its judgment of his underlying purposes and theories of government, it takes his measure and draws more conclusions from this single act than it does from his platform, his campaign pledges, his inaugural address or his first message to Congress. It represents in a vivid way the President's concept of the essential, vital and controlling organization of the executive government." See "The New Cabinet and Its Problems," *Review of Reviews*, April 1921, p. 382.

2. Roger Porter has used the term "adhocracy" to refer to an informal and changing policy organization that tends to neglect the need for overall policy coordination. See *Presidential Decision-Making: The Economic Policy Board*, (New York: Cambridge University Press, 1980). Graham Allison also uses the term in a discussion of the cabinet in "An Executive Cabinet," *Society*, (July/August, 1980), pp. 41–47, especially p. 44.

3. For a discussion of presidential personnel recruitment processes from Truman through Carter, see G. Calvin MacKenzie, *The Politics of Presidential Appointments* (New York: The Free Press Company, 1981), especially pp. 11–78. On the Reagan transition, see Laurin L. Henry, "The Transition: From Nomination to Inauguration" in Paul T. David and David H. Emerson, eds., *The Presidential Election and Transition, 1980–1981*, (Carbondale, IL: Southern Illinois University Press, 1983), pp. 195–218, especially pp. 200–207. For a detailed comparison of the cabinet recruitment efforts of Franklin Delano Roosevelt and Reagan, see Margaret J. Wyszomirski, "Roosevelt and Reagan: Cabinet Recruitment and Performance," paper presented at the Annual Meeting of the American Political Science Association, Washington, D.C., September 1984. For a comparison of the staffing of Franklin Delano Roosevelt

and Kennedy see Richard E. Neustadt, "Approaches to Staffing the Presidency: Notes on Franklin Delano Roosevelt and John F. Kennedy," *American Political Science Review*, vol. 52, no. 4 (December 1963), pp. 855–864.

4. This bears a resemblance to Richard Neustadt's perspective that presidential power is essentially persuasive in nature and that the ability to persuade requires "bargaining advantages." In that sense, "political capital" accrued through personnel recruitment can be regarded as one source of "bargaining advantage." However, this approach differs in emphasis from Neustadt in the sense that he regards the Department heads primarily as officers the president must bargain with (thus expending some of his political capital negotiating with them.) In contrast, I emphasize the utility of cabinet members in providing the president with assets that can enhance (or diminish) his ability to "bargain" with others. On Neustadt's approach see *Presidential Power* (New York: John Wiley and Sons, Inc., 1980), especially pp. 26–33.

Paul Light employs the idea of "political capital" as being "directly linked to the congressional parties" (p. 26). As Light uses the concept it refers to party support in Congress, an element that may, in turn, be affected by presidential public opinion ratings, electoral margin and professional reputation. See *The President's Agenda*, (Baltimore: Johns Hopkins University Press, 1983), especially pp. 25–33.

5. The idea of "preventive assistance" is Richard R. Fenno's, see *The President's Cabinet*, (Cambridge: Harvard University Press, 1959), pp. 208 and 220.

6. Arthur M. Schlesinger, Jr., *The Crisis of the Old Order*, (Boston: Houghton Mifflin, Co., 1957), p. 472.

7. For example, see Lloyd N. Cutler, "To Form a Government," *Foreign Affairs*, (Fall 1980): 126–143.

8. See for example, James L. Sundquist, "The Crisis of Competence in Our National Government," *Political Science Quarterly*, vol. 95, no. 2 (Summer 1980): 183–208.

9. Colin Campbell, *Managing the Presidency*, (Pittsburgh: University of Pittsburgh Press, 1986), pp. 55–6.

10. Edward Pendleton Herring, *Presidential Leadership*, (New York: Farrar and Rinehart, 1940), p. 92.

11. Elizabeth Dole is married to Senator Robert Dole, a moderate Republican who chairs the important Finance Committee and is an often-mentioned presidential hopeful. Margaret Heckler, a moderate Republican from Massachusetts, was defeated for re-election to the House in 1982, when redistricting pitted her against a Democratic congressional colleague who turned the election into a referendum on President Reagan's economic and military poli-

cies. As a Congresswoman Heckler has advocated women's rights and worked for the passage of legislation that addressed women's issues. While these actions brought her the endorsements of many women's groups, Heckler was never a leader of politically organized women. Furthermore, as an opponent of abortion, she forfeited the support of the National Women's Political Caucus.

12. The shift from an "establishment" to a "professional elite" in foreign policy has been persuasively recounted by I. M. Distler, Leslie H. Gelb, and Anthony Lake in *Our Own Worst Enemy, The Unmasking of American Foreign Policy*, (New York: Simon and Schuster, 1984), pp. 91–126.

13. Cutler, "To Form a Government."

CHAPTER THIRTEEN NOTES

1. See Terry M. Moe, "The Politicized Presidency," in John E. Chubb and Paul E. Peterson (eds.), *The New Direction in American Politics* (Washington: The Brookings Institution, 1985), pp. 235–272.

2. For this formulation, see Richard Rose, The President: A Chief but Not an Executive," *Presidential Studies Quarterly* 7 (Winter 1977): 5–20.

3. For some data on this, see Bert A. Rockman, *The Leadership Question: The Presidency and the American System* (New York: Praeger, 1984), p. 23.

4. Among others in this regard, see William A. Niskanen, Jr., *Bureaucracy and Representative Government* (Chicago: Aldine-Atherton, 1971); Richard P. Nathan, *The Administrative Presidency* (New York: John Wiley, 1983); Richard M. Nixon, *RN: The Memoirs of Richard Nixon* (New York: Grosset & Dunlap, 1978); Martin Anderson, *Revolution* (San Diego: Harcourt Brace Jovanovich, 1988); and Stuart M. Butler, Michael Sanera, and W. Bruce Weinrod (eds.), *Mandate for Leadership II — Continuing the Conservative Revolution* (Washington: The Heritage Foundation, 1984).

5. Nixon, *RN*, p. 768, *passim*.

6. See Richard Rose, *Managing Presidential Objectives* (New York: The Free Press, 1976).

7. Anderson, *Revolution*, p. 248.

8. Anderson, p. 246.

9. See Joel D. Aberbach, Robert D. Putnam, and Bert A. Rockman, *Bureaucrats and Politicians in Western Democracies* (Cambridge, Mass.: Harvard University Press, 1981), pp. 228–237, and Joel D. Aberbach and Bert A. Rockman, *The Administrative State in Industrialized Democracies* (Washington: American Political Science Association, 1985).

10. Interview #005.
11. Bert A. Rockman, "The Style and the Organization of the Reagan Presidency," in Charles O. Jones (ed.), *The Reagan Legacy* (Chatham, NJ: Chatham House Publishers, 1988), pp. 3–29.
12. This portrait seems to fit the British prime minister Mrs. Thatcher more definitively than the American president, Mr. Reagan. But it certainly does fit some of those around Mr. Reagan and some of his appointees in the departments. See Anthony King, "Margaret Thatcher: The Style of a Prime Minister," in Anthony King (ed.), *The British Prime Minister*, revised second edition (Durham, NC: Duke University Press, 1985), pp. 96–140.
13. See Richard Rose, "Loyalty, Voice or Exit? Margaret Thatcher's Challenge to the Civil Service," in T. Ellwein, J. J. Hesse, Renate Mayntz, and F. W. Scharpf (eds.), *Yearbook on Government and Public Administration* (Boulder, CO: Westview Press and Baden-Baden, West Germany: Nomos Verlag, forthcoming).
14. See Joel D. Aberbach and Bert A. Rockman, "Ideological Change in the American Administrative Elite." Paper prepared for presentation at The Workshop on Patterns of Elite Transformation in Western Democracies at the ECPR Joint Session, Rimini, Italy, April 5–10, 1988.
15. For discussions of this formulation, see Richard A. Chapman, "The Changing Administrative Culture in the British Civil Service," in Colin Campbell, S. J., and B. Guy Peters (eds.), *Organizing Governance: Governing Organizations* (Pittsburgh: University of Pittsburgh Press, 1988), pp. 167–182; Joel D. Aberbach and Bert A. Rockman, "Political and Bureaucratic Roles in Public Service Reorganization," in Campbell and Peters, pp. 79–98; and Rose, "Loyalty, Voice or Exit?"
16. For a very useful discussion of problems of civil service compensation, see Charles H. Levine, "Human Resource Erosion and the Uncertain Future of the U.S. Civil Service: From Policy Gridlock to Structural Fragmentation," *Governance* 1 (April 1988), pp. 115–143.
17. Interview #142.

CHAPTER FOURTEEN NOTES

1. M. P. Fiorina, "Flagellating the Federal Bureaucracy," *Society*, 20 (March/April 1983), p. 67.
2. J. D. Aberbach and B. A. Rockman, "Mandates or Mardarins? Control and Discretion in the Modern Administrative State," *Public Administration Review*, 48, (March/April 1988), p. 607.
3. P. Ingraham, "Applying Models of Political-Career Relationships

to Policy Implementation," A paper presented at the American Political Science Association's Annual Meeting, Chicago, IL, September 3, 1987.

4. *Ibid.*

5. *Ibid.*

6. *Ibid.*

7. *Ibid.*

8. W. H. Schmidt and B. Z. Posner, "Values and Expectations of Federal Service Executives," *Public Administration Review*, 46 (September/October 1986), p. 448.

9. *Ibid.*

10. James P. Pfiffner, *The Strategic Presidency: Hitting the Ground Running* (Chicago: The Dorsey Press, 1988), p. 104.

11. R. C. Kearney and C. Sinha, "Professionalism and Bureaucratic Responsiveness: Conflict or Compatibility," *Public Administration Review*, 48 (January/February 1988), p. 575.

12. J. D. Aberbach, B. A. Rockman, R. M. Copeland, "The Changing Federal Executive," a paper presented at the American Political Science Association's Annual Meeting, Chicago, IL, September 3, 1987.

13. S. Stehr, "Rethinking the Role of the Federal Career Executive," a paper presented at the American Political Science Association's Annual Meeting, Chicago, IL, September 3, 1987. FEIAA Newsletter, 1985.

14. Ingraham, *loc. cit.*

15. Henry Fairle, "After the Revolution," *The New Republic*, May 9, 1988, p. 15.

16. Brian Hogwood and B. Guy Peters, *Policy Dynamics* (London: Wheat Sheaf, 1983).

17. Donald Regan, *For the Record*, (New York: Harcourt Brace Jovanovich, 1988) excerpted in *Time* May 16, 1988, p. 38.

18. Ingraham, *loc. cit.*

19. Schmidt and Posner, *op. cit.*, 450. A. Northrop and J. L. Perry, "Change in Performance of the Federal Bureaucracy During the Carter-Reagan Transition: Evidence from Five Agencies," *Public Administration Quarterly*, (Winter 1986), p. 463, B. Rosen, "Crises in the U.S. Civil Service," *Public Administration Review*, 46 (May/June 1986), p. 210.

20. Schmidt and Posner, *loc. cit.*

21. *Los Angeles Times*, June 19, 1988.

22. P. W. Ingraham, "Building Bridges or Burning Them? The President, the Appointees, and the Bureaucracy," *Public Administration Review*, 47 (September/October 1987), p. 425.

CHAPTER FIFTEEN NOTES

1. American Academy of Political Science, *The Revolution, the Constitution, and America's Third Century*, 2 vols. (Philadelphia: University of Pennsylvania Press, 1980), II, 215.
2. Phillip G. Henderson, "Advice, and Decision: The Eisenhower National Security Council Reappraised," in R. Gordon Hoxie, ed. *The Presidency and National Security Policy* (New York: Center for the Study of the Presidency, 1984), pp. 175–176.
3. Statement of Zbigniew Brzezinski; September 16, 1981. Manuscript in Center for the Study of the Presidency.
4. R. Gordon Hoxie, ed. *The White House: Organization and Operations*. (New York: Center for the Study of the Presidency, 1971), pp. 194.
5. *The New York Times*, December 3, 1986.

CHAPTER SIXTEEN NOTES

1. On the earlier phase of the Reagan NSC, see McFarlane, Robert C. with Richard Saunders and Thomas C. Shull, "The National Security Council"; in R. Gordon Hoxie, ed., *The Presidency and National Security Policy* (New York Center for the Study of the Presidency, 1984); pp. 261–2.
2. Quoted in R. Gordon Hoxie, ed., *The White House: Organization and Operations* (New York: Center for the Study of the Presidency, 1971) pp. 118–19.
3. *Report of the President's Special Review Board*, February 26, 1987, p. IV-1.
4. Jackson, Henry M., ed., *The National Security Council.* (New York, Frederick A. Praeger, 1965) p. 44.

CHAPTER TWENTY NOTES

1. *Washington Evening Star*, October 30, 1944.
2. "A Post-Mortem on Transition Predictions of National Product," L. R. Klein, Journal of Political Economy, August 1946, pp. 289–308.
3. Public Law 304, 79th Congress, Sec. 4.
4. Edwin G. Nourse, *Economics in the Public Service*, pp. 376–377, Harcourt Brace, 1953.
5. Arthur F. Burns, *Frontiers of Economic Knowledge*, pp. 3–26, Princeton University Press, 1954.
6. *The New York Times*, April 6, 1953, p. 29.
7. U.S. Congress, Senate Committee on Banking, Hearings on the Confirmation of Arthur F. Burns as Chairman of the CEA, 83rd Congress, 1st session.

8. *The New York Times*, October 26, 1952, p. 78.
9. *Ibid*, December 14, 1960, p. 5.
10. Economic Report of the President, January 1965, p. 31.
11. *Ibid*, p. 32.
12. Economic Report of the President, January 1972, "Report to the President on the Activities of the Council of Economic Advisors During 1971."
13. Business Week, October 5, 1987, Washington Outlook, p. 47.
14. Anthony S. Campagna, U.S. National Economic Policy, 1917–1985 Praeger Publishers, p. 573.
15. "The Economic Approach to Public Policy," Ryan C. Amacher, Robert D. Tollison & Thomas D. Willett (eds.), Cornell University Press, 1976. See "A Modest Proposal" by Gordon Tullock, pp. 511–519.

CHAPTER TWENTY-TWO NOTES

1. For a review of the literature, see Kirsten Monroe, *Presidential Popularity and the Economy*. New York: Praeger, 1984.
2. For a development of this point, see Richard Rose. *The Post-Modern Presidency: the World Closes in on the White House*. Chatham, NJ: Chatham House, 1988, part three.
3. For a broad discussion, see Richard Rose, "The Political Appraisal of Employment Policies," *Journal of Public Policy* 7, 3 (1987), 285–305. For a case study, see David Stockman, *The Triumph of Politics*. New York: Harper & Row, 1986.
4. See Assar Lindbeck, "Stabilization Policy in Open Economies with Endogenous Politicians," *American Economic Review* 66, 2 (1976).
5. Samuel Morley and Erwin Hargrove, eds. *The President and the Council of Economic Advisers: Interviews with CEA Chairmen*. Boulder, Colo: Westview, 1984.
6. Isabel Sawhill, "Reaganomics in Retrospect," in John L. Palmer, ed., *Perspectives on the Reagan Years*. Washington, DC: Urban Institute, 1986, p. 109.
7. For details, see Richard Rose, *The Post-Modern Presidency*, chapter 5.
8. See e.g. William R. Allen, "Economics, Economists and Economic Policy," *History of Political Economy* 9, 1 (1977) pp. 48–88; Robert H. Nelson, "The Economics Profession and the Making of Public Policy." *Journal of Economic Literature* 25, 1 (1987), pp. 49–91.
9. See Aaron Wildavsky, *The New Politics of the Budgetary Process*. Boston: Little, Brown, 1988.
10. See John S. Odell, *U.S. International Monetary Policy: Markets, Power and Ideas as Sources of Change*. Princeton: Princeton University Press, 1982, and Yoichi Funabashi, *Managing the Dollar: From the Plaza*

to the Louvre. Washington, DC: Institute for International Economics, 1988.

11. John T. Woolley, *Monetary Politics.* New York: Cambridge University Press, 1984, p. 106. See also Donald F. Kettl, *Leadership at the Fed.* New Haven: Yale University Press, 1986.

12. Roger Porter, "Economic Advice to the President," *Political Science Quarterly* 93, 3 (1983) p. 415.

13. Richard E. Neustadt, *Presidential Power.* New York: John Wiley, 1960; James P. Pfiffner, *The Strategic Presidency: Hitting the Ground Running.* Chicago: Dorsey Press, 1987.

14. F. C. Mosher, W. D. Clinton and D. G. Lang. *Presidential Transitions and Foreign Affairs.* Baton Rouge: Louisiana State University Press, 1987.

15. Quoted in Stella Shamoon, "Markets: Where the Buck Stops," *The Observer* (London), 29 November 1987.

16. On a step in this direction in President Ford's Administration, see Roger Porter, *Presidential Decision Making: the Economic Policy Board.* New York: Cambridge University Press, 1980.

17. *Presidential Power* (3rd edition, 1980). p. 223.

CHAPTER TWENTY-THREE NOTES

1. Golden, William T. *"Government Military-Scientific Research: Review for the President of the United States, 1950–51."* 432 pages, unpublished. Available at the Harry S. Truman Library, Independence, Missouri 64050; the Herbert Hoover Presidential Library, West Branch, Iowa 52358; the Dwight D. Eisenhower Library, Abilene, Kansas 67410; and the American Institute of Physics. New York, New York 10017.

2. Bronk, Detlev W., "Science Advice in the White House: The Genesis of the President's Science Advisers and the National Science Foundation." *Science*, 11 October 1974. Vol. 186. pp. 116–121; reprinted in Golden, William T., ed., *Science Advice to the President* (New York: Pergamon Press, 1980). pp. 245–256.

4. *Genesis* 3:1–24.

5. Golden, William T., "Science Advice to the President: Past, Present, Future." *Proceedings of the American Philosophical Society.* Vol. 130. no. 3. 1986. pp. 325–329.

CHAPTER TWENTY-FOUR NOTES

1. Harold C. Syrett (ed.) and Jacob E. Cooke (assoc. ed.), *The Papers of Alexander Hamilton.* 26 vols. (New York: Columbia University Press, 1961–1979) x, p. 291.

2. Edward E. David, Jr., "Current State of White House Science Advising," in William T. Golden, ed., *Science Advice to the President* (New York: Pergamon Press, 1980), p. 55. See also Edward E. David, Jr., "Science Advising and the Nixon Presidency," in Kenneth W. Thompson, *The Presidency and Science Advising*, 3 vols. (Lanham, MD, 1986–87), III, p. 230.

3. Franklin A. Long, "New Perspectives in Science Advising," in Thompson, *op. cit.*, III, pp. 60–61.

4. Caspar W. Weinberger, "It's Time to Get S.D.I. Off the Ground," *The New York Times*, August 21, 1987, p. A.27.

5. R. Gordon Hoxie, *The White House: Organization and Operations* (New York: Center for the Study of the Presidency, 1971), pp. 173, 182.

6. James E. Katz, "Organizational Structure and Advisory Effectiveness: The Office of Science and Technology Policy," in Golden, *op. cit.*, p. 241.

7. Dwight D. Eisenhower, *The White House Years*, Vol. II, *Waging Peace, 1956–1961* (Garden City, New York: Doubleday & Company, 1965), p. 224.

8. A. Hunter Dupree, "A Historian's View of Advice to the President on Science: Retrospect and Prescription," in Golden, *op. cit.*, p. 179.

9. Harold C. Relyea, *The Presidency and Information Policy* (New York: Center for the Study of the Presidency, 1981).

10. William T. Golden, "A Department of Science: An Illusion-PSAC: A Prescription," in Thompson, *op. cit.*, III, 117, 119.

11. Hamilton, *Papers*, X. p. 291.

CHAPTER TWENTY-FIVE NOTES

1. November 19, 1988.

2. November 28, 1976.

3. Interview, MJK, April 24th, Washington, D.C.

4. Background interviews with reporters at the White House, March 27th, 1981.

5. Interview with Anne Wexler, Washington, D.C., MJK & MBG, January 13, 1981.

6. Interview with David Gergen, Washington, D.C., MBG & MJK, June 16, 1981.

7. Transcript, *The New York Times*, November 7, 1981.

CHAPTER TWENTY-SIX NOTES

1. Kathleen Hall Jamieson, *Packaging the Presidency: A History and Criticism of Presidential Campaign Advertising* (New York: Oxford University Press, 1984).

2. William C. Spragens, *The Presidency and the Mass Media in the Age of Television* (Washington: University Press of America, 1978); Spragens, *From Spokesman to Press Secretary: White House Media Operations* (Lanham, MD: University Press of America, 1980); see also Chapters 15–23, William C. Spragens, ed., *Popular Images of American Presidents* (Westport, CT: Greenwood Press, 1988).

3. Spragens, *From Spokesman to Press Secretary*, pp. 195–201.

4. Michael J. Robinson and Margaret A. Sheehan, *Over the Wire and on TV: CBS and UPI in Campaign '80* (New York: Russell Sage Foundation, 1983); see also William C. Adams, ed., *Television Coverage of the 1980 Presidential Campaign* (Norwood, NJ: Ablex Publishing Corp., 1983) and Santo Ingeyar and Donald R. Kinder, *News That Matters: Television and American Opinion* (Chicago: University of Chicago Press, 1987).

5. Larry Speakes, *Speaking Out: Inside the Reagan White House* (New York: Charles Scribner's Sons, 1988), pp. 243–245.

6. Speakes, *Speaking Out*, p. 136.

7. Speakes, *Speaking Out*, p. 65.

8. Correspondence between author and Professor George E. Reedy, Nieman Professor of Journalism, Marquette University, January 1988.

9. Spragens, *From Spokesman to Press Secretary*, pp. 228–234.

10. Hedrick Smith, *The Power Game: How Washington Works* (New York: Random House, 1988), pp. 341, 342, 390, 391. Smith contrasts the "fast start" of the Reagan team in 1981, alluded to in the Gergen interview, with the laggard beginning of 1985 which Smith finds more nearly comparable to Carter's start in 1977. By 1985 of course, Gergen had departed from the White House.

11. Interview with David R. Gergen, Editor, *U.S. News and World Report*, in Mr. Gergen's office, 2400 N. Street, N.W., Washington, D.C., November 30, 1987.

CHAPTER TWENTY-EIGHT NOTES

1. Jeff Fishel, *Presidents and Promises* (Washington, D.C.: CQ Press, 1985), p. 187.

2. Richard E. Neustadt, *Presidential Power* (N.Y.: Macmillan, 1980), p. 26.

3. Corwin as quoted in C. Crabb and P. Holt, *Invitation to Struggle* (Washington, D.C.: CQ Press, 1980), p. vii.

4. Harry Truman as quoted in Sidney Warren, *The American President* (Englewood Cliffs, N.J.: Prentice-Hall, 1967), pp. 33–38.

5. This, of course, is the argument made by Neustadt in his famous chapter 3, "The Power to Persuade" in *Presidential Power*.

6. See chapter 11 of *Presidential Power* entitled "Hazards of Transitions."

7. A splendid study of this successful effort is Mitchell Bard, "Interest Groups, the President, and Foreign Policy: How Reagan Snatched Victory from the Jaws of Defeat on AWACS," *Presidential Studies Quarterly* XVIII, Summer 1988, pp. 583–600.
8. For a summary of this new bargaining arena see Samuel Kernell, *Going Public* (Washington, D.C.: CQ Press, 1986).
9. Neustadt, p. 26.
10. For example, see Harold Barger, *The Impossible Presidency* (Glenview, Ill.: Scott, Foresman, 1984) and James L. Sundquist, "Congress, the President and the Crisis of Competence" in *Congress Reconsidered*, 2nd ed. Ed. by L. Dodd and B. Oppenheimer (Washington, D.C.: CQ Press, 1981), pp. 351–370.
11. Charles O. Jones, "Presidential Negotiations with Congress" in *Both Ends of the Avenue*, ed. by Anthony King (Washington, D.C.: American Enterprise Institute, 1983), pp. 100–126.
12. James P. Pfiffner, "The President's Legislative Agenda," *The Annals* (Sept. 1988).
13. In fact, the *CQ* Presidential success scores for the Reagan Administration trail those of other recent Administrations. See Charles O. Jones, "Ronald Reagan and the U.S. Congress: Visible Hand Politics," in *The Reagan Legacy*, Charles O. Jones, editor (Chatham, N.J.: Chatham House, 1988), pp. 52–56.
14. Stephen Wayne, "Congressional Liaison in the Reagan White House: A Preliminary Assessment of the First Year" in *President and Congress: Assessing Reagan's First Year*, ed. by Norman Ornstein (Washington, D.C.: AEI, 1987), p. 60.

CHAPTER TWENTY-EIGHT BIBLIOGRAPHY

Bard, Mitchell. "Interest Groups, the President, and Foreign Policy: How Reagan Snatched Victory from the Jaws of Defeat on AWACS" in *Presidential Studies Quarterly*, XVIII, Summer 1988, pp. 583–600.
Crabb, Cecil V. Jr. and Pat M. Holt. *Invitation to Struggle: Congress. The President and Foreign Policy*. Washington, D.C.: CQ Press, 1980.
Davis, Eric L. "Congressional Liaison: The People and the Institutions" in *Both Ends of the Avenue*, ed. by Anthony King. Washington, D.C.: American Enterprise Institute, 1983, pp. 59–95.
Destler, J. M. "Executive-Congressional Conflict in Foreign Policy: Explaining It, Coping with It," in *Congress Reconsidered*, 3rd ed. Ed. by L. C. Dodd and B. I. Oppenheimer. Washington, D.C.: CQ Press, 1985, pp. 343–63.
Edwards, George. *Presidential Influences in Congress*. San Francisco: Freeman, 1980.
Fishel, Jeff. *Presidents and Promises*. Washington, D.C.: CQ Press, 1985.

Fisher, Louis. *The Politics of Shared Power: Congress and the Executive.* Washington, D.C.: CQ Press, 1981.

Heginbotham, Stanley. "Dateline Washington: The Rules of the Games," *Foreign Policy,* No. 53 (Winter 1983–84); pp. 157–172.

Hoxie, R. Gordon. *The Presidency of the 1970's.* New York, N.Y.: Center for the Study of the Presidency, 1971.

————. *The White House: Organization and Operations.* New York, N.Y.: Center for the Study of the Presidency, 1972.

Jones, Charles O. "A New President, a Different Congress, a Maturing Agenda" in *The Reagan Presidency and the Governing of America.* Ed. by Lester Salamon and Michael Lund. Washington, D.C.: Urban Institute Press, 1984. pp. 261–87.

————. "Ronald Reagan and the U.S. Congress: Visible-Hand Politics" in *The Reagan Legacy,* ed. by Charles O. Jones. Chatham, N.J.: Chatham House Publishers, Inc., pp. 30–59.

————. *The Trusteeship Presidency: Jimmy Carter and the United States Congress.* Baton Rouge: Louisiana State University Press, 1988.

Kernell, Samuel. *Going Public: New Strategies of Presidential Leadership.* Washington, D.C.: CQ Press, 1986.

Neustadt, Richard E. *Presidential Power: The Politics of Leadership from Ford to Carter.* New York, N.Y.: Wiley, 1980.

Pfiffner, James. "The Reagan Budget Juggernaut: The Fiscal 1982 Budget Campaign," in *Public Administration: Concepts and Cases,* Richard Stillman, ed., 3rd. ed. Boston: Houghton-Mifflin, 1984, pp. 391–409.

————. "The President's Legislative Agenda," *The Annals of the American Academy of Political and Social Science.* (September 1988).

Shuman, Howard E. *Politics and the Budget: the Struggle Between the President and Congress.* Englewood Cliffs, N.J.: Prentice Hall, 1984.

Smith, Hedrick. "The President as Coalition Builder: Reagan's First Year," *New York Times Magazine,* (August 9, 1981).

Wayne, Stephen J. "Congressional Liaison in the Reagan White House: A Preliminary Assessment of the First Year," in *President and Congress: Assessing Reagan's First Year,* ed. by Norman Ornstein. Washington, D.C.: American Enterprise Institute, 1982, pp. 44–65.

————. *The Legislative Presidency.* New York, N.Y.: St. Martin's, 1978.

CHAPTER TWENTY-NINE NOTES

We are grateful to the following individuals for their constructive comments: George Berdes, Philip Brenner, Stanley Heginbotham, Robert Lockwood, Gale Mattox and Bruce Norton.

1. Louis Fisher, *The Politics of Shared Power: Congress and the Executive,* 2nd ed. (Washington, D.C.: Congressional Quarterly, 1987), p. ix.

2. An identically titled earlier draft of the article was presented as a paper at the International Studies Association Convention, Anaheim, California, March 25–29, 1986.

3. Cf., Morris S. Ogul, *Congress Oversees the Bureaucracy* (Pittsburgh, Pa.: University of Pittsburgh Press, 1976), pp. 5–9.

4. Another assumption affects attitudes toward consultation: the erroneous belief that Congress is a *bureaucracy* that manages operations and formulates policies. Those professing this view invariably find Congress inept. Consultation with such an allegedly irresponsible actor is thought to be, at best, hazardous. For a crisp detailing of distinctions between Congress and a classic bureaucracy see Stanley J. Heginbotham, "Congress and Defense Policy Making: Toward Realistic Expectations in a System of Countervailing Parochialisms," in Robert L. Pfaltzgraff, Jr., and Uri Ra'anan, eds., *National Security Policy: The Decision-making Process* (Hamden, CT.: Archon Books, 1984), pp. 251–55.

5. Thomas M. Franck and Edward Weisband, *Foreign Policy by Congress* (New York: Oxford University Press, 1979), pp. 6–8; Bayless Manning, "The Congress, the Executive and Intermestic Affairs: Three Proposals," *Foreign Affairs* 55 (January 1977): 306–324. But see John Rourke, *Congress and the President in U.S. Foreign Policymaking* (Boulder, Colo., Westview Press, 1983), p. 290.

6. Henry Kissinger, address to the American Society of Newspaper Editors, in *Department of State Bulletin*, May 5, 1975. See also Ronald Reagan, interview with Paul Duke, in *Public Papers of the Presidents of the United States—1982* (Washington, D.C.: U.S. Government Printing Office, 1983), p. 949.

7. U.S. Congress, House of Representatives, Committee on International Relations, Special Subcommittee on Investigations, *Report: Congress and Foreign Policy*, Committee Print, 94th Cong., 2d sess., 1977, p. 2; U.S. Congress, House of Representatives, Committee on Foreign Affairs [hereafter referred to as HFAC], *Strengthening Executive-Legislative Consultation on Foreign Policy* [hereafter cited as *Strengthening Executive-Legislative Consultation*], Congress and Foreign Policy Series, No. 8, Congressional Research Service [hereafter referred to as CRS], 1983, p. 14.

8. Paul B. Stares, *The Militarization of Space: U.S. Policy, 1945–84* (Ithaca, N.Y.: Cornell University Press, 1985), p. 225; U.S. Congress, HFAC, *Executive-Legislative Consultation on United States Arms Sales*, Congress and Foreign Policy Series, No. 7, CRS, 1982, p. 3; Richard Haas, *Congressional Power: Implications for American Security Policy*, Adelphi Paper 153 (London: International Institute for Strategic Studies, 1979), pp. 25–26; U.S. Congress, HFAC, *Executive Legislative Consultations on China Policy, 1978–79*, Congress and

Foreign Policy Series, No. 1, CRS, 1980; Dusko Doder, "Nunn: No Basis for Shift on ABM Treaty," *Washington Post*, March 14, 1987, p. A1; David Ottaway and David Hoffman, "Reagan Plan Lacks Bipartisan Support," *Washington Post*, July 5, 1987, p. A1.

9. Ronald Reagan, interview with Paul Duke, p. 949 (emphases added).

10. HFAC, *Strengthening Executive-Legislative Consultations*, p. 14; Robert E. Hunter and Wayne L. Berman, eds., *Making the Government Work: Legislative-Executive Reform* (Washington, D.C.: Center for Strategic and International Studies, Georgetown University, 1985), p. 7.

11. See U.S. Congress, Senate, Committee on Foreign Relations, *Congress, Information and Foreign Affairs*, CRS, 95th Cong., 2d sess., 1978, p. 97; IIFAC, *Strengthening Executive-Legislative Consultation*, p. 17; John F. Manley, "Presidential Power and White House Lobbying," *Political Science Quarterly* 93 (Summer 1978): pp. 255–75.

12. HFAC, *Strengthening Executive-Legislative Consultation*, pp. 17–18; HFAC, *Executive-Legislative Consultation on United States Arms Sales*, pp. 3, 36–39.

13. Richard F. Grimmett, "Arms Sales to Saudi Arabia: AWACs and the F-15 Enhancements," in HFAC, *Congress and Foreign Policy — 1981*, Committee Print, 97th Cong., 2d sess., 1982, pp. 24–48; HFAC, *Executive-Legislative Consultation on United States Arms Sales*, pp. 33–35.

14. See John Hart, "Congressional Reactions to White House Lobbying," *Presidential Studies Quarterly* 11 (Winter 1981): 86–88; Fisher, *The Politics of Shared Powers*, p. 61.

15. HFAC, *Strengthening Executive-Legislative Consultation*, pp. 16–17.

16. U.S. Congress, *Report: Congress and Foreign Policy*, p. 25; HFAC, *Strengthening Executive-Legislative Consultation*, pp. 60–63; Hart, "Congressional Reactions to White House Lobbying," pp. 83–86; HFAC, Executive-Legislative Consulation on Foreign Policy Strengthening The Legislative Side [hereafter cited as *Strengthening the Legislative Side*], Congress and Foreign Policy Series, No. 5, CRS, 1982, pp. 37–73.

17. HFAC, *Strengthening Executive-Legislative Consultation*, pp. 1, 18–19.

18. HFAC, *Strengthening the Legislative Side*, pp. 16–25.

19. *Ibid.*, pp. 17–22; U.S. Congress, *Report: Congress and Foreign Policy*, p. 7.

20. HFAC, *Executive-Legislative Consultation on Foreign Policy: Strengthening Executive Branch Procedures* [hereafter cited as *Strengthening Executive Branch Procedures*], Congress and Foreign Policy Series, No. 2, CRS, 1981, pp. 24–25, 52–53; HFAC, Subcommittee on International Security, Arms Control and Scientific Affairs and on Western Hemispheric Affairs, *Hearings: U.S. Military Actions in Grenada:*

Implications for U.S. Policy in the Eastern Caribbean, 98th Cong., 1st sess., 1983, pp. 4, 32 (concerning the Congressional Black Caucus); HFAC, *Strengthening the Legislative Side*, pp. 23–26.

21. HFAC, *Strengthening Executive Branch Procedures*, pp. 2, 46–51; HFAC, *Strengthening Executive-Legislative Consultation*, pp. 18–19; U.S. Congress, *Report: Congress and Foreign Policy*, p. 24.

22. Robert Lockwood, "Conceptualizing the National Security Policy Process: A Framework for the Analysis of Executive-Legislative Relations," In Duncan L. Clarke, ed., *Public Policy and Political Institutions: United States Defense and Foreign Policy — Policy Coordination and Integration* (Greenwich, Ct.: JAI Press, 1985), pp. 46–47.

23. Hunter and Berman, *Making the Government Work*, p. 20; HFAC, Strengthening Executive Branch Procedures, pp. 49–50; HFAC, *Strengthening Executive-Legislative Consultation*, pp. 19–20; HFAC, *Executive-Legislative Consultation on United States Arms Sales*, p. 37.

24. HFAC, *Strengthening Executive-Legislative Consultation*. pp. 3–5. See also Joseph T. Kendrick. "The Consultation Process: The Legislative-Executive Relationship in the Formulation of Foreign Policy," Ph.D. dissertation, George Washington University, 1979, chs. 7–8.

25. U.S. Congress, House of Representatives, Committee on International Relations, Subcommittee on Special Investigations, *Hearings: Congress and Foreign Policy*, 94th Cong., 2d sess., 1976, pp. 139, 142.

26. Patsy T. Mink, "Institutional Perspective: Misunderstandings, Myths, and Misperceptions: How Congress and the State Department See Each Other," in Thomas M. Franck, ed., *The Tethered Presidency: Congressional Restraints on Executive Power* (New York: New York University Press, 1981), p. 65.

27. Haas, *Congressional Power*, p. 30: HFAC, *Strengthening Executive-Legislative Consultation*, p. 40; U.S. Congress, *Hearings: Congress and Foreign Policy*, pp. 138–41, 180–82.

28. Mink, "Institutional Perspective . . .," p. 68.

29. *Ibid.*, pp. 73–74; William I. Bacchus, *Staffing for Foreign Affairs* (Princeton, N.J.: Princeton University Press, 1983), p. 30.

30. I.M. Destler, *Presidents, Bureaucrats and Foreign Policy* (Princeton, N.J.: Princeton University Press, 1972), pp. 70–71, 162–64; Leslie H. Gelb, "Why Not the State Department?," in Charles W. Kegley, Jr., and Eugene R. Wittkopf, eds., *Perspectives on American Foreign Policy* (New York: St. Martin's Press, 1983), p. 284; Bacchus, *Staffing for Foreign Affairs*, pp. 57, 100, 103.

31. U.S. Congress, *Report of the Congressional Committees Investigating the Iran-Contra Affair* [hereafter cited as *Report: Iran-Contra Affair*], H. Rept. 100–433, 100th Cong., 1st sess., 1987, p. 387.

32. "Closing Statements by Rep. Hamilton," *Washington Post*, July 22, 1987, p. A8.

33. *Report: Iran-Contra Affair*, p. 392.

34. Haynes Johnson, "Admiral's Goal: 'No Interference'," *Washington Post*, July 18, 1987, p. A1.

35. U.S. Congress, *Report: Congress and Foreign Policy*, pp. 18–19; Les Aspin, "Why Doesn't Congress Do Something?, *Foreign Policy* 15 (Summer 1974): 73; HFAC, *Strengthening the Legislative Side*, pp. 8–10; I.M. Destler, "Executive-Congressional Conflict in Foreign Policy: Explaining It, Coping with It," in Laurence C. Dodd and Bruce I. Oppenheimer, eds., *Congress Reconsidered* (Washington, D.C.: Congressional Quarterly Press, 1981), pp. 296–316.

36. HFAC, *Strengthening the Legislative Side*, p. 10; HFAC, *Strengthening Executive-Legislative Consultation*, pp. 40–42; U.S. Congress, *Hearings: Congress and Foreign Policy*, p. 3; Franck and Weisband, *Foreign Policy by Congress*, pp. 132–34.

37. David R. Mayhew, *Congress: The Electoral Connection* (New Haven, Ct.: Yale University Press, 1974), pp. 49–65.

38. Lockwood, "Conceptualizing the National Security Policy Process," pp. 408, 478; Richard Stubbing, *The Defense Game* (New York: Harper & Row, 1986), pp. 88–105. Other factors contribute to congressional micro-managment of defense programs, including development of an annual budget review process and the existence of standing subcommittees with specific substantive jurisdiction. Statutory restrictions on defense programs increased 233 percent between 1970 and 1985. During this period, the length of the Defense Authorization Act increased from 9 to 169 pages. U.S. Congress, Senate, Committee on Armed Services [hereafter cited as SASC], *Defense Organization: The Need for Change*, Staff Report, S. Prt. 99-86, 99th Cong., 1st sess., 1985, pp. 591–93.

39. Stanley J. Heginbotham, "Dateline Washington: The Rules of the Game," *Foreign Policy* 53 (Winter 1983–84): 158–60.

40. Destler, "Executive-Congressional Conflict in Foreign Policy," pp. 302–303; Zbigniew Brzezinski, testimony, U.S. Congress, Senate, Committee on Governmental Affairs, *Hearings: Relationship between Congress and the Executive in the Formulation and Implementation of Foreign Policy* [hereafter referred to as *Hearings: Relationship between Congress and the Executive*], Part I, 98th Cong., 2d sess., 1984, p. 68. Louis Fisher remarks that, "No better formula for legislative impotence has ever been devised than to allocate 'broad policy questions' to Congress and assign 'administrative details' to the executive,' and, "'Flexibility' is often a code word used by executive officials who want to be left alone." Louis Fisher, *The Politics of Shared Power: Congress and Executive* (Washington, D.C.: Congressional Quarterly Press, 1981), pp. 78, 104.

41. HFAC, *Strengthening Executive-Legislative Consultation*, pp. 4, 43–44.

42. Amos Jordon, statement, Senate Committee on Governmental Affairs, *Hearings: Relationship between Congress and the Executive*, p. 109; Franck and Weisband, *Foreign Policy by Congress*, pp. 100–103; Zbigniew Brzezinski, *Power and Principle: Memoirs of the National Security Adviser, 1977–1981* (New York: Farrar, Straus & Giroux, 1983), p. 126.

43. Manley, "Presidential Power and White House Lobbying," p. 270; William F. Mullen, "Perceptions of Carter's Legislative Successes and Failures: Views From the Hill and the Liaison Staff," *Presidential Studies Quarterly* 12 (Fall 1982): 532.

44. Edward Feigenbaum, "Staffing, Organization and Decisionmaking in the Ford and Carter White Houses," *Presidential Studies Quarterly* 10 (Summer 1980): 376; R. Gordon Hoxie, "Staffing the Ford and Carter Presidencies," *Presidential Studies Quarterly* 10 (Summer 1980): 378–401; HFAC, *Strengthening Executive-Legislative Consultation*, pp. 44–55; U.S. Congress, HFAC, *Congressional-Executive Relations and the Turkish Arms Embargo*, Congress and Foreign Policy Series, No. 3, CRS, 1981, pp. 19, 29.

45. Manley, "Presidential Power and White House Lobbying," p. 274; I. M. Destler, *Making Foreign Economic Policy* (Washington, D.C.: The Brookings Institution, 1980); Raymond Ahern, "Congress and Foreign Trade Policy," in U.S. Congress, HFAC, *Congress and Foreign Affairs-1979*, Committee Print, 96th Cong., 2d sess., 1980, p. 135.

46. U.S. Congress, HFAC, *The War Powers Resolution: A Special Study*, Committee Print, 97th Cong., 1st sess., 1982; Ellen C. Collier, *The War Powers Resolution: A Decade of Experience*, CRS, Report No. 84–44F, February 6, 1984; U.S. Congress, HFAC, *Executive-Legislative Consultation on Foreign Policy: Strengthening Foreign Policy Information Sources for Congress* [hereafter cited as *Strengthening Foreign Policy Information Sources*], Congress and Foreign Policy Series, No. 4, CRS, 1982, p. 1; Senate Committee on Governmental Affairs, *Hearings: Relationship between Congress and the Executive*, p. 8.

47. Norman J. Ornstein, Thomas E. Mann, Michael J. Malbin, Allen Schick, John F. Bibby, *Vital Statistics on Congress, 1984–1985* (Washington, D.C.: American Enterprise Institute, 1984), pp. 111, 143–46. There is also evidence that the corresponding enlargement of congressional staffs may have actually increased demands on legislators time. See Destler, "Executive-Congressional Conflict in Foreign Policy," pp. 304–305; Haas, *Congressional Power*, p. 10.

48. See Warren Christopher, "Ceasefire Between the Branches: A Compact in Foreign Affairs," *Foreign Affairs* 60 (Summer 1983): 1000.

49. See HFAC, *Executive-Legislative Consultation on China Policy, 1978–79*, p. 38; U.S. Congress, *Report: Congress and Foreign Policy*, p. 12.

50. HFAC, *Strengthening Executive-Legislative Consultation*, p. 46; HFAC, *Strengthening Executive Branch Procedures*, pp. 17–25; Franck and Weisband, *Foreign Policy by Congress*, pp. 284–85; Hunter and Berman, *Making the Government Work*, p. 16. See also HFAC, *Executive-Legislative Consultation on China Policy*, 1978–79, p. 25.

51. HFAC, *Strengthening Executive-Legislative Consultation*, p. 46; Franck and Weisband, *Foreign Policy by Congress*, pp. 210–26; Thomas E. Cavanagh, "The Dispersion of Authority in the House of Representatives," *Political Science Quarterly* 97 (Winter 1982-83); 623–37; Leroy N. Rieselbach, *Congressional Reform* (Washington, D.C.: Congressional Quarterly Press, 1986).

52. Cavanagh, "The Dispersion of Authority . . . ," p. 630; U.S. Congress, *Report: Congress and Foreign Policy*, p. 20; HFAC, *Strengthening the Legislative Side*, pp. 18–21. However, Louis Fisher notes that "earlier presidents complained that the *centralization* of power in Congress made it impossible to get bills past uncooperative committee chairmen. Legislative decentralization can be an opportunity, not an obstacle, because it opens up lines of communication." Fisher, *The Politics of Shared Power* (1987), p. 61.

53. Molly Moore, "Defense Oversight: War of the Watchdogs," *Washington Post*, October 12, 1987, p. A17.

54. SASC, *Defense Organization*, pp. 578, 582.

55. Haas, *Congressional Power*, p. 7; Cavanagh, "The Dispersion of Authority . . . ," pp. 630–31.

56. J. William Fulbright, "The Legislator as Educator," *Foreign Affairs* 57 (Spring 1979): 727; HFAC, *Strengthening Executive-Legislative Consultation*, pp. 5, 47–48; HFAC, *Strengthening Foreign Policy Information Sources*, pp. 2, 38–58; Charles McC. Mathias, "Ethnic Groups and Foreign Policy," *Foreign Affairs* 59 (Summer 1981): 975–96. Views differ about the weight to be accorded interest groups within the constellation of factors that generally affect major issues. Interest group influence may be overestimated or underestimated. Executive officials acknowledged retrospectively their own overestimation of the "China Lobby" in regretting their failure to give Congress prior notice of President Carter's normalization of relations with China. HFAC, *Executive-Legislative Consultations on China Policy, 1978–79*, p. 24. Those who are members of, or who identify normatively with, *successful ethnic* lobbies often (not always) *publicly* downplay their impact. Theodore Coloumbis and Sallie Hicks, for instance, largely discount the influence of Greek-American constituencies on congressional measures related to Turkey's invasion of Cyprus and the subsequent U.S. arms embargo. Sallie M. Hicks and Theodore A. Couloumbis, *"The 'Greek Lobby': Illusion or Reality?,"* in Abdul Aziz Said, ed., *Ethnicity and U.S. Foreign Policy* (New York:

Praeger, 1977), pp. 83–115. Professor Coloumbis worked closely with the "Greek Lobby." Sallie Hicks was his graduate student. Likewise, Edward Glick and Steven Spiegel, who find the unique U.S.-Israel relationship highly advantageous to both nations, deemphasize the role of the American Israel Public Affairs Committee (AIPAC) in U.S. policy toward Israel. Conversely, Paul Findley and Edward Tivnan, who find many aspects of this relationship inimical to U.S. interests, stress AIPAC's influence. Edward Bernard Glick, *The Triangular Connection: America, Israel and American Jews* (Winchester, Mass.: Allen & Unwin, 1982), pp. 95–106; Steven Spiegel, *The Other Arab-Israel Conflict: Making America's Middle East Policy, from Truman to Reagan* (Chicago, Ill.: University of Chicago Press, 1985), pp. 388–89; Edward Tivnan, *The Lobby: Jewish Political Power and American Foreign Policy* (New York: Simon & Schuster, 1987); Paul Findley, *They Dare To Speak Out: People and Institutions Confront Israel's Lobby* (Westport, Ct.: Lawrence Hill, 1985).

57. HFAC, *Strengthening Foreign Policy Information Sources*, p. 17. For an historical accounting of Congress' informational dependency on the executive and its implications see U.S. Congress, Senate Committee on Foreign Relations, *Congress, Information and Foreign Affairs*, CRS, 95th Cong., 2d sess., 1978. A senior Pentagon congressional liaison official said, "It is incredible the way we can mold what we wish to say [to Congress] to serve our own purposes." Confidential interview, April 14, 1986.

58. U.S. Congress, *Report: Congress and Foreign Policy*, pp. 8–10; HFAC, *Strengthening Executive-Legislative Consultation*, pp. 62–63, 144; Senate Committee on Governmental Affairs, *Hearings: Relationship between Congress and the Executive*, pp. 13, 101.

59. U.S. Congress, House of Representatives, Committee on Administration, *Reports to Be Made to Congress: Communications from the Clerk*, 98th Cong., 2d sess., 1984.

60. HFAC, *Strengthening the Legislative Side*, pp. 46–47. The utility of the latter "function" is illustrated by a provision of the Trade Act of 1974 that stipulated that Congress receive at least 90 days notice prior to the conclusion of trade agreements negotiated at the Tokyo Round of talks. Congress, given this opportunity to voice its concerns, then committed itself to vote implementing legislation, without amendment, within 90 days of submission. This "fast track" procedure contributed significantly to the easy passage of the Trade Act of 1979. Trade Act of 1974, 88 Stat. 1978, 19 U.S.C. secs. 2111, 2112, 2191; Chris Brantley, "The Trade Act of 1974: A Case Study of Executive-Legislative Relations," 1985 (mimeo); Robert C. Cassidy, Jr., "Negotiating About Negotiation: The Geneva Multilateral Trade Talks," in Franck, *The Tethered Presidency*, pp. 278–80.

61. HFAC, *Strengthening the Legislative Side*, pp. 48–50; Senate Committee on Governmental Affairs, *Hearings: Relationship between Congress and the Executive*, p. 79; U.S. Congress, *Report: Congress and Foreign Policy*, p. 6; PL 99–433, 100 Stat. 1066; *Congressional Record-House*, September 12, 1986, p. H6858.

62. U.S. Congress, *Report: Congress and Foreign Policy*, p. 14.

63. HFAC, *Strengthening the Legislative Side*, p. 55.

64. *Report: Iran-Contra Affair*, p. 378; Duncan L. Clarke and Edward L. Neveleff, "Secrecy, Foreign Intelligence, and Civil Liberties: Has the Pendulum Swung Too Far?", *Political Science Quarterly* 99 (Fall, 1984): 495; U.S. Congress, *Hearings: Congress and Foreign Policy*, p. 303. One troublesome issue is internal to Congress — the frequent difficulty experienced by legislators not on one of the two intelligence committees in gaining access to classified information held by these committees. See U.S. Congress, House of Representatives, Permanent Select Committee on Intelligence, *Adverse Report: Resolution of Inquiry with Respect to United States Military Involvement in Hostilities in Central America*, Rept. 98–742, 98th Cong., 2d sess., 1984; U.S. Congress, House of Representatives, *Rules of Procedure for the Permanent Select Committee on Intelligence* (Washington, D.C.: Government Printing Office, 1985); U.S. Senate, *Rules of Procedure for the Select Committee on Intelligence* (Washington, D.C.: Government Printing Office, 1981).

65. *Report: Iran-Contra Affair*, pp. 375, 378–82, 423–27; *Report of the President's Special Review Board* [hereafter cited as Tower Commission Report] (Washington, D.C.: Government Printing Office, February 26, 1987), p. IV-7; Bob Woodward, *Veil: The Secret Wars of the CIA, 1981–1987* (New York: Simon & Schuster, 1987).

66. Clarke and Neveleff, "Secrecy, Foreign Intelligence and Civil Liberties," pp. 506–508; Commission on the Organization of Government for the Conduct of Foreign Policy [Murphy Commission] *Report* (Washington, D.C.: Government Printing Office, 1975), pp. 201–202.

67. Zbigniew Brzezinski has offered a variant of the Zorinsky proposal. Brzezinski, *Power and Principle*, pp. 536–37; Zbigniew Brzezinski, "NSC's Midlife Crisis," *Foreign Policy* 69 (Winter 1987–88): 94–95. See U.S. Congress, Senate, Committee on Foreign Relations, *Hearings: The National Security Adviser: Role and Accountability*, 96th Cong., 2d sess., 1980, especially pp. 128–29; U.S. Congress, *Hearings: Congress and Foreign Policy*, pp. 49, 64, 53, 83, 110, 113.

68. Tower Commission Report, p. V-5; *Report: Iran-Contra Affair*, p. 425.

69. Lou Cannon and David Ottaway, "Carlucci, Aide in 4 Administrations," *Washington Post*, November 3, 1987, p. A16.

70. U.S. Congress, *Report: Congress and Foreign Policy*, p. 10; Lee Hamilton and Michael Van Dusen, "Making the Separation of Powers Work,"

Foreign Affairs 57 (Fall 1978): 37–38; HFAC, *Strengthening Foreign Policy Information Sources*, pp. 2, 68, 70.

71. HFAC, *Strengthening Executive-Legislative Consultation*, p. 64; U.S. Congress, *Report: Congress and Foreign Policy*, pp. 13–14.

72. HFAC, *Strengthening Foreign Policy Information Sources*, pp. 106–107. See also pp. 3, 7–26.

73. Ibid., p. 28. But see Destler, "Executive-Congressional Conflict in Foreign policy," p. 314.

74. Alton Frye, statement, U.S. Congress, *Hearings: Congress and Foreign Policy*, pp. 17–20, 26–27.

75. Hunter and Berman, *Making the Government Work*, pp. 27–28; Lockwood, "Conceptualizing the National Security Policy Process," p. 482; SASC, *Defense Organization*, pp. 588–89, 610.

76. U.S. Congress, Senate, Committee on Foreign Relations, *The Senate's Role in Foreign Affairs Appointments*, CRS, 97th Cong. 2d sess., 1982, pp. 1–3.

77. Hunter and Berman, *Making the Government Work*, p. 28.

78. HFAC, *Strengthening Executive Branch Procedures*, pp. 42–43, 73–76.

79. U.S. Congress, *Report: Congress and Foreign Policy*, pp. 11, 103, 133.

80. I. M. Destler, "State: A Department of 'Something More'," in Clarke, *Public Policy and Political Institutions*, pp. 98–99; HFAC, *Strengthening Executive Branch Procedures*, pp. 23–24, 60.

81. Stephen Hess, *Organizing the Presidency* (Washington, D.C.: The Brookings Institution, 1976), p. 209. See also James L. Sundquist, *Constitutional Reform and Effective Government* (Washington, D.C.: The Brookings Institution, 1986), pp. 168–74

82. HFAC, *Strengthening Executive Branch Procedures*, p. 45. But congressional staff are not afforded a similar opportunity to serve in the executive branch.

83. *Ibid.*, pp. 2, 43–45; Heginbotham, "Dateline Washington," p. 171.

84. Hunter and Berman, *Making the Government Work*, pp. 15–16; HFAC, *Strengthening Executive Branch Procedures*, p. 3.

85. Hunter and Berman, *Making the Government Work*, p. 9; SASC, *Defense Organization*, pp. 603–604.

86. On the benefits as well as the possible disadvantages of a biennial defense budget see "Report of a Working Group on the Congressional Defense Budget Process," in Barry M. Blechman and William J. Lynn, eds., *Toward a More Effective Defense: Report of the Defense Organization Project* (Cambridge, Mass.: Ballinger, 1985), pp. 109–110; SASC, *Defense Organization*, pp. 594–95, 602–603; *U.S. Defense Acquisition: A Process in Trouble* (Washington, D.C.: Center for Strategic and International Studies, Georgetown University, 1987), pp. 83–84; President's Blue Ribbon Commission on Defense Management [hereafter cited as Packard Commission], *A*

Quest for Excellence (Washington, D.C.: Government Printing Office, June 1968), pp. 25–26. The Packard Commission, which strongly endorsed a biennial defense budget, asserted (p. xvii): "Today, there is no rational system whereby the Executive Branch and the Congress reach coherent and enduring agreement on national military strategy, the forces to carry it out, and the funding that should be provided . . . "

87. "Report of the Working Group . . . ," p. 110.

88. *Ibid.*, pp. 110–11. See also Packard Commission, *A Quest for Excellence*, pp. 26–27; SASC, Defense Organization, pp. 599, 607–608.

89. For summaries of the many problems with these and similar proposals see Hamilton and Van Dusen, "Making the Separation of Powers Work," p. 36; Destler, "Executive-Legislative Conflict in Foreign Policy," p. 312; HFAC, *Strengthening the Legislative Side*, pp. 28–31; HFAC, *Strengthening Executive-Legislative Consultation*, p. 69.

90. Ottaway and Hoffman, "Reagan Plan Lacks Bipartisan Support," p. A1.

91. HFAC, *Strengthening the Legislative Side*, pp. 31–32; Hunter and Berman, *Making the Government Work*, pp. 19–20.

92. Richard E. Cohen, *Congressional Leadership: Seeking a New Role* (Beverly Hills, Calif.: Sage, 1980), pp. 58, 76, 78; Destler, "Executive-Congressional Conflict in Foreign Policy," p. 312.

93. U.S. Congress, *Report: Congress and Foreign Policy*, p. 4; HFAC, *Strengthening the Legislative Side*, pp. 19–20.

94. HFAC, *Strengthening Executive-Legislative Consultation*, pp. 140–41; HFAC, *Strengthening the Legislative Side*, pp. 3, 34.

95. Charles McC. Mathias, Jr., "Reflections on a System Spinning Out of Control," *Washington Post*, December 11, 1986, p. A21.

CHAPTER THIRTY NOTES

1. Lucius Wilmerding, "The Vice Presidency," *Political Science Quarterly*, 68 (March 1953), 40. More recently, in 1974, Arthur Schlesinger called for the abolition of the office of the Vice President and reliance upon a special election for Presidential succession. "Is the Vice Presidency Necessary?" *Atlantic*, May 1974: 37–44.

2. Paul Light, *Vice Presidential Power: Advice and Influence in the White House* (Baltimore: The Johns Hopkins Press, 1984), 63.

3. Stephen W. Stathis and Ronald C. Moe, "America's Other Inauguration," *Presidential Studies Quarterly*, 10 (Fall 1980), 550.

4. The swearing-in ceremonies for the President and Vice President were scheduled for the west front of the Capitol, but the extremely cold weather forced the ceremonies to be moved indoors to the

rotunda of the Capitol. Steven Pressman, "Reagan Calls Country 'Poised for Greatness,'" *Congressional Quarterly*, Jan. 26, 1985, p. 158.

5. For scholarly accounts of recent Presidential transitions, consult: Laurin Henry, *Presidential Transitions* (Washington: The Brookings Institution, 1960). Carl M. Brauer, *Presidential Transitions: Eisenhower Through Reagan* (New York: Oxford University Press, 1986). James P. Pfiffner, *The Strategic Presidency: Hitting the Ground Running* (Chicago: Dorsey Press, 1988). It is interesting to note that none of these accounts discusses Vice Presidential transitions.

6. By law in 1974, Congress created an official residence for the Vice President. 3 U.S.C. 111; P.L. 93–346; 88 Stat. 153.

7. U.S. Library of Congress, Congressional Research Service, "Presidental Transitions and the Presidential Transition Act of 1963," by Stephanie Smith. CRS Rep. 80–213GOV, December 1980.

8. U.S. Library of Congress, Congressional Research Service, "Federal Benefits to Former Presidents and Their Widows," by Stephanie Smith. CRS Rept. 85–173GOV, August 1985.

9. The use of private funds to supplement Federal funding was not unique to the Reagan-Bush transition. "Presidents Nixon, Carter, and Reagan all raised private funds for their transitions . . . ." U.S. Congress, Senate, Committee on Government Affairs, *Presidential Transitions Effectiveness Act*. S. Rept. 137. 100th Cong., 2d sess., Washington, 1988, p. 10.

10. U.S. Congress, House, Committee on Government Operations, *Presidential Transitions Effectiveness Act*, H. Rept. 532, 100th Cong., 2d sess., Washington, 1988. U.S. Congress, Senate, Committee on Governmental Affairs, *Presidential Transitions Effectiveness Act*, S. Rept. 317. 100th Cong., 2d sess., Washington, 1988.

11. Since 1977, the amount paid to the Vice President for expenses ($10,000) is not reported as income, while expenses reimbursed are not allowed as a deduction under the Internal Revenue Code (2 U.S.C. 31(a-1) and 26 U.S.C. 1, et. seq.; as amended by Public Law 95–94; 91 Stat. 661, Aug. 4, 1977).

12. Full and automatic Secret Service protection of the Vice President was not established until 1962. The same legislation extended this protection to the Vice President-elect and the officer next in line of succession when the Vice Presidency is unoccupied (76 Stat. 956). For a review of Secret Service protective responsibilities, consult: Frederick Kaiser, "Congressional Determination of Secret Service Protective Responsibilities," Congressional Research Service Memorandum, February 26, 1982.

13. For an extensive discussion of rules and procedures governing the operations of the Senate, consult: Walter J. Oleszek, *Congressional Procedures and The Policy Process*, 2d ed. (Washington: CQ Press, 1984).

14. Light, *Vice Presidential Power*, chapter 8.
15. Robert E. DiClerico, *The American President*, 2d ed. (Englewood Cliffs: Prentice-Hall, 1983), p. 374.
16. Light, *Vice Presidential Power*, p. 34.
17. Light, *Vice Presidential Power*, chapter 6. Stephen J. Wayne, *The Legislative Presidency* (New York: Harper and Row, 1978), chapter 4. Ronald C. Moe, "The Domestic Council in Perspective," *The Bureaucrat*, 5 (Oct. 1976): 251–272.

CHAPTER THIRTY-ONE NOTES

1. Carl M. Brauer, *Presidential Transitions: Eisenhower through Reagan* (New York: Oxford Univ. Press, 1986), p. 95.
2. See Marie D. Natoli, *American Prince, American Pauper: The Contemporary Vice Presidency in Perspective* (Westport, Ct.: Greenwood Press, 1985), ch. 1 for a fuller discussion of Hubert Humphrey's views and his vice presidential role in the Senate; see, too, for Agnew's experience.
3. Paul C. Light, *Vice Presidential Power: Advice and Influence in the White House* (Baltimore: Johns Hopkins Press, 1984), p. 40; for a fuller discussion of Nelson Rockefeller's role, see Natoli, *American Prince, American Pauper*, ch. 6 and Michael Turner, "Finding a Policy Role for the Vice President," unpublished Ph.D. Dissertation, State University of New York at Binghamton, 1978.
4. As quoted in Brauer, p. 202.
5. *National Journal*, June 20, 1981.
6. *Ibid.*
7. For a fuller discussion of vice presidential selection criteria, see Natoli, *American Prince, American Pauper*, ch. 2; Marie D. Natoli, "Vice Presidential Selection: The Political Considerations," *Presidential Studies Quarterly*, Spring, 1980.

    For a discussion of the Twenty-Fifth Amendment, see Natoli, *American Prince, American Pauper*, chs. 2, 3, 6 and Marie D. Natoli, "The Twenty-Fifth Amendment: Opening a Pandora's Box," *Presidential Studies Quarterly*, Fall, 1976.
8. Sidney Warren, *The Battle for the Presidency* (Philadelphia: Lippincott, 1968), p. 299.
9. For a fuller discussion of these cataclysmic events, see Marie D. Natoli, "Vice Presidency Gains—But Is Subject to Presidential Whim," *Atlanta Constitution*, September 29, 1981.
10. *New York Times*, September 29, 1977.
11. *New York Times*, December 21, 1980.
12. *National Journal*, June 10, 1981.
13. Ruth C. Silva's *Presidential Succession* (New York: Greenwood Press, 1968) provides a useful discussion of the questions which sur-

rounded presidential disability and succession, although the work is, of course, partly outdated; Birch Bayh's *One Heartbeat Away* (New York: Bobbs-Merrill, 1968) and John D. Feerick's *The Twenty-Fifth Amendment: Its Complete History and Earliest Applications* (New York: Fordham Univ. Press, 1976) are excellent accounts of the passage of the Amendment, with Feerick's work providing a thorough account of the 1973 and 1974 usage.

14. Alben Barkley, *That Reminds Me* (Garden City: Doubleday, 1954), *passim*.

15. Richard M. Nixon, *Six Crises* (Garden City: Doubleday, 1962), p. 144ff. discusses the politically delicate situation in which he found himself during Eisenhower's illnesses.

16. "Nixon's Own Story of Seven Years in the Vice Presidency," *U.S. News* 48 (May 16, 1960): 98–106.

17. Howard K. Smith, Oral History Interview, Eisenhower Administration Oral History Collection, Columbia University, New York, New York, pp. 369–60.

18. For a fuller discussion of this point, see Natoli, *American Prince, American Pauper*, p. 94ff.; p. 145ff; see also Nixon, *Six Crises*, p. 144.

19. *Ibid.*, p. 148ff.

20. Telephone interview with Kenneth P. O'Donnell, February, 1975; interview with Walter Jenkins, Austin, Texas, April 1973.

21. I asked this of Hubert Humphrey in a 1974 interview conducted in Washington, D.C. Humphrey's response: "One might have thought so—but apparently he didn't."

22. Interview, Hubert H. Humphrey, March, 1974.

23. Humphrey had been an early champion of a strong party position regarding advancement in the area of civil rights.

24. Hubert H. Humphrey, *The Education of a Public Man* (Garden City: Doubleday, 1976), p. 408.

25. Interview, Hubert H. Humphrey, March, 1974.

26. For a fuller discussion of Spiro Agnew as Administration Spokesperson, see Natoli, *American Prince, American Pauper*, ch. 5.

27. For a fuller discussion of Rockefeller's role vis à vis the Domestic Council, see Turner, "Finding a Policy Role."

28. Natoli, *American Prince, American Pauper*, p. 175.

29. See *Ibid.*, ch. 5, for a fuller discussion of Mondale's role.

30. See *Ibid.*, pp. 137, 161 for Bush and the "crisis management team."

31. See *Ibid.*, ch. 5 for a fuller discussion of Bush's role.

CHAPTER THIRTY-THREE NOTES

1. "Report of the Miller Center Commission on Presidential Disability and the Twenty-fifth Amendment." *Papers on Presidential Disability and the Twenty-fifth Amendment by Six Medical, Legal and Political Authorities*. Edited by Kenneth W. Thompson. Lanham, MD: University Press of America, 1988, p. 160.

2. *Ibid.*, p. 164.

3. *The Washington Post*, June 10, 1988, D1–3.

4. *Ibid.*

5. *Papers on Presidential Disability and the Twenty-Fifth Amendment*, p. 169.

6. *Ibid.*, p. 47.

7. *Ibid.*, p. 45.

8. *Ibid.*, p. 47.

9. *Ibid.*, p. 184.

10. *Ibid.*, p. 174.

11. *Ibid.*, p. 161.

12. *Ibid.*, p. 160.

13. *Ibid.*, pp. 160–61.

14. *Ibid.*, 161.

Index